6.95
C+H

68- 24832 (11/9/63)

THE PRESIDENTS' MEN

THE IRISH IN AUSTRALIA

THE
PRESIDENTS' MEN

White House Assistants of Franklin D. Roosevelt,
Harry S Truman, Dwight D. Eisenhower,
John F. Kennedy and Lyndon B. Johnson

PATRICK ANDERSON

1968
DOUBLEDAY & COMPANY, INC., GARDEN CITY, NEW YORK

Grateful acknowledgment is made to the following for copyrighted material:

ATHENEUM PUBLISHERS

Excerpts from *The Ordeal of Power*, by Emmet John Hughes; copyright
© 1962, 1963 by Emmet John Hughes; reprinted by permission.

DOUBLEDAY & COMPANY, INC.

Excerpts from the following: *Eighteen Acres Under Glass*, by Robert
Keith Gray; copyright © 1961, 1962, by Robert Keith Gray. *The Democratic Roosevelt*, by Rexford Guy Tugwell; copyright © 1957 by Rexford Guy Tugwell; reprinted by permission.

HARPER & ROW, PUBLISHERS

Excerpts from the following: *Firsthand Report*, by Sherman Adams. *The
Journals of David E. Lilienthal*; copyright © 1964, 1966, by David E.
Lilienthal. *This I Remember*, by Eleanor Roosevelt. *With Roosevelt*, by
Samuel I. Rosenman. *Roosevelt and Hopkins*, by Robert E. Sherwood;
copyright 1948, 1950 by Robert E. Sherwood. *Kennedy*, by Theodore
Sorensen. All reprinted by permission.

HOUGHTON MIFFLIN COMPANY

Excerpts from the following: *Anatomy of the State Department*, by Smith
Simpson. *The Age of Roosevelt*, by Arthur M. Schlesinger, Jr. *A Thousand Days*, by Arthur M. Schlesinger, Jr. All reprinted by permission.

DAVID MCKAY COMPANY, INC.

Excerpts from *My Twelve Years With John F. Kennedy*, by Evelyn Lincoln; copyright © 1965 by Evelyn Lincoln; reprinted by permission.

For Ann

CONTENTS

"The President needs help."

The Brownlow Committee, 1936

"Kings and great princes, even the wisest of them, have had their friends, their favorites, their privados, in all ages, for they have their affections as well as other men. Of these they make several uses; sometimes to communicate and debate their thoughts with them, and to ripen their judgments thereby; sometimes to ease their cares by imparting them; and sometimes to interpose them between themselves and the envy or malice of their people; for kings cannot err; that must be discharged upon the shoulders of their ministers; and they who are nearest unto them must be content to bear the greatest load. Remember then what your true condition is: the king himself is above the reach of his people, but cannot be above their censures; and you are his shadow, if either he commit an error, and is loth to avow it, but excuses it upon his ministers, of which you are the first in the eye; or you commit the fault or have willingly permitted it, and must suffer for it: and so perhaps you may be offered a sacrifice to appease the multitude. . . . Remember well the great trust you have undertaken: you are as a continual sentinel, always to stand upon your watch to give him true intelligence. If you flatter him, you betray him; if you conceal the truth of those things which concern his justice or his honor, you are as dangerous a traitor to his state as he that riseth in arms against him."

Sir Francis Bacon to Sir George Villiers, when the latter became the intimate of James I, 1610

THE PRESIDENTS' MEN

I. INTRODUCTION

In the course of writing this book I asked a man who served prominently on a recent President's White House staff if he would be interested in running for the Senate. His reply was candid:

"I had more power over national affairs in a few years in the White House than I could if I spent the rest of my life in the Senate."

Would he like to return to government in one of the Cabinet posts?

"Most of them aren't worth having," he said with a shrug.

These are overstatements—the gentleman quoted wouldn't turn down either a Senate or Cabinet seat, I suspect—yet they accurately reflect the tremendous influence over governmental affairs that has gravitated in recent years to the President's personal assistants.

The growth of the White House staff into a powerful instrument of government has been an inevitable result of the great expansion of the presidency itself that began in 1933 with Roosevelt's New Deal. The coming of the Welfare State at home and the Cold War abroad has all but overwhelmed the President with powers and responsibilities unimaginable forty years ago. The presidency has become, by any reasonable standard, an impossible job.

Fortunately, the presidency is an office of considerable flexibility. In the strict sense of the words, the President alone has power, and cannot delegate it, and his aides have only influence. But as a practical matter, leading presidential assistants do acquire considerable power, as the word is commonly used, even though they do not have the final accountability for their actions.

Traditionally, the members of the President's Cabinet have been the prime recipients of his delegated authority. Recent Presidents, however, have increasingly delegated authority to their most favored White House assistants, until several of those assistants have overshadowed the Cabinet executives. Essentially, the reason for this is that, as the federal government has grown, a centrifugal force has been pulling the Cabinet officers away from the presidential orbit, making them prisoners of their bureaucracies, giving them priorities and loyalties that may not be identical with the President's.

Cabinet members are still often chosen for political reasons—to repay a campaign debt, to please a religious or ethnic group—and they may or may not be men the President knows, likes, or trusts. It has often followed that Presidents, faced with complex issues on which they must make crucial decisions, have relied more heavily upon the judgment of their hand-picked personal staffs than on their Cabinet executives. The clear trend of the past thirty-five years is toward increased use of the staff to oversee the agencies and departments of government. This may not be a healthy trend, but it is an unmistakable one.

As the White House staff has increasingly challenged the influence of the Cabinet, it has also challenged the status of another time-honored source of advice for Presidents. These are the venerable figures who might be called Distinguished Outsiders—the Senator or party leader or prominent businessman to whom many Presidents have looked for sage counsel in time of adversity. The best known Distinguished Outsiders of this century have been Colonel E. M. House, who advised Woodrow Wilson, Bernard Baruch, who advised numerous Presidents, and, in recent years, Clark Clifford.

The complex, technical, fast-moving nature of today's government is inevitably reducing the importance of outside advisers. By sheer force of personality, the outsider may impress the President with general strategies, but to have a continuing impact, the adviser needs to be on the scene twelve hours a day, reading the cables, studying intelligence documents, sounding out the bureaucracy, digging deeply into the facts and figures a hard-pressed modern President needs. That is why the influence of outsiders is giving way to that of staff insiders— men like McGeorge Bundy, Bill D. Moyers, Theodore Sorensen, Joseph A. Califano, Jr.—whose value to the President rests less on their mastery of affairs of state than on their mastery of the endless details of state.

This book is about those insiders, men and women who worked on the White House staffs from Franklin Roosevelt's Administration to Lyndon Johnson's. My focus is on each President's inner circle, not on the entire Executive Office of the President, nor on such new presidential institutions as the Bureau of the Budget. Even in focusing on the inner circles, I have been arbitrary, as, for example, in my decision to discuss FDR's adviser Raymond Moley in detail and to mention

FDR's friend and speechwriter, Sam Rosenman, only in passing. Generally, I have concentrated my attention on those White House aides who wielded the most influence over national affairs, yet in several cases —as Harry Vaughan, Evelyn Lincoln, and Jack Valenti—I have examined the role of aides who, although of little or no substantive importance, seemed to me to dramatize some point about the relationship between Presidents and the people around them.

It would be impossible to write about the White House staff without devoting some attention to the mechanics of presidential leadership, to the differing ways various Presidents attempt to organize and administer their governments. This book, however, is not an attempt to analyze presidential administration as, for example, Richard E. Neustadt has done in *Presidential Power*. Rather, I have tried, without being entirely indifferent to institutional questions, to focus on presidential assistants as individuals, men who find themselves in a peculiar and delicate position, men who have an opportunity to wield great power and to make great mistakes.

A wonderful variety of men has made its way to the White House staff in recent years. There have been men of extraordinary ability, clowns, scoundrels, ruthless sons-of-bitches, men of rare sensitivity, even a hero or two. The one factor almost all of them have shared is uncommon ambition, a thirst for power and glory, even reflected power and glory, and a willingness to sacrifice friends, family, and personal health, often to suffer personal and political humiliation, in order to satisfy their ambitions. Sometimes their ambition is cloaked— the courtly manners of Clark Clifford or the determined modesty of Bill Moyers—in other cases, like those of Tom Corcoran, McGeorge Bundy, or Richard Goodwin, the ambition glistens like a dagger in the moonlight. In either event, the yearning is there, the desire to be near the center of decision, to have, in the current phrase, a piece of the action.

My interest in this subject began in the winter of 1965–66 when I wrote articles for the *New York Times Magazine* on three men who then adorned the White House staff, Lawrence F. O'Brien, Jack Valenti, and Bill Moyers. Three more diverse figures could hardly be found, but one striking point they shared was that each was better known to the public than most members of the President's Cabinet—better known, for example, than Secretary of the Treasury Henry H. Fowler, or Secretary of Commerce John T. Connor, or Postmaster General John A. Gronouski.

Amazing celebrity now accompanies service in the White House.

When Pierre Salinger returned to California in 1964 to seek the Democratic nomination for the U. S. Senate, a public-opinion poll revealed that eighty-five percent of the voters could identify him, whereas only thirty-five percent could identify his opponent, the State Controller, Alan Cranston. Similarly, when a leading pollster in 1966 attached Bill Moyers' name to a poll designed to rate public recognition of U. S. Senators, only three of the 100 Senators—Fulbright of Arkansas and the two Kennedys—proved to be better known nationally than the young Moyers.

Of course, Salinger and Moyers each served as presidential Press Secretary and were necessarily in the public eye, but other aides such as Sherman Adams, Sorensen, Bundy, and O'Brien have become equally well known as a result of countless newspaper and magazine articles and television appearances.

Essentially, the media's spotlights are focused on the President and necessarily illuminate the people around him. Some aides are singled out because they become exceedingly powerful; others, who have little to say about policy, are publicized because they are colorful or controversial, or simply because they are the President's intimates. The press and the nation realize instinctively that a President reveals himself by the sort of men he picks to be his close associates. A President assembling his staff, like a sultan choosing his harem, can indulge his whim—if we are to understand Lyndon Johnson, for example, we must understand how one man, within a few years' time, could bring into his official family four such diverse figures as Moyers, Valenti, Bobby Baker, and Marvin Watson.

A President's trusted aide can attain power and glory, but the power is precarious and the glory may become tinged with notoriety, for there are many dangers inherent in his position.

The scrutiny of the press will magnify both the aide's virtues and his faults. If he has a knack for putting his foot in his mouth, he can quickly make a fool of himself on a worldwide scale. On the other hand, if his President is a jealous master, praise from the press can be equally harmful to him, as aides to Roosevelt and Johnson discovered.

The aide must be willing to be used as a political lightning rod to draw criticism away from the President, for the President's political opponents, not ready to attack him directly, may find it convenient to blame his alleged misdeeds on his advisers. Over the years, the targets of such attacks have included Roosevelt's Rexford G. Tugwell and Harry Hopkins, Eisenhower's Sherman Adams, Kennedy's Arthur M.

Schlesinger, Jr., and Johnson's Bill Moyers and Marvin Watson. For such aides, the pain of suffering in silence is magnified by the fear that the President, to quiet the critics and protect his Administration, may make a political sacrifice of the controversial assistant.

The powerful presidential assistant will surely have enemies within the President's Cabinet, and he must regard them with extreme care, for whatever the Cabinet executive's real status within the Administration, he has an official, public status that reinforces his position. The presidential favorite must also live with suspicion and animosity from some congressional leaders; this has been the case at least since just after the 1932 election, when Sam Rayburn pointedly informed Raymond Moley, who was then Roosevelt's closest adviser, "I hope we don't have any —— Rasputins in this Administration!"

Finally, the aide will almost certainly develop an enemy or two among his fellow staff members—his rivals in the harem—for little has changed since the Earl of Rochester, poet and courtier of the English Renaissance, deplored "the mean policy of Court-Prudence, which makes us lie to one another all day, for fear of being betrayed by each other at night."

Most Presidents deliberately balance liberals against conservatives, intellectuals against non-intellectuals, on their staffs, and the certain result is friction, rivalry, and hostility. This is not done, as some have suggested, out of pure sadism on the President's part, but because a President will regard his staff as an important channel of ideas and information and he will want to ensure himself a clash of ideas.

All these forces play upon the White House favorite—a demanding President, the Cabinet, staff rivals, the press, congressional critics, a wife and family he too rarely sees—and the history of the White House is replete with men who, in one way or another, succumbed to the pressures. Indeed, although a President's staff can be a source of comfort and encouragement to him, he may be forgiven if he sometimes regards his assistants as a necessary evil, for the chances are excellent that one or more of them will embarrass him by some improbable indiscretion.

If there are dangers in being a presidential aide, there are also dangers in writing about them. One is that in viewing governmental affairs from the vantage point of the presidential assistant, rather than from the President's, one runs the risk of seeming to let the tail wag the dog. So it should be stressed, at this early point, that the final credit or blame for what happens in the White House is, and must be, the President's.

If he approves a policy or delivers a speech that is the work of one of his assistants, he makes it his own. Even if the aide makes some mistake of which the President has no knowledge, the President must be willing to bear the blame, if only because he gave the man too large a mandate or failed to exercise enough control over him.

Yet granting that, for example, Roosevelt must get final credit for his New Deal, or Johnson for his Great Society program, the fact remains that the New Deal would have been different without Tugwell and Corcoran, and the Great Society without Moyers and Califano. To ignore their contributions is to miss part of the story. It is, to be sure, a hard story to get at, for the White House is so constructed that credit flows upward and blame downward. The assistant cannot hope for much recognition, either from contemporary accounts or from history. The President's good works are carved in marble; his aides' are writ on water. Perhaps the most influential, and admirable, of the men discussed in this book was FDR's Harry Hopkins, a hero among heroes during the killing years of the Second World War. Yet his fame was fleeting; many members of my generation, asked to identify Harry Hopkins, would venture a guess that he once played shortstop for the Cardinals.

Today's White House aide generally fares better than Hopkins and his contemporaries. His role has achieved respectability. When he leaves the government, high-paying jobs await him. He may advance from the White House staff to the Cabinet, as Lawrence F. O'Brien and Clark Clifford have done, and as McGeorge Bundy, Bill Moyers, Ted Sorensen, and several others might do in the future. Or, he may try to convert the fame and experience he gained in the White House into a political career of his own, as Pierre Salinger and Ken O'Donnell did, and as O'Brien, Moyers, Sorensen, and others may in the future.

To appreciate the transformation that has taken place in the status of the White House staff, we need only look back to the early 1930s, when Franklin Roosevelt fashioned the modern staff system with such memorable figures as Louis Howe, Raymond Moley, Rexford Tugwell, Tom Corcoran, and Harry Hopkins.

II. THE ROOSEVELT STAFF

1. *Starting from Scratch*

Early in 1941, on the day before his third-term Inauguration, Franklin Roosevelt received in his White House office the man he had defeated for the presidency two months earlier, Wendell Willkie. It was a courtesy call, but Willkie's courtesy lapsed and he asked Roosevelt a blunt question about Harry Hopkins, the sick (half his stomach had been cut away to arrest cancer) and controversial New Dealer who was the President's permanent houseguest, closest friend, and most powerful adviser.

"Why do you keep Hopkins so close to you?" Willkie demanded. "You surely must realize that people distrust him and they resent his influence."

Roosevelt took no offense. Instead, he told Willkie gravely:

"I can understand that you wonder why I need that half man around me. But someday you may well be sitting here where I am now as President of the United States. And when you are, you'll be looking through that door over there and knowing that practically everybody who walks through it wants something out of you. You'll learn what a lonely job this is, and you'll discover the need for somebody like Harry Hopkins who asks for nothing except to serve you."

In this—in his loneliness, in his need for followers whose devotion was total—Roosevelt differed from no other man who has known the burden of the presidency. But in almost every other way, Roosevelt faced problems exceeding those of most other Presidents, save perhaps Washington and Lincoln. When Roosevelt took office, the fabled American economic system had collapsed, and it seemed as if the nation's political system might itself be the next to crumble. The voters had given Roosevelt a triumphant majority not because he had answers to the national catastrophe, but because he had promised to seek answers —to replace a blind faith in the old system with hopeful experimentation toward a new system.

To keep this pledge, Roosevelt needed help. He could buoy up the nation's hopes with his own indomitable confidence, but at heart the problem the nation faced was an economic one—there was much more to fear than fear itself—and Roosevelt was no economist. Thus, in his first term, he needed Raymond Moley and Rexford Tugwell to counsel him on economic policy, just as in his second term he needed the political skills of Thomas G. Corcoran, and in the third term he would rely heavily on the administrative troubleshooting of Harry Hopkins and Sam Rosenman.

In his need for the talents of such men, Roosevelt ran up against a simple, stubborn problem: the President had authorization to hire only four staff aides above the clerical level. These four jobs—there had been only two until Hoover's Administration—historically carried no particular prestige, and did not seem suitable for men like Moley and Tugwell. And in any event the slots were destined to be filled by Roosevelt's longtime followers, Louis Howe, Steve Early, and Marvin McIntyre.

The problem was no less real for being petty and bureaucratic, and Roosevelt solved it, as he solved so many others, by improvising. Men whom Roosevelt came to rely on heavily in his first two terms, men like Tugwell, Moley, and Corcoran, were given jobs in various government agencies but were on constant call to the President— White House aides in all but title. Later, Roosevelt took steps to expand the presidency into the institution we know today. He received congressional approval in 1939 to hire six Administrative Assistants—they of the famed "passion for anonymity." He created the position of Special Counsel to the President for his old friend Rosenman. He appointed the first Special Assistant to the President, Harry Hopkins. By the time he died, Roosevelt had started the evolution of the White House staff toward the large and powerful institution that now exists.

He did much more than create jobs. He filled them with men (and one woman) of such rare ability and dedication that they would continue over the years to be the standards by which future presidential aides would be measured. Dogged devotion to a President would be measured against Louis Howe. Exuberant political wheeling and dealing would call to mind Tommy Corcoran. A personal secretary who possessed canny insight into her boss's mind and moods would be compared with Missy LeHand. A White House aide who achieved both personal intimacy with the President and vast power in governmental affairs would inevitably be called another Harry Hopkins. (My research discloses that since 1945 an average of one presidential aide per year has been hailed by the press as the new Hopkins.)

It has often been said that Roosevelt used men, squeezed them dry, and ruthlessly discarded them. Louis Howe's biographer, Alfred Rollins, wrote: "Roosevelt's trail would be littered with the broken ambitions of men who had once thought themselves indispensable." The legend is only partly true. Men who tried to serve Roosevelt and at the same time nourish their own, independent ambitions—Moley, Corcoran, Jim Farley, John Nance Garner, Hugh Johnson—would inevitably find themselves on the outside looking in. But those who were willing to submerge their own fortunes entirely in Roosevelt's—Howe, Hopkins, Early, Missy LeHand—were protected by the President. The requirement was that they accept criticism without complaint, toil without credit, and accept unquestioningly Roosevelt's moods and machinations. One of Roosevelt's political ploys was to whisk controversial aides out of view at election time. Tugwell was sent to Europe during the 1934 congressional campaign and muzzled during the 1936 campaign. During the 1940 campaign, Corcoran was exiled to New York and Hopkins was forced to resign as Secretary of Commerce—but both afterward returned to favor. Roosevelt's aides had to learn to accept such indignities; if they couldn't, their days were numbered.

Roosevelt's aides were the victims of the most outrageous attacks from political and journalistic critics. The unhappy duty of bearing criticism for the President had traditionally fallen to Cabinet members, or to outside advisers, but during the New Deal it was largely transferred to Roosevelt's inner circle, notably Tugwell, Corcoran, and Hopkins. The criticism was inevitable, because the American people weren't accustomed to a White House palace guard with the shadowy status of Roosevelt's men.

It is oversimple to say that Roosevelt "used" his advisers as shields to criticism—the system used them, whether or not the President liked it. But it is true that he rarely spoke out publicly in their defense; he expected them to fight their own battles, or to suffer in silence if that suited his interests. And, while he may have regretted that they had to bear criticism for him, he was not in the slightest degree inclined to share any of his glories with them.

Once, in the late 1930s, one of Roosevelt's Administrative Assistants, James Rowe, chanced to have his name appear twice within a couple of months in the society pages of a Washington paper. The second time, Roosevelt told Rowe, in complete seriousness: "Jim, I'm the one who's running for office around here." Not until an FDR protégé, Lyndon Johnson, entered the White House would we have another President who so begrudged his helpers their press clippings.

Those who accepted Roosevelt's ground rules could be richly rewarded—by flashes of his incomparable charm, by the gaiety of the cocktail hour, by the warmth of Christmas with the Roosevelts, by involvement in the remaking of a nation.

The price was total dedication—not to the Democratic Party, or to liberal ideals or New Deal goals, but to Roosevelt personally, right or wrong, zigging or zagging, even when his means were most unsavory and his ends most unclear. The man who gave Roosevelt this degree of dedication first, and gave it to him longest, was the remarkable Louis Howe.

2. The Medieval Gnome: Howe

One day during Franklin Roosevelt's first term as President he sent his valet, Irwin McDuffie, to deliver a message to the wizened, sickly, chain-smoking man who lived in the White House's hallowed Lincoln Bedroom. Louis McHenry Howe listened impatiently to the message, then snapped at the valet: "You go back and tell the President I said to go to hell." McDuffie retreated in near-anguish and told his wife Lizzie, one of the White House maids, he couldn't possibly deliver such a reply to President Roosevelt. Lizzie promised to handle the matter and hurried to the President's room. "Mr. President," she reported, "Mr. Howe says that is a hell of a thing to do." The President looked up gravely. "Now, Lizzie, don't try to clean it up. You know very well that Louis said for me to go to hell, didn't he?" And Roosevelt lifted his great head and laughed aloud.

It is in the nature of Presidents to use many men, to need a few, and to love almost none. Franklin Roosevelt was loved by millions, and served by scores who idolized him, but throughout his political career he gave his fullest measure of affection, trust, and support to only a handful of men. The first was Louis Howe, the cynical, emaciated newspaperman-turned-politician who began plotting Roosevelt's road to the White House in 1912 and who, for the remaining twenty-four years of his life would be Roosevelt's political mentor, gadfly, court jester, alter ego, chief propagandist, sharpest critic, and closest friend. Their relationship, culminating with Howe's three years as Roosevelt's most intimate White House adviser, is without parallel in American politics.

On Election Night, 1932, when the dimensions of Roosevelt's landslide victory over Hoover had become clear, the President-to-be stood on a platform in the ballroom of New York's Biltmore Hotel, surrounded by cheering admirers and flanked by one big man and one small man. "There are two people in the United States more than anybody else who are responsible for this great victory," Roosevelt declared. "One is my old friend and associate, Colonel Louis Mc-Henry Howe, and the other is that splendid American, Jim Farley."

That splendid American Jim Farley—a big, bald, bluff political strategist who never forgot a face or a favor—was already well known to politicians, the press, and much of the public as the genial "Mr. Outside" of Roosevelt's political team. But "Colonel" Louis Howe, the shadowy Mr. Inside of the team, was a little-known quality. Now, with Roosevelt's affectionate endorsement, Howe's face was to become nationally known in the few years he had left to live.

And what a face it was. Howe, like Cyrano declaiming on his nose, sometimes delighted in stating the awful truth of it: "I am one of the four ugliest men, if what is left of me can be dignified by the name of man, in the State of New York. I am wizened in the Dickens manner. My eyes protrude because of so much looking. Children take one look at me on the street and run."

It was all too true. He was a small man, perhaps five feet five, never weighing much over 100 pounds. His tie was always awry, his fingers always stained and his suits ash-marked from smoking an endless chain of Sweet Caporal cigarettes. His thinning hair fell helterskelter over a wrinkled, parchment-like face; his nose was too big and his mouth too wide. Yet this homely little man was saved from outright ugliness by his eyes. They were large and brown and shrewd. Shrewd yet vulnerable, too, soft and deep like a deer's eyes; the eyes of a man who has seen much, suffered much, yet has kept the capacity to dream.

So he had. Howe had enjoyed a comfortable childhood in Saratoga, New York, as the son of a newspaper publisher. As a youth he enjoyed poetry and dramatics, but he bypassed college to go straight into the family paper. But by the time he was thirty, in the midst of a national recession, the paper failed, and Louis entered an agonizing decade as a not-quite-successful journalist, sometimes free-lancing, sometimes stringing for New York papers, usually broke and always worried about his ability to provide for his wife and children. This was his condition in 1911 when, while covering the New York legislature in Albany, he met Franklin Roosevelt, a twenty-nine-year-old first-term State Senator.

Their political partnership began informally with Howe advising Roosevelt and other young Turks who were defying their party's bosses. Then in 1912 Roosevelt employed Howe: first, to drum up support for Woodrow Wilson's nomination for President; later to manage Roosevelt's own campaign for re-election when he was floored by an attack of typhoid. In both cases, Howe proved an astute political technician, with particular talents for spotting issues, anticipating problems, handling the press, and using letter-writing as a political tool.

Their relationship was well stated by Alfred B. Rollins, Jr., in his book, *Roosevelt and Howe:* "After 1912 it would be impossible to think of Roosevelt or Howe without the other. They operated as parts of one political personality. They complemented each other in strengths and weaknesses. With smiles and warmth enough for both of them, the genial Roosevelt specialized in the high-level generalization, in persuasive speeches and personal charm in public contacts, and in the broad questions of public policy. Sardonic, cynical, shrewd, and chronically suspicious and worried, Louis Howe concentrated on the secret maneuver, the manipulation of the press, the organization of political loyalties and patronage hunger. . . . Roosevelt could absorb the credit, Howe the blame. But, between themselves, they understood that they rose and fell together."

When Roosevelt joined Wilson's Administration in 1913 as Assistant Secretary of the Navy, Howe went with him. Their partnership continued through Roosevelt's campaign for the vice presidency in 1920, his return to private life in 1921 (with Howe as his assistant when Roosevelt took an executive position with a large surety bonding house), Roosevelt's polio attack and long recuperation, and finally the high-level politicking that led to the Governor's Mansion in 1928 and the White House in 1932.

By then, Howe was much more than a political adviser; he was virtually one of the Roosevelt family. When the Roosevelts moved into the White House, it seemed altogether natural for Howe to settle in the Lincoln room. He complained that he would "rattle around like a pea in a pod" in the giant Lincoln bed, so he had a smaller bed put in the adjacent dressing room. Soon the room was wildly cluttered with Howe's paperwork, clothing, and countless half-filled packs of Sweet Caporal cigarettes.

Roosevelt put Howe in charge of organizing his White House staff. Howe's first act was to create for himself the new title of the Secretary to the President. Next, he gave Steve Early, the Press Secretary, and Marvin McIntyre, the Appointments Secretary, the lesser titles of Assistant Secretary to the President. Early and McIntyre, both friends of Roosevelt for a dozen years, were furious at this slight, but there was nothing to be done about it. Howe installed himself in an office next door to Roosevelt's office—then *he* was furious to learn that Roosevelt's personal secretary, Missy LeHand, had found herself a little cubbyhole office beside the Cabinet Room that was several prestige-laden feet closer to Roosevelt's office than his own.

Howe was fiercely jealous of his standing with Roosevelt. For many years he had been the number-one adviser. But as Governor, and then as President, Roosevelt had come to need other advisers with intellectual gifts Howe lacked. For the first time Howe found himself competing for Roosevelt's ear. When Roosevelt was Governor, Howe's archrival was the genial Sam Rosenman. Next, in the campaign of 1932, came the Brain Trusters, whose strange social schemes Howe was certain would lead Roosevelt to disaster. (Howe was the ultimate pessimist: he always wore both a belt *and* suspenders.)

Howe's competition with the newcomers was typified by an incident that occurred when Roosevelt received the Democratic nomination for President in 1932. Roosevelt had made the dramatic decision to fly to Chicago to accept the nomination in person. He carried with him a brilliant acceptance speech which he, Rosenman, Brain Truster Raymond Moley, and others had worked on for weeks. Howe, in his Chicago hotel room, had this speech read to him by telephone. He was furious. "Good God, do I have to do everything myself?" he asked a companion. "I see Sam Rosenman in every paragraph of this mess!" Howe frantically dictated his own version of the acceptance speech— a highly partisan, nonideological political document.

Howe met Roosevelt at the airport and thrust this speech into his hands. "Dammit, Louis, I'm the candidate," Roosevelt protested. But minutes later, when Roosevelt stood before the wildly cheering Democratic convention, he laid both speeches side by side on the speaker's rostrum. Deftly, he began reading Howe's introduction, then after one page he switched back to the eloquent Roosevelt-Rosenman-Moley speech. Jim Farley, who was listening to the speech over the radio with Howe, later wrote: "Louie was elated as his words came over the air and crushed when those of Moley were used for the rest of the speech."

Yet there was no shortage of work for Howe to do when he arrived in the White House. He was soon carrying a remarkable load for a man of his age and frail health, serving in a multi-sided capacity as public spokesman for the New Deal, behind-the-scenes administrator of several important programs, and ubiquitous presidential adviser, troubleshooter, and crony.

None of these roles is more amazing than Howe's emergence as a public spokesman. Howe had always been the mysterious, behind-the-scenes manipulator. His emergence seems to have been caused both by a long-suppressed love of the limelight and by a desire to counter what he felt to be the politically damaging influence of the Brain Trusters. Howe was devoutly anti-intellectual. "I'm no mastermind," he once said. "These masterminds are usually too intellectual to convince anyone but themselves, and being so superior they never get the viewpoint of the man in the street."

Howe flattered himself, probably correctly, that he understood the man in the street. With Roosevelt's blessing, he was soon accepting invitations to write magazine articles and to appear on the radio.

He wrote eight major articles for the *Saturday Evening Post*, *Woman's Home Companion*, *American Magazine*, *Liberty*, and *Cosmopolitan*. Some of the articles gave "intimate" portraits of Roosevelt; the ones that ventured into policy areas tended toward bland generalizations: "What is a balanced government as applied to these United States . . . ? In a general way a balanced government means a government of equal opportunity."

Howe made his radio debut in February, 1933, with a talk on the role of the Secret Service. Radio was Howe's best medium; his looks were no handicap, and his warm, cultured voice made him almost as effective a radio performer as his chief. In the spring of 1933 Howe was signed to make a series of thirteen radio appearances at $900 each. Although ostensibly a spontaneous question-and-answer exchange on government programs, Howe and the announcer in fact followed a carefully prepared script, with Howe having a veto over every word. (Sometimes he cleared the scripts with Roosevelt.)

Howe always downplayed his own importance; naturally, the result of this was to enlarge his legend. The more he denied being a kingmaker, the more he was hailed as one. Howe drew upon forty years in journalism and politics to carefully create his reputation. Once he crossed out of a radio script the accurate statement that he read little except newspapers and detective stories, but left in such phrases as "gnomelike," "planning under cover like a benevolent mole"; "it would be absurd to call him a kingmaker."

While Roosevelt's liberal advisers were being denounced for leading the country to ruin, Howe became a popular, rarely criticized public figure. Partly this was because the press associated him, correctly, with the conservative clique around Roosevelt, along with Farley, Secretary of State Cordell Hull, and Vice President John Nance Garner. But it was also because he so brilliantly presented himself to the public as the gruff but lovable, outspoken but loyal, intelligent but practical, grand old man of the Roosevelt Administration.

Howe loved the attention. The benevolent mole gloried in the peacock's role. His colonelcy was of the Kentucky variety, bestowed during the 1932 campaign for political, not military, maneuvers, and he laughed louder than anyone when White House correspondents gave him a tin sword and cocked hat to denote his military status. But he did nothing to discourage the use of the title; Colonel Howe sounded a great deal like Colonel House, a not unflattering comparison. He had calling cards printed, in deference to his growing legend, reading "Col. Louis Rasputin Voltaire Talleyrand Simon Legree Howe." When a journalist tagged him "the medieval Gnome," he for several days answered his phone with "Hello, this is the Medieval Gnome." It was noted that, although his workaday suits were as ill-fitting and ash-flecked as ever, he could dress as elegantly as a lord for the White House dinners he now proudly attended.

Even as Howe emerged in 1933–34 as a public figure, he was busy behind the scenes as the *de facto* administrator of two key New Deal programs, the Civilian Conservation Corps (CCC) and the Subsistence Home Experiment. Both were potentially explosive and Howe's role in running them reflected Roosevelt's trust in his political judgment. As it turned out, the CCC was a success and the Subsistence Home Project a fiasco. Howe deserved some credit for both results.

In typical Roosevelt fashion, the CCC was an administrative monstrosity. FDR hoped to put a quarter-million unemployed boys and men to work on conservation projects by the summer of 1933—within months of his inauguration. To achieve this goal, it was agreed that the Army would house and supervise the men; the Forest Service, National Park Service, and Army Engineers would devise their work projects; the Labor Department would handle recruiting; and a union official named Robert Fechner would coordinate the whole operation. Howe's job was to coordinate Fechner.

Howe's biographer Rollins wrote, "Roosevelt had no intention of allowing the CCC wars to reach him personally. He dumped the whole problem of police and management on Louis's desk. It nearly killed Fechner, it drove Howe to distraction, but it worked."

Fechner was expected to clear all important decisions with Howe. Fechner's press releases were approved—or rejected—by Howe. Howe used his White House influence to press the War Department for fast action on proposed flood-control projects. He kept a close eye on CCC hiring. He visited many of the camps, and was delighted to find one CCC-built road called "Louis McHenry Howe Boulevard." Only one shadow of scandal touched the CCC. Howe carelessly approved the purchase of 200,000 toilet kits without competitive bidding; however, he neatly passed the buck to the luckless Fechner and was absolved of all blame by a Senate investigating committee.

The Subsistence Homes program was another mess. The real power was held by Howe and Mrs. Roosevelt, both of whom were enthusiastic about the concept of building self-sufficient rural communities in which unemployed men and their families would work at gardening and light industries. Howe and Mrs. Roosevelt were determined to make a showcase of the first project, Arthurdale, in West Virginia. For a year, Rollins writes, he was "pouring over statistics on concrete, electricity, crops, and lumber, personally negotiating with General Electric for pumps and refrigeration, personally ordering prefabricated houses, personally shopping around to find out whether concrete blocks or hollow tiles were better-suited for foundations."

But it didn't jell. There was opposition within the government, and much more from private industry. At least one Senator denounced the scheme as Communistic. Everything went wrong. When Howe ordered fifty prefabricated houses from the navy for Arthurdale, they turned out to be thin-walled summer cottages and, worse, too small for the foundations that were already in place. Providing water for Arthurdale proved difficult. The Bureau of the Budget disliked Arthurdale's corporate structure. The nominal director of the program, tired of being bossed by Howe, resigned in public protest. To climax the troubles, in August of 1934, *The Washington Post* ran a devastating photograph of a tiny prefabricated house sitting on an outsized foundation ten feet from its chimney.

Soon after this, Howe began to withdraw from the Subsistence Homes project, perhaps because of his failing health, perhaps at Roosevelt's suggestion. In the spring of 1935, the entire operation was made a part of Rex Tugwell's new Resettlement Administration and, like many another government fiasco before and since, it soon faded quietly from view.

Howe's colorful public role detracted from the fact that he was a highly valued political adviser. On strategic questions, on issues of public policy, Roosevelt's vision had far outstripped his old mentor. But on political tactics, on personalities and publicity and patronage, Howe remained Roosevelt's most valued counselor. Howe's role was often a negative one; for two decades he had seen it as his mission to restrain an impetuous Roosevelt from acts of folly. Thus, although he lacked political dogma, he tended to be an ally of conservatives in the Administration. (In 1936, his dying words to Vice President Garner would be: "Hold Franklin down!")

Yet Howe could just as easily take the liberals' side if politics so decreed. In the summer of 1934, San Francisco was hit by a violent general strike while Roosevelt was on a vacation cruise. Hull, Attorney General Cummings, and others wanted Roosevelt to return and use force to break the strike. Secretary of Labor Frances Perkins believed that such action would only make a bad situation worse. Howe sided with Miss Perkins' moderate counsel, and he sent a telegram to Roosevelt advising him: "*Only danger San Francisco strike is that Mayor is badly frightened and his fear infected entire city.*" His advice proved to be sound.

Howe conformed to no political pattern. His cynicism and caution would now and then give way to bursts of idealism that stunned even Roosevelt. One day in the spring of 1934, Roosevelt remarked to David E. Lilienthal, who headed the Tennessee Valley Authority: "You know, Louie Howe sits over there at the house like a gnome, thinking. Out of every ten ideas he gets, one is likely to be very good. That's a good percentage, isn't it—one idea out of ten? Well, he had an idea that probably isn't any of your business or mine. It was to clear out the slums and poor housing, and build a city the way it ought to be built. Instead of doing patchwork here and patchwork there, have a place where you could say to the country, 'This is how it should be done.' How does that strike you? Perhaps we could do that in the Tennessee Valley—say at Nashville—what kind of a city is that? Of course, you have the Negro conflict there, don't you?"

Perhaps the strangest example of Howe's political troubleshooting came in May 1933 when the 6000 man Bonus Army descended on

Washington. Roosevelt was determined not to make the kind of mistake Hoover had made when he sent the army to disband a previous Bonus Army the year before. Instead, he provided the marchers with food and housing, and instructed Howe to visit the campsite and make sure the veterans were decently cared for. Yet Howe knew the mood in the camp was ugly; the marchers were grimly awaiting some sign or message from the White House.

The climax came one rainy afternoon when Howe invited Mrs. Roosevelt to go for a drive, as they often did for a chance to talk undisturbed. Howe proceeded to the Bonus Army encampment and, as he later told the story, this exchange followed:

"Louis, what is this place and what are we going to do here?"

"This is where the Bonus Army is quartered, and you are going in there and talk to those men, get their gripes, if any, make a tour of the camp and tell them that Franklin sent you out to see about them. Don't forget that—be sure to tell them that Franklin sent you."

"But Louis, what are you going to do?"

"I'm going to take a nap," he said. And he did, as she left the car and walked alone toward the camp. She performed magnificently, walking through ankle-deep mud to shake hands, talk, and sing with the old soldiers. Afterward, one veteran said, "Hoover sent the army: Roosevelt sent his wife." Presidents pray for words like those to be spoken of them.

But did Roosevelt send his wife? Or was it Howe's idea? No one seems quite sure: Roosevelt's biographer credits Roosevelt; Howe's biographer credits Howe. There is no doubt that Howe was cynical enough to have thought of it, and one can only speculate on whether Roosevelt was cynical enough to have approved sending his wife to soothe the angry Bonus Marchers. The device has the aura of Howe about it, for he had taken Mrs. Roosevelt's political education in hand as early as the 1920 vice-presidential campaign, and she had limitless trust in Howe's political wisdom. She said of the 1938 congressional campaign with its luckless attempt to purge anti-Roosevelt Democrats: "If there were political mistakes in this campaign, some of them, I think, might have been avoided if Louis Howe had been alive. After Louis Howe's death, Franklin never had a political adviser who argued with him, when he really disagreed, and yet still gave him unquestioned loyalty."

Howe's health, delicate for years, was in a steady decline by 1934. Toward the end of that year more and more of his administrative duties began to be taken up by others. He continued to chain-smoke, and he continued to be plagued by fits of coughing and labored breathing. In the early months of 1934 he was bedridden with pneumonia. He disobeyed doctor's orders by leaving the White House to attend the Gridiron dinner in April, and late that summer he horrified his friends by turning up in Portland, Oregon, to greet the President after a Pacific cruise. By January 1935 he was again bedridden, and in March his condition seemed critical. On March 19, 1935, Howe's daughter, after seeing him unconscious in an oxygen tent, wired her husband: "No hope beyond twenty-four hours." Later that day Howe awoke complaining: "Why in hell doesn't somebody give me a cigarette?" Soon he was on the phone telling Harry Hopkins how to run his relief agency.

Mrs. Roosevelt nursed him, and his wife, Grace, came from their Fall River, Massachusetts, home to stay in the White House. Howe continued to work in his room, but it soon was clear that he needed hospital attention, and he was moved to the U. S. Naval Hospital in August 1935.

Even there he busied himself with politics. He had a plan to produce a movie which would explain the U. S. Constitution to the man in the street (and find its goals quite similar to those of the New Deal). He proposed a Good Neighbor League to demonstrate Roosevelt's concern for minority groups. Bernard Baruch advanced the money to start this league, and it was later successfully incorporated into the Democratic campaign of 1936.

Roosevelt often visited Howe's bedside, where he was lectured about the evils of Huey Long, Father Coughlin, and Mussolini. Farley, Ickes, and others in the Administration were also frequent visitors. Howe's old adversary Moley, still a part-time presidential speechwriter, would bring speech drafts for Howe's perusal now out of respect rather than necessity. As Howe's condition worsened there would be times when he would call government officials and make unreasonable requests. Roosevelt issued instructions that Howe was to be treated with the utmost respect and that only the President himself was authorized to countermand Howe's orders. There were moments of clarity, too. Once when a friend tried to raise Howe's spirits by saying he would be back on his feet in time for the 1936 campaign, Howe shook his head and said: "No, I will not be there. Franklin's on his own now."

He died in his sleep on the night of April 18, 1936, while the President was attending a Gridiron dinner. Roosevelt, learning the news upon his return to the White House, ordered flags to half-mast and a state funeral in the East Room of the White House for his old companion. Later the Roosevelts would journey to Fall River to attend Howe's burial.

Howe holds a special niche in the pantheon of presidential aides. He was not the most brilliant or effective assistant who ever served a President. His most important contributions to Roosevelt's career were made before he became President. By the time they arrived in the White House, Howe's failing health and the narrowness of his background limited the role he could play. Yet he made a unique and immensely valuable contribution to Roosevelt's political fortunes and personal well-being. Always nagging, doubting, questioning, probing, Howe was a constant reminder to Roosevelt of his own fallibility. He was a faithful friend to a man who was destined to have few friends. And, for all his cynicism, Howe set a standard of dedication which few other presidential aides, in Roosevelt's time or since, would equal. In 1921, soon after Roosevelt's polio attack, Howe had declared: "By God, Franklin will be President, legs or no legs!" That was his dream, and, incredibly, he lived to see it come true.

3. The Professor: Moley

Raymond Moley in 1932 was a forty-six-year-old Columbia University professor whose long face, dark brows, jutting nose and sly smile conspired to give him the visage of a canny but benevolent hawk. The adjectives would have pleased Moley, for he viewed himself as a man blessed both with political sophistication and social conscience. His political instincts had asserted themselves early: at the age of twenty-one he had been elected mayor of the village of Olmsted Falls, Ohio. Later, as a specialist in the administration of criminal law, he conducted pioneering studies of police, prosecution, and the courts in several states. These achievements won him a professorship at Columbia in 1923; he was a man on the move in academic circles.

Still there was little reason to suspect, as the nation anxiously awaited the presidential election of 1932, that Professor Moley was about to become one of the most influential men in the United States. Yet that is what he did. He captured Franklin Roosevelt's ear; he served for a dozen intoxicating months as Roosevelt's most-heeded policy adviser; and in the end he left a mark on the New Deal (the *first* New Deal, Moley would be quick to say) that not even his abrupt fall from power could erase. Moley burst across the political heavens like an errant skyrocket; few men have soared so high so fast, or fallen so far so soon.

Louis Howe first brought Moley into the Roosevelt circle. Howe's nominal job in the 1920s, the cover for his ceaseless politicking, was as director of the National Crime Commission. Howe hired Moley to write some reports for the commission and was impressed by him. When Roosevelt became Governor, he named Moley to the New York Commission on the Administration of Justice, and the hard-working professor soon caught the eye of Roosevelt's other top adviser, Sam Rosenman.

Early in 1932, when Rosenman urged Roosevelt to call in some university professors to coach him on national issues, Moley's was the first name he suggested. Moley brought in two colleagues from Columbia, economist Rexford G. Tugwell and law professor Adolph A. Berle, Jr. The Brain Trust—Louis Howe coined the term with no charitable intent—was born.

Tugwell has given us an indelible picture of that short-lived but remarkable institution at work. The time was the spring of 1932; the place, the Governor's Mansion; those present, Roosevelt, Rosenman, Moley, Berle, Tugwell, and Basil (Doc) O'Connor, Roosevelt's former law partner. Tugwell wrote:

"Those meetings, we can claim, contributed to the fitting of Franklin for the presidency. We were able, Berle and I, with Ray abetting and Sam and Doc O'Connor looking on approvingly, to lead an exceptionally agile mind to a level of discussion adequate to the circumstances.

"That level, of course, was theoretical. We pressed him to grapple with the complex realities of industrial life, to move beyond his reasonable but oversimple reactions which were obviously insufficient as guides to policy. He went with us toward a comprehension of large-scale technology, the forces it had created and the consequences of allowing it to escape regulation—or rather of allowing its management to be gathered into a few privately controlled ganglia. This we linked up with the price system, the network of credits, and the handling of commodities and services. Everywhere we probed for weaknesses and dangers and felt for such possibilities as there might be for leverage. We exposed for him the private wars going on among the titans of industrial society. Each strove to exploit the other. Some succeeded and, in doing so, overbalanced the system. That, essentially, was our explanation of the current trouble. It was one he seemed to accept. . . .

"Franklin's progress in gaining an understanding of matters about which he had heretofore thought only in the oversimple way of an educated and well-informed amateur was so remarkable that by June a notable weakness was transformed into an all-round competence. He knew what it was he expected to say about most of the issues he was likely to have to meet in the campaign, and he was well on the way to shaping a system of policy to be used when the presidency was attained."

The overriding fact facing Roosevelt as he neared the presidency was that the American economy had collapsed. The national income was less than half of what it had been four years earlier. Almost thirteen million Americans—nearly one-fourth of the labor force—could not find work. Mass starvation was at hand; perhaps revolution. The American system had broken down, and it was Roosevelt's job to make it work again. This was why the members of the Brain Trust—principally Moley, Tugwell, and Berle—achieved such importance. Roosevelt was no economist; they were. They had an economic philosophy they believed would bring national recovery, and which seemed to Roosevelt to make such sense (although he was certainly never such putty in their hands as the self-impressed Tugwell's statement above would indicate). Their philosophy was, however, one that broke sharply with tradition.

In American political life, there had traditionally been two views of the proper relationship between business and government. The dominant one was *laissez faire*, the faith that business was by its nature good and government should simply leave it alone. That was Herbert Hoover's view.

The second traditional view was that of the Progressives, the rural reformers whose leading spokesman in the 1930s was Supreme Court Justice Louis Brandeis. Their view was that business is by its nature evil, and the job of government is to minimize its evil by keeping business small through "trust-busting" policies.

Moley, Tugwell, and Berle offered a third alternative, one that seems commonplace today but was radical in 1933. Government, they said, should neither ignore business nor attack it, but should *work with business* to achieve a healthy economy. The idea common to the three Columbia University professors was that government must accept the economic integration that industrialization had brought to America, abandon the old Progressive idea of trust-busting, and accept a co-ordinating and planning role to make the nation's magnificent but Depression-idled industrial plant produce the bounty of which it was capable. Instead of passing laws to make it illegal for businessmen to cooperate with each other, they wanted government to help businessmen work together to direct the flow of resources, to cut down murderous competition, to prevent overpricing and overproduction. The Progressives wanted government to tell business what it could not do; the Brain Trust wanted government to tell business what it could do.

Within this general consensus, the Columbia professors differed sharply among themselves as to the exact nature of the new "business-government partnership." The more conservative Moley saw it as a business-dominated partnership, one that would restore investor confidence in the economy. Tugwell, at the other extreme, envisioned substantial government control of business: "I thought of industrial leaders meeting under government auspices and determining quotas, prices, and schedules. I thought of competition modified, of speculation outlawed by formal agreement, of resources and materials marshalled and flowing toward uses determined on the principles of national need."

But despite their differences, the Brain Trusters' belief in government-business planning was to dominate the first two years of the New Deal. Then, in 1935, Roosevelt decided that the business community did not want to cooperate with him, and he began to shift from economic planning to old-style Progressive trust-busting. This shift marked the line between what are now called the First and Second New Deals. Personnel would shift with policy: Moley and Tugwell would depart, and a Brandeis disciple, Tom Corcoran, would replace them as Roosevelt's leading adviser.

But for Moley, in the crucial months between Roosevelt's election and his inauguration, these problems were far in the future. During the campaign he had emerged as the acknowledged leader of the Brain Trust, and in the pre-Inaugural period he was (as *Newsweek* called him) the "one-man reception committee through whom ideas had to go to reach Roosevelt." Congressional leaders flocked to his rooms in the Carlton Hotel with ideas for the New Deal's legislative program. A joke circulated in which one of Roosevelt's oldest friends pleaded: "Franklin, can you do me just one favor? Can you get me an appointment with Moley?"

Moley played a multi-sided role in this period. He was Roosevelt's intermediary with potential Cabinet members. He opposed Tugwell and others who favored the "grand gesture" of reducing European war debts; the politician in Moley perceived the folly of canceling foreigners' debts while millions of Americans were struggling with their own debts at home. Moley collaborated with Roosevelt on the early drafts of the Inaugural Address—and was later piqued when Roosevelt claimed to have written it himself in one four-hour spurt of creativity. It was Moley whom Roosevelt selected to accompany him on an ice-cool conference with Hoover and his Secretary of the Treasury, and since Roosevelt knew almost nothing about the topic of the conference, European war debts, he let Moley do most of the talking. In later years, Moley would say that one of his most important contributions was to save J. Edgar Hoover's job. According to Moley, Louis Howe and several political bosses wanted to oust Hoover to open up FBI jobs for patronage, but he talked Roosevelt out of it.

For all his new-found power, Moley repeatedly told Roosevelt he sought no government position and intended to return to Columbia as soon as possible. (Of the other Brain Trusters, Rosenman stayed in New York to serve on the state Supreme Court; Berle declined a federal post but helped with legislation during the Hundred Days; and Tugwell became an Assistant Secretary of Agriculture. The Brain Trust never met as such after the 1932 election, but the name continued to be applied to virtually anyone who advised Roosevelt.)

Roosevelt, as Moley later recalled it, implored him to stay by his side and outlined an extraordinary role for him to play: "No one in the Administration would have a more intimate relationship with the President. No one, except himself, would have more to do with making policy. . . . The time had come to begin translating policy into action. My authorization seemed to make me Roosevelt's *de facto* minister of the moment."

Offered such a glimmering vision of power, Moley at length agreed to take a job with the Administration. There still remained the question of just what job he would fill. Clearly, he was to be Roosevelt's right-hand man. Roosevelt told Moley he had considered him for a slot called Administrative Assistant to the President, but rather than upset the ever-jealous Louis Howe, he had resolved to abolish that position altogether. But he had another idea for Moley. He had discovered that almost no specific duties were required by law of the Assistant Secretaries of State. Here was a perfect base of operations for Moley— it would give Moley status, freedom to work directly with Roosevelt, and an office just a stone's throw from the White House.

Moley protested. The new Secretary of State, Senator Cordell Hull of Tennessee, would resent a subordinate who was closer to the President than he. "Hull knows all about it," Roosevelt assured him. "There'll be no misunderstanding with him." In the end, Moley agreed. He could not argue with the President. Besides, it occurred to him that the State Department needed someone at the top who understood the New Deal—Hull didn't—and who understood it better than he himself? So Moley took the job. He lasted for six months.

Strictly speaking, Moley was not a White House aide—he was an Assistant Secretary of State. But in 1933 there was no provision for a presidential aide of Moley's type, no tradition that influential policy advisers should be attached to the White House staff. Moley was the first of this new breed, one that would later include such men as Clark Clifford, Sherman Adams, McGeorge Bundy, and Bill Moyers. During Moley's brief career in Washington, he was a White House aide with a State Department title. A few years later such a fiction would not be necessary.

These had been heady times for Moley, and old associates found him not unchanged by the experience. Rosenman told Henry Morgenthau: "To think that Ray Moley used to stand outside my office six months ago with the hope that I would pass on some of his papers to Governor Roosevelt. This morning he acted as if he was running the government and that Roosevelt was carrying out Moley's suggestions." A Washington joke, parodying the hymn, was "Moley, Moley, Moley, Lord God Almighty . . ."

Washington might joke, but Moley's power was real as the Hundred Days began. He met with the new President for fifteen minutes each morning to discuss the issues of the day. He was credited with persuading Roosevelt to depart from the gold standard. On most new legislative proposals—and there were scores of them—he was the White House liaison with Congress and the government agency involved. Roosevelt made the big policy decisions himself, but he would let others work out details. And to Roosevelt, Moley once noted, "details" might involve, for example, whether the CCC should enroll 250,000 men or 500,000. More than thirty years later, Moley would grimace as he thought back to these days; he spoke of it as a "frightening" time, a time of "tearing responsibility."

Much of Moley's influence was through the people he brought into the Roosevelt circle. He had recruited Tugwell, who played a key role in shaping farm policy, and Berle, who dominated Roosevelt's handling of the railroad and banking problems. Too busy to help draft the all-important National Industrial Recovery Act, Moley delegated that task to General Hugh Johnson who went on to be NRA's flamboyant administrator. It was Moley who summoned Felix Frankfurter to draft the securities legislation, and Frankfurter in turn called upon his friends Tom Corcoran and Ben Cohen.

Moley and the other advocates of government-business planning won two great victories during the Hundred Days. On March 16 Roosevelt's farm message called for federal regulation of agriculture; two months later in the National Industrial Recovery Act Roosevelt called for the organization of industry and commerce under federal authority. Those two decisions—to seek central management of agriculture and industry —determined the shape of the First New Deal.

As the Hundred Days drew to a close, Moley's views seemed triumphant. Yet a few years later he complained bitterly that he had seen the Roosevelt Administration "lurch between the philosophy of controlling bigness and the philosophy of destroying bigness, between the belief in a partnership between government and industry and the belief in trust-busting. . . . I had no way of knowing in May of 1933 that Roosevelt had not the slightest comprehension of the difference between the two sets of beliefs."

Moley was wrong, of course. Roosevelt understood the difference between the two philosophies. It was Moley who did not understand Roosevelt. Schlesinger suggested the failure of understanding between them when he wrote:

"For Moley and the others, national planning tended to be almost an end in itself; for Roosevelt, it was a means to an end. Seeing people and not ideologies—specific cases rather than general principles —Roosevelt freely indulged in contradictions which drove logical men to despondency. . . . Roosevelt transcended systems for the sake of a more complex vision of America, which included elements of coordination and of decentralization, of nationalism and internationalism. . . ."

Moley might in time have adjusted to the realities of political compromise, but he didn't have the chance. The beginning of the end had come when he crossed paths with Cordell Hull.

He had thought, when Hull's name was first mentioned as a possible Secretary of State, that the old Tennessean would be hopelessly out of place in the New Deal. He later wrote with exquisite irony: "I had nothing but pity for the guilelessness that might lead Hull to walk with eyes wide open into a difficult, perhaps an intolerable situation." Someone was walking guilelessly into an intolerable situation, but it was not Hull.

The new Secretary of State was sixty-two years old and had been in Congress for more than a quarter century. A Southerner and a Jeffersonian, he had championed the income tax and the inheritance tax. But his lifelong crusade, the cornerstone of his philosophy, was opposition to what he called "the king of evils"—the protective tariff.

And on that issue the stiff-necked old Tennessean was in direct opposition to Moley, who was doing his best to convince Roosevelt that the New Deal's domestic programs *needed* the protection of a tariff. To Moley, Hull's dream of free trade was a worthy long-term goal, but tariffs were an immediate necessity.

A clash between Moley and Hull was inevitable, yet when it came, it was less over the tariff question than the simple fact that Hull didn't like Moley and considered him an affront to his authority. The press had been quick to spot the incongruity of Moley's position at State and to speculate that he had his eye on Hull's job. Moley went out of his way to assure Hull that this was not true, but his protestations of good will only made the old man more suspicious. After one such assurance, Hull dryly commented: "Moley at least has the subject on his mind."

The climax came in London in the summer of 1933 at the International Monetary and Economic Conference, a gathering which is memorable only as one of the splendid fiascoes in the history of international relations. The issues at the ill-fated conference included tariffs, war debts, exchange restrictions, currency stabilization, and the gold standard.

In retrospect, it can be seen that American participation in this conference could not have been successful if the nation's six-man delegation had consisted of six Alexander Hamiltons, which it emphatically did not. Hull headed the American delegation despite his opposition to the Administration's tariff position. One member of the American delegation was a drunken Senator who sometimes brandished a bowie knife. The head of the delegation's staff was a man so enamored of intrigue that he enraged the British Prime Minister by taking out his secretary and trying to pry state secrets from her.

At the end of June, with the American delegation—and the entire conference—in disarray, Roosevelt dispatched an eager Moley to London as his "liaison officer." It was everywhere assumed that Moley was Roosevelt's personal spokesman, come to take over from Hull. The New York *Times* astutely warned that the "professor *ex machina*" would only add to the confusion. Hull was furious as newspapermen and foreign officials (including the British Prime Minister) rushed to see Moley. Moley's sincere attempts to play down his role were futile. At one point Hull bitterly told the younger man he had surrendered a lifetime seat in the Senate only to be humiliated at his hands. Moley tried to make peace with Hull, but the embittered Tennessean would have none of it; he wrote in his diary: "I decided to give him [Moley] all the rope he might want and see how long he would last in that London situation."

Moving into action, Moley entered negotiations that resulted in his urging Roosevelt to subscribe to an innocuous, face-saving declaration proposed by the gold-standard countries, one that simply looked to the eventual restoration of the gold standard as a measure of international exchange.

Suddenly Moley was struck by a double-barreled blast. First, Roosevelt rejected the Moley-approved declaration. Next, and infinitely worse, Roosevelt issued a public statement that came to be known as "The Bombshell" for its impact on the London Conference. The conference, Roosevelt declared, was exhibiting "a singular lack of proportion and a failure to remember the large purposes" for which it had been called. Apparently Roosevelt got the idea he was being pressured by the gold-standard nations and the international bankers, and decided to show them who was boss. But in so doing he seemed to have publicly repudiated Moley. Moley sailed home in dismay while Hull stayed in London and did a creditable job of salvaging the wreckage of the conference.

Moley's pride was hurt, as well as his reputation. "There were stories that I'd planted spies within the delegation," he wrote later. "There were stories that I'd betrayed official secrets to spies—French and Chinese, male and female—in the traditional dime-store novel manner."

The worst was yet to come. Shortly before Moley left London he decided to urge Roosevelt to appoint an entirely new delegation. Unable to reach the vacationing President by telephone, Moley sent a cable which said of the Hull-led delegation: "PITTMAN IS THE ONLY MEMBER OF DELEGATION ABLE INTELLECTUALLY AND AGGRESSIVELY TO PRESENT YOUR IDEAS." Moley had marked this cable "top secret, for the President's eyes only," yet a copy somehow found its way to Hull's desk. That was the end.

"That pissant Moley!" Hull roared. "Here he curled up at my feet and let me stroke his head like a huntin' dog and then he goes and bites me in the ass!"

Using somewhat more formal language, Hull wrote in protest to Roosevelt: "Moley was secretly sending code messages to you about my incapacity to function here. He was at the same time pretending absolute loyalty of friendship and of official attitude toward me." Reports circulated that Hull had told the President to choose between him and Moley.

When Moley saw Roosevelt upon his return to Washington, neither man mentioned the London fiasco. Moley privately felt Roosevelt owed him an apology. He had begun to think of resigning, but he realized it would look better if he stayed on his job for a while. He was already engaged in negotiations to become editor of a new national magazine, and he perceived the public-relations benefits of bowing out gracefully. He did not know that Roosevelt was thinking along the same lines. Forced to choose between a brilliant but thin-skinned professor and a Secretary of State whom both he and Congress held in the highest regard, Roosevelt made the obvious decision. "It has been characteristic of the New Deal to send officials far away from Washington on long expeditions when awkward situations present themselves," Moley wrote later. "That technique was first tried out on me."

Moley noted that this gambit was also used on NRA Administrator Hugh Johnson, who resigned rather than embark on an unexpected tour of Europe. Moley attributed this scheme to Louis Howe.

"Louis' scheme for me in July, 1933, was more ingenious," Moley continued. "In fact, it was a product not only of his political acumen, but of a romanticism induced by a lifetime of reading detective stories. Louis told me that he had been talking with Secretary Ickes about the administration of criminal justice in Hawaii; a certain *cause célèbre* [the Massie rape-murder case] a short time before had revealed pretty incompetent conditions there. . . . Would I not, in short, go to Hawaii for three months? I would not, I said. Louis did not give up, however. In a few days he came through with another plan. This time it was presented to me by the President."

The new plan was for Moley to be assigned to the Justice Department to help draw up legislation to cope with a recent rash of kidnapings. This was a plausible plan and Moley agreed to it. The press accepted the switch at face value—there was no talk of Moley's being forced out by Hull. After a few months Moley resigned from government to become editor of the new magazine, *Today*, which later merged with *Newsweek*.

One editorial likened Moley's exit from the Roosevelt Administration to Lucifer's fall from Heaven. Moley acidly replied that the analogy belittled the editorialist's own profession, since his "fall" had been from government to journalism.

Actually, Moley's break with the Administration was a friendly one. Roosevelt was not angry with Moley; he simply found it inconvenient to keep him in the official family. Moley continued to serve Roosevelt from time to time as an adviser and speechwriter. But during the next few years Moley's political views were becoming increasingly conservative, his magazine writing often criticized the New Deal, and he was seen less and less at the White House. Moley believed Roosevelt was making a serious mistake by breaking with the business community and returning to trust-busting policies, and his intellectual honesty required him to speak bluntly, even if it meant losing his influence with Roosevelt.

The final break came during the 1936 campaign. Moley, Tom Corcoran, Stanley High, and Sam Rosenman were at the White House drafting Roosevelt's acceptance speech one evening, and they dined with the President and Missy LeHand. Rosenman later described the scene this way:

"That night in the small family dining room, for the first and only time in my life, I saw the President forget himself as a gentleman. He began twitting Moley about his new conservatism and about the influence of his 'new, rich friends' on his recent writings, which had been very critical of the Administration. Moley responded with what I thought was justifiable heat. The President grew angry, and the exchanges between them became very bitter. We all felt embarrassed; Missy did her best to change the subject but failed. Their words became more acrimonious. . . . I am sure that Roosevelt soon felt sorry for what he had said; but I could not see how the two of them could ever resume their earlier friendship. They never did."

Roosevelt and Moley lunched together two years later, but the meeting was strained and they never met again. But if Moley had lost a friend, he had found a calling. He never returned to teaching, for journalism proved to be the ideal outlet for his well-reasoned conservatism and his polished prose. Today, in his eighties, he remains a regular columnist for *Newsweek,* a very cordial, very conservative old man whose age has not dulled the sharpness of his mind or of his pen. He is quick to say that he came out ahead for his Washington experience. It took him from academic life, made him a national figure, and led him to a rewarding career as an author and political journalist. Yet Moley will admit, too, when he reflects on the awful responsibilities, the criticisms, the back-stabbing, the jealousies that accompanied his political power, that even now, more than thirty years later, he still cannot bear to spend a night in Washington, D.C.

Moley's brief career as a presidential adviser abounds with cautionary value for his successors. Rule One—it might be called Moley's Law—would be "Don't tangle with Cabinet members." Today, as then, Cabinet officials often have a political following—as Hull emphatically did. They have been confirmed by the Senate. Several Cabinet offices have, since the founding of the Republic, enjoyed widespread public veneration. The Secretaries are, in short, hard men to dislodge. None of this is true of the White House staff members. They have only the good will of the President, a singularly ephemeral blessing.

A presidential favorite can undercut a Cabinet member in an infinity of ways. He can cultivate allies on the Secretary's staff and conspire with them on policy matters. He can talk against the Secretary to the President. He can leak damning information about the Cabinet officer to the press. He can delay or distort the Secretary's messages to the President. But in all of this the aide is wise to stay in the shadows; to cover his tracks; to avoid a direct confrontation.

Moley made three tangible errors. First, he should never have taken the job under Hull. Second, he should have avoided the London Conference. Finally, he should never have put on paper—in the cable to Roosevelt—his low opinion of Hull. Any President might have second thoughts about a man who would make that mistake.

It is interesting to note where Moley himself placed the blame for his fall from grace. He might well have blamed himself, but human nature being as it is, he could not do that. The next logical step would have been to blame Roosevelt, but Moley chose not to do that either.

Instead, Moley placed most of the blame on Louis Howe. He credited Howe, first, with sabotaging Roosevelt's original plan to place him on the White House staff; second, with persuading Roosevelt to place him at the State Department in the hope that a conflict with Hull would result; and, third, with persuading Roosevelt to issue the "Bombshell" message that so embarrassed Moley at the London Conference.

Howe was a devious man, but Moley surely overestimates his influence in his own downfall, which was caused not by Howe's plots, but by his own unfortunate lapses of judgment.

Even without the confrontation with Hull, Moley would probably not have lasted long. He is quick to admit that he was never a team player. It was difficult, almost impossible, for him to subjugate himself to another man's interests, even those of the President of the United States. Individualism is an admirable quality but it is not always helpful to those who would serve a President. Moley was thin-skinned; his feelings were hurt when Roosevelt embarrassed him at the London Conference. He should have known better. To suffer without cause is the loyal aide's fate; kings cannot err. Moley understood the principle but he was not willing to live with the reality.

4. *The Whipping Boy: Tugwell*

Raymond Moley lasted six months with the Roosevelt Administration but his friend Rexford G. Tugwell was not so lucky. He lasted four years. During those years, while playing a dual role as Assistant Secretary of Agriculture and as a wide-ranging presidential adviser, Tugwell was the victim of one of the most vicious, most effective smear campaigns in the annals of American journalism. It is part of the political ethos that Presidents must have men around them to serve as shields to criticism, and this unhappy role fell to Tugwell. The young professor became the New Deal's whipping boy. He was soon known to millions of newspaper readers as Rex the Red, a Communist, a fascist, an anarchist, a would-be Lenin, a traitor, a madman lusting for power, "a third-rate Voltaire trying to be a second-rate Rousseau"—in sum, an impractical, overeducated, arrogant, ruthless, inefficient yet somehow vastly danger-ous enemy of the American Way of Life.

Tugwell did not volunteer for this assignment, but in retrospect he seems to have been destined for it. One reason was simply his availability. In the earliest days of the New Deal, its critics lumped Tugwell, Moley, and Berle together; one New York political writer was moved to verse:

> "School days, school days
> Good old Golden Rule days,
> Moley and Tugwell and Dr. Berle
> Telling us how to run the worl' . . ."

But Moley and Berle (whose name, incidentally, rhymes with "early") were soon safely back in New York, and Tugwell was left to shoulder all the anti-intellectual criticism alone.

A second reason for Tugwell's troubles was that he *was* arrogant, at least with that overwhelming majority of the citizenry he considered his intellectual inferiors, a group that unfortunately included most mem-bers of Congress. Tugwell was too handsome, too professorial, too enamored of six-syllable words. The liberal Texas Congressman Maury Maverick gave this account of a talk with Tugwell:

"He used more professorial language and said something about 'avert-ing a revolution.' I was going blind.

"Then, to prove his point, he said: 'And the workers and farmers, combining their genius and (another word I couldn't get), and they shall form a nodule. . . .'

"I blew up completely.

"I said, 'Rex, I am sore and insulted, and do not want to hear any more.'

" 'Why?' he asked.

" 'What in God's name is a nodule?' I said.

" 'A nodule is . . .' began Rex.

" 'Stop! Stop!' I shouted. 'Don't tell me. Whenever you use a word that I don't understand, it makes me mad. I am an American! The word nodule is not understood by the American people, nor is it understood by me, which makes it worse . . . Nodule my eye! Put your speech in simple language. I never heard of a nodule before. Besides, it sounds like sex perversion.' "

But the real reason for the attacks on Tugwell went far deeper than his looks or his vocabulary. Never before had a man reached a position of such influence over national affairs who was so passionate and articulate a champion of the public interest over the interests of private profit. The vested interests soon sensed that Moley was no threat to them, but Tugwell was their natural enemy. As a writer and professor, and as a presidential adviser, Tugwell fought for the small farmer against the big landowners, for the consumer against dishonest advertising and dangerous food processing, for the unemployed worker and his family against the indifference of big business, for the national forests and streams against the industries that were polluting and destroying them. Tugwell was the sort of radical intellectual who had traditionally operated outside the political mainstream, and conservatives were outraged to see him at the pinnacle of national policy-making.

For the same reason Moley was made Assistant Secretary of State, Tugwell was made Assistant Secretary of Agriculture under Henry Wallace, whom he greatly admired. Unlike Moley Tugwell took an active role in departmental affairs. As Assistant Secretary of Agriculture, he was in a position to influence farm recovery, to aid the small farmer and sharecropper, to work for soil conservation, and to promote various other causes that interested him. One of his responsibilities was to oversee the Food and Drug Administration, then a part of the Department of Agriculture. Tugwell had long protested the "robbery of consumer deception"; he wanted the people to have "freedom from fakes," i.e., deceptive advertising. Ever before he took his new office, he had written in his diary: "I'll do the best I can for the consumer regardless of politics; I won't compromise on this." What Tugwell did not understand, and would learn at high cost, was that a refusal to make political compromise was not necessarily the best way to help the consumer.

It was Tugwell's advocacy of consumers' interests that first inspired widespread criticism of him. With Roosevelt's approval, he had a new Food and Drug Act written and sent to Congress in June 1933. This legislation, soon dubbed the Tugwell Act, set high standards for the labeling and advertising of drugs. It vigorously opposed, someone commented, the God-given right of free enterprise to sell horse linament as a cure for cancer.

The problem was that Tugwell had no political sense. His boss at Agriculture, Wallace, was no better off, and Roosevelt was too busy to worry about the timing and presentation of a food and drug bill. Tugwell's first blunder came even before his bill was introduced. He issued an administrative order reducing the maximum amount of poisonous-spray residue allowable on fruits and vegetables. Immediately fruit growers protested to their Congressmen, and resistance to the Tugwell Act began to stiffen even before it reached Congress.

The Tugwell Act united the drug, advertising, and newspaper businesses into one of the most potent lobbies in Washington history. The drug and advertising people were worried about having to tell the truth about their products, and the newspapers were worried about losing advertising, truthful or otherwise. The lobby's strategy was soon clear: discredit the Tugwell Act by discrediting Tugwell. Unfortunately, Tugwell proved to be ripe for abuse, and he soon advanced from being a whipping boy for those who opposed consumer protection to being a whipping boy for those who opposed any of the liberal aspects of the New Deal.

Tugwell's enemies found an abundance of ammunition to use against him in his own voluminous writings. They joyously unearthed (and had read on the Senate floor) a woeful Whitmanesque poem he had written in college, one that said in part:

> "I am strong
> I am big and well-made
> I am muscled and lean and nervous
> I am frank and sure and incisive . . .
>
> I am sick of a nation's stenches
> I am sick of propertied czars . . .

I have dreamed my great dream of their passing
I have gathered my tools and my charts
My plans are fashioned and practical
I shall roll up my sleeves—make America over!"

Tugwell's economic writings caused more trouble than his poetry. He had an unfortunate habit of referring to his economic theories as "collectivism"—a word that the average American equated with Russian Communism. His writings were studded with calls for economic "revolution" that sounded ominous out of context. Once the Food and Drug Act had brought Tugwell to national attention, the McCormick-Patterson press—the Chicago *Tribune*, the New York *Daily News*, and the Washington *Times-Herald*—led the attack. Day after day the *Tribune* carried on its front page a cartoon picturing (as Tugwell later recalled it) "a college teacher in mortar board and flapping gown offering ridiculous advice to wiser and more experienced men than he." The Hearst and Scripps-Howard papers joined the assault, and the drug/advertising/press lobby sent thousands of canned (i.e., pre-written) anti-Tugwell editorials to small-town papers across the nation.

At the same time, there was a widespread blackout on magazine and newspaper coverage of the new Food and Drug Act. Editors would get the word from the advertising managers and there would be either hostile coverage or no coverage. In a survey of Washington correspondents, Leo Rosten asked for comment on this statement: "Most papers printed unfair or distorted stories about the Tugwell Pure Foods Bill." The result: forty-nine agreed, twenty-three disagreed. The manager of the United Features Syndicate told Tugwell in December, 1933, that it was becoming very hard to sell his articles.

The sheer weight of the onslaught forced Tugwell and his supporters to the defensive. In December, 1933, the Washington *Daily News* editorially *denied* that Tugwell was a socialist or a fanatic. A friendly Baltimore *Sun* columnist defended Tugwell and other intellectuals in government as "intelligent and decent citizens." Secretary Wallace told reporters: "You may not realize it, and some of you apparently do not, but you are insisting on erecting a mythical man."

The newspapers gave extensive coverage to charges by Dr. William Wirt, school superintendent in Gary, Indiana, that Tugwell was the leader of a revolutionary plot within the government. As Dr. Wirt explained it to a fascinated congressional committee, the plotters were using Roosevelt as a Kerensky, but Tugwell was soon to emerge as the Lenin of a Red dictatorship in America. This tale was given heightened interest because Dr. Wirt claimed that it had been told to him by government officials who were part of the plot. Tugwell's friends had a different explanation. They said that Dr. Wirt had one evening fallen in with a group of young New Dealers who, finding him both a bore and a reactionary, had pulled his leg with tales of a Tugwell conspiracy.

The Food and Drug Act bogged down under congressional opposition (it did not pass until 1938), but the anti-Tugwell hysteria flamed higher than ever in May, 1934, when Roosevelt nominated him for a promotion from Assistant Secretary to Under Secretary of Agriculture. The promotion involved little new authority but it clearly denoted symbolic support from Roosevelt. (It also involved a much-needed raise from $7500 to $10,000.)

The Senate hearing on Tugwell's promotion was low comedy. The opposition was led by South Carolina's stem-winding Senator "Cotton Ed" Smith, who declared that he was against Tugwell's promotion because the professor had never been a dirt farmer with mud on his boots. ("He is not a graduate of God's Great University," Smith said.) However, Tugwell responded that he had in fact worked in his father's orchard during his college vacations and therefore did have a history of muddy boots. In the end Roosevelt made a deal with Smith by which a friend of the Senator's with a murder record became a U. S. Marshall and Tugwell became Under Secretary of Agriculture. The confirmation vote was 53–24. Afterward, Sinclair Lewis gave a party for Tugwell.

The celebration was short-lived. In the summer of 1934, Tugwell abruptly broke off a Midwestern speaking tour and returned to Washington; Roosevelt had recalled him because Congressmen had complained to Jim Farley that Tugwell would offend farmers in the Midwest and thereby hurt them in the fall's elections. Roosevelt therefore dispatched Tugwell to Europe to perform various missions during the last two months before Election Day.

But in 1935, Roosevelt gave Tugwell another pat on the back: he made him director of the Resettlement Administration, which was to take 15,000 impoverished farm families and give them a new start on government land in forty-four of the forty-eight states. Needless to say, this new assignment, with its aura of Russian-style collective farming, only stirred up more controversy. The New Republic wrote in December, 1935: "The efforts to drive Rexford G. Tugwell out of Washington are now more vigorous than at any time during the

Roosevelt Administration." It was rumored that he was about to be eased out with an appointment to a foreign post, and that Farley had warned Roosevelt that in 1936 he could "lose with Tugwell or win without him."

Roosevelt's decision during the 1936 campaign was not to exile Tugwell to Europe as he had in 1934, but to order him to silence. He was not to make speeches or statements. He was not to answer charges made against him. Tugwell resented this, particularly because he thought it was unnecessary. In retrospect, it is clear that the Roosevelt landslide of 1936 could have survived a few Tugwell speeches. He wrote later: "I was through unconditionally when Roosevelt agreed with Farley to keep me quiet and hidden during the 1936 campaign. I had worked hard and I was entitled to speak."

Tugwell's campaign silence by no means silenced his critics. The Republican National Committee demanded his ouster. William Randolph Hearst denounced the "Tugwell Bolsheviks" around Roosevelt. In August, the *Saturday Evening Post* carried a vicious attack written by Alva Johnson. He said at one point:

"Tugwell's influence has been potent in the President's class-hate and anti-business policies, which are generally thought to be vote-getters. . . . Tugwell is an undoubted drawing card with Communists, Socialists, and dillettante earth-shakers."

The *Post's* hatchet-job did contain this perceptive comment:

"Roosevelt is the hero and Tugwell the villain of the piece. Admirers of the President are not inclined to regard Roosevelt as in any way responsible for Tugwell. Roosevelt is the dear, good little Queen; Tugwell the wicked Prime Minister. Conservative farmers, who love private property and hate the idea of revolution, seem to regard Tugwell as an evil of spontaneous origin, a natural calamity like dust storms or seventeen-year locusts, for whom no political party can be blamed. In this way Tugwell serves his chief effectively as a shield against criticism. If there were no Tugwell to take the punishment, it might land on Roosevelt."

There was much truth in the analysis.

Roosevelt's attitude toward Tugwell as the attacks on him mounted is far from clear. Tugwell was well aware that the criticisms were undercutting his influence at the White House. By 1935, Roosevelt was seeking Tugwell's advice less and less. He wished Roosevelt would speak out in his defense (as Moley had wished after the London Conference) but he understood the President's policy of letting his men fight their own battles. He wrote of Roosevelt showing "irritation" at the attacks on him, Harry Hopkins, and other New Dealers—irritation directed at the men suffering the attacks as well as at their critics. Tugwell wrote with a shadow of bitterness that Roosevelt "can be seen in retrospect to have allowed his policy to be shaped by a desire to escape from" the right-wing criticisms.

On the other hand, Tugwell's promotion in 1934 and his assignment to head the Resettlement Administration in 1935 were clear gestures of presidential support. Probably Tugwell's slow drift out of presidential favor had less to do with the attacks on him than with the social and political forces (notably the Supreme Court's striking down of NRA and AAA) that were forcing the President to abandon Tugwell's policies of economic planning in favor of orthodox Progressive trust-busting.

Roosevelt unquestionably liked Tugwell and admired his courage, but this did not stop him from following Farley's advice and muzzling him at election time. Tugwell's biographer, Bernard Sternsher, asks why Roosevelt, with his keen political sense, ever let Tugwell sponsor the Food and Drug Act in the first place. Similarly, one might ask why Roosevelt was so insensitive as to put Moley in the impossible position of working for Hull. The answer in both cases is simply that Roosevelt did not employ the same elaborate guile in computing the futures of other men that he did in plotting his own.

Tugwell suffered in silence through the 1936 election campaign, and submitted his resignation a week after the election victory. In later years he could look back with pride to his substantial contributions to the New Deal. Neither he nor Moley, in later years, believed the New Deal had done all it should have, yet their impact on it was considerable. They had gone to Roosevelt in 1932 with the then-radical notion that government should work with business, not against it, to bring a better deal to the American people. They first persuaded an American President to unlimber government, to rush in where traditionalists feared to tread, and government has moved in this direction ever since. On the other hand, Roosevelt did not follow the exact paths that either of them wanted. Moley wanted government to encourage businessmen, but after the honeymoon of 1933–34 government would not again pamper business to Moley's satisfaction until the Eisenhower years. Tugwell, for his part, wanted government to regulate business much more than it did, and to go farther in fighting for the public interest.

Tugwell's influence exceeded Moley's because the flow of national history was on Tugwell's side. His concern for conservation, for the consumer, for the sharecropper, for the public interest, would be carried forward in future years by Senators like Kefauver of Tennessee and Douglas of Illinois, and in the growing efforts in the 1950s and 1960s to protect the public from cancer-causing cigarettes, dangerous drugs, unsafe automobiles, deceptive advertising and packaging, air and water pollution. The fact that government in the 1960s increasingly speaks on behalf of the public interest is in large part due to Tugwell's "radical" influence on Franklin Roosevelt in 1932–36.

But Tugwell paid a high price to advance his vision of America. His public reputation was ruined. A stigma of radicalism had stuck to him that he would never entirely shake off. He noted bitterly that during his final year in Washington some of his old New Deal colleagues would praise his courage—and would avoid being seen in public with him. The cruelest blow was that he couldn't return to Columbia: "I wasn't reputable. I was a crackpot. My resignation was written out. My greatest humiliation was that the propaganda about me had even 'gotten' the faculty at Columbia."

Tugwell's first job after leaving Washington was as a vice president of the American Molasses Company, which was owned by his friend Charles Taussig, a prominent backer of the New Deal. Tugwell was promptly attacked by some liberal journals for having sold out to big business. A year later he became chairman of the New York City Planning Commission. In 1941 Harold Ickes was instrumental in persuading Roosevelt to make Tugwell the governor of Puerto Rico, a position he kept until 1945. Eventually Tugwell returned to teaching and writing.

He emerged from his ordeal bloody but unbowed. He had not known what he was getting into when he came to Washington, but he soon learned the rules of the game and he played the game with courage. He stated those rules in a memorable passage in *The Democratic Roosevelt* on the relationship between a President and those who serve him:

"All his co-workers are subordinate and they are expendable. But that, he assumes, they must expect. It is a hazard they must accept in taking the King's shilling. The sovereign is not required to explain or to regret the sacrifice of his servants. It is for the nation and therefore in a cause not to be compromised because of any man's pride or convenience."

5. The Hatchet Man: Corcoran

"The way to get ahead," an all-conquering Tommy Corcoran would tell friends in his days as Franklin Roosevelt's fair-haired boy, "is to fish in troubled waters."

Corcoran fished brilliantly in the swirling crosscurrents of 1935–40, when FDR was beset by an army of opposition: from Congress, from the Supreme Court, from big business, even from old allies like Jim Farley and Raymond Moley.

Corcoran, still in his thirties (he was born in 1900), replace Moley as a speechwriter and idea man, and replaced Farley as a political operative. He recruited scores of young lawyers into government jobs and thus created an all-seeing intelligence network to keep him—and, through him, Roosevelt—informed of the plots and counterplots of scheming New Deal officials. Through his close ties with Justice Louis Brandeis and Harvard's Felix Frankfurter, Corcoran symbolized the Second New Deal's return to Progressive trust-busting, just as the departed Moley and Tugwell had symbolized the First New Deal's fling with government-business economic planning.

Corcoran did not stumble into this prominence by chance. He was a young man whose towering ambitions were fully equaled by wide-ranging abilities. Few men ever brought more raw talent to the service of a President. His agile mind had been sharpened by a first-rate education (he led his classes at Brown University and Harvard Law School), by a year in the coveted post of law clerk to Justice Oliver Wendell Holmes, and by five years with a leading Wall Street law firm. His intellect was very nearly matched by his charm. A witty, outgoing, quick-smiling Irishman, Corcoran disarmed Washington's leading figures—in time, even the President—with his storytelling, his singing, his piano- and accordion-playing.

His youthful stamina was another asset. Corcoran could outstrip other men by the sheer ability to work days and nights on end without rest. Most of all, Roosevelt appreciated Corcoran's sure grasp of politics. Corcoran knew, as men like Moley and Tugwell never would, that noble ends must often be attained by ignoble means. He could be as ruthless as he could be charming. Years after he left the White House, he told a historian:

"There isn't enough time to explain everything to everyone, to cajole everyone, to persuade everyone, to make everyone see why it has to be done one way rather than another. If a President tried to do this, he would have no time left for anything else. So he must deceive, misrepresent, leave false impressions, even sometimes, lie—and trust to charm, loyalty and the result to make up for it. . . . A great man cannot be a good man."

Nor, he might have added, can a great man's intimates always hope to be remembered as good men. Corcoran's rise to power brought him enemies and ceaseless controversy. Senators resented the cold-eyed way he bartered for their votes with New Deal patronage; a Congressman once drew applause from the House when he declared, "I am getting very well fed up with Mr. Thomas Corcoran!" Tugwell viewed him as an unscrupulous hatchet man. Early and McIntyre resented his influence with Roosevelt. Mrs. Roosevelt never entirely trusted him. Farley, during Roosevelt's attempt to "purge" conservative Democrats in the 1938 party primaries, spoke bitterly to the President of Corcoran's "dirty party-splitting work."

Farley's remark is a key to Corcoran's value and his ultimate difficulties. It was absurd for Farley to blame Corcoran for the purge. Corcoran had directed it with enthusiasm, but the responsibility was entirely Roosevelt's. Yet here the exquisite protocols of politics come into play. Farley, however great his fury, would never direct such words at the President. Again, there had to be a third-party to bear the blame for Roosevelt. That, in time, became Corcoran's job. He did the dirty work and he took the heat. By 1940, Corcoran had made too many powerful enemies. Roosevelt, in one of those computer-like calculations that master politicians make in the blink of an eye, realized the young Irishman had outlived his usefulness, so he sighed and waved his cigarette holder and sent him on his way.

During his heyday, Corcoran wielded a far-ranging, free-wheeling power that few presidential aides have ever matched. Backed up by his scholarly, retiring alter ego, Ben Cohen, Corcoran served as the President's speechwriter, legislative draftsman, top lobbyist, political fixer, policy adviser, hirer and firer, and frequent companion.

Corcoran did more than achieve power; he became a legend. He did it not by seeking publicity, but by shunning it. Reporters thought him the best news source in Washington, but they got his tidbits only by agreeing never to mention his name. Corcoran understood the uses of mystery, and the corresponding follies of publicity-seeking. His lowly official status as a lawyer for the Reconstruction Finance Corporation was no hindrance to his celebrity. Word of his authority spread—perhaps exaggerated in the early days—via the governmental grapevine. His "This is Tom Corcoran calling from the White House" always got his calls through.

The tales they told of Tommy the Cork were without number.

Congressman Maury Maverick liked to tell of the time Tommy was waiting to see him when a prominent journalist happened to enter the room. Corcoran, with his instinct for anonymity, raised his newspaper to cover his face. The reporter sat down and was intrigued by the mysterious spectacle of a man sitting for five, ten, twenty minutes with a motionless newspaper covering his face. Then Maverick came to the door, called, "Come in, Tommy," and a red-faced Corcoran had to reveal himself.

They told, too, of Corcoran's being asked about a report that he had just come from a political meeting with New York Mayor La Guardia. It must have been some other Tom Corcoran, he replied with a perfectly straight face.

A New England Senator told of Corcoran's coming to his office to argue for a bill he opposed. Discovering the Senator to be back in his home state, Corcoran called him long-distance—and let the $20 charge be billed to the Senator's office.

Stanley High, Corcoran's co-speechwriter in the 1936 campaign, recalled how Corcoran appeared late at a party given by a leading government official, shook hands with his host, glanced around the room, whispered to High, "This doesn't fit into my scheme," and vanished into the night.

Another Senator always mentioned a tense moment during the battle over Roosevelt's court-packing plan when Corcoran told him:

"Just wait until the heat is turned on."

"What heat?" demanded the indignant Senator.

"The heat of reason," Corcoran laughed, and dashed away.

The Corcoran of those days was a short, square, fast-moving young man with a high, broad forehead, large ears, blond, wavy hair, a quicksilver smile, an engaging manner, an infectious enthusiasm, and a gleam in his eye that seemed to proceed more from the fires of ambition than the heat of reason. His critics observed that his Irish charm was generally reserved for those who could advance his career, and he was well aware that he was widely resented.

Part of his legend was the fact that Corcoran, a bachelor until his late thirties, had little use for married men among his inner circle. "Married men have divided loyalties," he would say. One of his favorite tricks was to schedule conferences with opposing lawyers for the late evening, on the theory that by midnight married men will agree to almost anything to get home.

Corcoran's high spirits infected others. When a reporter asked about a report that Corcoran would replace Farley as chairman of the Democratic National Committee, Roosevelt punned joyously:

"You can call it tommyrot. . . . That refers to your story, you see, and not to Mr. Corcoran." (Laughter)

Corcoran's career was a sure, steady progression toward power. After five years with a Wall Street law firm (a Democratic firm in that heavily Republican precinct) he went to Washington during the final months of the Hoover Administration as counsel for the newly established Reconstruction Finance Corporation. He took this post as a last-minute substitute for an older member of his firm, and it caused him no ideological torment to join a Republican Administration. Indeed, there was a certain ambiguity about Corcoran's politics, one that did much to aid his success in the years ahead. Nominally a Democrat, Corcoran was acceptable to the Hoover Administration because of his Wall Street ties, yet he viewed himself as a Progressive, for he had been deeply influenced by the careers of such men as Justice Holmes, Mayor Fiorello La Guardia of New York City, and Senators George Norris of Nebraska, Robert LaFollette of Wisconsin, and Edward Costigan of Colorado.

In the early months of the New Deal, it was Corcoran's intimate knowledge of the Street that carried him into the presidential orbit. Most New Dealers knew little about Wall Street except that they were against it; Corcoran was not violently against it, but he had an insider's knowledge of all its faults and weaknesses, and this knowledge was his steppingstone to power. In April of 1933, Ray Moley asked Felix Frankfurter, then still a law professor at Harvard, to draft legislation to curb fraud in the sale of securities. Frankfurter assembled a task force that included two of his favorite former students, Corcoran and Cohen. Their skillful drafting of the Securities Act of 1933 led them into the drafting of the Securities Exchange Act of 1934, and later the Holding Companies Act of 1934.

Corcoran first won Roosevelt's personal attention in 1934 when he was chosen to testify on the Stock Exchange Act before the Senate Banking and Commerce Committee. The bill, which proposed to regulate speculation on the Stock Exchange, was the object of intense resistance from the financial community, and in an unprecedented move, the Senate Committee allowed not only its own members, but the general counsel of the New York Stock Exchange to cross-examine the Administration witness, Corcoran. The thirty-four-year-old lawyer more than held his own in the exchange, and afterward Roosevelt called him in high spirits and exclaimed, "By God, you're the first man I've had who could handle himself on the Hill."

Later, Roosevelt would have more reason to be grateful for his trust in Corcoran's legal skill, for while other key New Deal measures were declared unconstitutional by the Supreme Court, all the Corcoran-Cohen bills survived the judicial scrutiny.

As Corcoran was impressing Roosevelt with his legal knowledge, his social skills were impressing Roosevelt's influential secretary, Missy LeHand. She sensed that Corcoran's charm, storytelling, and singing would be welcome diversion for FDR, and she added his name to the select list of people she invited to the small parties she sometimes gave for Roosevelt at the White House. She was right—Roosevelt did enjoy Corcoran's company—but in later years Corcoran would insist that writers had made too much of his ballad-singing and piano-playing. As Corcoran recalls it, his personal intimacy with Roosevelt was overrated and was never basic to his influence in the New Deal. The secret of his success, he says, was that he was a damn good corporation lawyer.

Throughout Roosevelt's first term, Felix Frankfurter had urged him to appoint a younger man as an all-purpose assistant who could relieve him of some of the burdens of the presidency. Frankfurter's candidate for this assignment was Corcoran, and by 1935 the younger man was moving swiftly into that role.

One of the reasons for Corcoran's success was his skill as a writer. During the campaign of 1936, he and Cohen, along with Sam Rosenman and Stanley High, constituted Roosevelt's basic speechwriting team. Corcoran, a skilled phrasemaker, was credited with such well-remembered phrases as "a rendezvous with destiny" and "an instinct for the jugular." His antibusiness bent was reflected in Roosevelt's scornful denunciation of "desperate men with their backs to the wall." And Corcoran's love of Dante resulted in Roosevelt's unforgettable declaration that:

"Governments can err, Presidents do make mistakes, but the immortal Dante tells us that divine justice weighs the sins of the cold-blooded and the sins of the warmhearted in different scales. Better the occasional faults of a government that lives in a spirit of charity than the consistent omissions of a government frozen in the ice of its own indifference."

Corcoran's power, however, flowed less from his ability to draft legislation or to write speeches than from his exceptional talent as a catalyst. He was a man in perpetual motion. His only official office was at the Reconstruction Finance Corporation, and he was rarely seen in it. Instead, he moved about Washington like a secret agent, turning up now here, now there, seeking out the ideas of all sorts of political figures: Ickes, Hopkins, Joe Kennedy, Brandeis, Farley, Jesse Jones, Henry Wallace, John Nance Garner. In addition to these figures, Corcoran's supply of intelligence was bolstered by dozens of young lawyers (usually sent down from Harvard by Felix Frankfurter) he had placed in government jobs and who reported to him faithfully on the plots and problems at their agencies. Unburdened by the administrative responsibilities of Hopkins or Tugwell, blessed with the physical stamina that was denied Louis Howe, far more able than Farley or Garner to grasp the new political ideas of a decade in ferment, Corcoran was simply (save only Roosevelt) the best-informed man in Washington. Like Roosevelt, he was an activist; like Roosevelt, he shunned dogma for experimentation. This meeting of minds afforded Corcoran, during the four or five years of his heyday, an enormous power; his was less the power to command, although he did not mind giving commands, than the power to pull together ideas from other men and serve them up to a President who wanted and needed ideas for no less a purpose than the remaking of a nation.

The complex role played by Corcoran and other New Dealers in influencing—or, in many cases, attempting to influence—Roosevelt's actions is illustrated by the long, heated debate on what the Administration should do about the 1937–38 recession. In the late summer of 1937 a wave of selling hit the stock market and carried stock prices to new lows. Unemployment rose. "We are headed right into another depression," Roosevelt's jittery Secretary of the Treasury, Henry Morgenthau, warned him. "The question is, Mr. President, what are we going to do about it?"

Roosevelt had followed no fixed star in economic matters. His only policy had been experimentation. He had tried rigid economy, shifted to heavy spending, then reduced spending. He had swung between spending on relief and spending on public works. He had toyed with Moley's economic nationalism, then with Hull's economic internationalism.

Now, as the 1937 crisis worsened, he procrastinated. When Congress met in mid-November he spoke of the seriousness of the situation, but the legislative program he sent down contained no new economic measures to deal with the crisis.

Meanwhile, two opposing factions within the Administration were fighting for the President's ear. Conservatives, led by Morgenthau, insisted that a balanced budget would end the recession by restoring business confidence. They counted on Roosevelt's deep-rooted yearning for a balanced budget. Inability to achieve that goal had not weakened his belief in it.

The second group, headed by Corcoran and including Solicitor General Robert H. Jackson and numerous New Deal economists, incorporated two overlapping views on the recession. Corcoran and some other Brandeis advocates blamed the recession on abuses by business and therefore called for a stepped-up program of trust-busting. Keynesian economists in the group saw increased spending as the solution. The two views were not at all incompatible.

Corcoran's strategy, as leader of this coalition, was to counter Morgenthau's influence by building pressure on Roosevelt's left for trust-busting and government spending. Harry Hopkins, seriously ill but still Roosevelt's most intimate adviser, was an on-and-off ally of the Corcoran clique. Spending always appealed to Hopkins.

The conservatives drew first blood when Morgenthau in a major speech on November 10 declared the Administration positively intended to balance the budget. Corcoran's forces were chilled to learn that Roosevelt had read over this speech in advance and made no objection to it.

But no positive action followed and Hopkins returned from a December trip with the President convinced he might look with favor on a trust-busting campaign. Encouraged, Corcoran called upon Solicitor General Jackson (a Corcoran protégé and his choice for the Presidency in 1940 if Roosevelt retired) to deliver several antimonopoly speeches. Unfortunately, Jackson's first two, self-written speeches caused no ripple in the press. Then Corcoran and Cohen wrote a third, hard-hitting speech for Jackson, and Corcoran arranged prime-time radio for its delivery. The third speech clicked, and front-page news stories stirred up talk of new, antibusiness policies. Hauling out his big guns, Corcoran called upon Ickes to deliver one of the fighting speeches for which he was justly famed. Ickes responded with a memorable denunciation of the "sixty families" who controlled the American economy.

The Corcoran-Jackson-Ickes call for antimonopoly action had been made without presidential blessing, but with hopes of achieving it. It was a dangerous game, and Corcoran waited nervously while days and weeks passed with no sure sign from the uncommitted and inscrutable Roosevelt. Then one day a conservative visitor denounced Ickes in a talk with Roosevelt, and Roosevelt responded with solid support for the Secretary. The news spread like wildfire among Corcoran's forces. The President's mood, it seemed at last, coincided with their proposed policies. Corcoran hurried to insert antimonopoly passages into the President's forthcoming State of the Union message, and also a promise of a separate message on monopolies.

But victory was not complete or even assured. Big business might be blamed for the recession, but there were still two opposing courses of action open to Roosevelt. The old Moley-Tugwell policy of joint government-business economic planning was being urged by many persons, such as the president of U. S. Steel. In January, to Corcoran's dismay, Roosevelt declared that the way to end the recession was for everybody to get together and plan production and consumption. Corcoran pressed trust-busting on Roosevelt so often that the President passed word through Missy LeHand that he was tired of being "nagged."

Corcoran, discouraged, left for a skiing trip to Canada. Then his cause received an unexpected boost. In March, the stock-market decline turned into a roller-coaster drop. Hopkins reported to Roosevelt at Warm Springs that businessmen were so worried they would not oppose new government spending to boost the economy. Hopkins, sensing that the moment was right, pressed Roosevelt to meet the crisis with large-scale spending.

Roosevelt returned to Washington from Warm Springs and told Morgenthau he was going to scrap budget balancing for a policy of increased spending. Morgenthau vainly threatened to resign. Corcoran was called in to help draft a three-billion dollar spending program and a fireside chat to explain the program. Two weeks later Corcoran helped draft a message in which Roosevelt asked Congress to study the concentration of economic power in American industry and its effect on economic competition. The legislation passed quickly. Then, unpredictably, the recession ran its course, and the economy began to inch upward again.

In the end it had been Hopkins, who had played a waiting game, whose arguments (combined with the worsening economic situation) carried the day with Roosevelt. Yet it was Corcoran by his vigorous (and personally dangerous) advocacy of trust-busting and spending who had dramatized and held open the alternative course. In November, when the budget-balancers seemed about to triumph, Corcoran had thrown himself into the breach. Without Corcoran's marshaling of Jackson and Ickes, without his plotting and "nagging," neither the public nor the President would have been conditioned to accept the course of action that was ultimately followed. He was the activist, the advocate who was willing to gamble all his chips, to take large chances to win large victories. He fished the troubled waters.

It was a short step from drafting legislation to fighting for it on Capitol Hill. Corcoran was increasingly involved in congressional affairs, and by 1936 he had emerged as FDR's number-one emissary to the Senate.

Corcoran's lobbying for the New Deal would make him many powerful enemies, yet he was drawn to the passion and conflict of the congressional arena like a moth to the flame. Rosenman: "Nothing was more to Tommy's liking than the political manipulation involved in trying to get votes for legislation pending in the Congress, trying to get recalcitrant Congressmen into line, and helping Congressmen who had incurred enmities by their support of the President. It was all strong food for his love of political excitement, his feeling for political power, and his satisfaction in promoting the aims of the New Deal."

Corcoran was never a total success on Capitol Hill, despite his energy and his intelligence. For one thing, he was just a little too young to please some Senators. (The nickname Tommy, however affectionately intended by his friends, was used cuttingly by his enemies to underscore his youth and supposed immaturity—just as Senator Kennedy's "Bobby" would be used three decades later.) Some Senators found Corcoran too ingratiating; one complained that he called him "sir" twice in one sentence. Others resented the guile that was not well hidden by Corcoran's genial exterior. "When you want two loaves, you've got to ask for four," was a Corcoran maxim; thus, he would sometimes ram a severe bill through one House of Congress to use in bargaining with the other.

It was Corcoran's ill-fortune to be closely identified with two of Roosevelt's most controversial and ultimately disastrous political ventures: the court-packing attempt* of 1937 and the attempted purge of reactionary Democrats in 1938.

Corcoran had been kept off the drafting of the court-packing plan

---

* Up to January, 1937, the Supreme Court had struck down nine of eleven major New Deal programs; the only two to survive were the Tennessee Valley Authority and the devaluation of gold. The ages of the nine Justices at that time were Brandeis, 80; Van Devanter, 77; McReynolds, 75; Sutherland, 74; Hughes, 74; Butler, 70; Cardozo, 66; Stone, 65; and Roberts, 61. On February 5, two weeks after his second inauguration, Roosevelt sent to Congress a bill to give him the right to appoint a new Justice, up to a total of fifteen, for every Justice who refused to retire at full pay within six months of reaching the age of seventy. Widespread public opposition to this plan led to a bitter, 168-day legislative battle, ending with the bill's defeat by a ten to eight vote in the Senate Judiciary Committee. After that the bill was dropped. However, Roosevelt won in the long run. While the legislative fight was in progress, the Court approved two key New Deal measures by five to four votes: The Wagner Act and Social Security.

because he did not get along with Attorney General Homer Cummings. When the plan was unveiled, it tore Corcoran between his deepest loyalties. On the one hand was his devotion to Roosevelt. On the other hand, court-packing, with its implication that justices over age seventy were less than competent, was a cruel slap at his old mentor, Justice Brandeis, and at the memory of Justice Holmes. Corcoran did not hesitate; he waded into the battle on Roosevelt's behalf.

At one point, as congressional resistance stiffened, Roosevelt asked Corcoran for his assessment of the Senate sentiment. Corcoran's response was candid—he thought the court-packing plan was doomed. He believed that Roosevelt, who had come to see himself as politically invincible, resented his pessimism, and in later years, Corcoran marked that conversation as the start of his fall from favor.

In 1938, Corcoran was equally involved in the attempt to purge anti-New Deal Democrats by backing their more liberal opponents in party primaries.

Party professionals like Farley and Bronx boss Ed Flynn were furious at this plan, which violated Roosevelt's old rule of never interfering in party primaries. But Corcoran and Hopkins urged Roosevelt to attempt the purge, and Corcoran was to become more identified with it than anyone except the President himself.

In later years, Corcoran would say that the 1938 purge had been Hopkins' scheme, one he sold to Roosevelt in the hope of eliminating several conservative Democrats who he knew would stand in the way of his (Hopkins') dream of becoming the Democratic nominee for President in 1940 if Roosevelt stepped down.

Almost without exception, the 1938 campaign ended in disaster for FDR. Cotton Ed Smith in South Carolina, Millard Tydings in Maryland, Walter George in Georgia, and Pat McCarran in Nevada were all re-elected despite the President's opposition. Corcoran's identification with the scheme made him the natural target for politicians who were outraged by the campaign but did not want to attack Roosevelt directly. The victorious Senators Tydings and George spoke scathingly of "little Wall Street lawyers who want the power to say who shall or who shall not be Senators." Other Senators, whatever their politics, resented the thought that the young Corcoran might at any time direct his talents and the President's power toward their destruction. The resentment continued for many years.

Corcoran's way of riding roughshod over his opponents made him many enemies in the Executive Branch, too. When he tried to help his friend Ickes make the Tennessee Valley Authority a part of the Department of Interior, Corcoran clashed with the TVA director, David Lilienthal.

Corcoran and Lilienthal, two of the New Deal's most talented young men, were natural rivals. The TVA director was idealistic, introspective, precise, a little pious; Corcoran was his opposite: ultrarealistic, outgoing, guileful, an improviser. The day after one angry meeting with Corcoran, Lilienthal jotted in his journal:

"Tom has changed a great deal since the last time I talked to him at any length—several years ago. Then he had the appearance and the lingo of a campus leader—very youthful, full of zest and fun, but essentially the sophomore. There is something hard and tough in his appearance and manner now, and it all came back to me—the resemblance to the hard-bitten tough-guy cynical ward leaders, in Chicago. This was confirmed by his sliding from one position to another, and paying not the least attention to anything I might say, plus his loss of temper, in the course of our discussion. The hardness of expression should have 'scared' me, I suppose, for I can see him throwing enough knives in my back to make me look like a porcupine."

Next Lilienthal criticized the erratic way Roosevelt often chose to use his men:

"What a curious kind of a government it all is. Tom doesn't seem to realize that the method of which he is so extensive a practitioner of trying to slip things through, without adequate consideration and discussion, may have a good deal to do with the growth of that practice among others. It never seems to occur to him that he could be of greater help to the President if he would help in setting up adequate machinery to insure *study* and all-round *consideration* of such problems. . . ."

Late in 1936, Roosevelt had mentioned to both Corcoran and Ickes his intention of naming Corcoran as his personal counsel, the post later created for Sam Rosenman. But, as Corcoran made more and more enemies, this appointment never materialized. Within the White House, Corcoran had enemies in Steve Early and Marvin McIntyre. In 1939, when Early announced to the press the addition to the White House staff of six new Administrative Assistants, he declared in reply to a reporter's question that this meant "the brain trust was out of the window." This was widely taken to mean that Corcoran and Cohen were out the window. Corcoran was furious at Early, who he believed had planted the question with the reporter to take a crack at him.

Corcoran's downfall in 1940 had several causes. One was that he had lacked the final degree of commitment, the ultimate unquestioning dedication, that Roosevelt demanded. Corcoran told his confidant Ickes in

1935 that he was so discouraged with Roosevelt's lack of leadership that he might leave the government, and three years later, Ickes wrote "Tom Corcoran is thoroughly disgusted with the lack of aggressive leadership the President has been displaying recently." Such heresy could not be hidden from so watchful a master as Roosevelt.

Moreover, it was in the nature of Corcoran's work—as a political hatchet man—that he would soon have to go. In the 1940 political campaign, Roosevelt eased him out of the White House to go to New York City and work with the Citizens Committee for Roosevelt.

Tugwell, who disliked Corcoran, gave Harry Hopkins much of the credit for Corcoran's ouster. Tugwell wrote that, during the late 1930s, Corcoran's "talents, his energy, his lack of scruple were just what was needed. By 1940, he had outlived that usefulness. When the third term was definitely in prospect, but before the campaign was started, he was allowed to understand what he had conveyed to so many others—that his departure would be welcome. And so he went.

"Hopkins' part in this is quite understandable. Corcoran was his only remaining rival for Franklin's trust and affection. He was vigorous and ebullient. Hopkins, sick and driven, made a sorry contrast. In his mind, I think, it had become an intolerable rivalry. So Franklin was caused to hear from many prompted visitors, as had happened once to Moley, later to me, and at other times to others, that Corcoran was a handicap. He irritated the politicians; he presumed on his White House credentials; he was a political liability. . . .

"That Hopkins planted these stories cannot be proved. But that somehow he was responsible for Corcoran's departure seems obvious. Moreover, it is likely that Franklin knew all about it. He was through with the contriving Irishman. Perhaps he felt himself surrounded too closely by Corcoran's picked people. Perhaps he thought there had been too much Brandeis. . . . There would, anyway, be less need of intriguers and hatchet men of the Corcoran type now."

Sam Rosenman, closer to the scene, gives this account:

"Tom's disregard for bruised feelings had made him a lot of enemies, and his ruthlessness and aggressiveness had aroused the antagonism of important political leaders such as Jim Farley and Ed Flynn. In fact, nearly all the Democratic national political leaders in the country had become bitter at him. . . . They carried their complaints to the President; several of them threatened to walk out unless Tom quit. And it is true that Tom's zealousness was sometimes embarrassing to the President. Finally Roosevelt decided that Tom should not be permitted to do all the things he had been doing. . . . In 1941, he left the government. He is now a prosperous Washington lawyer—quite a different person from the fighting, jolly New Dealer I used to know."

Corcoran's own memory of his departure from the government is somewhat different. He says that he had intended to leave after the 1936 election, but then he got caught up in Roosevelt's court-packing fight because no one else wanted anything to do with it. His exile to New York during the 1940 campaign, he says, was only in part because of the political enemies he had made; another reason was that Roosevelt didn't trust his New York political leaders, Farley and Flynn, and wanted Corcoran in New York to keep them honest.

Corcoran in 1940 was forty years old, recently married, and broke, and for all these reasons the financial security of private law practice appealed to him. Yet there was one government job that he coveted —Solicitor General, the government's chief advocate before the Supreme Court. He says that Roosevelt had many times promised this prize to him but never delivered. Corcoran had made so many enemies in the Senate that his confirmation there was by no means certain. And in later years, Corcoran added another element to the story. Roosevelt, he said, informally polled the members of the Supreme Court on their reaction to Corcoran's appointment as Solicitor General. Four Democrats were for him, four Republicans were against him, and the swing vote went to his old mentor, Justice Felix Frankfurter—who cast the deciding vote against him! Corcoran refuses to give the details of this incident.

Roosevelt offered to make him Under Secretary of the Navy, but a conflict arose with Secretary of the Navy Frank Knox. Roosevelt also offered him a job on the White House staff, but Corcoran felt that after six years he deserved more than that.

So in 1941, he left the government and began the practice of law in Washington. Looking back, he says that he has no complaint about Roosevelt's treatment of him. He mentions an affectionate letter of farewell the President wrote to him, and points out that Roosevelt called upon him, as a private citizen, to carry out several wartime assignments. During the war, Roosevelt asked—ordered, Corcoran says—him to join the Justice Department staff, but Corcoran would not do so unless he was made Solicitor General, so he remained a private citizen.

Corcoran hung up his lawyer's shingle a few blocks from the White House and scored immediate, enormous financial success. Yet in a broader social and political sense, Corcoran was less than a total triumph as a lawyer. Much of his success, obviously, was based on his friendships with scores of prominent government officials, and this sort of influence is open to varying kinds of interpretations. A congressional committee looked into one government decision Corcoran was involved in, and a Republican Congressman denounced Corcoran as "the biggest influence-peddler in Washington." Those were strong words, but it was true that the wheeler-dealer reputation he had acquired while serving Roosevelt stayed with him in later years and served to cloud his accomplishment. Certainly his transition from presidential adviser to Washington lawyer was not as smoothly managed as Clark Clifford's a decade later, and Clifford no doubt profited by Corcoran's experience.

There was, moreover, an outpouring of bitterness among Corcoran's old New Deal associates as they watched him grow rich serving the private interests he had fought so fiercely during the 1930s. A hostile *Saturday Evening Post* writer summed this up with cruel accuracy:

"Corporations have no soul, but they have the sweetest dispositions in the world. . . . Big Business always forgives and forgets. As soon as Tommy left the government, Big Business clasped him to its bosom and poured fortunes into the hand that had so often cudgeled it."

Finally, Corcoran's post-government career was marred by a widespread belief that—despite Corcoran's protestations to the contrary—Roosevelt had used and then discarded him. Jonathan Daniels, Roosevelt's Administrative Assistant and Press Secretary during the war years, wrote of seeing Corcoran at a Washington party in 1946. He was the life of the party, singing and playing his accordion, while others whispered about the huge legal fees he had been receiving. Daniels quotes another man who knew Corcoran as saying: "It hurts to be dropped as Tommy was dropped, especially in Washington. And he can't prove he still has power except by fees. . . . He wanted to be Solicitor General of the United States. Now he's only getting rich."

6. The Inner Circle: LeHand, Early, Watson

Bill Moyers once commented in his days as the kingpin of Lyndon Johnson's staff: "Any President has to have around him some people who are so unquestioningly loyal that their very loyalty is a source of strength to him." Moyers was referring to Johnson's hero-worshiping aide of that period, Jack Valenti, but his point was true of every President. Each President wants some aides whose primary function is not to criticize or analyze but to believe and serve.

Roosevelt was fortunate to have a White House inner circle that combined high ability with total loyalty. The hard core of this palace guard consisted of two men and a woman who first served Roosevelt during his vice-presidential campaign in 1920: Steven T. Early, his Press Secretary, Marvin H. McIntyre, his Appointments Secretary, and Marguerite Alice (Missy) LeHand, his personal secretary.*

This trio, along with Louis Howe, were charter members of a group called the Cuff Links Gang, so titled because at the end of the 1920 campaign Roosevelt had given each of the men a pair of cuff links engraved "FDR" on one side and with the recipient's initials on the other side. Throughout the 1920s the Cuff Links Gang and other Roosevelt intimates would gather at Hyde Park each year on Roosevelt's birthday. After he became President, Roosevelt gave similar cuff links to all his top appointees, a gesture that John Kennedy would later imitate with his PT-109 tie clasps. But possession of the engraved cuff links in later years did not signify membership in the real inner circle of the Cuff Links Gang. Only a very few late-comers achieved that intimacy; they included Roosevelt's military aide, Major General Edwin M. (Pa) Watson, and his number-two secretary, Grace Tully.

Roosevelt's inner circle wielded a power not easily defined. If they rarely advised on policy, they often advised on people, which can amount to the same thing. They gave Roosevelt unbiased judgments and sometimes blunt criticism. They could be vital allies to Cabinet members and other New Deal officials. Their main contribution to Roosevelt was more personal than political. Presidents, no less than other men, like to play poker, to go fishing, to sip good whisky, to swap stories, and exchange laughs. They enjoy the company of attractive, admiring women. They become depressed and want someone to share their troubles. After years in the political jungle, they like to think they have a few friends whose loyalty is absolute.

The three posts called Secretary to the President that were filled by Howe, Early, and McIntyre represented more than a century's evolution of the White House staff—an evolution that Roosevelt would sharply accelerate. In fact, Roosevelt's predecessor, Herbert Hoover, had doubled the size of the President's administrative staff from two to four—an extravagance that caused a "national sensation" according to one observer. In addition to these four top aides, Hoover was assisted by two military aides, and some forty clerks, typists, and messengers.

Earlier Presidents had managed with much less. When Benjamin Harrison was President, in 1889–93, his staff was so small it could be

---

* In 1920 Roosevelt and Governor James M. Cox of Ohio were the Democratic candidates opposing Republicans Warren G. Harding and Calvin Coolidge.

housed on the second floor of the White House, next to the first family's living quarters. Until William McKinley's term, at the turn of the century, the President had to pay part of his staff expenses out of his own pocket. This resulted in the practice, which still exists, of having some presidential aides paid by the other agencies. Another enduring practice was begun by George Washington when he hired his young nephew, Howell Lewis, as "a writer in my office . . . at the rate of three hundred dollars a year." Andrew Jackson hired his nephew, Andrew Jackson Donelson, as his secretary, and later both Franklin Roosevelt and Dwight Eisenhower would employ their sons as White House aides.

Before the New Deal, little prestige had gone with being one of the President's Secretaries (a nineteenth century term that best translates today as Administrative Assistant). The government was smaller, the President could have more intimate dealings with his Cabinet, and his personal aides had traditionally confined themselves to fixing appointments, overseeing clerical work, and answering inquiries from the press. Still, given the right chemistry between President and aide, it was always possible for a Presidential Secretary to achieve political importance.

Two of the most influential of the Presidential Secretaries served in the early years of this century. The first was George B. Cortelyou, who after three years as President McKinley's stenographer became his Secretary when the incumbent, John A. Porter, broke down under the strain of the Spanish-American War. Cortelyou, who was only thirty-eight years old, proved to be as skilled at politics as at stenography. His smartest political move was persuading McKinley to stop Mark Hanna from trying to block Theodore Roosevelt's nomination as McKinley's running mate in 1900. The McKinley-Roosevelt ticket was victorious, and only six months after Inauguration, on September 6, 1901, McKinley was shot by the anarchist Leon Czolgosz. McKinley lingered near death for eight days and Cortelyou was virtually Acting President. After the death, Cortelyou eased young Roosevelt's takeover as President. Roosevelt soon showed his gratitude by making Cortelyou the first Secretary of the new Department of Commerce and Labor.

Cortelyou's successor in the $5000-a-year post of Secretary to the President was his assistant, William Loeb, Jr., another talented and ambitious stenographer. Roosevelt later credited Loeb with inspiring the investigations that led to the discovery of frauds by the American Sugar Trust at the New York Customs House. In 1908 Roosevelt dispatched Loeb to the Republican National Convention to mastermind the nomination of his handpicked successor, William Howard Taft (much as thirty-two years later another Roosevelt would dispatch another intimate adviser, Harry Hopkins, to mastermind Henry Wallace's nomination as the Democratic nominee for Vice President). One other Presidential Secretary who became a political adviser of note was Wilson's Joe Tumulty, but the loyal Tumulty was barred by Mrs. Wilson from the President's side during his period of greatest need—his final illness.

When Franklin Roosevelt entered the White House in 1933 he had—thanks to his predecessor—legal authority for three Secretaries and an Administrative Assistant, plus the various clerical jobs. He chose not to fill the Administrative Assistant's position. He told Raymond Moley he had thought of putting him in the post, but decided not to lest he arouse the jealousies of Louis Howe. Another reason was probably that Roosevelt didn't want Moley or any other newcomer locked into a job that close to him.

But Roosevelt had no hesitation about filling the three Secretary-ships with Louis Howe, Mac McIntyre, and Steve Early, or about putting Missy LeHand in the position available for the President's personal secretary. These were people who had been tested over the years and whose dedication was total. Soon a newcomer, military aide Pa Watson, would gain acceptance in their inner circle. After Louis Howe's death in 1936, Early, McIntyre, Watson, and Miss LeHand carried on until either their death or Roosevelt's ended their service. Several members of this durable and talented inner circle merit a closer look.

Anyone who has been around Washington very long comes to know a breed of women who are invariably found sitting at desks just outside the offices of Very Important Men. These are the politicians' hard-working, generally very bright, always fiercely loyal personal secretaries. Each year scores of capable young women are drawn to the world of politics by the promise of excitement, by the possibility that, in this world of ambitious young men, one day their prince will come along. Sometimes he does. Senators and Congressmen from time to time marry their secretaries, and during the New Deal the highly eligible bachelor Tommy Corcoran eventually married his secretary. More often than not the politician's girl Friday finds herself wedded only to her work. The long hours required by her job generally forbid much of a social life, passes are more frequent than proposals, and eventually spinsterhood at the heart of public affairs may seem preferable to married life in suburbia.

Missy LeHand became the prototype of this breed, its best example, its ultimate success story. Missy came to have a tremendous influence with Roosevelt. He would follow her advice and accept her criticism. Probably only Mrs. Roosevelt and Louis Howe had a fuller understanding of Roosevelt's mind and moods than Missy. Stanley High, a speechwriter for Roosevelt during the 1936 campaign and later a critic of the New Deal, wrote of her: "Missy is the one indispensable member of the secretarial entourage. She not only understands what the President is driving at—and approves of it—she understands the President. No one else breaks in on him with so little hesitation or knows so well when breaking in would not be judicious. Her disapproval of a person or a course of action is more difficult to overcome than that of anyone else, save only Mrs. Roosevelt."

Missy's service on Roosevelt's staff began as a secretary during his 1920 campaign for the vice presidency. She was in her early twenties. After Roosevelt was struck by polio the next year, Missy was hired to live at Hyde Park as his secretary. She also lived with the Roosevelts in the Governor's Mansion at Albany and in 1933, like Louis Howe, she moved into the White House as a matter of course. She occupied a small bedroom-sitting room apartment on the third floor and during Mrs. Roosevelt's frequent absences from the White House, Missy served as hostess at social affairs. When she thought Roosevelt needed diversion she would arrange small dinner parties and invite men like Corcoran, Hopkins, Watson, and Early.

Gay and charming, Missy handled Roosevelt's personal finances, swam with him in the White House pool, did his Christmas shopping for him, hounded him into taking his cough medicine, and in countless ways injected into his life "an essential femininity" (in Schlesinger's phrase) that might otherwise have been lacking. Missy played this role, which amounted to that of an assistant First Lady, with the approval of Mrs. Roosevelt, whose travels kept her away from the White House much of the time.

Mrs. Roosevelt's affection for Missy was not entirely uncritical; she once wrote:

"Missy was young and pretty and loved a good time, and occasionally her social contacts got mixed up with her work and made it hard for her and others. To me she was always kind and helpful, and when I had to be away she took up without complaint the additional social responsibilities thrust upon her."

Mrs. Roosevelt felt that some ambitious political figures, notably Tom Corcoran, cultivated Missy's friendship to gain access to the President, but as she later wrote of the younger woman:

". . . though occasionally someone fooled her for a time, I always waited for enlightenment to come, with confidence born of experience."

Missy was an attractive woman—"handsome" was an adjective often used by writers—with large blue eyes, prematurely graying hair, and strong, intelligent features. She was thirty-seven when she entered the White House in 1933, and she was never at a loss in dealing with world figures. It was once reported that the bachelor Prime Minister of Canada was smitten with Missy while visiting the White House, but nothing ever came of this or similar reports. She never married.

There are many examples of Missy's influence. Roosevelt's political adviser Edward J. Flynn gives the following account of the selection of Homer S. Cummings to be Attorney General after the sudden death of Roosevelt's first choice, Senator Thomas J. Walsh:

"When this news (of Walsh's death) came, Missy LeHand . . . and I were in the room. . . . Missy said that perhaps Homer Cummings would be a good appointment.

"The President-elect hesitated, for Cummings was down for Governor General of the Philippines. The longer Roosevelt thought about it, however, the more he resolved that at least a temporary appointment of Cummings would be an excellent solution for his needs."

Cummings served as Attorney General until 1939.

The New Deal was nothing if not an assemblage of prima donnas—Harold Ickes, Henry Morgenthau, Hugh Johnson, Cordell Hull, Harry Hopkins—and one of Missy LeHand's primary duties was to soothe the injured egos of these often irate officials. Roosevelt believed in government by friction. He constantly pitted his highest officials against one another, gave them overlapping jurisdictions, alternately praised and damned them—partly because it amused him and partly because he believed competition increased performance. At times, as hurt feelings multiplied and threatened resignations piled up, the entire machinery of government seemed to teeter on the brink of catastrophe. Missy, and to a lesser extent Marvin McIntyre and Pa Watson, served to hold hands, to soothe feelings, to lubricate the official machinery, to be friends in court to the anxious officials.

Missy suffered from a heart condition and was forced to retire in 1943. She went to live with her sister in their hometown, Somerville, Massachusetts, and she died in a Boston hospital on July 31, 1944,

at the age of forty-six. Arthur Krock, who had known and admired
Missy for more than a decade, wrote on the day of her death:

"Missy moved calmly and graciously but always watchfully at the
leader's side . . . ever on guard to restrain Mr. Roosevelt from yielding
to any impulse or normal human failing she felt was inconsistent
with the talents and ideas in which she believed so firmly. . . . Her
influence upon the President was very great and constructive."

A few days after Roosevelt took office in 1933 he held his first press
conference. More than 100 reporters, most from newspapers hostile
to him, crowded into his office. They were delighted to learn that
Roosevelt had radically changed the ground rules of the press conference. No longer, as in Hoover's time, would questions have to be
submitted in writing in advance. No longer would the President's replies be attributed only to "a White House spokesman." A new system
prevailed whereby some replies were attributed to the President and
others were either unattributed or entirely "off-the-record." Under
these new rules Roosevelt jumped into a frank, free-wheeling discussion of the banking crisis. He clearly enjoyed the give-and-take
with the press as much as the reporters. At the end of the conference,
for the first time in memory, the newspapermen broke into spontaneous
applause.

This new deal in press relations was largely the handiwork of
Roosevelt's hard-driving, hot-tempered press secretary, Steve Early.
Before accepting the job, Early demanded Roosevelt's assurance that
he would cooperate in a liberalized press policy. As a former Washington reporter, Early knew that Hoover's practice of playing favorites
among the correspondents made him innumerable enemies, so he urged
Roosevelt to play fair with everyone. He knew, too, that many government press officers were kept in humiliating ignorance of high-level
affairs, so he demanded a guarantee of full access to the President,
and similar access for the Cabinet members' press officers.

Early brought impressive credentials to the job of Press Secretary.
Born in Crozet, Virginia, in 1889, he began his newspaper career
with the United Press bureau in Washington in 1908. After a few
years he switched to the Associated Press and he was covering the
State-War-Navy beat when Franklin Roosevelt arrived at the Navy
Department in 1913. He served successively as an infantry captain
and an editor of *Stars and Stripes* during World War I, and upon his

return to Washington, he went directly into Roosevelt's 1920 vice-presidential campaign.

His next job, as if to underscore his lack of political ideology, was as publicity director for the U. S. Chamber of Commerce, but he quit after a year and rejoined the AP. In 1923 he scored a famous news beat by slipping down the fire escape of a San Francisco hotel and notifying his office of President Harding's death six minutes before the official announcement was made. In 1927 he became Washington representative of Paramount News and he was still there when the call came from Roosevelt to join his White House staff.

Early tried to stay out of politics, but he inadvertently provoked a major political incident during Roosevelt's 1940 campaign against Wendell Willkie. On October 28, just a few days before the election, Early and a group of newsmen were returning to the presidential train in New York's Pennsylvania Station after a speech by Roosevelt. They were stopped outside the station by security-minded policemen who refused to let them in even after Early identified himself. Angered, Early started to push his way past the policemen. Two of them pushed back and when a third, a Negro named James Sloan, joined the melee Early's knee struck him in the groin.

The kneeing was particularly painful to the forty-two-year-old Sloan because he had undergone a hernia operation only three months earlier. Early, as a Southerner, was immediately suspected of racial prejudice. Early's story was that his leg had merely been lifted upward involuntarily as the policemen pushed him backward.

Whatever the truth, Republican leaders sniffed a potent political issue. If one of Roosevelt's close associates could be pictured as anti-Negro, perhaps Harlem (where Sloan lived) could be swung to the Republican column; in a close election Harlem might swing New York and New York might swing the nation. Various Negroes for Willkie began issuing statements deploring the incident. Heavyweight champion Joe Louis visited Sloan's bedside before dashing off for a round of pro-Willkie speeches. (The Democrats had Jack Dempsey in their corner.) District Attorney Tom Dewey ordered an investigation of the incident. On Election Eve, candidate Willkie condemned Early for "the irresponsible act" of "kicking in the stomach a Negro policeman."

Roosevelt was worried. He ordered Sam Rosenman to ascertain the facts of the matter. Some of Roosevelt's advisers thought Early should be fired. Roosevelt called a White House meeting with Rosenman and Harry Hopkins present. Early asked Don Richberg, a former New

Deal official, to attend the meeting on his behalf. Harry Hopkins told Richberg at the outset: "Don, you are here as a friend of Steve. Steve and I are good friends, also, but I have only one interest in this matter, and this is what is going to help or hurt FDR."

It was agreed that Early would issue a statement declaring that he had not struck Sloan intentionally, but nonetheless apologizing to the policeman. This was done. Then, the day before the election, the incident was permanently closed when the bedridden Sloan issued this statement:

"I know that all this fuss would not be made over me if this was not election time. . . . If anybody thinks they can turn me against our great President, who has done so much for my race, they certainly are mistaken. . . . I am voting for Franklin D. Roosevelt for President."

After Roosevelt's death Early stayed on for a few months as a Special Assistant to President Truman. But he was broke after thirteen years in the White House at a salary never exceeding $10,000, and he soon resigned to accept a $25,000 post as a vice president of the Pullman-Standard Car Manufacturing Company. As he left the government, Truman presented Early with the Distinguished Service Medal. Early promised that he would always be "on call." The call came in April, 1948, when Early became Under Secretary of Defense. Early went back to private life in September, 1950, but returned to the White House briefly in December after Truman's Press Secretary, Charlie Ross, died at his desk. Early himself died of a heart attack on August 11, 1951, the last survivor of Roosevelt's original Cuff Links Gang.

The King's Court must always have its Fool, but (as readers of Shakespeare's *King Lear* will recall) the Fool need not always be a fool. Roosevelt's court jester was Major General Edwin M. (Pa) Watson, his military aide starting in June, 1933, and after mid-1938 one of the three Presidential Secretaries as well. Watson was a big, jovial Virginia storyteller who loved a joke, even a joke on himself.

But Watson's easy-going exterior was misleading. Schlesinger calls him a "complex and subtle" figure who, although no New Dealer, understood the social implications of the New Deal far more than his co-workers Early and McIntyre. Grace Tully, a sharp-eyed observer of the White House circle, wrote: "The bluff exterior fooled many outsiders into thinking Pa was just a court jester but some of them had occasion to back away and think again when he moved into operation."

Watson's dual role as military aide and Presidential Secretary made him one of Roosevelt's steady companions. He had the distinction of being the only man in the armed services authorized to salute with his left hand—because Roosevelt so often leaned on his right arm at official ceremonies. He had a genius for gently removing long-winded visitors from the President's office. Watson served as an effective liaison with the War Department, and as an army man he helped balance the President's well-known favoritism for the navy.

Yet Watson clearly recognized that the most valuable contribution he could make to Roosevelt was to divert his mind with jokes and laughter—to play the fool, if need be. Roosevelt liked to tease his associates and he found in Watson an ever-ready target for his barbs.

The two raconteurs shared a love of the outdoors. Roosevelt loved to belittle Watson's skill as a fisherman and hunter. Once when Watson killed two turkeys with one shot, the President solemnly filed written charges that the birds were blind. Watson, also in writing, demanded a court-martial. Roosevelt countered that a trial would cost the government too much and that the charges were therefore dropped. It was the sort of elaborate, corny joke that Roosevelt loved.

Watson's father, a Virginia tobacco planter, had once photographed his young son astride a pony to advertise a new brand of chewing tobacco he called the Little Edwin plug. When Roosevelt heard this story he laughed until he cried, and he thereafter delighted in calling the hefty Watson "Little Edwin."

Harold Ickes tells of a poker party incident which showed the lengths Watson would go in giving Roosevelt a laugh:

"Colonel Watson and McIntyre got into a fierce argument about a twenty-dollar bill which McIntyre insisted he had paid Watson at the outset for chips. They got so eloquent about it that all the rest of us became hilarious. We almost had to recess the poker game to give these two men a free forum to express what each thought of the other."

It never occurred to the humorless Ickes that Watson had pocketed the gullible McIntyre's twenty-dollar bill precisely to provoke the scene that followed.

Watson was introduced to the Roosevelt circle by Admiral Cary T. Grayson, who was Woodrow Wilson's doctor and close friend, and was himself a Virginia storyteller of distinction. Watson, after outstanding service as an artillery commander during World War I, had served on Wilson's staff at the Versailles Conference. He and Grayson became friends, and a dozen years later Grayson recommended Watson to be Roosevelt's military aide. Watson was an instant success.

James MacGregor Burns describes a tension-filled scene in Roosevelt's office during the 1940 Democratic convention. The delegates had drafted Roosevelt for a third term but were rebelling at his choice for Vice President, Henry Wallace. Furious, Roosevelt wrote out a statement rejecting the nomination and gave it to Sam Rosenman to polish. Presumably the statement was to be issued if the convention rejected Wallace. Outside the President's office Watson pleaded with Rosenman to tear up the statement. "I don't give a damn who's Vice President and neither does the country," he shouted. "The only thing that is important to this country is that fellow in there."

Rosenman went ahead with his rewrite job and when he returned to the President's office Watson was almost in tears. Missy LeHand, who opposed the third term because she feared for Roosevelt's health, was all smiles at the prospect of his refusing the nomination. Then the convention nominated Wallace and—with Watson smiling now, and Missy LeHand in tears—Roosevelt prepared to deliver his acceptance speech.

Like McIntyre, like Missy, like Hopkins, like Roosevelt himself, Pa Watson was a casualty of the war. He died of a heart attack on board a military cruiser on February 20, 1945, while returning with Roosevelt from the Yalta Conference. He had suffered previous heart attacks fourteen months earlier at the Teheran Conference and three months earlier at the Quebec Conference. "I shall miss him almost more than I can express," a grieving Roosevelt said at Watson's death. "There was never a cloud between us in all these years. He helped me greatly. . . . It was his sense of duty and determination to see the war through that made him insist on taking this trip with me."

Every President would have his favorite staff jester—Truman's Harry Vaughan, Eisenhower's Thomas E. Stephens, Kennedy's Dave Powers and Pierre Salinger, Johnson's Jack Valenti—but perhaps none of Watson's successors would match him in mingling good sense and underlying dignity with his high spirits.

Louis Howe's death in the spring of 1936 left vacant one of the three positions as Presidential Secretary. Roosevelt filled the post early in 1937 with his twenty-nine-year-old son, James Roosevelt, who had been singled out as his father's political protégé. Jimmy Roosevelt was by then already well known for his enjoyment of fast cars, pretty girls, and café society. Jimmy's appointment to the White House staff was vigorously opposed by his mother, and by Louis Howe. But the President overruled them, asking: "Why should I be deprived of my eldest son's help and of the pleasure of having him with me just because I am President?"

Jimmy Roosevelt would have had to possess the highest degree of tact and political skill to succeed in the White House. His father had tossed him into the ocean of big-time politics on a sink-or-swim basis and, unfortunately, Jimmy sank. His year and a half in the White House was distinguished mainly by friction, criticism, and ill will. Congressmen were annoyed when he spoke of the President as "Father"; the newspapers made embarrassing references to the "Crown Prince"; other presidential aides were jealous of his special status and critical of his talents.

Corcoran, in particular, resented Jimmy's influence. After a talk with Corcoran, Ickes wrote in his diary of March 1938: "He is bitterly disappointed about the bad influence of James Roosevelt. According to him, James Roosevelt is willing to sacrifice the whole New Deal in order to make himself Governor of Massachusetts. . . . Jimmy has his father's ear at all times. When the President is tired or discouraged, Jimmy is at hand to say what may be influential. Jimmy has no political ideals, he is not a liberal, and he is trying to make a place for himself in public life."

James MacGregor Burns wrote that during FDR's fight with Congress over the court-packing plan "James made promises that seemed to have special authenticity but in fact did not; the efforts of the other aides on the Hill were undermined, and congressional friction and bitterness increased."

James Roosevelt and his father were closer during this eighteen-month period than at any other time in his adult life, but the young man paid a high price for this intimacy. By mid-1938 he had developed a serious case of ulcers and had to undergo surgery. Also, in this period, his first marriage was breaking up. He never went back to his White House post, although he was far from finished with politics. In 1954 he was elected to Congress in Los Angeles, and after a decade in the House he resigned to become a member of the U.S. delegation to the United Nations. Later he returned to private business.

By the end of Roosevelt's first term it was clear that the three Presidential Secretaries couldn't handle the volume of work pouring in to the President.* This was true despite the fact that each of the three had one or more assistants. By 1937 the government included some 150 departments and agencies, and about 50 of them reported directly to the President. Seeking a way out of this snarl, and others, Roosevelt appointed a Committee on Administrative Management, chaired by Louis Brownlow, to suggest ways to reorganize the presidential apparatus.

Among the recommendations made by this committee was the provision for a number of new Presidential Assistants to expand the presidency into a genuine institution. These new assistants, the report urged, should not be officials in their own right, but should virtually be extensions of the President himself. They should have, the committee said in a famous phrase, "a passion for anonymity." FDR liked this phrase and often used it.

This recommendation was incorporated into the Reorganization Act of 1939, which gave the President authority to hire six Administrative assistants at $10,000 per year. These new assistants, the legislation said, were to be presidential fact-finders, but were not to be decision makers or have authority over agency officials. In fact, they inevitably acquired the not-too-subtle authority that goes with speaking in the President's name.

Roosevelt was slow to fill these new posts. Perhaps his son's unhappy experience in the White House had impressed the President with the need to select his aides with the utmost care. By the spring of 1941, he had filled five of the new posts with men from a variety of backgrounds. Lauchlin Currie, whose specialty was economic matters, was drafted from the staff of the Federal Reserve Board. Lowell Mellett, an outspoken liberal and the former managing editor of the *Washington News*, was made head of the Office of Government Reports, and as such was chief propagandist for the New Deal. William H. McReynolds, who was put in charge of government personnel problems, was a career bureaucrat.

Former Senator Sherman Minton of Indiana dealt mainly with congressional relations. James H. Rowe was a young lawyer from Harvard who had been an assistant to Jimmy Roosevelt and then to Pa Watson. In later years, Rowe and Tom Corcoran were law partners in Washington.

* When James Roosevelt succeeded Louis Howe, Early and McIntyre were at last given the full title "Secretary to the President," thus dropping the "Assistant Secretary" status that Howe had imposed on them. White House staff titles have always been highly flexible; today's Appointments Secretary and Press Secretary, for instance, are actually Special Assistants who are given those designations purely for convenience.

For the most part, these new aides maintained the prescribed passion for anonymity. However, one of them, James Rowe, did bequeath to posterity a classic statement of the relationship between Presidents and those who serve them. Rowe was explaining to Roosevelt his proposal for the best way to shift a certain government official from one agency to another. Roosevelt had a different idea, and Rowe, who felt he had thoroughly investigated the matter, declared: "Mr. President, you should do it my way and not yours." Roosevelt replied:

"I do not have to do it your way and I will tell you the reason why. The reason is that, although they may have made a mistake, the people of the United States have elected me President, not you."

7. The Man Who Came to Dinner: Hopkins

Men who would serve a President should study the career of Harry Lloyd Hopkins, who for a dozen tumultuous years walked the razor's edge of that exacting service. Hopkins was an Iowa harness-maker's son, a social worker by trade, and a politician by instinct, who spent his life in an eminently successful quest for power. There was a time, in 1938–39, when he dared dream of succeeding his friend and patron, Franklin Roosevelt, as President of the United States. Failing that, Hopkins settled for a different dominion. For the last six years of Roosevelt's life Hopkins was his closest friend and most valued adviser; as such, he was probably the most powerful presidential aide who ever lived.

Hopkins' friend, co-worker in government, and biographer, the playwright Robert Sherwood, summed up his remarkable role when he wrote:

"The extraordinary fact was that the second most important individual in the United States government during the most critical period of the world's greatest war had no legitimate official position nor even any desk of his own except a card table in his bedroom. However, the bedroom was in the White House."

At least five factors helped enable Hopkins to achieve his unique position. One was simply that Hopkins sought power relentlessly; he was a perpetual schemer who would undercut his friends, bully Mrs. Roosevelt, stop at nothing to preserve his intimacy with the President.

Second, his abilities matched his ambitions; he was a brilliant administrator, an indefatigable man of action whom Winston Churchill dubbed

"Lord Root of the Matter" for his ability to pierce to the heart of any problem.

Third, Hopkins had served Roosevelt since 1930 and his understanding of the President's mind and moods was excelled by no man—and equaled perhaps only by two women, Mrs. Roosevelt and Missy LeHand. Along with everything else it is helpful for presidential intimates to be mind readers, and Hopkins more than anyone else could anticipate Roosevelt's needs and fulfill them. Fourth, the timing was right: Roosevelt desperately needed a deputy and alter ego to help him bear the awful physical and mental pressures of the war years.

Fifth and finally, Hopkins was given power because like Louis Howe in earlier years he was willing to make a total commitment to Roosevelt's cause. Others held back because of pride, ideology, or personal political ambitions. Hopkins was never much bothered by ideology, his political ambitions had vanished with his health in 1939, and his pride had become pride in serving Roosevelt. Moreover, after his trip to England in January, 1941, opened his eyes to the magnitude of Hitler's evil, Hopkins became a man with a mission: To serve Roosevelt was to serve all humanity. It was a cause a man might die for. Hopkins' friend Marquis Childs wrote that after visiting England Hopkins seemed ". . . relieved, happy almost, at having found something in which he could abandon his own personal destiny; submerging himself in a task of immeasurable magnitude and immeasurable risk."

There were personal reasons, too, for Hopkins' dedication to Roosevelt. His life had not been a happy one. His first marriage ended in divorce; his second wife died of cancer. His eighteen-year-old son was killed in combat during the war. His reputation was darkened by a decade of intense political criticism. Alimony and medical bills kept him virtually penniless during his years in Washington. Finally, he was in wretched health, often near death, during the last six years of his life. Given all this, the affection of Franklin and Eleanor Roosevelt became the one joy of his life. Rexford Tugwell describes a scene in the White House on Christmas Eve, 1939, which poignantly illustrates this fact:

"The stockings now were hung, and the children went unwillingly to bed. Among them, I might note, was one small girl who was not a Roosevelt. She was the daughter of Harry Hopkins—and of his beloved wife Barbara who had died of cancer. Of all the gathering, she was the one most closely held in Eleanor's protective arms, and it was she who had the warmest grandfatherly kiss. Harry, gaunt and ill, was unnerved. On such occasions he was overcome by loneliness in spite of the kindness of his great friends. The rest of his life would be given to proving in his own way the depth and reach of his gratefulness."

The road to the White House had begun in Sioux City, Iowa, where Hopkins was born in 1890. He graduated from Iowa's Grinnell College and was remembered there as an average student and above-average campus politician. He thought of entering newspaper work, but instead accepted a job one of his professors arranged in a New York City settlement house. His energy, his concern for society's underdogs, and his political instincts won him rapid advancement as a social work administrator. In 1930, as the Great Depression settled over the nation, the forty-year-old Hopkins became chairman of Governor Franklin Roosevelt's Emergency Relief Administration.

He did his job well, and when Roosevelt became President, Hopkins became head of the Federal Emergency Relief Administration. In his first two hours in his new post Hopkins spent $5 million, and thereby launched his legend as a prodigious spender of the taxpayers' dollars. Later that year he managed the Herculean feat of putting four million men to work in the Civil Works Administration in two months. Afterward he told Roosevelt: "Well, they're all at work, but for God's sake don't ask me what they're doing."

Hopkins once summed up his administrative philosophy in four words: "Hunger is not debatable." If people were hungry, government's job was to feed them—fast—and if a few dollars went down the drain in the rush that was too damn bad. This philosophy pointedly differed with that of Hopkins' archrival as a relief administrator, Secretary of the Interior Harold Ickes, who would agonize for weeks over every detail of a relief project before letting go any federal funds. Roosevelt respected Ickes' prudence, but it was Hopkins' zeal to help people fast that won his deeper affection.

Any man who spent public funds with Hopkins' abandon was sure to become a target of the New Deal's critics, and Hopkins helped speed the process with his sharp tongue. Once in a congressional hearing when an annoying Republican Congressman told him, "I'm not trying to persecute you," Hopkins shot back: "Oh, hell, you're intellectually incapable of persecuting anybody." When a reporter told Hopkins that congressional leaders were saying he was no politician, he cracked: "Tell 'em thanks for the compliment." Once in a press conference he lashed out at welfare critics as "too damn dumb" to understand the programs; he was widely reported as having said "people are too damn dumb" and this phony charge hounded him for years.

Hopkins rose steadily in Roosevelt's favor throughout the 1930s. At first Mrs. Roosevelt was his patroness. She was deeply interested in his relief programs and he took care to keep her well informed. Roosevelt soon came to appreciate Hopkins as an effective administrator who took the political heat without complaint. Roosevelt found, too, that Hopkins was a good companion, one with a breezy, irreverent humor much reminiscent of Louis Howe.

The Hopkins of the early 1930s was a slender, rather boyish-looking man, quick to laugh or crack a joke, a bit too flip for some tastes but generally viewed as a man of considerable charm. Newspapermen liked his candor, wit and lack of pretention. He worked in his shirt-sleeves, loathed bureaucratic procedures, and ran to dandruff.

To know Hopkins only from his pictures is to see a man who seemed to pass from youth to old age overnight. Before his 1937 operation, he had seemed a young man—at least ten years younger than he was. After his ill-health began, and the pressures of the war years, he became a frail, gaunt, hollow-eyed man—an old man, suddenly looking ten years older than his fifty-odd years. Jonathan Daniels remembered him as a "dingy grasshopper"; FDR in 1941 spoke of him as a "half man"; Truman described him as looking like a cadaver in the weeks after Roosevelt's death.

But in the good years of the mid-30s Hopkins could indulge his fondness for high living. Like his boss, he enjoyed the company of witty, well-born, talented people. He liked nightclubs and racetracks—a fact that was widely noted in the press, and that Mrs. Roosevelt viewed as a regrettable flaw in an otherwise sterling character. Roosevelt seems to have been amused by it. Hopkins sometimes accompanied young Jimmy Roosevelt on excursions into café society. For a time after the death of Hopkins' second wife there were rumors of a possible romance between him and Roosevelt's daughter Anna, who was then divorced.

Hopkins spent Election Night 1936 drinking champagne in the elegant Iridium Room of the St. Regis Hotel in New York, surrounded by Republicans who were smoldering with anger at Landon's defeat. When one of Hopkins' companions, columnist Dorothy Thompson, put aside her Landon button and proposed a toast to the President, the others ignored her. Hopkins was delighted at the Republicans' anger, and even more delighted at the thought of making them much more angry in the four years ahead.

Hopkins' relief agency had spent some $6 billion in the first term and would spend another $4 billion in the second. The bulk of this money went to the standard make-work jobs—the leaf-rakers, the construction workers who critics said were always leaning on their shovels instead of digging with them. Hopkins also became something of a patron of the arts. Artists have to eat like everybody else, he said, and made room in WPA for thousands of unemployed writers, dancers, painters, actors, and musicians. His Federal Theater Project presented, among other things, T. S. Eliot's *Murder in the Cathedral* and an all-Negro *Macbeth*. Hopkins, although he did not advertise the fact, had a lifelong love of poetry and literature. While visiting England, he wrote moving letters to his wife describing his thrill at visiting Keats's home and the county-side of which the poet had written.

But poetry was secondary. As Hopkins rose in favor, Roosevelt in-creasingly tutored him in political manipulation, and Hopkins was a willing pupil. He became a key figure, along with his rival Corcoran, in the attempted purge of conservative Democrats in the 1938 primaries.

The presidential sun shone most brightly on Hopkins in mid-1938 when talk began that Roosevelt was grooming him to be the Democratic candidate for President in 1940. The rumors reached a peak on Christmas Eve, 1938, when Roosevelt named Hopkins to be Secretary of Com-merce. Here was a job that would give Hopkins the prestige of Cabinet status and also enable him to woo the political support of the nation's businessmen. The Hopkins boomlet also included frequent photographs with Roosevelt, increased speechmaking, and an audacious attempt to re-establish himself as a native son of Iowa by leasing a farm near Grinnell. This last ploy moved Ickes to comment: "There is hardly anyone I know whom I would less spontaneously associate with farm life than Harry."

There are several possible reasons why Roosevelt encouraged Hopkins' presidential hopes—and Hopkins, in later years, freely admitted that he hungered for the presidential nomination and did everything he could to win it. First, had Roosevelt stepped down after two terms, Hopkins probably would have been one of two or three liberals he might have backed to keep the nomination from going to Hull, Farley, Garner, or some other conservative. Or, Roosevelt may have reasoned that if he was to seek a third term in 1940, Hopkins would make a convenient stalking horse to draw criticism and to remind Democrats, by comparison, that there really was no one to fill the Chief's shoes. Or, Roosevelt may have been considering Hopkins for the vice-presidential nomination; certainly he would not have offended conservatives any more than the eventual choice, Henry Wallace.

Whatever Roosevelt's motives—and Hopkins was as much in the dark as anyone—they came to naught when illness carried Hopkins close to death in September, 1939. Doctors at Mayo Clinic gave Hopkins only weeks to live. Two years earlier doctors had cut away half his stomach to halt cancer; the result had been a multiplicity of digestive problems.

Roosevelt resolved that his friend would not die. As the instrument of his resolve he turned to an institution in which he had limitless faith: the U. S. Navy. Hopkins was moved to the U. S. Naval Hospital in Washington, where he became a guinea pig for countless drugs and injections designed to replace the acids missing from his digestive system. The experiments were successful. Hopkins would never again be entirely well; he would spend the rest of his life taking pills and injections; but he would live for six historic years.

Because of his health, Hopkins made precious few visits to the Department of Commerce during his eighteen months as its Secretary. One of those visits fell on May 10, 1940, which coincidentally was the day the German armies launched their blitzkrieg against the Low Countries. When he finished his business at the Commerce Department, Hopkins went next door to the White House to have dinner with Roosevelt. He felt so sick that Roosevelt persuaded him to stay overnight at the White House. He ended up staying there for three and a half years. (However, he did not inspire the Broadway comedy, *The Man Who Came to Dinner*, as Missy LeHand sometimes said; it was written several years earlier.)

One of Hopkins' first assignments after he moved into the White House was to engineer Roosevelt's third-term nomination at the Democratic convention in Chicago in mid-July. In so doing, Hopkins superseded both the departed Corcoran and Farley, who had broken with Roosevelt over the third term. At the Chicago convention, it was Hopkins who broke the news to outraged Democratic politicians that the ex-Republican Henry Wallace was to be the vice-presidential candidate —and Hopkins who gave Wallace a tongue-lashing when he naïvely proposed to appear before the angry delegates to accept the nomination.

A few weeks later, on August 22, Hopkins submitted his resignation as Secretary of Commerce. Poor health was the stated reason for his resignation, but the real reason was political. Hopkins had become a double-barreled liability to Roosevelt's campaign against Wendell Willkie. First, because as a non-functioning Secretary of Commerce he was a sure target of Republican criticism. Second, because in doing Roosevelt's dirty work at the Democratic convention he had made countless enemies high in his own party.

So Hopkins resigned, took an apartment in New York, and talked vaguely of doing some writing. It is not clear whether he really thought he was out of the presidential circle for good. Roosevelt's letter accepting his resignation had stressed their continued friendship: "You may resign the office—and nothing else. Our friendship will and must go on as always." Yet an emotional, highly personal handwritten letter Hopkins sent Roosevelt, recalling their good times together, seemed to indicate that Hopkins did indeed think the good times were over. This letter said in part:

"A public letter of resignation is almost a vulgar institution. Why don't you abolish it? At any rate, I have told you little that is in my mind and heart as I leave the government's service.

"I think of the things that have made my years with you the happiest time of my life. The first exciting days—the exhaltation of being part of government—our first formal dinner at the White House when I met Cardozo and another (when) Bob Jackson tried to sell me some old underwear—and Cocos Island—did you ever see anything so green? Then there were those cigarettes in my pocket—it seems to me in all decency you should forget that one.

"And one day you went to church with me when the going wasn't so good—and life seemed ever so dark.

"Those nine old men—a better fight none of us ever took in.

"And there was always New Year's Eve—and the warm glow of Auld Lang Syne—with champagne. That's about the only time we get champagne around your house. Or am I wrong . . . ?

"I presume Henry Morgenthau will ever go to the bathroom when he gets ahead—and 'Dollar Watson' will ever talk about the Powder River.

"The cheese store on 42nd St.—and fresh fish in Iowa—and maps and rivers and forests and Admirals and dams and power plants—funny things that no President ever talked about before.

"All of these things I think of—and Mac and Steve and Tommy and Ben and Rex and Felix and Sam and Missy—and I know they are important because I remember them—and they are good.

"This letter is simply to say that I have had an awfully good time—and to thank you very much."

It was a lover's letter of farewell, and as such letters often do, it seemed to hint very softly that this need not be farewell forever. A few weeks later the separation ended. Hopkins was called to Washington as a campaign speechwriter and soon he moved back into his old two-room suite in the southwest corner of the second floor of the White House. There, as a private citizen, he entered the final and most remarkable phase of his career.

With the election won Roosevelt could concentrate on the urgent problem of how to continue to aid Britain's stand against Nazi Germany despite the fact that the British government had virtually exhausted its dollar credits. Roosevelt conceived his plan for the lend-lease program in December, and during the Christmas holidays he spoke with Hopkins of the countless military and political matters he urgently needed to discuss with Churchill. He thought it unwise for him to meet personally with Churchill until the lend-lease bill had passed Congress.

"How about me going over, Mr. President?" Hopkins suggested.

Roosevelt vetoed the idea, but Hopkins refused to give up. He had Missy LeHand and Felix Frankfurter pursue the idea with the President. A week later Roosevelt abruptly told a press conference—without first telling Hopkins—that he was sending Hopkins to Britain as his "personal representative" to maintain "personal relations between me and the British government." Two days later, on January 5, 1941, Hopkins was en route.

Roosevelt had several motives for his action. He wanted to establish more personal contact with Churchill. He wanted a size-up of Churchill and the men around him. He wanted to do what he could to bolster British morale. Another purpose of the trip that might have been in Roosevelt's mind was expressed by Hopkins in an off-the-record interview in London with Edward R. Murrow: "I suppose you could say I've come here to try to find a way to be a catalytic agent between two prima donnas."

Hopkins met with the King and Queen, and held long sessions with Britain's military and political leaders, but his main accomplishment was to lay the groundwork for his warm personal relationship with Churchill. Hopkins had long believed that Roosevelt was the greatest man in the world; he soon decided that Churchill was close behind. This did not mean he was blind to Churchill's faults, any more than he was to Roosevelt's. (Once, during a dinner at the Casablanca Conference, a smartly dressed British marine hurried in to hand Churchill a cable; Hopkins later saw the cable, judged its message to be less than urgent, and noted in his diary that Churchill had probably staged the interruption for dramatic effect. Similarly, Roosevelt had once ordered Hopkins to scatter some papers—any papers—over his desk because Wendell Willkie was coming to see him and he wanted to look busy.) But whatever the foibles of his two heroes, Hopkins knew that the lives and freedom of millions depended upon the closest possible cooperation between them. He knew, too, that theirs was a delicate and potentially explosive relationship. Probably the secret of his remarkable success as a middle-man was that he did not just try to represent Roosevelt's interests to Churchill; instead, he tried the more dangerous task of serving two masters.

Hopkins put on a bluntness in his dealings with Churchill that he would not have dared use with Roosevelt. It is epitomized in a (probably apocryphal) story that was told about his first meeting with the British leader. Churchill, knowing Hopkins was a social worker and hoping to gain his sympathy, was said to have made a long speech in which he stressed that Britain was fighting for the Forgotten Men of all the world. When he finished Hopkins said dryly: "Well, Mr. Prime Minister, neither the President nor myself gives a damn about what you've been saying. All we're interested in is how we can beat that son of a bitch in Berlin."

Hopkins' visit boosted the morale of many Englishmen who were beginning to wonder if America was indifferent to their desperate plight. When Hopkins quoted from the Book of Ruth—"Whither thou goest, I will go . . . even unto the end"—at a dinner he attended with Churchill, word of it spread across England in days. Another time he was the guest of honor at a dinner given by Lord Beaverbrook for leading members of the London press. One of the editors present later wrote:

"Hopkins rose, looking lean, shy and untidy, grasping the back of his chair. . . . He told us of the anxiety and admiration with which every phase of Britain's lonely struggle was watched from the White House, and of his own emotions as he traveled through our blitzed land. His speech left us with the feeling that although America was not yet in the war, she was marching beside us, and that should we stumble she would see we did not fall. . . .

"None of us British journalists who had been listening to the man from the White House was in any illusion about the peril which encompassed our land. But we were happy men all; our confidence and our courage had been stimulated by a contact for which Shakespeare, in *Henry V*, had a phrase: 'A little touch of Harry in the night.'"

Hopkins' trip impressed him, and through him Roosevelt, with the determination of the British to stand against the Germans. He wrote to Roosevelt: "The people here are amazing from Churchill down, and if courage alone can win the result will be inevitable. But they need our help desperately and I am sure you will permit nothing to stand in the way." Similarly, his first trip to Russia—in August, 1941, just after the German invasion—convinced him that Stalin's armies would hold out against the advancing Germans. His firm belief in this was important, for American and British military calculations were then being made on the assumption that the German army would defeat Russia in two or three months. Hopkins' reports that Russia would hold, and his continuing advocacy of maximum military assistance to Russia, had a far-reaching impact on Anglo-American military decisions.

Hopkins got on well with Stalin. The U. S. Ambassador to Russia said in July, 1941, that Stalin spoke to Hopkins with "a frankness unparalleled in my knowledge in recent Soviet history." Hopkins abhorred Communism—a feeling that was reinforced by his first-hand view of Russian totalitarianism—but he was strongly pro-Russian in the war because: "They're killing Germans." Stalin viewed Hopkins as a man of his word, a man who got things done. Averell Harriman noted at the wartime conferences that Hopkins was one of the few men in the world Stalin would cross a room to shake hands with.

But if Hopkins won Stalin's respect, he won Churchill's affection. Robert Sherwood wrote of his first meeting with Churchill: "He paid glowing tribute to Harry Hopkins, speaking of 'the great heart that is within that frail frame.' His eyes welled over with tears when he said this." Later, when Hopkins' youngest son was killed during the invasion of the Marshall Islands, Churchill sent his friend a beautiful scroll which read:

Stephen Peter Hopkins

Age 18

"Your son, my lord, has paid a soldier's debt:
He only liv'd but till he was a man;
The which no sooner had his prowess confirmed
In the unshrinking station where he fought,
But like a man he died."

Shakespeare

To Harry Hopkins from Winston S. Churchill
13 February, 1944

Hopkins made five trips to England during the war and also met with Churchill at the wartime conferences and during Churchill's trips to Washington. The Prime Minister had full access to Roosevelt, but as a matter of mutual convenience Hopkins became his day-to-day link with the President. Hopkins was the buffer between the two men, the mutual friend who made excuses and eased tensions on both sides of the Atlantic.

An unspoken arrangement was reached whereby Churchill could informally present new proposals to Roosevelt through Hopkins, and not run the risk of their being officially rejected by Roosevelt. Churchill would cable his proposals to Hopkins with the comment: "If you think well of it, perhaps you will ask our great friend for his opinion on this proposal. . . ." Hopkins would then discuss the matter with Roosevelt. If Roosevelt disapproved, Hopkins would tell Churchill he didn't think the time was ripe to air his new idea. If Roosevelt approved the idea, however, Hopkins would urge Churchill to go ahead with his proposal. It was an extraordinary and elaborate fiction, a face-saving device pure and simple, but a necessary and effective one.

One example of this arrangement in operation came in 1943 when five U. S. Senators returned from a world tour and made critical statements about British use of lend-lease materials. Churchill sent Hopkins the advance text of a rebuttal he planned to deliver in the House of Commons. Roosevelt feared that such a rebuttal would cause him political problems in Congress, so he had Hopkins suggest to Churchill that he cancel his plans, which the Prime Minister did.

Hopkins' intimacy with Churchill and Stalin soon made him virtually indispensable to Roosevelt; in effect, these friendships became a unique power base from which he could increase his influence in Washington. One of Hopkins' critics commented that the way for him to go on living at the White House was to be always on the verge of leaving for England.

When Hopkins made his first trip to England in January 1941 he was simply a private citizen acting at the President's request, but he was soon on the White House payroll as a $10,000 Special Assistant to the President on the lend-lease program. Hopkins was to be the real head of the lend-lease program for several years, although other men would have the administrator's title. When Roosevelt and Churchill set up the Anglo-American Munitions Assignment Board, Hopkins was made its chairman. He thus had the overwhelming responsibility for allocating, on a worldwide basis, the supply of war material to the U.S. and British armed forces.

Throughout 1940 and 1941 Roosevelt was under heavy pressure to appoint a single top assistant to run the defense mobilization effort. The names of Justice William O. Douglas and Senator James F. Byrnes were often mentioned. Roosevelt refused. There would be no Czar, he said. He seems to have feared that such a figure—an Assistant President —would undercut his own authority, and possibly emerge as a rival for Democratic leadership. Hopkins, for his part, knew that an able, energetic executive like Douglas or Byrnes would soon rob him of his hard-won power. So Roosevelt's and Hopkins' interests coincided perfectly: neither wanted a rival, so they worked together to keep power securely in their own hands.

One man whom both Roosevelt and Hopkins knew they could trust was Roosevelt's old friend and speechwriter Sam Rosenman, and he was increasingly called upon as a presidential troubleshooter in the early war years. In August, 1941, Roosevelt asked Rosenman, who was then still serving on the New York Supreme Court, to draft a reorganization plan to prepare the government for wartime production; the result was the Supply, Priorities and Allocations Board. Later, Rosenman was involved in setting up the National Housing Authority, the War Manpower Commission, the Office of War Information, and the Office of Economic Stabilization.

In September, 1943, Rosenman resigned from the court and was named Special Counsel to the President, the same title he had held during Roosevelt's governorship. The creation of the post caused some controversy in Congress, since the President already had one lawyer he could call upon—the Attorney General. The White House argued that Rosenman, as Special Counsel, would aid the President with *personal* matters, whereas the Attorney General was concerned with *governmental* matters. The distinction was spurious, for Rosenman was less a legal adviser than a presidential troubleshooter who happened to be a good lawyer. But the creation of a prestigious position in the White House for a lawyer was important, and in later years men of such talent as Clark Clifford and Theodore Sorensen would fill it.

Hopkins, with no serious rivals as the President's favorite, was in a position of incredible strength.

Scores of wartime agency administrators reported to him, officially or unofficially; "Can you get the HH on it?" was a bureaucratic byword. Whereas other White House aides have had to fear the wrath of Cabinet members and other high officials, Hopkins was often able to bring about the appointment of his chosen men to key positions. Sometimes he deliberately pushed ineffectual men into high government jobs because he knew they wouldn't be a threat to him.

One such case was Edward R. Stettinius, the genial, aristocratic former board chairman of U. S. Steel. In September, 1941, Hopkins had Stettinius named as administrator of the lend-lease program; thus, in effect, he became Hopkins' front-man for dealings with Congress. In 1944, when ill-health finally forced Cordell Hull's retirement as Secretary of State, Roosevelt was inclined toward Byrnes as his successor, but Hopkins persuaded the President to name Stettinius instead.

The appointment of Stettinius as lend-lease administrator was a good example of Hopkins' style. It was he, not Roosevelt, who offered the job to Stettinius. Didn't the President want to talk it over with him, Stettinius asked. That wasn't necessary, Hopkins said. So Stettinius accepted the post and a few days later he got a letter from Roosevelt that made it painfully clear just where he stood: "Harry Hopkins is, of course, familiar with the administration of Lend Lease, and I hope you will consult with him and with me where matters of major policy arise."

Not all the men Hopkins pushed were mediocrities. He promoted General George Marshall's appointment as chairman of the Joint Chiefs of Staff. Averell Harriman was a Hopkins protégé. But Hopkins was ruthless if he felt his authority was being challenged. If his fellow speechwriters Rosenman and Sherwood seemed to be gaining too much presidential favor, he would undercut them by seemingly agreeing with them on some important issue and then talking against them in private with Roosevelt. When he sensed that his original patroness, Mrs. Roosevelt, wished he would move out of the White House, he was so rude to her that she decided to leave him alone, which was exactly what he wanted. For a time in 1943 Hopkins hoped to replace seventy-six-year-old Henry L. Stimson as Secretary of War, and he was the apparent source of a rash of newspaper stories saying Stimson was senile, losing his grip, and otherwise ripe for retirement. Stimson's popularity with Congress foiled this plot, however.

Hopkins of course felt that he had the purest of motives for his endless scheming: he believed that no one else could serve Roosevelt as well as he himself. Certainly there was much truth in this. Even victims of Hopkins' plots respected his ability. Stimson wrote in his memoirs, "It was a Godsend to have Harry Hopkins in the White House." Hopkins also had the respect of military leaders who might have resented his influence in their field. General Eisenhower later wrote: "He had a grasp of the broad factors in military problems that was almost phenomenal." General Marshall wrote to Hopkins upon the latter's retirement from government: "Time after time you have done for me things I was finding it exceedingly difficult to do for myself and always in matters of the gravest import."

Here was the heart of Hopkins' power: he got things done. He could speak bluntly to Churchill or Stalin, Eisenhower or Marshall, because he had the drive, the authority, and the knowledge of Washington to break through the innumerable wartime bottlenecks. No detail of the war effort was too small to escape Hopkins' attention. Here is part of a memo—one of thousands of such memos—he wrote to the head of the War Shipping Administration:

"Are our merchant ship repair facilities used on a twenty-four-hour basis? Is there adequate personnel in these facilities? What inducement is there to the companies to finish the job with all possible speed? What are the general terms of the contract? Is it on a cost-plus basis? What are the average hours worked by employees in merchant ship repair yards? Are you satisfied with the security of the stevedoring?"

George Kennan provides a vivid picture of Hopkins at work during his wartime heyday. Kennan, then a little-known foreign-service officer, had returned to Washington from Portugal convinced American policy toward that country was dangerously misdirected, but unable to get anyone to listen to him. Finally he outlined his fears to Admiral William D. Leahy. Then, Kennan writes:

"Admiral Leahy listened patiently, and I believe with some astonishment, to what I had to say. He told me that the man I should see was Harry Hopkins, and arranged for me to be taken at once to Hopkins' office. Hopkins lost no time on politeness or pleasantries. For the better part of an hour he paced up and down and cross-examined me as though I were a suspected criminal. The questions were sharp, skeptical, and menacing in tone. I realized that if I failed to pass this test, things would not go well with me. When he had asked his fill of questions, he pondered a brief moment and then asked 'Where are you staying?' I told him. 'You go back there,' he said, 'and don't let yourself get out of reach of the telephone.' Shortly after I arrived at the home where I was a guest, the telephone rang. It was Hopkins, instructing me to return at once to the White House. This time I was taken through a different set of corridors, asked to pass through a different door, and found myself, to my consternation but also to my relief, alone in a room with the President of the United States."

Hopkins' role as wartime expediter was once summed up in a note Roosevelt scribbled to him about a navy foul-up in delivering desperately needed airplanes to Russia: "Say to them from me: Hurry, Hurry, Hurry!" Another time a defense contractor was delaying the delivery of planes and Hopkins tipped off the press so damning pictures would be made of the grounded planes. The frustrations of Hopkins' job were many; he once said: "Decisions to go ahead are made by the President and the Prime Minister and all the generals and admirals and air marshals—and then, a few months later, somebody asks, 'Where are all those landing craft?' or 'Whatever became of those medium bombers we promised to China?' and then you start investigating and it takes you weeks to find out that the orders have deliberately stalled on the desk of some lieutenant commander or lieutenant colonel down on Constitution Avenue." Hopkins' unprecedented power stemmed from his ability to find and blast loose that stalled paper on that obscure desk. Roosevelt set long-term goals, and Hopkins worried about short-term means. Hopkins grasped the issues of the war, but at bottom his influence rested on his unexcelled talent as a "nuts-and-bolts man."

Hopkins married Mrs. Louise Macy in the White House on July 30, 1942, with the President serving as his best man. Mrs. Macy was an attractive, vivacious young woman, a former writer for *Harper's Bazaar*, who had met Hopkins through mutual friends when she was seeking a job in the war effort. Hopkins had no intention of letting his marriage interfere with his status as the White House's permanent houseguest. He knew Mrs. Roosevelt wished he would move out, so he raised the issue with her on a "You-don't-mind-if-we-stay?" basis that left little choice but her consent.

Thus Hopkins maintained an intimacy with Roosevelt that only Louis Howe in earlier years had equalled. The two men usually had lunch, pre-dinner cocktails, and dinner together. They were lunching together in the Oval Room when news of the Pearl Harbor attack came. Hopkins would listen patiently to Roosevelt's favorite risqué jokes, although he had heard them many times before. He would endure Roosevelt's weakness for bizarre cocktails, including one siege of gin and grapefruit juice. In return, Hopkins alone could break in on Roosevelt at any hour. Hopkins was once said to have told a friend: "I don't give a damn who sees Roosevelt during the day. I see him at night, the last half-hour before he goes to bed. People forget how lonely a President is, how often he sits alone, eats alone, thinks alone. I see the Chief when he is alone and tired, and a half-hour then is worth two hours any other time."

Yet Hopkins was never entirely secure in Roosevelt's favor during the war years. The main reason for this was that the interests of any man, any friend were secondary to Roosevelt's overriding commitment to winning the war. Whenever it seemed that Hopkins was not physically able to carry his share of the war effort, his stock dipped accordingly, friendship or no. Secondly, Hopkins' position was precarious because Roosevelt had always been a difficult friend to keep, a master whose jealousy was almost womanish, a companion who was always conscious of the gulf between a President and those who serve him. Louis Howe had done so much for Roosevelt that in his last

years the President would forgive his old mentor almost any indiscretion; Hopkins' position was never that secure.

Sherwood writes of a time when Hopkins made a slurring remark
about Wendell Willkie "and Roosevelt slapped him with as sharp a
reproof as I ever heard him utter. He said, 'Don't ever say anything
like that around here again. Don't even think it. You of all people
ought to know that we might not have had lend-lease or selective
service or a lot of other things if it hadn't been for Willkie.'" Arthur
Krock tells of a meeting in which Hopkins interrupted Roosevelt on
some point and declared: "Oh, no, you're wrong about that, Mr. President," only to have Roosevelt glare at him in silent fury until Hopkins
backed down and said *he* had been wrong. (Krock, recalling the
cautious, subtle way that Hopkins would observe Roosevelt's moods
and humor Roosevelt's whims, was reminded of a comment by Bottom in *As You Like It:* "I will roar you as gently as any sucking
dove.")

Mrs. Roosevelt once wrote of Hopkins: "He gave his opinions
honestly, but because he knew Franklin did not like opposition too
well—as who does?—he frequently agreed with him regardless of his
own opinion, or tried to persuade him in indirect ways. . . . This was
not as valuable a service as forcing Franklin, in the way Louis Howe
did, to hear unpleasant arguments."

Two factors worked against Hopkins as he sought to maintain and
expand his power. One was his health. He often had to be hospitalized for several weeks after his exhausting trips abroad. An operation and slow recuperation kept him out of action for the first six
months of 1944, an absence from which his influence never fully recovered.

His second handicap was an endless torrent of politically inspired
criticism. In 1943, the Chicago *Tribune* carried an ingenious article—
one of hundreds like it—comparing Hopkins (". . . a lean, gangly
figure with thinning brown hair and dandruff . . . his face twisted by
a sardonic grin . . .") with the Russian court plotter Rasputin. Included were superimposed pictures of the two intriguers. Another time
a *Tribune* editorial titled "Hopkins' Slimy Hand" asserted that he
was trying "to turn the War Department into a global political organization."

The notion that the world loves a lover did not hold true in Hopkins'
case. His marriage to Mrs. Macy only inspired endless critical rumors
and newspaper items. It was widely reported that Hopkins had com-
mandeered a navy ship for a honeymoon cruise; actually he honey-

mooned on a farm in Connecticut. Lord Beaverbrook was rumored to have given Hopkins' wife a $500,000 emerald necklace, presumably to repay Hopkins for favoring the British in the allocation of military supplies. Stories spread of angry scenes in the White House involving Mrs. Roosevelt and Mrs. Hopkins, and there was some truth in them. Over the years the rumors and criticisms did their job. Robert Sherwood wrote a few weeks after Hopkins' death: "The very name Harry Hopkins became a sort of symbol of dark dealings in high places."

In the late summer and fall of 1944 a shadow fell between Roosevelt and Hopkins. Sherwood wrote of this period: "Roosevelt's need for Hopkins' counsel and even more for his companionship was no longer so great that the President was willing to defy the criticism which invariably arose in the hostile press whenever Hopkins took Hull's place at an important conference." As a result, Hopkins did not attend a Roosevelt-Churchill meeting in Quebec in September. The next month Roosevelt pointedly neglected to appoint Hopkins to a high-level committee on post-war lend-lease to Britain, despite the fact that lend-lease had been Hopkins' jurisdiction for three years.

The break was not complete, nor permanent, nor did it even come to the attention of the press, yet it was very real, as Hopkins later told Churchill and Sherwood. Roosevelt thought Hopkins no longer had the strength to play a large part in the war effort. Also, Hopkins' enemies had been busy talking against him to Roosevelt during his long illness in the early months of 1944. Finally, the approach of the 1944 election was a factor, for it was almost second nature by then for Roosevelt to put his controversial aides on the back burner during election campaigns.

Yet Hopkins managed to win his way back into Roosevelt's favor. Sherwood suggests two reasons. One was that during Hopkins' out-of-favor period, Roosevelt had given tentative approval to the ill-conceived Morgenthau Plan, a proposal to reduce post-war Germany to an agrarian state; Roosevelt probably felt this was exactly the sort of blunder from which Hopkins' skeptical scrutiny would have protected him. Apparently the fact that Morgenthau was an old friend of Roosevelt's had intimidated the staff members who should have warned the President against such a misguided proposal.

The other incident that helped revive Hopkins' influence occurred in early October 1944. Churchill and Stalin had scheduled a meeting to discuss postwar spheres of influence in the Balkans. Roosevelt was unable to attend the meeting because of the U.S. elections. Hopkins feared that Churchill would presume to speak for the absent Roosevelt and that Stalin would think the U.S. was disinterested in the postwar political situation. On October 3, Hopkins was shocked to learn that Roosevelt was sending a cable to Churchill which seemed to imply that the Prime Minister could speak for him. Hopkins rushed to the White House communications center. Far overstepping his authority, he ordered the officer on duty to hold up the cable. Then he hurried to Roosevelt's bedroom and told him what he had done and why. Roosevelt realized he had been saved from a serious mistake and immediately cabled Stalin: "I choose to consider your forthcoming talks with Mr. Churchill merely as preliminary to a conference of the three of us."

Hopkins returned to power, and it was at about this time that he was able to engineer the appointment of his ally Stettinius as Secretary of State. In January, 1945, Roosevelt sent Hopkins to London to spend a few days with Churchill smoothing over some Anglo-American differences prior to the Yalta Conference. The mission was successful, but was followed by an unsuccessful meeting with General de Gaulle in Paris. By the time Hopkins reached Yalta he was so exhausted that he had to be carried about on a stretcher. He was able to attend only the major meetings at Yalta, but he kept in close touch with the proceedings. From his sickbed Hopkins backed Churchill in persuading Roosevelt that France had to be given a role in the postwar occupation of Germany. Another time, Hopkins persuaded Roosevelt to tone down a statement critical of de Gaulle.

When the Yalta Conference was over, Hopkins was too sick to return to the U.S. by ship with Roosevelt and decided instead to fly back. Roosevelt was annoyed to lose Hopkins' company on his voyage and, Sherwood wrote, "the President's good-bye to him was not a very amiable one." They never saw each other again.

Hopkins entered the Mayo Clinic and was still there when Roosevelt died in Warm Springs on April 12. The next morning Hopkins phoned Sherwood. "There was no sadness in his tone," Sherwood recalled later. "He talked with a kind of exaltation as though he had suddenly experienced the intimations of immortality. He said, 'You and I have got something great that we can take with us all the rest of our lives. It's a great realization. Because we know it's *true* what so many people believed about him and what made them love him. The President never let them down. That's what you and I can remember. Oh, we all know he could be exasperating, and he could seem to be temporizing and delaying, and he'd get us all worked up when we thought he was making too many concessions to expedi-

ency. But all of that was in the little things, the unimportant things—
and he knew exactly how little and unimportant they really were. But
in the big things—all of the things that were of real, permanent importance—he never let the people down.'"

Hopkins went to Washington for the funeral and stayed there, although desperately ill, to brief the new President on the international
situation. Truman recalled: "I, too, trusted him implicitly, and unless
his health had been seriously impaired I hoped that he would continue with me in the same role he had played with my predecessor."
In May, Truman sent Hopkins on a dramatic mission to Moscow to
talk to Stalin about Russian objections that threatened to wreck the
United Nations Charter Conference in San Francisco. This final undertaking was successful: Hopkins got the needed concessions from
Stalin.

Shortly before Hopkins left for Moscow, he and Sam Rosenman
had a talk at the White House. Rosenman asked Hopkins what he
would do after he returned from Moscow. "I don't know," Hopkins
replied. "I don't have a job." Rosenman, recalling this many years
later, shook his head sadly. "Harry had a lot of rich friends who entertained him when he was in the White House—and he did a lot
for them—but they never offered him a job afterward."

As it happened, David Dubinsky, president of the International Ladies
Garment Workers Union, had offered to secure for Rosenman an appointment as the $25,000 a year chairman of the New York clothing
industry. This chairmanship was largely an honorary post that involved arbitrating occasional disputes in the clothing industry. Rosenman couldn't accept the position because he had agreed to stay in the
White House for an indefinite period to help Truman get started. He
suggested to Dubinsky that he offer the job to Hopkins, and the
union leader agreed. "I sent Harry a cable in Moscow telling him not
to worry, he had a job," Rosenman recalls. "He cabled back and said
he'd take it."

Hopkins resigned from government on July 2. He and his wife
moved to New York, where he planned to spend much of his time
writing a book, or books, about his years with Roosevelt. But in November he was hospitalized. On January 29, 1946, he died in Memorial
Hospital with his wife at his bedside. The cause of death was hemo-
chromatosis, which results from inadequate digestive equipment. He
was fifty-five and he had outlived Roosevelt by nine months. His friend
Sherwood wrote: "Hopkins had spent so much time at death's door

during the past nine years that the final act of passing through must have been for him pretty much a routine matter."

Expressions of sorrow came to his widow from all parts of the nation and the world. Perhaps the one that would have meant the most to Hopkins came from his old comrade-at-arms Winston Churchill, who wrote:

"I have been present at several great conferences where twenty or more of the most important executive personages were gathered together. When all discussion flagged and all seemed baffled, it was on these occasions he would rap out the deadly question: 'Surely, Mr. President, here is the point we have got to settle. Are we going to face it or not?'

"Faced it always was and, being faced, was conquered."

III. THE TRUMAN STAFF

1. *A Maddening Mixture*

Harry Truman's White House staff seemed in many ways to be the very opposite of Franklin Roosevelt's.

Roosevelt's had been disorganized but powerful; Truman's was relatively well organized but possessed far less power.

Roosevelt's was marked by loyalty up—unwavering loyalty to the President from aides who were often manipulated and kept in the dark. Truman's was marked by loyalty down—the President's defiant support of men whose misdeeds caused his Administration to be smeared with scandal.

Roosevelt often seemed to be plotting against his aides, playing them off against one another; in Truman's White House most of the plotting was done by the aides, as opposing factions fought an underground battle to shape the President's decisions.

Roosevelt's aides, whatever else one might think of them, were unusually able men; Truman's staff was a maddening mixture of talent and mediocrity. Two Washington correspondents, Robert S. Allen and William V. Shannon, declared: "Harry Truman's White House staff has a double distinction: in size, it is the largest in history, and in ability it is the weakest in decades." Even a leading member of the Administration, AEC chairman David Lilienthal, noted in his journal in 1951 that Truman "has close about him—since Clark Clifford left two years ago —as sorry a bunch of third-raters as I have seen in many a moon."

When Truman was thrust into the presidency in April, 1945, he instinctively turned for help to the men he knew best: old friends and political allies from Missouri, and men who had served on his Senate staff.*

From St. Louis, to be military aide and naval aide, respectively, came Harry Vaughan, Truman's friend since the First World War, and James K. (Jake) Vardaman, the Mississippi Senator's son, who had become a political supporter of Truman's. Vardaman would soon be promoted to the Federal Reserve Board, but not before he brought into the White House a young lawyer friend from St. Louis to be his aide, Clark Clifford.

Also from St. Louis came Charles G. Ross, Truman's boyhood friend, later a Pulitzer Prize winning Washington correspondent for the St. Louis *Post-Dispatch,* who became a popular but not outstanding Press Secretary.

From Kansas City, Missouri, came Edward D. McKim, an insurance executive, another World War I buddy of Truman's, who was made Chief Administrative Assistant to the President and rumored in the press to be the new Harry Hopkins; but McKim proved to have no aptitude for politics and he soon returned to Kansas City.

Donald Dawson, another Missourian, had worked his way up to the position of personnel chief for the Reconstruction Finance Corporation when Truman called him to be the White House's top man on personnel. The President's personal physician, Brigadier General Wallace H. Graham, was another Missourian. His personal secretary, the gracious Rose Conway, came with him from the Senate staff.

For an Appointments Secretary and political operative, Truman turned to one of his Senate aides and favorite companions, tall, thirty-seven-year-old Matt Connelly.

When the White House needed a legislative draftsman, Truman chose a young North Carolinian, Charles S. Murphy, whom he had first known as a Senate legislative assistant.

To handle labor disputes, and day-to-day liaison with the domestic agencies, Truman hired Dr. John Roy Steelman, a big, jovial native of Arkansas, and gave him the title of The Assistant to the President. Steelman recruited another Southerner, David Stowe, a thirty-nine-year-old former North Carolina schoolteacher, to be his deputy.

---

* Most accounts picture Truman as thunderstruck by Roosevelt's death and his own accession to the presidency. One account to the contrary was written by Robert L. Riggs, Washington correspondent for the Louisville *Courier Journal,* in *The New Republic* of April 11, 1955, in which he describes an off-the-record dinner with the then Vice President: "There was Harry S Truman, seven days before he took the oath as President, sitting with us and, in a shy manner, making it clear to all that he had no doubt he would be in the White House before many months had passed."

Three holdovers from Roosevelt's staff were David Niles, formerly an aide to Harry Hopkins, who dealt with minority groups; thirty-one-year-old George Elsey, a military aide who became a researcher and writer for Truman; and William Hassett, who handled routine correspondence.

Finally, of course, Truman's staff included a few men who were not Missourians, not Southerners, not cronies, not old Senate aides, not holdovers, but were simply men whose talents were uncovered and put to use. One was David Bell, who was discovered working for the Bureau of the Budget and recruited to Charles Murphy's staff (and in the 1960s served as AID Director, Budget Director, and vice president of the Ford Foundation). Another was David Demarest Lloyd, a lawyer and lobbyist for the ADA whom Clark Clifford recruited as a White House speechwriter during the 1948 campaign. Lloyd had the distinction, in 1950, of becoming the first man to have a novel published while he was working in the White House. The novel, *Son and Stranger,* received excellent reviews, although it had nothing to do with politics. Rather, it concerned a middle-aged American couple whose son was killed in Europe during the Second World War.

Truman in June 1950 brought one man of unquestioned stature and ability to his staff, Averell Harriman. Harriman was Ambassador to Russia when Truman entered the White House, and Truman later made him Ambassador to England, Secretary of Commerce, and director of the Economic Cooperation Administration. It was from the last-named post that Truman recalled Harriman to be his Special Assistant, a title that had not been used since Hopkins left the White House.

Truman wanted Harriman to be a high-level coordinator of military, diplomatic, and intelligence affairs, a role that Clark Clifford had performed until his resignation six months earlier. Inevitably, Harriman was compared with his late friend Hopkins, a comparison he curtly dismissed with: "Truman isn't Roosevelt and I'm not Hopkins."

Probably Truman had a secondary motive in summoning Harriman to the White House: to use Harriman's prestige to offset the growing reputation of the White House staff as an assembly of cronies and second-raters. Truman and Harriman were often photographed together: at the Army-Navy football game, at the baseball opener, on cruises, at Key West. The publicity may have served Truman's purpose, but more than anything else the pictures underscored the immeasurable distance between the Missouri-born President and the Eastern Establishment that Harriman so elegantly symbolized. One picture lingers in the memory: a grinning Truman in a multi-colored Hawaiian sport shirt and jaunty golf cap, and close by a solemn Harriman, looking like a misplaced polo captain in his white shirt, black sweater, and white sport coat.

Their union was cordial, but brief. Harriman was restless in the White House. In November, 1951, he left to become Director of Mutual Security; in 1954 he ran successfully for Governor of New York.

Throughout Truman's presidency, such attention as his staff received was focused almost exclusively on two contrasting subjects. First, there was Clark Clifford, an extraordinarily talented man, one whose intelligence, subtlety, and instinct for power earned him a place with Hopkins, Adams, Sorensen, and Moyers among the most influential of all White House aides. On the other hand—in pointed contrast to Clifford's glittering and highly praised performance—was the Missouri Gang, the presidential cronies whose various indiscretions helped create "the mess in Washington."

Robert Cutler, the Boston banker who later served on Eisenhower's staff, once visited Truman's White House in the company of Gordon Gray, Secretary of the Army. Cutler gives this jaundiced but probably accurate picture of the scene:

"The anteroom in which sat Matthew Connelly, the Appointments Secretary, was in those days filled with hangers-on, smoking cigars, wearing their hats, talking confidentially in small groups. One of these figures was Major General Harry Vaughan, dressed in uniform, his garrison cap as usual slightly off center, who greeted us warmly as 'Gordon' and 'Robert' (my first meeting)."

I. F. Stone, a journalist with a habit of stating unpleasant truths about Washington more bluntly than anyone else, wrote of the Truman Administration:

"The composite impression was of big-bellied, good-natured guys who knew a lot of dirty jokes, spent as little time in their offices as possible, saw Washington as a chance to make useful 'contacts,' and were anxious to get what they could for themselves out of the experience. They were not unusually corrupt or especially wicked. . . . They were just trying to get along. The Truman era was the era of the moocher. The place was full of Wimpys who could be had for a hamburger."

Yet Clifford's glamor and the Missouri Gang's notoriety were not all of the story. A third important fact was that quietly, behind the scenes, the White House staff was functioning as a genuine presidential institution. Roosevelt had created the institution; Truman expanded and perpetuated it.

Truman, modest about himself, was immodest about the office he held, and he moved in numerous ways to protect and expand its prerogatives. He created the National Security Council; he created the Central Intelligence Agency to gather intelligence data for the President; he created the Council of Economic Advisers to give himself new sources of economic advice; he created the Atomic Energy Commission to place responsibility for atomic development securely in the President's grasp.

He was similarly innovative in shaping his personal staff. The two most important staff offices in Truman's White House were those of The Assistant to the President and the Special Counsel; Truman created the former and allowed the latter to evolve into an important legislative and policy-shaping institution.

The key fact about Truman's White House, however, is that Truman believed in administering his government through his Cabinet officials, not through powerful White House operatives in the Corcoran-Hopkins tradition. Truman once put his feeling succinctly: "I propose to get Cabinet officers I can depend on and have them run their affairs, and when I can't depend on them I'll keep on firing Cabinet members until I can get that kind." He was as good as his word: in seven and a half years Truman had twenty-four men in his Cabinet, compared with Eisenhower's sixteen in eight years.

Truman's belief in a strong Cabinet, plus the fact that he attracted only one empire-builder, Clark Clifford, to his inner circle, resulted in making Truman's staff rank with Eisenhower's as the least powerful in recent years. He expected his staff to render personal service to him rather than to be a shadow Cabinet exercising vast powers throughout the government. Even Clifford's primary importance lay in his intellectual and political influence on Truman, rather than in the authority he exercised over the executive departments.

Richard E. Neustadt, who served for a time on Truman's staff, comments in *Presidential Power*:

"Truman's methods in the White House followed forms somewhat like Eisenhower's to results somewhat like Roosevelt's. In theory Truman was as much committed as was Eisenhower to straight lines and tidy boxes on the organization chart, and to 'completed staff work.' But in practice Truman had more feel for personalities than jurisdictions, and his instinct was to improvise arrangements around problems rather than to work through fixed procedures. In dealing with his staff he set no precise lines of demarcation or of hierarchy; those he did establish he was likely to ignore. . . . His office was decked out with many of the trappings of what later became known as a staff system, but he, himself, remained incurably informal and accessible. . . . He loved to make decisions. Unlike Eisenhower he was not disposed to keep away from them and unlike Roosevelt he had little inclination to defer them once he got them."

Truman, preoccupied with foreign affairs and domestic politics, had little time to devote to the departments and agencies concerned with domestic programs. He expected his Cabinet Secretaries to shoulder their own burdens, and insofar as that was impossible he looked to The Assistant to the President, John Steelman, to plant his solid 215 pounds between the President and unwanted details. Steelman's presence in the White House resulted from the fact that Truman's first Secretary of Labor, Lewis Schwellenbach, a former Senator and federal judge, was utterly without experience in the field of labor. As the rash of postwar strikes began, Truman was in desperate need of advice on labor relations, and at Schwellenbach's suggestion, the man he turned to was Steelman.

Born in Arkansas, educated at Vanderbilt, Harvard, and the University of North Carolina, Steelman taught economics at the Alabama College for Women until, in 1934, he chanced to meet Secretary of Labor Frances Perkins at an economic conference. She offered him a job in Washington, and within a few years he had worked his way up to be head of the Federal Conciliation Service. In the fall of 1945 he accepted Truman's invitation to come to the White House as a special consultant on mediation problems. Steelman lacked the intellectual graces of a Moley, a Corcoran, or a Hopkins, but he worked hard, he knew his business, and until Schwellenbach was replaced, he functioned as *de facto* Secretary of Labor.

In June, 1946, Truman promoted Steelman to Director of the Office of War Mobilization and Reconversion (OWMR).

Six months later, Truman abolished OWMR and gave Steelman the new title of The Assistant to the President with roughly the same responsibility for dealing with the domestic departments of government. There was one crucial difference: The OWMR director had statutory powers over Cabinet members; The Assistant to the President would have to use persuasion.

As Steelman recalls it, he employed a good deal of amateur psychology in his dealings with the Cabinet. At Cabinet meetings, he says, he would remain silent until Truman asked him if he had any comments; then he would declare that he only wanted to second what Secretary So-and-so had said a few minutes earlier. This manuever, he says, invariably won him the trust of the Cabinet officials.

Another of Steelman's ploys came when Cabinet members had some problem they wanted to take to the President. Steelman recalls: "I would tell them, 'Well, I think the President would want you to do so-and-so, but why don't you talk to him about it?' They would almost always say, 'No, there's no use wasting his time; I'll just do as you suggest.' I always kept the door to the President wide open, so they didn't often want to come in."

There has never again been anyone quite like Steelman in a position of such authority in the White House. He lacked the intellectual ability, the political experience, the personal finesse, and the ideological under-pinnings that have marked other notable aides. His distinguishing char-acteristics were a capacity for work and an overwhelming heartiness. Robert S. Allen and William V. Shannon found him: ". . . red-faced, pushing, opportunistic . . . a congenital glad-hander . . . a bombastic hack." Others were offended by Steelman's jovial evasiveness on the issues and his crude attempts to manage the news to his own advantage. But Steelman had support where it counted. Something in his back-slap-ping, country-boy manner appealed to Truman, and the criticisms of Steelman, like those of Harry Vaughan, probably strengthened his posi-tion with the President rather than hurt it.

One of Steelman's proudest claims was that he was "non-political." Actually, Steelman's cautious and conciliatory manner led him to become the main White House ally of the Administration conservatives who were led by Secretary of the Treasury Snyder. At the same time in 1946 that Steelman was emerging as the conservative spokesman, the other rising star on the President's staff, Clark Clifford, was becoming the leading liberal.

Clifford and Steelman were natural rivals, not only because of poli-tics but because of their contrasting personalities. Yet it was an unequal competition, for Clifford was a vastly more subtle and effective operator than the blustering Steelman. More important, however, in giving Clifford the edge over his rival, was that his pragmatic liberalism struck a more responsive chord with Truman than Steelman's cautious conservatism.

An instance of the Steelman-Clifford conflict came late in 1946 as Truman neared a showdown with John L. Lewis, the defiant head of the United Mine Workers. The fight had begun in January when Lewis presented the mine owners with an unprecedented demand: a ten-cent royalty on every ton of coal mined, to be used to provide medical and retirement benefits for the miners. The mine owners rejected the de-mand, and on March 30 some 400,000 miners in twenty-one states went on strike. With the mines closed, it was only a matter of time until the nation's business would grind to a halt, for coal provided the power for ninety-five percent of all locomotives and supplied sixty-two percent of all electric power. After Truman's personal attempts at a settlement failed, he seized the mines on May 21 and put them under the operation of Secretary of the Interior Julius Krug. In effect, Lewis was then bargaining with the government instead of the mine owners. A week later the government agreed to a new contract giving the miners a five-cent royalty on each ton of coal. Truman, following the advice of Steelman and others, had chosen to appease Lewis.

Appeasement didn't work. In October, two weeks before the 1946 congressional elections, Lewis repudiated the contract and threatened a new strike. At that point a heated debate erupted within the Administration on the way to handle Lewis. It was not a simple liberal *versus* conservative argument—presumably the "liberal" view would have been pro-Lewis—but rather a question of power, the power of the President *versus* the power of a defiant labor leader. Steelman, who prided himself on his good relations with Lewis, urged a compromise with Lewis. Clifford urged a fight to the finish, and says:

"It was a very sharp, clear conflict. John Steelman counseled working out some kind of an arrangement with Lewis. The trouble was that the only arrangement you could work out was on Lewis' terms. Steelman and some of the others were really afraid that the President would be licked if he locked horns with Lewis on this issue. The rest of us argued that the President would have to take him on sooner or later, and the longer we put it off, the worse it would be.

"I took the position that we were in a very critical period, the national economy was in a delicate state of balance, and Lewis had chosen to challenge the government. I felt we could not cave in. The President had to meet the challenge and fight it through. The debate went on for days. After the matter had been argued strenuously, President Truman decided to fight. And he fought and won."

Once Truman decided to fight, the Justice Department devised a strategy that involved securing a court injunction against Lewis and culminated with a $3.5 million contempt-of-court fine against the UMW and total victory for Truman.

A similar pattern continued throughout Truman's first term. The liberals, led by Clifford, wanted the President to take a liberal line—on wages, on Taft-Hartley, on housing, on civil rights—and, if Congress defied him, to take his case to the people in 1948. The conservatives, including Steelman, urged Truman to go slower, to avoid offending powerful interests, to stick to the middle-of-the-road. Truman chose to follow the liberal advice, and with his "Give-'em-hell" campaign of 1948, managed his miraculous victory over Thomas E. Dewey.

The fight between Clifford and Steelman was bureaucratic as well as political. In theory, the Special Counsel's Office dealt with the government departments on "forward planning" (i.e., legislation) and the office of The Assistant to the President dealt with operational (i.e., day-to-day) affairs. In reality the line between the two offices was never clearly defined and there was a continuing struggle between them.

When Clifford resigned in January 1950 to enter private law practice, his hand-picked successor as Special Counsel was Charles S. Murphy. Truman had first known Murphy as a young Senate legislative draftsman, and he brought him to the White House in 1947 to work on legislation. The tall, quiet Murphy had been one of Clifford's ideological allies and was the logical choice to succeed him.

As Special Counsel, Murphy lacked Clifford's charisma or his taste for power, but he was widely viewed as the most able member of the generally lackluster staff of Truman's final term. After spending the Eisenhower years practicing law in Washington, Murphy returned to government in 1961 as Under Secretary of Agriculture in the Kennedy Administration, and was later Lyndon Johnson's appointee as chairman of the Civil Aeronautics Board. Like Clifford, if on a less majestic scale, Murphy has remained an influential and respected behind-the-scenes figure in the inner councils of the Democratic Party.

Clifford, Murphy and a few others were the bright spots on Truman's staff—and it took all their talents to offset the dim view the nation, and history, took of some other staff members who were known collectively as the Missouri Gang.

2. The Missouri Gang

In the years since Harry Truman left the White House a generation of Americans has come along to whom "the mess in Washington" is only a Republican rallying cry from a far-off political campaign. This is unfortunate, for the charges in 1952 of a mess in Washington were not just election-year rhetoric. There most emphatically *was* a mess, involving specific corruption and a general laxness of ethical standards, and responsible Democrats were as concerned about it as Republicans. Unscrupulous men enriched themselves at the taxpayers' expense, often with the aid of government officials, and in time some of them went to prison for their crimes. Scandals in the Bureau of Internal Revenue and the Reconstruction Finance Corporation (RFC) shook the confidence of millions of Americans in their government, and helped bring the Republicans to power in 1953. Public concern was intensified by unmistakable evidence that in several cases the stain of corruption reached into the White House itself.

It is no pleasure to poke through the Truman Administration's dirty linen; it stinks to high Heaven. It lacks even the redeeming grace of grandeur. We may be sure that if such men as Tom Corcoran or Clark Clifford had turned their talents to larceny they would at the very least have stolen California. But the Truman Administration's mess was a record of petty graft: mink coats and deepfreezes, free hotel visits and cheap "fixes," two-bit operators getting rich because they had friends in the White House.

It is far more pleasant to dwell on the glories of the Truman Administration: the Marshall Plan, the Truman Doctrine, the creation of NATO. Certainly these accomplishments far outweigh the fact that Truman's Appointments Secretary was sent to prison for fixing a tax case, or that his military aide was so dim-witted as to accept the gift of seven deepfreezes, or that his personal physician dabbled in the commodities market and lied about it, or that one of his secretaries was given an $8500 mink coat in anticipation of services to be rendered by her influence-peddling husband.

Yet even if these and other indiscretions may not weigh heavily in the long sweep of history, they are not without significance. They point up the myriad pressures and temptations that play upon men who are suddenly given vast power. They are an enduring reminder of the varieties of human weakness, the foibles of character that lead one man to sell himself for cash, another for compliments, a third for political capital. They underscore the fact that a President's friends can do him infinitely more harm than his enemies. The misdeeds of the Truman staff dramatize the fact that in any Administration the man at the top is the ultimate moral arbiter. His acts or omissions set the tone. If he is overly tolerant, or short-sighted, or gullible, or simply dishonest, there is every likelihood that some of his intimates will yield to the temptations that beset every man who stands in proximity to presidential power.

The inner circle of Truman's staff—the men whose ties with the President were as much social and personal as they were official and political—consisted of Harry Vaughan, Matt Connelly, Donald Dawson, Dr. Wallace Graham. Other intimates included Secretary of the Treasury

John Snyder, Postmaster General Robert Hannegan, and George Schoeneman, a close friend of Hannegan's who served on the White House staff in 1945 and was made Commissioner of Internal Revenue. Schoeneman resigned in July 1952 amid tax scandals that caused sixty-six employees of the Bureau of Internal Revenue and the Justice Department to be fired, and nine of them to be sent to prison.

These were Truman's cronies. Charlie Ross was an old and intimate friend; Clifford, Steelman, and Murphy were valued employees and frequent companions—but Vaughan, Connelly, Dawson, Graham, and Snyder were the men Truman most liked to have around in his off-duty hours to drink with, to joke with, to play poker with, to reminisce with. Truman was a good friend to these men. He lifted them to power, he trusted them, he stood behind them when they were under fire. Some of them were good friends to Truman, too, but it was a blot on his Administration when others let him down.

Harry Vaughan became the best-known of all Truman's intimates, for it was his misfortune to become a one-man symbol of the mess.

Partly this was because Vaughan made the mistake of accepting the seven much-publicized freezers from a Chicago businessman he had befriended. Partly it was because Vaughan used his White House influence to abet the lucrative activities of an odious little influence-peddler and perjurer named John Maragon.

But mainly Harry Vaughan became a symbol because he is so admirably suited to serve as one, because he is an instantly recognizable sub-type of *homo Americanus*, part George Babbitt and part Willie Loman, a man whose sunny smile and hearty handshake can any day be found in countless Elks Clubs and National Guard armories from coast to coast. Harry Vaughan is a loud, jovial, boastful, crude, cunning, not-too-bright, rather likable buffoon. He is a denizen of poker-parlors and a dabbler in local politics, a drinker of bourbon and a teller of tales. He is everybody's bachelor uncle, the one who turns up for Christmas dinner each year three sheets to the wind, the one whose off-color tales draw blushes from the ladies and guffaws from the men. He is, in short, a one hundred percent, red-blooded, All-American Regular Guy—and Harry Truman loved him for it.

They had trained for World War I together at Fort Sill, Oklahoma, and served in the National Guard in the 1920s and 1930s. Vaughan was never much of a success in the business world—he was a tea salesman for ten years before he hitched his wagon to Harry Truman's star—but he worked on Truman's 1940 campaign for re-election and afterward went to Washington as the Senator's secretary. He served in the South Pacific during the war, and after being injured in a plane crash, he returned to Washington and was made the War Department's liaison to the Truman Committee. When Truman became Vice President, Colonel Vaughan became his military aide. To the infinite distress of the professional military establishment, National Guardsman Vaughan remained Truman's military aide for seven and a half long years, and advanced to the rank of Brigadier General.

During Vaughan's first days in the White House some history-conscious journalists hailed him as the Louis Howe of the Truman Administration. Vaughan soon shattered their illusions by unveiling his rare talent for speaking with his foot in mouth. In one memorable address to a group of Presbyterian ladies in Alexandria, Virginia, Vaughan settled the respective merits of Presidents Roosevelt and Truman with a gastronomical metaphor ("After a diet of caviar, you like to get back to ham and eggs"), and dismissed Churchill as "a garrulous old man."

Once Vaughan unburdened himself of the opinion that the country hadn't had a decent Secretary of Commerce since Herbert Hoover. Another time he drew criticism for accepting a decoration from Argentine dictator Juan Perón. Later, when reporters pressed him to explain how he could afford to take his family on a vacation to Guatemala, he told them to lay off because: "After all, I am the President's military aide and you guys will want favors at the White House someday."

Soon, when trouble broke around the White House, Press Secretary Charlie Ross would shake his head sadly and say: "Cherchez le Vaughan."

Vaughan was a crony, but he also had responsibility. First, he was military aide, a liaison man with the War Department. Second, Truman made Vaughan his liaison with J. Edgar Hoover on FBI matters. Third, Vaughan was coordinator of veterans' affairs, and as such empowered to cut red tape to help servicemen.

It was Vaughan's fourth capacity—as an untitled administrative troubleshooter—that led to trouble. The word soon spread in political circles that Vaughan was a good man to know in the White House. Vaughan delighted in playing the role of the fellow who could get things done. He had a towering disdain for bureaucratic red tape, and was seemingly unaware that most of the red tape exists to protect the taxpayers from being fleeced by just the sort of shady dealers who were besieging him for favors. In the postwar years, there were fortunes to be made in surplus war commodities, and Vaughan's word carried weight with the military officials who were in charge of military surplus. A few phone calls from Vaughan might be worth hundreds of thousands of dollars.

Vaughan himself tells the story of a man who came to him for help in purchasing surplus oil tankers. Vaughan helped him swing the deal and the man realized a huge profit. Afterward, the man offered Vaughan $15,000 as a reward for his assistance. Vaughan turned it down, and the man then tried to give him his new Buick. Finally, Vaughan says, he let the man give him a box of good cigars to show his gratitude.

In August, 1949, Vaughan was a star witness at a Senate subcommittee's investigation into the activities of the Washington influence-peddlers who were known as "five-percenters." The five-percenters were men whose livelihood was their supposed influence with high government officials. They promised defense contractors and others who sought to do business with the government that they could get their projects approved. In return, they wanted five percent (and sometimes much more) of the take. Two of Harry Vaughan's good friends were a big-time five-percenter named Colonel J. V. Hunt and a small-time five-percenter named John Maragon.

Colonel Hunt had once been with the Quartermaster Corps, and he boasted of friendships with almost all the army brass. His luxurious offices were decorated with autographed pictures of Harry Truman and most of his Cabinet members. Hunt delighted in impressing his clients by picking up the phone and calling Harry Vaughan in the White House. Hunt told one prospective client, "Have no doubt of it, General Vaughan is Harry Truman's friend, and I am one of General Vaughan's closest friends." It was true; thanks to Vaughan, Hunt was a frequent White House visitor.

The repurchase of the Lido Beach Hotel in Long Beach, New York, from the Navy was typical of one of Hunt's deals. The Navy had paid $1.3 million for the Lido. Its former owners wanted it back and agreed to pay Hunt a $50,000 fee plus a percentage to get it; he did, for $635,000, and cleared $86,000 on the sale.

Vaughan was instrumental in the winter of 1947–48 in enabling some of Hunt's friends to get special approval to use scarce building materials to reopen the Tanforan Race Track near San Francisco. On January 12, 1948, Vaughan made a trip to the Housing Expediter's office to discuss the deal; the next day Hunt's friends were given permission to use $150,000 worth of building materials to rebuild their track.

Vaughan apparently saw nothing wrong with Hunt's enriching himself off the government. Once when reporters quizzed Vaughan about his friend, he snapped back: "Why pick on Hunt when there are three hundred people in Washington in the same business?"

One of the least distinguished of that three hundred was Vaughan's other friend, John Maragon. Maragon was a sharp-faced little man whose fast tongue and limitless audacity had carried him from a job as a ticket agent for the B & O Railroad to a lucrative business as a five-percenter and sometime visitor to the White House.

Vaughan and Maragon met before the war when the former was on Truman's Senate staff and the latter was the B & O Railroad's ticket agent on Capitol Hill.

Vaughan had hardly settled in the White House before he was using his new-found eminence to do favors for his old friend Maragon. Maragon was an on-and-off employee of the Albert Verley perfume company of Chicago. On May 1, 1945, Vaughan wrote this letter on White House stationery: "To Whom It May Concern: This will serve to introduce Mr. David A. Bennett, owner of Albert Verley & Co. of Chicago, Illinois, who is contemplating travel in Europe. Mr. Bennett is a prominent businessman of Chicago and is entitled to the courtesies of American officials abroad."

Bennett and a companion traveled to Europe and back on Air Transport Command planes at a time when such facilities were supposedly reserved for military use, particularly for bringing home wounded soldiers. They brought back forty-one kilos of perfume essence valued at $53,405. Presumably this gave Verley & Co. a distinct advantage in competing with perfumers who were unable to make special trips to Europe.

On July 14, 1945, Maragon and two other men flew to Europe via military planes on another trip for the Verley perfume company. Returning through customs, Maragon declared a package which he said contained four bottles of champagne worth $40 which he was taking to the White House. He waved a White House pass and protested furiously when customs inspectors insisted on opening the package. It contained perfume oils valued at $2225. This attempted smuggling carried a maximum fine of $10,000; six months later customs officials accepted Maragon's offer of a $1500 settlement.

Next, on August 3, 1945, Vaughan sent this note to the U. S. Passport Bureau: "Mr. John F. Maragon, executive for the Albert Verley Co.

in Chicago, is arranging to visit the continent, including the northern part of Italy, for the purpose of re-establishing negotiations for essential oils for the above company." Later, a passport official penciled onto the note: "Col. Vaughan informed Mrs. Shipley that the President is personally interested in Maragon's trip to Italy—Col. S. agrees that he is 1-D." 1-D signified a top priority rating for persons traveling with presidential authority.

It was the Verley perfume company that paid $2625 to give seven deepfreezes to Harry Vaughan in the summer of 1945. Vaughan kept one for himself and gave the other six to the White House; the Little White House in Independence, Mo.; Fred Vinson, the Secretary of the Treasury (who sent it back); Reconversion Director John Snyder; Jake Vardaman; and Matt Connelly.

Vaughan helped Maragon gain appointment as a member of the U.S. mission to oversee the Greek elections. Maragon was employed at a $5600 a year salary, plus $15 a day expenses, from November 1945 until March 1946. He remained on the perfume company's payroll at $1000 a month. By all reports he was a terrible nuisance on the mission. In moments of stress he would pull out a snapshot of himself with Harry Truman and warn that he was reporting directly to the White House. Eventually he was sent home.

Late in 1946 Maragon made a deal with officials of the Allied Molasses Co. of New Jersey whereby he would get $2000 if he could induce the Department of Agriculture to lift a ban on allocations of molasses to Allied. The ban had been placed because of a wartime violation of food orders in which Allied had exceeded its quota of rationed molasses by 771,000 gallons with a shipment to Pepsi-Cola.

A young Agriculture Department lawyer named Herbert Hathorn testified at the Senate's five-percenter hearings that Colonel Harry Vaughan of the White House called him one day and—after saying he had already spoken with the Secretary of Agriculture—urged Hathorn to help get Allied Molasses a new allocation of 500,000 to 1,000,000 gallons of molasses. "We Democrats have to stick together," Hathorn said Vaughan told him.

Hathorn testified that when he told Vaughan he could do nothing to help Allied Molasses, Vaughan warned that he was a very close friend of the President and he could get Hathorn's job.

When Vaughan testified, he said he could remember no conversation with Hathorn. Perhaps, he suggested, someone else had called Hathorn and impersonated him. Further testimony revealed that Vaughan and Maragon had continued to bother other Agriculture Department officials about Allied Molasses' quota, although no special concessions were made.

The Senate hearings also revealed that during the 1946 congressional campaigns Maragon collected some $2500 in campaign contributions and turned it over to Vaughan; included were donations from one of the men for whom Vaughan had interceded in the Tanforan Race Track deal, and another from a man who had called upon Vaughan to win a pardon for a friend convicted of illegal liquor sales. In 1948, Maragon went into the surplus property business with an English entrepreneur and Vaughan was soon busy writing letters of introduction for him to military officials.

And so it went, *ad nauseam*. Time after time Maragon would turn up in high places—at the War Department, at the Maritime Commission—with an interest in a government ruling or government contract, and letting it be known that his good friend General Harry Vaughan at the White House was personally concerned with the matter. Maragon had a White House pass and he would sometimes come to Vaughan's office to place telephone calls; if his clients weren't in, he would leave word for them to "call me at the White House."

In his testimony before the Senate five-percenter investigators Maragon repeatedly invoked the Fifth Amendment rather than answer questions about his finances. Senate investigators said he had $119,608.61 deposited in three banks although he had been reporting only about $6000 per year on his income-tax returns. He answered enough questions, however, to be convicted of perjury and sentenced to a jail term of eight months to two years. In 1954, Maragon turned up in Washington again as part of Senator Joe McCarthy's entourage.

The irony of Vaughan's involvement with the five-percenters is that, while they obviously were profiting mightily from his good will, there is no evidence that Vaughan himself profited (except for one deep-freeze, one box of cigars, and occasional meals, drinks, and hospitality). The favors he so lavishly distributed in exchange for good fellowship and flattery he could no doubt have sold for hundreds of thousands of dollars had he been so disposed. But the indications are that Vaughan was a dumb but not dishonest man who was made a fool of in the classic pattern of the country bumpkin and the city slickers. Vaughan had come a long way from St. Louis, but he still had a long way to go.

Men who make it to the White House tend to be exceedingly realistic students of the world as it is. By the same token, men who are chosen for a President's Cabinet are often those who have come up through the political process—Governors, Senators, Congressmen—and learned over the years to weigh every word, to ponder every move, to exhibit a flawless façade.

That is the rule, but every now and then a political innocent slips through the system. Most often he is a presidential crony who is brought into the White House for old times' sake; sometimes he is a Cabinet official who is chosen for some special, non-political talent. In either event, he comes, dewy-eyed, an Alice in Wonderland; and he is barely settled in his office when he discovers a glittering new world spread out before him. Limousines and private planes await his call. Suave diplomats, celebrated bureaucrats, and solemn military commanders arrive to brief him on affairs of state. He is eagerly sought as a speaker, a writer, a social lion. Breathless society columnists record his every utterance, and respectful political writers seek his views on world problems.

Dazzled by his sudden eminence, the newcomer is tempted to forget he is a creature of circumstance and view himself, instead, as a man of destiny. Unlike the seasoned politician, he is blind to the contempt behind the bureaucrat's smile, the amused cynicism behind the journalist's polite inquiries, the impersonality of the limousines, the helicopters, and other amenities of power. He is unaware that nothing so pleases a bureaucrat as a White House functionary whose head can be turned by flattery, or so delights a Washington journalist as a man in power who is destined to make a fool of himself, or so amuses the congressional hierarchy as a new boy in the White House who is riding for a fall. The newcomer breathes the heady winds of acclaim and plucks the fruit of sudden power; only too late does he find he has been living in a fool's paradise.

So it was with Harry Vaughan, a man singularly lacking in finesse, in good judgment, in the imagination to see the inevitable consequences of his impulsive acts. He only saw his bigger-than-life reflection—a big man, a puller of strings, a doer of favors, a cutter of red tape, a hell of a fellow. Yet his case was far from unique. It was, rather, an exaggerated instance of an eternal problem. Men far more sophisticated than Harry Vaughan would stumble over the same hurdles. Eisenhower's first Secretary of Defense, the likable Charles E. Wilson, had risen to become president of the largest corporation in the world, General Motors, yet he was unable to see the political dynamite in his own off-hand remarks. First came his declaration that what was good for our country was good for General Motors, and vice versa; then his comment, when asked about the problem of unemployment, that he'd "always liked bird dogs better than kennel-fed dogs . . . you know, one who'll get out and hunt for food rather than sit on his fanny and yell." All this prompted James Reston to speculate that Charlie Wilson had invented the automatic transmission (at General Motors) so he'd have one foot free to put in his mouth. After Vaughan, the next White House crony to stir up controversy with his ill-chosen phrases was Lyndon Johnson's irrepressible friend Jack Valenti, who became most famous for his "I-sleep-better-each-night" speech.

Yet the risk of verbal blunders is far less significant than the risk of ethical transgressions. The moral pressures at the White House level are tremendous. So much power is concentrated there, so many decisions involving millions of dollars are made there, so many outsiders are enriched by those decisions, that in time the functionary may find it cruelly unjust that he should work so hard, for such a small salary, with little recognition and no provision for his future. There has never been a shortage in Washington of lobbyists, influence-peddlers, and assorted entrepreneurs eager to seek favors from the presidential intimate and glad to reward him, in whatever manner he prefers, for his assistance. The temptations are of a sort that most men never confront in their lifetimes; to resist them requires—if simple political prudence will not suffice—a positive understanding that the functionary, for all his sudden authority, must remain the servant of the people, and that the real rewards of his service must be other than financial. Such an understanding requires a philosophical turn of mind not always found in politicians and their friends; perhaps the real surprise of recent years is that, as far as we know, the transgressions committed by White House aides have been so petty.

Throughout his tribulations, Vaughan had Truman's full support. The President's only known concession to Vaughan's growing notoriety was to order him to keep out of sight during the 1948 campaign. Once Truman called newspaper columnist Drew Pearson an "SOB" for criticizing Vaughan. He declared that the Senate five-percenter investigation was unfair to Vaughan. He defiantly promoted and decorated Vaughan while he was under fire, and in time the former National Guardsman rose from Colonel to Brigadier General.

Vaughan's influence on the substance of the Truman Administration was negligible. He does, however, deserve this footnote to history: it was at his urging that Winston Churchill's famous "Iron Curtain" speech was delivered at Westminster College in Fulton, Missouri, Vaughan's old alma mater. And back there, in his home country, Vaughan remains a hero to many old friends and acquaintances despite the efforts of Republicans and the Eastern press to darken his good name. A young woman who taught for a year at Westminster College told me of seeing a child in a soldier suit at play near the college campus. "Who are you?" she asked the child. "General Eisenhower? Or General MacArthur? Or General Westmoreland?" The boy shook his head, drew himself to attention, and announced: "I'm General Harry Vaughan."

Soon after leaving the White House, Vaughan went into retirement on his military pension, which amounts to some $13,000 annually, and he now lives in a comfortable home on a hilltop overlooking Alexandria, Virginia. He says he and Mr. Truman correspond often. Vaughan often recalls the time during the five-percenter investigations when he offered to resign as military aide to spare the President embarrassment. As he recalls the scene in Truman's office: "He got up and walked over and put his arm around my shoulder. He said, 'Harry, they're just trying to use you to embarrass me. You go up there and tell 'em to go to hell. We came in here together and, God damn it, we're going out together!'"

And so they did.

If Harry Vaughan was the most conspicuous member of Truman's White House circle, Appointments Secretary Matt Connelly was the least conspicuous. Connelly was once described by a journalist as a man who could walk a tightrope with chewing gum on one shoe, which is an elaborate way of saying he was a very cool operator. Yet in the long run it was Connelly, the cool, behind-the-scenes operator, who provided the most tangible, most damning evidence of corruption among the Truman staff.

Connelly was a janitor's son from Clinton, Massachusetts. He graduated from Fordham College in 1930, held low-paying jobs in New York City, and moved to Washington in 1935 with his wife and child. He found a job as a WPA investigator, and later got a job on Senator Harry Truman's committee investigating wartime government management.

Connelly and Truman hit it off from the start. Connelly was a likable, easy-going young man who fit in well with the Truman circle. He had a knack for politics and he knew how to keep his mouth shut. During Truman's second term, Connelly was put in charge of a two-man congressional-relations team that foreshadowed the more elaborate efforts of General Wilton B. Persons in the Eisenhower Administration and Larry O'Brien during the Kennedy Administration. Reporters tended to like Connelly, but because he rarely talked for the record, they wrote very little about him.

When Truman left the White House, Connelly entered the public-relations business in New York. He might have dropped from public view altogether had not a federal grand jury indicted him in December 1955 for conspiring to defraud the government. Indicted with him in the conspiracy were T. Lamar Caudle, Truman's one-time Assistant Attorney General in charge of the Justice Department's tax division, and a Kansas City lawyer named H. J. Schwimmer. In addition to the general charge of conspiracy against Connelly, the indictment included specific charges of bribery and perjury.

The charges stemmed from the case of a St. Louis businessman named Irving Sachs who in 1951 had pleaded guilty to evading payment of $118,142 in federal income taxes. Sachs was fined $40,000 and spared a prison term on the ground of ill health. The grand jury asserted that Schwimmer, acting as Sachs' lawyer, had bribed Connelly and Caudle, and that they had first tried to stop the prosecution of Sachs' tax case, and then managed to prevent his imprisonment.

Connelly asserted his innocence and countercharged that the Republican Administration had timed his indictment to coincide with the 1956 elections: "There is a little group of willful men now in power in Washington. They have called Harry S Truman a traitor. Now, because of my association with him, they are calling me a crook."

A federal court jury in St. Louis found Connelly guilty as charged in June 1956 and he was sentenced to two years in prison and fined $2500. The jury found that Connelly had received a topcoat, two suits, and an oil royalty worth some $7500 for his part in the fix. (Connelly said he had paid Schwimmer $750 for the oil royalty and didn't know it was worth ten times that amount.) After unsuccessfully appealing his case, Connelly entered the federal prison in Danbury, Connecticut, on May 5, 1960, and was released some six months later, on November 12. On November 22, 1962, President Kennedy granted Connelly a full pardon, reportedly at Harry Truman's request. (T. Lamar Caudle was also convicted and served a brief prison term; he was given a pardon by President Johnson on August 18, 1965.) Throughout Connelly's ordeal, his old White House associates stuck by him; it is an article of faith in the Truman circle that Matt Connelly was framed by the Republicans.

After his release from prison Connelly returned to the public-relations business in New York.

Donald Dawson, unlike either Vaughan or Connelly, was a man of proven executive ability. He had come to Washington in 1933 and had risen to a top job in the Reconstruction Finance Corporation (RFC) when Truman recruited him to the White House to be the Administration's personnel chief. Once the husky, outgoing Dawson might have been promoted to the chairmanship of the RFC, but at Truman's request he agreed to remain in the White House. Another time he was reportedly in the running to fill the presidency of the New York Stock Exchange, but chose to stay with Truman.

Yet Dawson, for all his talents, was also caught up in the mess. A Senate investigation into the scandal-ridden RFC named Dawson as a leader in an influence ring that exercised authority over the RFC's often-dubious million-dollar loans. It was revealed that Dawson had accepted favors from RFC loan recipients. Senator J. William Fulbright, who headed the investigation, charged that Dawson's friendship and influence were responsible for the incredibly lucrative activities of an influence-peddler named E. Merl Young.

The Fulbright investigation (Fulbright headed a special subcommittee of the Senate Banking and Currency Committee) in the spring of 1951 revealed the RFC to be shot through with influence-peddling and politically motivated loan-making. The Fulbright subcommittee charged that Dawson ". . . apparently exerted considerable influence over certain Directors of the RFC. . . . Investigation by the subcommittee indicates that close personal relationships exist between Dawson, Merl Young, Rex Jacobs, James Windham, and RFC Directors Dunham and Willett. These friends, with others, constitute a group who appear to have exercised influence over the RFC."*

The Senate subcommittee charged that RFC Directors Dunham and Willett were virtually Dawson's puppets because they feared he would fire them if they did not do his bidding.

Dawson insisted that he had no influence over the decisions of the RFC Directors; Senator Fulbright commented ironically on Dawson's modesty: "All you say is that your relationship with these people is purely social; that you have no influence over them whatsoever. My point is that you may not have been conscious of having any influence with them, because you are a very modest man, you feel that you are only an assistant in the White House. My feeling is that they (RFC Directors Dunham and Willett) took everything you had to say as of

* Merl Young was Dawson's close friend and an influence-peddler; Jacobs was the president of a firm that received a $3 million RFC loan; Windham was an aide to RFC Director George E. Allen who resigned when the loan was made to the Jacobs company and became its treasurer.

greatest importance; that you had the power of life and death over them in an economic sense; that is, the job of Mr. Willett was completely dependent upon your approval. If you did not submit his name to the President, he would not be reappointed. These are factors which most of us in political life know to be a fact."

Dawson readily admitted that on three separate visits to Miami Beach, totaling twenty days, he stayed for free in a thirty-dollar-a-day room in the Saxony Hotel, which had recently received a $1.5 million RFC loan. He said he saw nothing wrong with this.

Dawson also conceded he had several times been a guest in the Florida estate of Rex Jacobs, whose company had received a $3 million RFC loan. He said however that he never discussed business matters while visiting with Jacobs. Committee investigators found in influence-peddler Merl Young's files a copy of a letter from James Windham to Rex Jacobs dated June 12, 1950, concerning a wildcat oil venture in Gaines County, Texas. The letter listed six persons as being involved in the venture:

Rex C. Jacobs	20%
James C. Windham	20%
E. Merl Young	20%
Phil Regan	20%
Donald Dawson	10%
William Boyle	10%

Phil Regan was a former movie and radio entertainer who was active in politics; Boyle was chairman of the Democratic National Committee. Dawson admitted he had discussed the $120,000 oil deal with Jacobs but said he had not participated in it because he didn't have enough money.

Dawson was also questioned closely about his relationship with Merl Young. Young and his wife had first come to Washington during the 1930s, soon after he graduated from high school in Jericho Spring, Missouri. He had become a $1080 government messenger, and his wife, Lauretta, took a job as a stenographer with Senator Harry Truman. When Young returned from wartime service, his wife was working in the White House and he was able to get a $4500 job with the RFC. There he resumed his friendship with Don Dawson, the RFC's personnel director, and he soon achieved a government job rating of GS-13, with a salary of $7193 and duties as an RFC loan examiner.

Young's fast-moving career was helped by the widespread, although erroneous, impression that he was related to President Truman, whose mother's maiden name was Young. He soon decided the RFC could not satisfy his ambitions. In 1948, soon after approving a $37 million RFC loan to the Lustron Corporation, a manufacturer of prefabricated houses, he took an $18,000 job as a Lustron vice president. A few months later he also went on the payroll of another RFC debtor, the F. L. Jacobs Company, at $10,000 a year. Both companies granted him lavish expense accounts, and his 1949 income was above $40,000.

Young was also busy as a free-lance "expediter" of RFC loans. A Dallas lawyer who represented a firm seeking a $10 million RFC loan testified that Young offered to help secure the loan for a $10,000 fee plus $7500 a year for ten years—a total fee of $85,000. Young teamed up with a Washington lawyer named Joseph Rosenbaum whose specialty was helping clients get RFC loans. Rosenbaum showered Young with gifts and unsecured loans worth hundreds of thousands of dollars. The best-known (but far from the biggest) of these was a royal pastel mink coat worth $8500 for Young's wife, Laurette, the White House secretary.

When Young testified before the Fulbright subcommittee he denied everything—he was not an influence-peddler; he had no influence; he had not offered to help get the Dallas lawyer the RFC loan; he had paid for his wife's mink coat himself; he was just a young American in the Horatio Alger tradition who was getting ahead through luck and pluck. On the basis of this testimony, he was convicted of perjury and sent to jail.

The Fulbright subcommittee's report charged that Merl Young's amazing money-making stemmed from "the influential atmosphere which surrounds him" and gave Donald Dawson much of the credit for creating that atmosphere. Dawson in his testimony acknowledged a "good friendship" with Young, but denied that he had in any way helped advance his friend's career. This caused an exasperated Senator Fulbright to declare:

"There is no other explanation that we can find of his being able to retain a position of $18,000 with Lustron with a very large expense account and also a position with the F. L. Jacobs Company with a large expense account. If his influence or if his power to obtain salaries did not run to his association and close friendship with you, I cannot tell where it did run to."

President Truman did not share Senator Fulbright's concern about Dawson's ethics. Truman denounced the Senate investigation as "asinine" and, at a press conference a few days after Dawson's testimony, the President dramatically pointed to Dawson and said he stood by him. Dawson, in return, stayed on with Truman until the end of his term. In fact, as Dawson recalls it, he was the last member of the Truman staff to leave the White House: "I watched the Inauguration Ceremony on television in the President's office. When Eisenhower raised his hand and took the oath of office, I got up and walked out the door." Soon Dawson, who had studied law at night during the 1930s, founded a successful Washington law firm.

At the time of the Communist takeover in Hungary, the noted actress-singer Ilona Massey had come to Washington to urge Truman to intervene. Before seeing the President, she first talked with Dawson, and this meeting led to courtship and marriage. After making one more film, Miss Massey retired from show business. She and Dawson now live in Bethesda, Maryland, just outside Washington, in a home that is a showplace for antiques and paintings they have collected from throughout the world.

There are other instances of questionable activities by members of Truman's staff. For example, on October 5, 1947, Truman denounced those persons who were speculating on the commodity exchange. A few days later his personal physician, Missouri-born Brigadier General Wallace H. Graham, issued a White House press release admitting that he had been engaged in commodity speculation (with a recent profit of $6165) but had withdrawn from them as a result of the President's statement. Commodity speculation by government officials is, of course, an extremely questionable practice, since the Department of Agriculture has secret information on commodity prices.

When called to testify before a Senate Committee in January, Graham admitted that he had in fact continued his commodity speculations until December 18. He admitted of his press release: "That was not an accurate statement." He blamed his inaccuracy on ignorance. He had withdrawn from wheat speculation—to move into cotton and cottonseed oil speculation, because he was unaware that cotton and cottonseed oil were "commodities."

There was no suggestion that Graham had obtained special information from the Department of Agriculture. But there were obvious ethical questions about the propriety of his speculations, and his clumsy attempt to mislead the press only made the matter worse. Despite all this, however, he remained in Truman's good graces.

The question remains: Why?

Why did Truman, a man of unquestioned personal integrity, tolerate highly questionable behavior by those closest to him? Why didn't he let Vaughan resign, or fire General Graham, or keep a closer rein on Dawson and his friend Merl Young? (For the record made it clear that Truman knew Merl Young and knew about his high-paying job with Lustron.) Why did Truman, a close student of American political history, tolerate a mess that has caused his Administration to be compared with those of Grant and Harding?

It has often been said that Truman was betrayed by his friends, and in a literal sense that is true. But in a deeper sense Truman was betrayed by himself; he was a victim of inevitable consequences of his own imperfect nature. This is not to say there is any simple, all-embracing key to President Truman's tolerance of wrongdoing, but to say that the key must be sought in the man himself, not in those who so poorly served him.

Truman once said that his entire political career was based upon his World War I experience, upon the friends he made and the lessons he learned. It was as an army captain under fire in France that Harry Truman first learned that he was as brave and as capable as the next man. He learned, too, the rule that says an officer must always stand by his men. Perhaps he learned that rule too well; in later years he seemed to confuse standing by Harry Vaughan when he was under fire from Drew Pearson with standing by the men of the 35th Division when they were under fire from the Germans at Meuse-Argonne and Verdun.

After the war, he was a failure as a businessman; his success came in politics. It must have galled Truman that he owed his political success to the corruption-ridden Pendergast machine. But he kept quiet, he kept his hands clean, he learned to mind his own business. That may be another lesson he learned too well. The most simple, most harsh explanation of Truman's tolerance is just this: You can take the politician out of the county courthouse, but you can't take the county courthouse out of the politician.

But it is not that simple. Another reason Truman stood by Vaughan and the others was no doubt simple political tactics: If you fire a man, you in effect admit wrongdoing; if you keep him, you can continue to deny it. More than by politics, however, Truman seems to have been motivated by stubborn loyalty to his friends. It was a sadly misguided loyalty, for Presidents owe a loyalty to the nation that transcends any allegiance to erring friends. Roosevelt understood this instinctively; Truman would not recognize it. Truman's dilemma was complicated by the fact that his nature was more sentimental than that of any of the other recent Presidents. It is often helpful for a President to be a ruthless son-of-a-bitch, particularly in his personal relationships; this, for better or worse, Truman was not.

Newbold Morris, the Republican reformer from New York City whom Truman hired early in 1952 to try to weed out corruption in government—and summarily fired two months later—once told a story that casts light on Truman's feelings about his erring friends. While appearing on the "Meet the Press" television show, Morris had made critical remarks about Harry Vaughan. Morris saw the President a few days later and Truman told him he did not hold against him his criticisms of Vaughan. Then Truman pointed to a small piece of sculpture on his mantelpiece. "Do you know who gave that to me?" he asked. "Harry Vaughan's daughter did. She made it, and she's just graduating from art school. I have a daughter, too, you know, and Harry Vaughan is my friend. You say what you want about him—that's what you're here for—but Harry Vaughan is still my friend."

There was, of course, another side to the story. Clark Clifford once commented, when asked to explain this tolerance of wrongdoing: "President Truman was loyal to his friends, and that was that. And for whatever trouble it may have caused him, he was repaid ten times by the loyalty he was given in return. We'd have died for him."

No one knows exactly how much Truman knew of what was going on. He could hardly have been totally unaware of it if the RFC, under Donald Dawson's direction, was making politically motivated loans, or if Harry Vaughan was bestowing countless favors under the banner "We Democrats have to stick together." Dawson and Vaughan were only following the oldest rule of politics: to help one's friends. And Truman desperately needed all the friends he could get if he was to win re-election in 1948.

Yet can he have known it all? With the incredible burdens of his first term—the A-bomb, the end of the war, the start of the cold war, labor unrest, economic reconversion, fights with Congress, the uphill fight for re-election—Truman had little time to be a watchdog over his friends. Nor had he the inclination; it was his manner to trust his aides too far, to assume their honesty, to give them a job and not look over their shoulders.

Perhaps he awoke one morning after his Inauguration in January, 1949, and realized that something was terribly wrong, that things had gotten out of hand. Perhaps the scope of it, the history-making reality of it, only began to dawn on him with the five-percenter investigations of 1949 or even the RFC investigations of 1951. Perhaps by then he really did not want to know the truth.

3. *The Golden Boy: Clifford*

Clark Clifford is a gorgeous man, smooth as silk and tough as nails; the White House may never see his like again. For four years he was the Golden Boy of the Truman Administration. Young, handsome, intelligent, charming, intensely political, Clifford seemed to have stepped to the political stage from the pages of one of Scott Fitzgerald's stories. He dazzled the President, the press, and the entire political cosmos, and when he returned to private life early in 1950 he could look back on two remarkable achievements.

First, after entering the White House as the unknown friend of a friend in 1945 he had swiftly become Harry Truman's most influential all-round adviser and, as such, one of the four or five most important White House aides in history. As a liberal, as an internationalist, and as a political strategist, Clifford had left his mark on Truman's domestic and foreign policies and on his miraculous 1948 election victory.

Second, Clifford wielded power with such finesse that he avoided the political and public-relations pitfalls that have beset so many other presidential aides. He left the White House with his reputation intact, respected by conservatives and admired by liberals. He went on to start a Washington law practice that soon made him the most financially successful lawyer of his generation, probably of all time.

Clifford's financial success was combined with continued influence within the Democratic Party. He was a friend and valued adviser to such leading figures as Senators Robert Kerr, Stuart Symington, John Kennedy, and Lyndon Johnson. His role as a behind-the-scenes adviser to Presidents ended abruptly early in 1968 when Lyndon Johnson named him to replace Robert McNamara as Secretary of Defense. The appointment capped a remarkable career; Clifford must rank as one of the most successful—perhaps the most successful—of all the talented and ambitious men who have struggled in the shadows of presidential power.

Clifford's was a conventional, upper-middle-class background. He was born on Christmas Day, 1906, the son of an official of the Missouri

Pacific Railroad. He grew up in St. Louis, where his mother's brother, Clark McAdams, for whom he was named, was a famous crusading editor of the St. Louis *Post-Dispatch*. He was a big man on campus at St. Louis' Washington University, where he received his undergraduate and law degrees. In 1930, he married Margery Pepperell Kimball of Boston, whom he met while touring Europe in the summer of 1929.

One of Clifford's friends in St. Louis was Jake Vardaman, a businessman and friend of Senator Harry Truman. When Truman became President in April, 1945, he summoned his friend Vardaman to be White House naval aide. Vardaman in turn summoned his friend Clifford—then a naval officer stationed in San Francisco—to be the naval aide's aide. Clifford was then thirty-eight years old and had met Truman only twice, both times very casually.

Clifford's swift rise to intimacy with Truman was based on the same qualities of self-assurance and political judgment that have marked his career ever since. He first caught the eye of Sam Rosenman, FDR's Special Counsel, who had stayed on to help Truman. Clifford began helping the overworked Rosenman with speechwriting and legal matters. Truman soon took a liking to the hard-working and self-confident young naval officer, and in January 1946, when Vardaman was promoted to another job, Clifford became the President's Naval Aide—a naval aide who was more involved in political and legislative matters than naval affairs.

One event that did much to win Clifford the President's favor came in May, 1946, when two railroad unions rejected Truman's demand that they call off a nationwide strike. Truman, infuriated, decided to ask Congress for increased strike-breaking authority and to seek national support with a radio address. He scribbled out a speech and gave it to Charlie Ross, his Press Secretary, to have typed. Ross read the notes in horror. The speech was shrill, rambling, undignified, and corny.

Truman's speech lashed out at various union leaders as liars and Communists. He denounced a "weak-kneed" Congress for lacking the "intestinal fortitude" to pass labor legislation. Finally, he appealed to "you men who are my comrades in arms, you men who fought the battles to save the nation just as I did twenty-five years ago" to support the President and "Let's give the country back to the people. Let's . . . hang a few traitors and make our own country safe for democracy. Come on, boys, let's do the job!"

Fortunately, Press Secretary Ross could bluntly tell the President his speech just wouldn't do. Clifford was given the delicate task of rewriting the presidential prose. He recalls, "The points President Truman wanted to say just couldn't be said. I tempered it a bit with Charlie Ross' moral assistance. It was a tough speech."

Actually, Clifford rewrote the speech entirely, giving it a dignity of tone that had been entirely lacking from the original draft. It was, as Clifford says, still a tough speech, for at the outset it compared the crisis threatened by the railroad strike with the crisis brought on by the Japanese sneak attack on Pearl Harbor. But from that point the new speech moved to strengthen Truman's moral position by stressing the havoc the railroad strike would wreak on the nation and on the world.

Truman delivered this speech in a dramatic appearance before Congress, and he was rewarded with total victory. His threat to draft the strikers into the army forced the union leaders to capitulate, and the tone and content of his speech won wide approval. Truman realized that Clifford and Ross had saved him from a serious blunder. A few weeks later he promoted Clifford again, this time to be Special Counsel.

Clifford had not been in his new job very long before he sensed he was caught up in nothing less than a full-scale battle for the President's mind. Truman's liberalism was an uncertain quality, rooted in instinct rather than ideology—he viewed many important New Dealers as "crackpots"—and when he became President many conservatives were confident he could be won over.

Two of the leading conservative spokesmen within the Administration were Truman's old friend John W. Snyder, a Missouri banker who was made Secretary of the Treasury, and John Steelman, the labor specialist who had become The Assistant to the President. Clifford soon emerged as the liberals' spokesman, both because of his physical proximity to the President and because of his unusual powers of persuasion. His allies included Oscar Chapman, the Under Secretary (and later Secretary) of the Interior; Oscar R. (Jack) Ewing, director of the Federal Security Agency; Leon Keyserling, a member of the Council of Economic Advisers; and Charles S. Murphy.

Clifford says candidly: "If I rendered any service to President Truman in five years it was as the representative of the liberal forces. I think our forces were generally successful. We had something of an advantage in the liberal-conservative fight because I was there all the time. I saw the President often, and if he wanted to discuss an issue, I was at hand."

Oscar Chapman recalls: "Clark would say to one of us, 'The President has confidence in you on that subject. You present the case to him and

I'll back you up.' Clark always knew exactly how far he could go with Truman."

Late in 1946, the liberals began to meet at least once a week to plan how they could most effectively influence the President's course of action. Clifford once gave this account of the meetings:

"The idea was that the six or eight of us would try to come to an understanding among ourselves on what directions we would like the President to take on any given issue. And then, quietly and unobtrusively, each in his own way, we would try to steer the President in that direction.

"Naturally, we were up against tough competition. Most of the Cabinet and the congressional leaders were urging Mr. Truman to go slow, to veer a little closer to the conservative line. They held the image of Bob Taft before him like a bogeyman. We were pushing the other way, urging him to boldness and to strike out for new, high ground. He wasn't going to pacify that Republican Congress, whatever he did.

"Well, it was two forces fighting for the mind of the President, that's really what it was. It was completely unpublicized, and I don't think Mr. Truman ever realized it was going on. But it was an unceasing struggle during those two years, and it got to the point where no quarter was asked and none was given."

Clifford's leadership of the liberal forces was based upon his growing intimacy with the President. "The whole relationship between the President and me was a highly personal one," he recalls. "It developed because there was a vacuum in the White House. We were both from Missouri. He was comfortable with me." The vacuum Clifford filled in Truman's inner circle was both personal and political. Personally, Clifford is a man of vast charm and self-assurance; his voice is always soft, his manner always confident. He has the lawyer's equivalent of a perfect bedside manner, and he was able to provide just the sort of encouragement, reassurance, and counsel that Truman needed to meet the incredible pressures of his first term as President.

It was Clifford's peculiar talent to be able to interpret Truman to liberals and intellectuals, and vice versa. Clifford was the only Truman aide who spoke both the language of Missouri and the language of Harvard and Wall Street as well. Clifford was the only man Truman brought to the White House who could communicate easily with men like Dean Acheson, James Forrestal, and David Lilienthal, and it was natural that Clifford would become their ally and spokesman within the White House. Lilienthal, the idealistic Midwestern lawyer who directed the Tennessee Valley Authority for Franklin Roosevelt, and was Truman's choice as first head of the Atomic Energy Commission, wrote in his journal of October 23, 1946, soon after meeting Clifford: "I have come to have a very high opinion of him—clear-headed, decisive, and with none of the maneuver complex, none discernible at least, that so marred some of his predecessors." Clifford and Lilienthal became close friends, and in December, 1948, after spending an evening with Clifford, Lilienthal thought about Clifford's usefulness to Truman. Truman, he wrote, "came out of the Middle West kind of progressivism, a kind of twentieth-century version of Populism—against Wall Street, the railroads, Big Business, etc., and hence he used the words and ideas of Teddy Roosevelt, Norris, Bryan, the elder La Follette, and could not communicate with the more recent progressives with their great emphasis on language that seemed to him highfalutin and crackpot. I said all this because I thought Clark's influence on the course of the President had been so very, very great because he caught on about this aspect of the President, and had found a language, a terminology, and an atmosphere in which the President could express those deep-rooted Populist, insurgent ideas."

Truman admired Clifford's charm and finesse, but another side of the young man's nature appealed to him as well. Clifford's cordial manner is the velvet glove that conceals the iron hand. He is an exceedingly tough political pragmatist. Essentially he and Truman shared the same unsentimental view of power politics—the young lawyer instinctively, the older man on the basis of long years in political life. Time after time, in conflicts with adversaries as diverse as John L. Lewis, Thomas E. Dewey, and Joseph Stalin, others would urge Truman to go slow, to compromise, but Clifford would advise him to stand and fight. No advice could have been better calculated to appeal to Truman's own deepest instincts.

Clifford's first major service to Truman came in November 1946 when, as has already been described, John L. Lewis tried to double-cross the government and Clifford urged Truman to fight it out with the union leader. Truman followed this advice and won. Clifford later said: "I think you can put your finger on winning this showdown with Lewis as the moment when Truman finally and irrevocably stepped out from the shadow of Roosevelt to become President in his own right."

However, Clifford's influence had begun before the fight with Lewis. In September, 1946, Truman told a press conference he had approved a forthcoming speech by Secretary of Commerce Henry Wallace;

in fact, Truman had only glanced at the speech and was unaware of its criticisms of U.S. foreign policy. The speech infuriated the Secretary of State, James F. Byrnes, and resulted in Truman's firing of Wallace a few days later. Clifford warmly approved this firing—he viewed Wallace as the sort of fuzzy-thinking New Dealer that Truman's Administration could do without—but he played no significant role in the decision. However, in the aftermath of the fiasco, he and Press Secretary Ross were able to persuade Truman never to approve a speech until his staff had studied it, and to begin saying "no comment" at his press conferences when issues were raised about which he was ill-informed.

In June, 1946, Clifford and Office of Price Administration (OPA) director Paul Porter successfully urged Truman—over the protests of Cabinet and congressional leaders—to veto an unenforceable new OPA bill. A year later, the issue was whether or not Truman should veto the Taft-Hartley labor bill, which bore the name of "Mr. Republican," Senator Robert A. Taft, and was considered by labor leaders to be a sharply repressive measure. Clifford and other liberals were urging a defiant presidential veto, one designed to regain labor support lost by the Administration's crackdowns on the 1946 railroad and coal miner's strikes.

Leon Keyserling recalls the liberals' campaign for a veto:

"One of our early major projects was to have the President veto the Taft-Hartley Bill. We worked this over for several sessions, because not all of us were together on this at the outset. . . . Well, we thrashed this out for two or three meetings, and in time we all came to see it the same way. The President was getting tremendous pressure from his congressional leaders to sign the bill, also from every member of his Cabinet except one, the Secretary of Labor. For a time, I think the President was inclined to go along with them. But in time our viewpoint prevailed and he did veto the bill."

In May, 1948, Clifford and Chapman persuaded Truman to override State Department objections and grant immediate recognition to the new state of Israel. They hoped a dramatic gesture of support to Israel would be repaid by Jewish votes and campaign contributions that fall. Eventually, Truman agreed: By his command, U.S. recognition was extended exactly sixteen minutes after Israel officially became a state. The inter-administration struggle leading up to this greased-lightning diplomacy was highlighted by a clash between Clifford and Secretary of State George Marshall, who opposed instant recognition for Israel. At a preliminary meeting on the subject, Marshall even resented the fact that Clifford was present. "Mr. President," he protested, "this is not a matter to be determined on the basis of politics. Unless politics were involved, Mr. Clifford would not even be at this conference. This is a very serious matter of foreign policy determination." Clifford, although furious, remained silent, but he recalled angrily: "He said it all in a righteous God-damned Baptist tone." Clifford's viewpoint eventually prevailed.

The liberal group's pressure on Truman stemmed from a belief that his only hope of re-election in 1948 was to go to the people with a clearcut liberal record. In November, 1947, Clifford submitted to Truman a remarkable forty-three-page memorandum outlining the strategies he believed might bring about Truman's re-election.

Drawing upon talks with and memos from former FDR aide James Rowe and other liberal friends and political leaders, Clifford began:

"The basic premise of this memo—that the Democratic Party is an unhappy alliance of Southern conservatives, Western progressives, and big-city labor—is very trite, but it is also very true. And it is equally true that the success or failure of the Democratic leadership can be precisely measured by its ability to lead enough members of these three misfit groups to the polls. . . ."

Clifford predicted, correctly, that Tom Dewey would again be the Republican candidate. He then proceeded to his one major misjudgment—his Southern strategy: "It is inconceivable that any policies initiated by the Truman Administration, no matter how 'liberal,' could so alienate the South in the next year that it would revolt. As always, the South can be considered safely Democratic. And in formulating national policy, it can be safely ignored." Truman, therefore, "has no real necessity for getting along with the Southern conservatives. He must, however, get along with the Westerners and with labor if he is to be re-elected. Therefore, political and program planning demands concentration upon the West and its problems, including reclamation, floods, and agriculture."

Clifford feared that Henry Wallace, whom Truman had fired from his Cabinet and who was running as a third-party, "Progressive" candidate, might lure a decisive number of liberal votes away from Truman. He wrote of Wallace:

"Wallace's mysticism has increased while his humility has decreased —so now he has a Messianic belief that he is the Indispensable Man. Wallace is gambling for high stakes. He hopes to defeat President Truman by splitting the Democratic Party and then inherit its leadership so he can be the candidate in 1952.

"Every effort must be made *now* jointly and at one and the same time—although, of course, by different groups—to dissuade him and also to identify him and isolate him in the public mind with the Communists."

On organized labor: "It is dangerous to assume that Labor has nowhere else to go in 1948. *Labor can stay home.* . . . The labor group has always been politically inactive during prosperity. When they are well fed they are not interested. They will probably be well fed in 1948.

"Labor leaders should be invited to the White House to flatter them —but to talk on *general* issues. To invite advice on specifics, and then not follow it, is to court trouble."

On intellectuals: "The 'right' may have money, but the 'left' has the pen. If the intellectual can be induced to back the President, he will do so in the press, on the radio, and in the movies. He is the 'idea man' for the people."

On key issues: "The High Cost of Living will be the most controversial issue of the 1948 campaign—indeed, the only domestic issue. Whichever Party is adjudged guilty of causing it will lose the election. . . . The Administration's recommendations—in the State of the Union Message and elsewhere—must be tailored for the voter, not the Congressman; they must display a label which reads 'No Compromises.' "

On civil rights: "It would appear to be sound strategy to have the President go as far as he feels he possibly could go in recommending measures to protect the rights of minority groups."

The Democratic National Committee must have a new chairman, and there must be new faces within the Administration itself. The South and West have traditionally been united by fear of Wall Street, Clifford wrote, and they were bothered by the abundance of Wall Street names within the Administration, such as Harriman, Forrestal, Lovett, and Mc-Cloy. More progressives should be named to high office, men like young Bob La Follette, even if the Senate refused to confirm some of them.

Truman's enemies had created a false impression, Clifford wrote, that "Everything good about Administration foreign policy is Marshall; everything bad is Truman." To combat this, Truman should make more speeches on foreign affairs, and should announce more foreign policy decisions himself, rather than letting them be announced at the State Department.

"The public has a tremendous interest in its Chief Executive and is invariably hungry for news about him," Clifford wrote. "It does not want those stereotyped gestures so done to death in past years. No one really cares any more about a round-the-world flyer, or the little girl with the first poppy of the Disabled Veterans, or the Eagle Scout from Idaho." But the President might invite Albert Einstein to lunch at the White House and then explain at his next press conference that they had talked about the peaceful uses of atomic energy. Another good luncheon guest would be Henry Ford II, then a dashing young tycoon. Or the President might comment in his press conference on an important current book he was reading.

"A President who is also a candidate must resort to subterfuge," Clifford advised. "He cannot sit silent; he must be in the limelight. . . . He must resort to the kind of trip Roosevelt made famous in the 1940 campaign—the 'inspection tour' . . . No matter how much the opposition and the press pointed out the political overtones of those trips, the people paid little attention, for what they saw was the Head of State performing his duties."

In conclusion, Clifford made the point that he fervently believed justified all the subterfuge, the cynicism, the flattery, the hypocrisy, the deception. The end, he said, justified any means employed in Truman's behalf—"because the future of this country and the future of the world are linked inextricably with his re-election."

Clifford's memorandum is a classic political document, and one that provides us with brilliant insights into its author. Clearly, behind Clifford's courtly Southern manner is a man who views without sentiment and without illusion the large political forces and petty personal ambitions that men must master who would succeed within the democratic system.

Clifford's role in Truman's foreign policy decisions was probably best described by one of his colleagues who termed it "as big as he could make it." Clifford was intensely interested (and still is today) in foreign policy, but he was overshadowed by such towering figures as George Marshall, Dean Acheson, and James Forrestal. He filled a vacuum in Truman's personal and political affairs, but there was no such vacuum in foreign affairs. What he could—and did—do was become the ally and advocate of such internationalists as Secretary of State Acheson, Secretary of Defense Forrestal, and Under Secretary of State Robert Lovett. He had breakfast one morning a week with Forrestal. He wrote the legislation creating the Defense Department, the CIA, and the National Security Council. He was White House liaison with both State and Defense, and his role as presidential speechwriter gave him access to all foreign-policy matters. He drafted, for instance, one of Truman's most significant speeches, the March 12, 1947, message to Congress asking $400 million in aid for Greece and Turkey.

One of Clifford's most important involvements in foreign affairs came in the summer of 1946 when Truman asked him to prepare a summary statement on the status of U.S. relations with Russia. The assignment came at a crucial time, a time when the U.S. government was making a historic shift in foreign policy. The dream of postwar cooperation with Russia was beginning to fade. In February, George F. Kennan, then a little-known diplomat stationed in Moscow, had caused a sensation with the 8000-word telegram he had dispatched outlining the harsh realities of Russia's ambitions. It was, as Kennan saw it, "one of those moments when official Washington, whose states of receptivity or the opposite are determined by subjective emotional currents intricately imbedded in the subconscious . . . was ready to receive a given message."

Truman had read Kennan's telegram, but apparently he wanted an appraisal of U.S.-Russian relations that was more broadly based and that was the work of someone known to him. Clifford wrote his seventy-page memorandum after talks with Acheson, Marshall, Forrestal, Lovett, and other officials, and he gave it to Truman on September 24. Truman's first response, upon reading it, was to order Clifford to put all copies of the document under lock and key.

The Clifford memorandum began:

"The gravest problem facing the U.S. today is that of American relations with the Soviet Union. The solution of that problem may determine whether or not there will be a third World War. Soviet leaders appear to be conducting their nation on a course of aggrandizement designed to lead to eventual world domination by the U.S.S.R. Their goal, and their policies designed to reach it, are in direct conflict with American ideals, and the United States has not yet been able to persuade Stalin and his associates that world peace and prosperity lie not in the direction in which the Soviet Union is moving, but in the opposite direction of international cooperation and friendship. . . .

"The key to an understanding of current Soviet foreign policy is the realization that Soviet leaders adhere to the Marxian theory of the ultimate destruction of capitalist states by Communist states."

Next, in a lawyer-like documentation of his charges, Clifford devoted some thirty pages to Russia's postwar domination of Eastern Europe, to her numerous violations of postwar agreements, and to the Soviet-American dispute over reparations from the Axis nations. Then, drawing upon U.S. intelligence reports, Clifford described Russia's postwar military build-up and her worldwide espionage network.

As long as Russia continues this aggressive policy, Clifford said, "it is highly dangerous to conclude that hope of international peace lies only in 'accord,' 'mutual understanding,' or 'solidarity' with the Soviet Union."

Here was the heart of the memorandum: "The language of military power is the only language which disciples of power politics understand. The United States must use that language in order that Soviet leaders will realize that our government is determined to uphold the interests of its citizens and the rights of small nations. Compromises and concessions are considered by the Soviets to be evidence of weakness."

The memorandum was not entirely devoted to the realities of power politics. It called for cultural, intellectual, and economic interchange to demonstrate to the Soviets that peaceful coexistence is possible. But for the most part the memorandum anticipated a long, twilight struggle:

"The Soviet government will never be easy to get along with. The American people must accustom themselves to this thought, not as a cause for despair, but as a fact to be faced objectively and courageously. . . ."

Clifford's memorandum closed by advocating policies of containment and aid:

"The United States should support and assist all democratic countries which are in any way menaced or endangered by the U.S.S.R. Providing military support in case of attack is a last resort; a more effective barrier to Communism is strong economic support. . . .

"In conclusion, as long as the Soviet government adheres to its present policy, the U.S. should maintain military forces powerful enough to restrain the Soviet Union and to confine Soviet influence to its present area. All nations not now within the Soviet sphere should be given generous economic assistance and political support in their opposition to Soviet penetration."

It would be unwise to place too much emphasis upon the impact of one document in moving Truman toward the Cold War policies he so resolutely followed. Yet the Clifford memorandum does give an excellent picture of the state of mind in high levels of the government in mid-1946 as the U.S. moved toward such major decisions as the Marshall Plan, the creation of NATO, and the defense of Korea. The document shows how Kennan's view, with its stress on political containment of the Russians, was swept aside by the doctrine of military containment. Finally, the document is of interest because Clifford's view of international relations was formed in 1946, and there were many echoes of the hard-line advice he gave Harry Truman then in the advice he was giving Lyndon Johnson twenty-two years later when he became Secretary of Defense.

Insofar as possible, Clifford operated in strict secrecy within the White House. "I never made a public appearance or went on radio or television or made a speech," he says. "I was an adviser to the President and that was all I wanted to be." But as Clifford's importance soared throughout 1946 he received more and more attention. This interest climaxed when he played a key role in the Administration's victory over John L. Lewis in December. A few days after that victory, Press Secretary Charlie Ross told a reporter in mock dismay: "All I do around here is answer questions about the great Clark Clifford." Clifford was pictured as the young David who had slain the Goliath of John L. Lewis.

Interestingly enough, most of the early stories about Clifford either said little about his politics or else mistakenly portrayed him as a conservative influence on Truman. As a *Saturday Evening Post* writer put it: "Because of his opposition to the expansion of world Communism, his distrust of Henry Wallace, and his leading role in averting the coal and railroad strikes, New Dealers consider Clifford reactionary."

Clifford did nothing to enlighten the press about his politics, for he knew that to be tagged a liberal would only win him powerful enemies in the press, the bureaucracy, and Congress. Moreover, he was not a liberal in the New Deal mold; he shared with Truman a belief that many of the New Dealers were dreamers who had little understanding of politics.

Because Clifford kept his politics a mystery, the press wrote instead about one fact he could not conceal—his good looks. Not since Warren G. Harding (and not again until John F. Kennedy) had so much been written about the physical charms of a man in public life. For Clifford at forty was a striking figure. Six-feet-two, a trim 185 pounds, broad-shouldered and narrow-waisted, always elegantly dressed, with blue eyes, an open, handsome face, and wavy golden hair—this made infinitely more pleasing copy than Clifford's role in the veto of Taft-Hartley. *Life* magazine, for instance, devoted nearly half of an article on Clifford to his looks and sartorial excellence. Among other tidbits, *Life* revealed that Clifford's enemies had been spreading a malicious rumor that he had his hair curled.

Robert S. Allen and William V. Shannon summed it up: "Glamorous Clark Clifford is one of those people who is too good to be true. His face is too handsome, his blond hair too evenly waved, his smile too dazzling, his voice too resonant, his manner too patently sincere. . . . Somewhere there must be a flaw, a glaring weakness, an idiosyncrasy. But so far Washington hasn't discovered it."

Clifford's was—and is—among the most flawless public façades ever seen in Washington. Even the most able men in public life, when exposed to the relentless scrutiny of Congress and the press, usually prove to be a bit *too* something. McGeorge Bundy is a bit too intellectual, Robert McNamara a bit too self-assured, Sargent Shriver a bit too glib, Lyndon Johnson a bit too cornpone, and so on. Clifford, however ambitious he might be personally, however ruthless he might be politically, maintained a near-perfect public posture. Blessed with Southern charm, but not burdened with Southern political prejudices, he managed to be confident without being cocky, intelligent without being arrogant, persuasive without being domineering, courteous without being ingratiating, friendly without being folksy. In short, he left his critics very little to snipe at. One might grumble—as some observers did, and still do—that it was all an act, but if so it was a beautiful act, and a very hard one to fault.

Clifford grew weary of the stories about his good looks, just as Tom Corcoran had grown tired of stories about his ballad-singing, and Bill Moyers would tire of stories about his background in the Baptist ministry. But in the last analysis it is highly useful for any presidential aide to have some idiosyncrasy to divert the attention of the press from the true nature of his duties. In Clifford's case, for instance, it was better for the press to be writing about his wavy hair than to be probing into more basic facts—i.e., that he was scheming to brand Henry Wallace a Communist, to use Albert Einstein to polish the President's image, and to sell the South down the political river.

There are, of course, inherent dangers in any presidential aide's getting a better press than his boss, but Clifford found Truman infinitely tolerant on this score. One evening they both attended an annual Gridiron Club dinner, at which leading Washington newspapermen annually roast Administration officials in song and skit. One particularly rough skit portrayed Truman as a stooge for an all-powerful Clark Clifford. Clifford was furious and humiliated, and when it was over, he told Truman he couldn't begin to express how sorry he was about the incident.

Truman replied: "It wasn't your fault, Clark. What could you do about it? They're just jumping over your back to get at me."

Clifford recalled years later: "I could have thrown my arms around him and kissed him."

The years with Truman were a time of profound growth and personal decision for Clifford. He came from a liberal family background, but his interests had always been more social and professional than political. Suddenly he found himself in a position to influence decisions that affected the lives of millions of people in America and throughout the world. It was a moving experience. One night in October, 1947, he expressed his deepest feelings in a talk with David Lilienthal. He told Lilienthal that before he entered the White House he had always thought that what he wanted out of life was to make a lot of money and to have a big house and a lot of servants. But, Clifford told Lilienthal, after his experiences of the past year, he would never again be content with such unimportant goals; making money suddenly seemed far less important than using his talents to help create a better America and a better world.

It was a moment of transcendent idealism for Clifford—and it did not last much longer. His devotion to Truman carried him through the campaign of 1948; he fought with all he had, believing in his heart he was fighting for a lost cause. Yet Truman's incredible victory brought Clifford little personal joy, for his mood had changed, and he had sensed a change in those around him. Clifford had seen the mess develop, the five-percenters, the favors, the deals, the friends-of-friends, and after the election victory of 1948 he sensed a new intensity as the lobbyists and influence-peddlers probed to find the soft spots in Truman's inner circle. He saw the weakness in some of the men around him, and he even feared it in himself. One night in December of 1948, Clifford had another long talk with Lilienthal, and his mood was very different from the one expressed fourteen months earlier. Lilienthal wrote in his journal:

"Clark seemed tired and very thoughtful. He spoke in a worried tone—quite unusual for him—about the conflict within the President's own family about future policy, between the conservatives and the 'forward-lookers.' He said he was 'tired, awfully tired; not physically, but emotionally, psychologically.' Felt that the lift that came from doing new things, of learning, is no longer there. He spoke of the awful exhibition one sees around the White House of self-seeking, etc., and seemed rather depressed by it, not as if it were something new but that he was getting his fill of it. I was struck with the way he spoke of the dangers of being in the midst of such great power and influence, and its effect on people, adding, 'Every once in a while I notice it in myself, and I try to drag it out in the open.'"

Clifford had by then decided to leave the government, but he could not do so all at once. There was, first of all, the hectic and unexpected business of translating Truman's political victory into a legislative program. First of all, there was an Inaugural Address to be written. And in the course of writing that address, Clifford helped bring into being one of the Truman Administration's most talked-about foreign ventures, the technical assistance program that came to be known as Point Four.

Several months earlier, during the heat of the campaign, a State Department aide who couldn't gain the interest of his superiors had sent Clifford a memo that described a modest technical assistance program under way in Latin America and suggested its expansion on a worldwide basis. Clifford had promptly forgotten about this memo, but he remembered it as he searched the government for new ideas to add to the Inaugural Address. He recalls: "We'd just won the greatest election upset in history and the President said, 'We've really got to have an outstanding Inaugural Address.' I began to think about what we could do to seize the attention of the world. Then—BONG!— I thought of that memo. I got it out of my desk and showed it to the President."

Truman liked the idea—it was no more than that—and approved its inclusion in the address. The details, he said, could come later. Because his Inaugural listed four points on which U.S. foreign policy should be based—the United Nations, the Marshall Plan, the North Atlantic Alliance, and the "bold new plan" for worldwide technical assistance— the new plan was dubbed Point Four. Truman's announcement was an even bigger publicity success than he and Clifford had expected. "When he delivered that speech, Point Four rang round the world," Clifford recalls. "My God, the press it got in foreign nations!" World leaders entertained visions of U.S. support for dozens of TVA-style development programs around the globe. Their dreams were in vain; Point Four, hampered by opposition in both Congress and the State Department, never attained more than modest dimensions. However, by 1953, the Point Four program did have a budget of $155 million for projects in thirty-three countries, and it stands as a memorable example of the power of an alert White House aide to cut through red tape and gain presidential support for good ideas that might otherwise be lost.

Once the first months of the new term were past, Clifford began to make plans for his departure from government. He was tired, broke, and increasingly disillusioned by the signs of corruption he saw around him. His $12,000 salary as Special Counsel was substantially less than he had been making in law practice before the war, and to make ends meet he had been borrowing from a wealthy St. Louis friend.* By 1949, he owed his friend some $25,000.

He told Truman of his decision to return to private life in mid-1949. It was said at the time that Clifford hoped Truman might make him Attorney General but that for various reasons this was not possible. One other opportunity that Clifford had declined came early in 1948 when he was visited by a group of prominent Missouri Democrats who promised him their support if he would return to run for the Senate. It was a crucial decision, for Clifford as a Senator would no doubt have become a leading figure in the party and probably a presidential contender (as his friend Symington later did), but Clifford turned down the opportunity. Electoral politics seemed to him too risky a business—he preferred to work behind the scenes—and he had decided that when he left the White House he would pursue his first dream: to achieve vast wealth through the practice of law.

His departure from the White House in January 1950 was mourned by liberals. *The Nation* magazine said, "Clifford has been the mainstay of the Fair Deal, the author of its best presidential speeches, and the originator of its most impressive strategies." *The New Republic* declared, "Clifford's retirement as Special Counsel further weakens Our Side in the White House. . . . Clifford knew the score. In many ways he was the strongest liberal influence in the Presidential entourage. He and Oscar Chapman helped toward fixing the seemingly hopeless Truman 1948 campaign on the polestar of New Dealism."

Clifford moved quickly from being the fair-haired boy of the liberal press to being the fair-haired boy of the conservative corporations. Among the clients who flocked to his Washington law office in his first year of practice were the Radio Corporation of America, Phillips Petroleum, Standard Oil, the Pennsylvania Railroad, and entrepreneur Howard Hughes. In April, 1951, Lilienthal entered in his journal this vivid picture of Clifford's success:

"Lunched with Clark Clifford. He told me the whole details of his

---

* In October, 1949, Congress approved pay raises for the White House staff. The Special Counsel's increase was from $12,000 to $20,000; The Assistant to the President from $15,000 to $20,000; the three Presidential Secretaries from $10,000 to $18,000; and the five Administrative Assistants from $10,000 to $15,000.

last year, his first year of law practice after leaving the White House. It is a simply unbelievable story. He practices alone; his partner died two and a half months after they began; he hired four young lawyers; five stenographers. In this establishment—a one-man performance—he earned probably as much as any professional man in the country, amusement field included, and more than any lawyer. He said he came out even on the year, after paying off his debts . . . buying a house, outfitting a law office, etc. He was uneasy about what will happen after Truman is out, if he is; wonders if he will keep any of his clients—which is nonsense, as he is a very able man with or without Truman.

"He looks like the wrath of God, ten years older than two years ago. Troubled with his stomach, his nerves, wakes up at three A.M. How can this have happened to him, who never had any limit on how hard he could work? I told him what I had said when his wife raised the same questions with me months ago; that this was nonsense; he was selling his only asset of health and family life for too little; that he ought to cut down and give attention to capital gains possibilities. He has a sense of insecurity (financial) that is hard to fathom, considering the facts. He is a fine man, did a great job with the President, best man in the White House since I've known about things. I told him he must remember he will be expected to render public service again, somebody must keep his hand in, as Clark Clifford, not as Harry Truman's helper."

Clifford's success did not lessen when the Republicans took control of the government in 1953 or at any time thereafter. In 1967, President Johnson, who often cites Clifford's financial success as proof of his good judgment, told some friends that the lawyer's income for the past year had been $1.2 million. Clifford, the fighting Fair Dealer of 1945–50, had gone on to become one of the richest lawyers in America.

Clifford's support of his friend Stuart Symington for the 1960 presidential nomination did not lessen John Kennedy's respect for him. After Kennedy won the nomination, he asked Clifford to analyze for him the problems he would face in taking over the government if he won the election, and how he should organize his White House staff. On the day after the election, when Eisenhower suggested that Kennedy name someone to be liaison between their two Administrations, Kennedy immediately chose Clifford.

Kennedy named Clifford to be a member of the Foreign Intelligence Advisory Board, and consulted extensively with Clifford and other board members about the reorganization of the CIA after the Bay of Pigs disaster. In 1962, when Kennedy reached a showdown with the major steel companies over their price increase, he again turned to his lawyer. Knowing that the steel executives knew and respected Clifford, Kennedy sent him, along with Secretary of Labor Goldberg, to outline the government's position to them. After the steel companies rescinded the price increase, Kennedy told Paul Fay: "If any one person deserves the credit for having the steel companies see the light, it has to be Clark Clifford. Since he represents so many of them here in Washington, he had immediate entree. Can't you just see Clifford outlining the possible courses of action the government could take if they showed signs of not moving?"

For all this, Kennedy offered Clifford no major appointment. Clifford was a decade older than Kennedy, and, superficially at least, his style was not the style of the blunt, hard-charging New Frontiersmen.

Clifford's position vis-à-vis the White House changed significantly after Johnson assumed the presidency, for while Kennedy had admired Clifford, Johnson needed him.

The two men had known one another since 1948, when Clifford was Special Counsel to Truman and Johnson was a young Texas Congressman running for the Senate. Yet over the 1950s the two men, although friendly, were not intimate. Indeed, there was a cooling between them in 1959 when Clifford threw his support to Symington for the Democratic nomination.

But one evening during Johnson's first week in the presidency, he called Clifford and asked him to come to the White House. Clifford arrived at 5 P.M. and stayed for five hours discussing with Johnson the burdens of the presidency. Johnson wanted Clifford's advice as someone who had served four years in the White House, but soon from their political discussions a close personal relationship developed. This intimacy was based on Johnson's respect for Clifford's judgment and discretion, on the fact that they are contemporaries, with many friends and memories in common, and most of all on the fact that, despite surface differences, they are much alike. Johnson is histrionic and high-powered, Clifford soft-voiced and subtle, but they share the same ultrapragmatic view of politics.

One member of the Johnson circle says, comparing Clifford's role with that of another Johnson adviser, Justice Abe Fortas:

"The President has greater respect for Clark's political judgment than he does for Abe's. He admires Abe's warm, human qualities, but he knows Abe's heart is on fire with liberal causes, so he discounts his advice accordingly. The President likes to get advice from men like Clark who are cold and shrewd and aren't swayed by moralistic arguments. The President knows that Clark understands the nature of the Presidency—he realizes that a President may sometimes do what is right but he must always do what is necessary."

During 1965–67, Clifford always insisted that he sought no appointment to any office. But it was difficult to talk to him and not sense that he wanted very badly to be either Secretary of State or Secretary of Defense. The unfolding drama of Vietnam challenged and excited Clifford; he believed his experience in international affairs, begun in the late 1940s, could help resolve the crisis of the late 1960s. Clifford had made his millions, now he wanted the responsibility and the place in history that only a Cabinet position could make possible.

He got his wish. In mid-January of 1968, Johnson announced that on March 1 Clifford would replace Robert McNamara as Secretary of Defense. This appointment made possible the climactic moment of Clifford's career—his vital role in Johnson's decision, announced on March 31, to reverse U.S. policy in Vietnam.

In the high-level debates about Vietnam in 1965-67 Clifford had been an effective advocate of a hardline policy. He had supported military escalation and opposed bombing pauses and peace overtures, which he believed the enemy would only regard as signs of weakness.

Yet in February and March, as Clifford plunged into his new job, something remarkable happened: He changed his mind about Vietnam. Johnson had instructed Clifford to direct a full-scale, government-wide review of Vietnam policy, and as Clifford probed deeper and deeper into the realities of the war, he began to have doubts about his previous positions. At that time, General Westmoreland was seeking another 200,000 men. Clifford had supported previous troop increases but now he began to fear that continued escalation was a bottomless pit. His hawkishness began to give way to his pragmatism and he decided that the U.S. must limit its commitment in Vietnam.

However, although Clifford had changed his thinking, Dean Rusk, Walt Rostow, and General Westmoreland had not changed theirs. Thus, in the last two weeks of March Clifford found himself engaged—as he so often had twenty years earlier with Truman—in an all-out battle for the mind of a President.

One milestone in this battle was a March 13 Cabinet meeting at which Clifford presented a blunt and somber review of the state of the war in the aftermath of the Tet offensive. For the next two weeks Clifford fought to get his new view translated into policy. He told Johnson that a partial bombing halt, made unilaterally, might prompt peace talks. His advocacy was a major factor in producing Johnson's historic March 31 speech, which served notice that the U.S. would not make another major troop increase in Vietnam, and also announced a limited halt in the bombing, thus making possible the Paris peace talks.

(Clifford, however, was not consulted about Johnson's decision not to seek re-election; the President told him of that only fifteen minutes before he delivered his speech.)

Apparently, Clifford's very credentials as a hawk, along with his reputation for realism, enabled him to succeed where the doves had failed and move Johnson toward a negotiated settlement of the war. If this is true (and much remains to be learned about the policy debates of that March), Clark Clifford has surely earned a place as not only one of the most spectacular but one of the most significant political figures in Washington history.

IV. THE EISENHOWER STAFF

1. *A Passion for Organization*

Dwight D. Eisenhower brought to the presidency—as he is not adverse to pointing out—an unprecedented amount of organizational experience. after spending much of his military career as a staff officer, he rose during the Second World War to be the Supreme Commander of the mightiest army in history. After the war he had been, successively, Chief of Staff of the U. S. Army, president of Columbia University, and Supreme Commander of the NATO forces in Europe. Moreover, he had specific knowledge of White House organization, gained in a decade of dealing intimately with Presidents Roosevelt and Truman and their staffs. He had not been terribly impressed with what he had seen, however, as he made clear in his memoirs:

"For years I had been in frequent contact with the Executive Office of the White House and I had certain ideas about the system, or lack of system, under which it operated. With my training in problems involving organization it was inconceivable to me that the work of the White House could not be better systemized than had been the case during the years I observed it."

As President, Eisenhower began in the White House a system of organization far more elaborate than those used by Roosevelt, Truman, Kennedy, or Johnson. Unfortunately, his organizational system has tended to be either ridiculed—as an attempt to "institutionalize" or "automate" the presidency—or to be overlooked, because of the fact that one controversial aide, Sherman Adams, came to so dominate the entire White House machinery. Yet Eisenhower's system of staff organization was an entirely valid experiment, and if it had several shortcomings, it also had numerous virtues. Above all, it suited Eisenhower's needs.

Before looking at the innovations Eisenhower brought to the White

House, it should be noted that he continued most of the traditional staff offices that had grown up during the Roosevelt and Truman Administrations.

There was, to begin with, the Press Secretary, a post filled for eight years by a genuine genius in political image-making, James C. Hagerty.

There was a Congressional Relations Office—the first one to operate openly as such—directed by Eisenhower's old friend Major General Wilton B. Persons, who had headed the Pentagon's Congressional Relations in 1933–48. In creating this office, Eisenhower gave official recognition to the semiofficial function performed under Truman by Matt Connelly and under FDR by various troubleshooters.

There was the Special Counsel's Office, headed successively by Thomas E. Stephens, a New York lawyer, Bernard M. Shanley, a New Jersey lawyer, Gerald D. Morgan, a lawyer with Capitol Hill experience, and David Kendall, a Michigan lawyer. During the Eisenhower era the Special Counsel's Office surrendered the speechwriting and administrative functions it had held under Rosenman, Clifford, and Murphy, and concentrated on legal and legislative matters.

The post of Appointments Secretary was filled by Thomas E. Stephens (who was Special Counsel only briefly), who doubled as unofficial White House jester.

These were the traditional White House offices and they functioned under Eisenhower more or less as they had in the past. Eisenhower's innovations came in creating or perfecting four staff instruments:

1) The position of The Assistant to the President, in which Sherman Adams served as Eisenhower's chief of staff;

2) The formalization of the National Security Council system, and the appointment of a Special Assistant for National Security Affairs;

3) The creation of two new positions—the Staff Secretary and the Secretary to the Cabinet—to systemize paperwork coming to and going from the White House, and to enable the Cabinet to function as a formal advisory council to the President;

4) The creation of numerous posts of Special Assistant to the President to enable Eisenhower to bring in prominent outsiders to advise him on specialized matters.

The essence of Eisenhower's system of administration was his belief in the delegation of authority. Eisenhower would not have used that word; he would say he delegated "work," not "authority," but most observers believed that, as a practical matter, Sherman Adams inherited a good measure of presidential authority along with the presidential workload. What Eisenhower could not delegate, of course, was responsibility.

Eisenhower believed, and no doubt correctly, that the people had elected him President to deal with major decisions, particularly in foreign affairs, to plot strategy rather than tactics. In the early months of Eisenhower's presidency, Secretary of Defense Charles E. Wilson made the mistake of coming to the President too often for advice on the operational details of his department. Finally Eisenhower told him bluntly: "Look here, Charlie, I want *you* to run Defense. We *both* can't run it. And I *won't* run it. I was elected to worry about a lot of things other than the day-to-day operations of a department."

Another time, Eisenhower said of Adams: "A man like that is valuable because of the unnecessary detail he keeps away from the President. A President who doesn't know how to decentralize will be weighed down with details and won't have time to deal with the big issues." Eisenhower molded the NSC into an elaborate and powerful instrument to bring foreign affairs issues before him for determination. To free himself for maximum involvement in foreign affairs, he delegated to Adams unprecedented authority over the domestic affairs of government, over political decisions, and over administrative matters.

Eisenhower's concept of efficient organization differed sharply from that of any other recent President. There was, to begin with, his preference for dealing, as much as possible, with the single chief of staff, rather than giving a half-dozen aides equal status and equal access to him, as other Presidents have done. Eisenhower's concept of good staff work decreed that he not be involved in a problem until it had reached a point of decision; one of Adams' rules to the staff was that no ideas or problems were to be taken to the President unless accompanied by a recommendation or a solution.

It was Eisenhower's lifelong preference to get and give ideas in conversation rather than in writing, and a result of this was that he tended to give generalized instructions which left the "details" to others. Adams writes: "Eisenhower was not much of a reader. He was impatient with the endless paperwork of the Presidency and always tried to get his staff to digest long documents into one-page summaries, which was sometimes next to impossible."

One matter in which Eisenhower's preferences differed markedly from other Presidents' concerned speeches. One imagines Ken O'Donnell going to Kennedy, or Marvin Watson to Johnson, with the news that, say, the American Legion has invited the President to speak at its national convention. They would first discuss whether the President should speak before that organization and, if so, what he should talk about. A speechwriter might be called in, given some general ideas, and assigned to prepare a first draft. The procedure was much different in Eisenhower's White House.

Adams relates an instance when Secretary of Agriculture Benson wanted the President to address the Future Farmers of America. Republican National Chairman Len Hall agreed that the speech would be useful politically. They went to Adams, who called in speechwriter Gabriel Hauge and Agriculture Department experts to determine what the President might say. Hauge wrote a first draft, discussed it with Adams, and wrote a second draft. All this time, nothing had been said to Eisenhower about the proposed speech. Adams explains: "Until an acceptable working draft had been prepared and tentative plans drawn up by myself and the staff, he would not want to know. I found out early in the game that Eisenhower expected anyone who proposed a speech to him to have the reasons for making it thoroughly thought out, a draft on paper, and the trip phased into his calendar. . . . We had to have a finished draft in shape and into the President's hands at least two weeks before it was to be delivered so that he could put it into his desk drawer and brood over it at his leisure. The preparation usually meant days, sometimes weeks, of staff work."

In the day-to-day business of the White House, Eisenhower's concept of sound staff work was reflected in the efforts of two officials whose posts he created, the Staff Secretary and the Secretary to the Cabinet. These two "Secretariats," as they and their staffs became known, working under Adams' general supervision, were intended to bring maximum efficiency to the daily business of government. The two offices were set up in 1953 with General Paul T. Carroll, who had served under Eisenhower at SHAPE, as Staff Secretary, and Maxwell Rabb, a lawyer and former Senate aide to Henry Cabot Lodge, as Secretary of the Cabinet. After General Carroll died in 1954, he was replaced by another military man who soon won Eisenhower's high regard, Colonel (now Lieutenant General) Andrew J. Goodpaster. Eisenhower's son, Major John Eisenhower, became Assistant Staff Secretary in 1958.

Eisenhower liked visual presentations, and in 1954 he had his staff system put in diagram form on a series of charts so it could better be explained throughout the government. A typical chart is headed SPEEDING ACTION THROUGH STAFF OPERATIONS and uses a series of arrows to indicate White House ASSIGNMENT followed by agency PREPARATION followed by REVIEW: BY SECRETARIAT . . . BY WHITE HOUSE ASSISTANTS

followed by presidential decision, followed by White House staff RE-
PORTING followed by agency ACTION.

Other charts stressed the need for "Lateral Coordination" and out-
lined the use of The Route Slip, The Suspense List, and The Covering
Brief. The questions to be asked by the Staff Secretary were explained
as: IS IT NECESSARY? . . . IS IT RESPONSIVE? . . . IS IT READY FOR ACTION?
. . . IS IT TIMELY? . . . IS IT CONSISTENT? . . . HOW WILL IT BE FOL-
LOWED UP?

To some readers, perhaps, these charts, with their exhortations for
TIME SAVED . . . FULL INFORMATION . . . BRIEF–ONCE–RIGHT . . . , may
call to mind those pages in the Boy Scout Handbook that counsel a lad
to be TRUSTWORTHY . . . LOYAL . . . HELPFUL. . . .

Yet, like the admonitions of the Scout Handbook, the maxims on
these charts were not without wisdom and utility, or so it must have
seemed to Eisenhower, for as soon as he had seen the charts he ordered
the two efficiency experts to ship them to Camp David. There, ten
days later, climaxing a weenie roast for the Cabinet, the two efficiency
experts again made their visual presentation, and when they finished
Eisenhower declared, "That's the way I want it to be." And that's the
way it was.

The function of the Staff Secretary's office was to serve as a clearinghouse for all papers and documents coming into the White House.
It had been customary in previous Administrations for papers to descend
on the President from all directions. The Staff Secretariat provided
a semblance of order. Papers were checked for "lateral coordination"—
i.e., to make sure that all interested departments and agencies had been
given a chance to express their views on an issue. Important papers
would make their way to Adams, who generally decided what went
on to the President.

The point was that by the time a proposal reached the President
it would be fully processed. All views would be affixed, all issues
explored, all alternatives considered. The President, after reading the
one-page covering brief, usually prepared by Adams, and reading as
much of the accompanying documents as he cared to, was presented
with a complete, clear-cut decision. He would not be bothered with
the scores of details and possible alternatives that had gone into shaping
the decision.

Eisenhower was determined not to be bothered by what he considered
unnecessary details. He writes in his memoirs: "Whenever I had to
make a decision that properly belonged to a subordinate I admonished
him at once, but if he failed again it was time to begin looking for a

replacement." This attitude did not encourage members of the White House staff to take problems to the President; it was safer to take them to Adams.

While the Staff Secretary was overseeing day to day paperwork, the Secretary to the Cabinet handled preparations for Eisenhower's weekly Cabinet meetings. His work reflected Eisenhower's belief that the President's Cabinet should be a formal, highly respected advisory body. It appalled Eisenhower that FDR and Truman had called Cabinet meetings in a hit-or-miss fashion, generally using them for formless bull sessions or presidential monologues. Similarly, Eisenhower's successor, Kennedy, convened his Cabinet as seldom as possible, and once said he saw no reason to seek the views of the Secretary of Health, Education and Welfare on matters that did not concern his department.

Eisenhower's view was quite different. Three beliefs undergirded his use of his Cabinet, and the first was that his Cabinet members were not specialists but statesmen—men (and one woman) with broad experience in the affairs of government and of business.

Second, Eisenhower understood that we have today less a government of departments than a government of programs, and he viewed the Cabinet as a coordinating mechanism to resolve interdepartmental disputes at the highest level. If two departments were in disagreement about some program that cut across their bureaucratic lines—foreign aid, say, or employment programs—the issue could be debated in the Cabinet session; then, after the President had publicly stated the resolution he desired, it became difficult for the departments to evade action.

Third, the Cabinet meetings, which averaged about one every two weeks and lasted from two to three hours, provided direct communication between the President and his lieutenants of government—between the Supreme Commander and his theater commanders—with no palace guard coming between them. A Cabinet member who sought to see the President at other times would probably run afoul of Adams' stern protectiveness, but the Cabinet meeting guaranteed him a day in court. Certainly the Cabinet members wanted to see the President more often (they always do, in any Administration) and certainly they wanted to talk to him in greater privacy, but that was not Eisenhower's preference.

The Cabinet Secretary's job was to ensure maximum productivity from each Cabinet meeting. Preparations began weeks in advance with the drawing up of an agenda. In doing this, the Cabinet Secretary worked with executive assistants to the Cabinet members. Often, the White House aides would spot issues and controversies that the departments did not want on the agenda. Such disputes were carried to Adams for decision. From time to time, issues would be excluded from the agenda by Adams, only to come up in Cabinet meeting discussions and be greeted with the angry presidential question: "Why wasn't this on the agenda?"

Once the agenda was set, the Cabinet Secretary would solicit papers from the various departments outlining their positions on matters to be discussed. These were circulated to all Cabinet members. The President was also given a folder containing briefing papers a day or two in advance of the Cabinet meeting, but members of the Cabinet Secretariat say that their impression was that Eisenhower usually didn't read these papers. The Cabinet system was never as well staffed or as carefully structured as the NSC system. The latter, with the extensive preliminary work by the Planning Board staff, was structured toward very specific decision-making; the Cabinet meetings tended more toward general discussion and broad statements of policy by the President.

In the weeks after Eisenhower's election, as he and Adams discussed the sort of White House staff operation they should have, they debated the merits of a staff of generalists—"versatile troubleshooters," Adams called them—as against a staff of specialists in various areas of government. In theory, Eisenhower preferred a staff of generalists, with specialists assigned to the various departments. In practice, one of Eisenhower's innovations in the White House was the appointment of an unprecedented number of White House "Special Assistants" who could advise him on specialized issues and could communicate his wishes to the bureaucratic experts whose influence they often supplanted.

Under Kennedy and Johnson, "Special Assistant to the President" became the regular title given to top White House assistants, but under Eisenhower the Special Assistants tended to be really special. Eisenhower had the pick of the Republican Party in general and the business community in particular, and he was often able to attract to the White House men with national reputations in business or politics. Because of Eisenhower's popularity, and because of the credentials of the men involved, there was no outcry when the President vastly expanded the size of the White House staff, as there had been when Roosevelt and Truman expanded it. In addition to Eisenhower's regular White House staff, some twenty-five or thirty of these Special Assistants were appointed by Eisenhower, and they unquestionably brought a vast amount of special skills and experience into the presidential offices. The problem was that men of such prominence were often frustrated by the anonymity of staff work, by the evasions of the bureaucracy, by the financial sacrifices involved, and by the dominance of Adams in domestic matters and Dulles in foreign affairs. As a result, many of the Special Assistants stayed only a year or two—barely time enough to learn the rules of the game.

A partial list can suggest the level of these special advisers:

Clarence B. Randall, retired chairman of the board of Inland Steel, was a Special Assistant for Foreign Economic Policy during most of Eisenhower's two terms as President.

Meyer Kestenbaum, former president of Hart, Schaffner & Marx, was a Special Assistant on administrative and intergovernmental affairs in 1955–60.

Stanley M. Rumbough, Jr., a prominent industrialist, a national co-founder of Citizens for Eisenhower in 1952 (and then-husband of actress-heiress Dina Merrill) was a Special Assistant for six months in 1954.

Robert E. Merriam, a forty-year-old Chicago business executive, Republican politician, and author (his account of the Battle of the Bulge was a favorite of Eisenhower's) became Deptuty Assistant to the President for Interdepartmental Affairs on September 10, 1958, and continued in that post for the remaining twenty-eight months of Eisenhower's presidency.

Edward Peck Curtis, a vice president of Eastman Kodak, was a Special Assistant for Aviation Facilities for fifteen months in 1956–57.

Robert Cutler, president of Old Colony Trust Company in Boston, served two terms as Special Assistant for National Security Affairs, the first in 1953–55, the second in 1956–58.

Val Peterson, the former Governor of Nebraska, was made an Administrative Assistant after the two Senators from Nebraska refused to approve his appointment as Ambassador to India; two months later he was promoted to be federal Civil Defense Administrator.

Harold E. Stassen, the onetime Governor of Minnesota, was a Special Assistant on disarmament negotiations in 1955–58, but his influence fell after he tried to block Vice President Nixon's renomination in 1956.

Fred Seaton, the former Senator from Nebraska, was a Special Assistant for fifteen months in 1955–56, prior to his appointment as Secretary of the Interior.

C. D. Jackson, an official of the Luce Publications, later publisher of *Life* magazine, was a Special Assistant for thirteen months in 1953–54 on matters relating to Cold War propaganda and psychological strategy. His early departure was reportedly caused in part by conflicts with Dulles over the national strategy toward Russia—Dulles being a hard-liner, Jackson favoring a more flexible approach.

Two talented presidential assistants whose brief careers in the White House seemed to epitomize the problems of the Eisenhower era were Nelson A. Rockefeller, the multimillionaire and future Governor of New York, and Emmet John Hughes, a writer for *Fortune* and *Life* magazines in the 1950s, later a columnist for *Newsweek* in the 1960s.

Rockefeller, who had worked on Inter-American Affairs under both Roosevelt and Truman, became Under Secretary of Health, Education and Welfare in July 1953. After C. D. Jackson resigned in mid-1954, Rockefeller joined the President's staff as a Special Assistant (and this was Eisenhower's phrase) for Cold War Strategy. Press Secretary Hagerty made it clear at the outset that Rockefeller's responsibilities would be "much broader" than Jackson's had been, and Eisenhower in a letter of appointment gave Rockefeller a sweeping mandate to "work for increased understanding and cooperation among all peoples."

The fanfare attending the forty-six-year-old Rockefeller's appointment on December 16, 1954, did not go unnoticed at the State Department, which continued to consider itself in charge of Cold War Strategy, and whose two top officials, Secretary Dulles and Under Secretary Herbert Hoover, Jr., would soon clash head-on with the new appointee.

Rockefeller set to work with his customary zeal, and during his fast-moving year in the White House he had a hand in many foreign policy decisions. He helped shape the Administration's Atoms for Peace proposal. He helped push through the U.S. agreement to put up money for Egypt's Aswan Dam. Probably his most important contribution was in developing and sponsoring the Open Skies proposal (as the press later dubbed it) that Eisenhower extended to the Russians at the Geneva Conference in July 1955.

When Rockefeller went to work, U.S.-Russian efforts toward disarmament were at a standstill. Proposals for aerial surveys to enforce disarmament agreements were not new, but none of them had ever overcome the Russian fear of foreign overflights. Rockefeller, in preparation for the Geneva Conference, set up a panel of outside experts to study various disarmament possibilities.

The American dilemma on disarmament was how to maintain nuclear strength, yet convince the world that America was a peaceful nation. Rockefeller's panel decided that Eisenhower could accomplish this dual objective by presenting at Geneva a revived plan for aerial inspection and the exchange of military information. A proposal to this effect went to Eisenhower on June 10, and he greeted it with enthusiasm. Secretary Dulles was less enthusiastic, and when Eisenhower reached Geneva in July he had still not made up his mind on proposing the Open Skies plan.

While Eisenhower debated his course of action in Geneva, Rockefeller was in Paris winning support for his plan. Harold Stassen, the Special Assistant for Disarmament, was already behind him, and he was able to win over the Deputy Secretary of Defense, Robert B. Anderson, and the Chairman of the Joint Chiefs of Staff, Admiral Arthur W. Radford.

On the first day of the conference, a Monday, Russian Premier Bulganin submitted a plan for limiting military forces. Rockefeller immediately sent a message to Eisenhower urging him to submit the Open Skies plan as a countermeasure that might seize the initiative for the U.S.; Anderson and Radford sent a similar message to Dulles. Dulles quickly summoned Rockefeller and Stassen to Geneva. Eisenhower tried out the Open Skies plan on Sir Anthony Eden, who was enthusiastic. Eisenhower decided to introduce the plan personally.

It received worldwide acclaim. The Russians greeted it with cautious interest, and even such an anti-American journal as France's *Le Monde* remarked: "Eisenhower, whose personality has long been misunderstood, has emerged as the type of leader humanity needs today."

But Open Skies, and the entire "spirit of Geneva" were to prove fleeting. In part, they—along with Rockefeller's career in the White House—were to be victims of Eisenhower's heart attack, which struck in late September, just two months after Geneva. Rockefeller's influence within the government depended on a close relationship with Eisenhower. After the heart attack, when access to the bedridden President was sharply restricted, Secretary of State Dulles could see him, Rockefeller could not, and the latter's importance fell accordingly.

It was during this period that Rockefeller fought and lost the battle that prompted his resignation. The issue was money for foreign aid (or "mutual assistance," as it was then called). Rockefeller wanted bold programs to develop backward nations. He was supported by Stassen and by Vice President Nixon. They were opposed by a quartet that came to be known as the "4-H Club"—Herbert Hoover, Jr., Budget Director Roland Hughes, Secretary of the Treasury George Humphrey, and Foreign Aid Director John B. Hollister. This group held that there was no need to increase foreign aid because the recipient nations couldn't effectively spend any more money than they were already getting.

Rockefeller was unable to see the President and plead his case until December 5. The President struck a compromise between Rockefeller and the budget-balancers. Rockefeller, dissatisfied, resigned on December 31.

Although the foreign-aid dispute was apparently the immediate cause of Rockefeller's resignation, there were reports that Dulles was furious at the young adviser's "meddling," and had told Eisenhower he must choose between the two of them. Emmet Hughes attributes to Eisenhower the comment that: "Well, it's true that there's no department so jealous of its prerogatives as State. And even Foster's hackles rise when he thinks someone is butting in. Why, when Nelson Rockefeller was on the White House staff here, producing ideas in this area, he got Foster so fuming that I just had to do something about it."

In the long view, Rockefeller's losing fight with the State Department recalled Raymond Moley's downfall in 1933 and foreshadowed Richard Goodwin's fate in 1962. More immediately, the episode was the making of a governor, for Rockefeller reportedly vowed as he left the White House that his next entry into public life would be in elective office, where he could call his own shots. He was, of course, one of the few Republican candidates to withstand the Democratic landslide in the elections of 1958.

Emmet Hughes was, like Rockefeller, a liberal, an internationalist, and a sophisticated student of political affairs. His service to Eisenhower was brief. He was a speechwriter in the 1952 campaign,* an Administrative Assistant (i.e., speechwriter) in January–October 1953, and an intermittent visitor to the White House through the remainder of Eisenhower's terms. Hughes's role in the Eisenhower Administration would have been long since forgotten but for one key fact: He was keeping a record of all his talks with Eisenhower and all the Cabinet meetings and strategy sessions he attended. His notes became, in 1963, a "political memoir" called *The Ordeal of Power*.

Hughes's book is the most vivid, most persuasive portrait of Eisenhower we have; the President emerges as a complex, contradictory, multidimensioned leader—hot-tempered, modest, humorous, profane, compassionate, often fluctuating between decision and indecision, always endowed with enormous resources of physical and moral strength.

Hughes's candor, however, served to alienate him permanently from Eisenhower and his inner circle. Hughes is variously dismissed as a frustrated Secretary of State (aren't we all?) and as an uppity journalist who didn't know his place. In one sense, however, Hughes knew his

---

* Hughes is credited in several accounts, including his own, with first having the idea that Eisenhower should promise to go to Korea if elected.

place very well. He knew, as Clark Clifford had in the previous Administration and as Ted Sorensen would in the next one, just how much influence a speechwriter can wield if he is both subtle and persistent.

Despite Eisenhower's passion for organization, there was room for broken-field running within his White House, and Hughes, like Rockefeller, made a stab at it. A good example is Hughes's role in the debate that preceded Eisenhower's speech, "The Chance of Peace," delivered on April 16, 1953.

The first stirrings of this important policy statement came in mid-March as Eisenhower and Hughes were discussing some routine speech assignments. Stalin had died a few days earlier, and Eisenhower began to talk of his hopes for an end to the Cold War. He told Hughes:

"Look, I am tired—and I think everyone is tired—of just plain indictments of the Soviet regime. I think it would be wrong—in fact, asinine—for me to get up before the world now to make another one of those indictments. Instead, just one thing matters: What have *we* got to offer the world? What are *we* ready to do, to improve the chances of peace?"

Eisenhower talked on in this vein, deploring the burden on mankind caused by the investment of national wealth into armaments instead of into homes, schools, and hospitals. Hughes, although deeply moved by Eisenhower's words, pointed out that his idea of beginning a "peace offensive" ran directly counter to Secretary Dulles' no-negotiations, hardline stance toward the Russians. Eisenhower brushed this aside and Hughes—hoping to keep alive the presidential mood—quickly suggested a meeting the next day to discuss a major address incorporating Eisenhower's ideas.

Besides the President and Hughes, the meeting was attended by Dulles, his brother Allen Dulles, director of the CIA, and by C. D. Jackson, the Cold War propagandist. Secretary Dulles, Hughes says, contributed a "dry and dubious acquiescence" to the speechwriter's proposal to draft a speech challenging the Russians to work for peace. Allen Dulles was surprisingly favorable to the idea. More surprisingly, perhaps, Jackson was critical and suggested that the Russian leaders would be unimpressed by "bourgeois talk about schools and hospitals."

But Eisenhower retorted: "Damn it, I don't know that you're right, basically. I remember that in one four-hour session I had with Stalin, damn near all he talked about was the essential things his people needed—homes and food and technical help. When he talked about seven people to a room in Moscow living quarters, he seemed to me just as anxious as you or I would be in looking at an American slum problem.

Hell, these boys *have* to think in material terms. It's all they believe in."

With that, Hughes had his permission to go ahead with the proposed speech. He also had a target date in mind—Eisenhower's April 16 appearance before the American Society of Newspaper Editors. He pushed ahead, aware that to turn the President's admirable generalities into a specific statement of policy, he would have "to guard it from the ambushes of policy debate and bureaucratic scrutiny."

He worked closely with Eisenhower on draft after draft, showing copies only to the Dulles brothers and Jackson. Secretary Dulles grumbled from first to last. "I think there's some real danger of our just seeming to fall in with these Soviet overtures," he said at one point. Hovering unmentioned in the background was the specter of McCarthyism, and the realization that any presidential "peace" overture might well be denounced as "soft on Communism."

But Eisenhower's enthusiasm continued, the speech was written— only to be threatened five days before delivery by an objection from an entirely unexpected quarter. Sir Winston Churchill had been sent an advance text of the speech. In a message to Eisenhower, he applauded the speech as "grave and formidable," but then questioned its timing and suggested that the President "bide your time" and leave the next move up to the Russians. Hughes suspected that Churchill simply wanted to ensure that he, not Eisenhower, took the initiative in dramatic Western peace initiatives.

As a result of Churchill's message, Hughes found himself—at a meeting with the President, Milton Eisenhower, Allen Dulles, and Under Secretary of State Bedell Smith—standing alone in support of the speech. He gives this account:

"To my dismay, however, Bedell Smith, while repeating the State Department's warm collective approval of the actual text of the speech, nonetheless felt obliged to report Dulles' general doubt as to the 'need' for *any* speech. Milton Eisenhower . . . suggested that the speech should, perhaps, completely eliminate any challenges to the Soviets and 'simply say what we are willing to do.' This, of course, would have upset all balance in the 'grave' declaration. And impatiently, with that air of resignation which at times seemed almost to engulf him, the President broke in: "Well, maybe Churchill's right, and we can whip up some other text for the occasion.' In what I felt was a desperate appeal, I recalled my own opposition to a premature speech; I argued that now there was sufficient clarity to the Soviet temper to allow us to address it with some precision; and I warned finally against greeting all recent events merely with impassive silence. As minutes passed, the conversation slowly, almost imperceptibly, began to revert to the substance of the speech, not the question of its delivery."

Finally the speech was delivered on April 16. It said in part:

"Every gun that is fired, every warship launched, every rocket fired signifies, in the final sense, a theft from those who hunger and are not fed, those who are cold and are not clothed. . . .

"This government is ready to ask its people to join with all nations in devoting a substantial percentage of the savings achieved by disarmament to a fund for world aid and reconstruction. . . .

"We are ready, in short, to dedicate our strength to serving the needs, rather than the fears of the world. . . .

"What is the Soviet Union ready to do . . . ?

"We aspire to this: the lifting, from the backs and the hearts of men, of the burden of arms and of fears—so that they may find before them a golden age of freedom and of peace."

The speech was a national and international success. The New York *Times* called it "magnificent and deeply moving"; Richard Rovere declared that Eisenhower had "firmly established his leadership in America and re-established American leadership in the world." Not until Kennedy's American University speech, ten years and two months later, would an American President again so eloquently express mankind's dream of peace. Yet if we are to believe Hughes the speech would never have been delivered but for his stubborn opposition to the Secretary of State's inability to see any need for it, of Winston Churchill's inscrutable objections, of Milton Eisenhower's doubts about the speech's contents, and of the President's own readiness to chuck the whole project five days before the delivery date.*

In a pointed afternote to the speech episode, Hughes sharply indicts what he viewed as the unimaginative quality of Eisenhower's staff by describing a staff discussion of the speech the next day. He does not identify the individual staff members, except to say that Adams was not among them:

"The White House staff meeting stirred with delight over the press reaction to the President's speech. The group did not waste time or emotion on the substance of the declaration, its implications for our practical diplomacy, its demands for further acts to prove its intent. . . . Instead, the talk was of more immediate matters:

"A.: 'This speech is just what this Administration needed—in fact,

---

* Eisenhower, in his memoirs, makes no mention of Hughes's involvement in the speech, or of any doubts he might have entertained about delivering it.

we were needing it goddam bad. It really gets us off our backs—
and off the ground.'

"B.: 'The problem's more than that. Now that we've gotten this lift—
how do we *stay* up?'

"C.: 'I think it's pretty obvious what we need. One speech isn't
enough. We got to follow up. We need *another* speech. Only this one has
to do for us in *domestic* affairs what we've just done in *foreign*
affairs. If we could just get the same sex appeal into this other speech as
there was in yesterday's . . .'

"A.: 'We simply have to get into our setup a really first-class *public
relations* man. . . .'"

Hughes has here put his finger on the bothersome aspect of the Eisenhower staff. His inner circle was loyal and efficient, his Special Assistants
had impressive credentials, but the group as a whole seems to have
rarely performed the most important service a staff can give a President: being a source of ideas, of imagination, of stimulation.

Eisenhower's Cabinet was dominated by two men who were not only
devoid of new ideas, they were positively hostile to them—Humphrey,
the leading adviser in economic affairs, and Dulles, the architect of
foreign policy. Conceivably, the White House staff might have provided
a balance to the negative influences of Dulles and Humphrey. Some,
like Hughes and Rockefeller, tried, failed, and left. Of those who remained, the three closest to Eisenhower—Adams, Hagerty, and Persons—
were not men of creative imagination.

As Richard Rovere wrote, Eisenhower's White House "contained a
man of enormous popularity and authority, but it was also a place in
which the novel, the unexpected, and the unforeseen were seldom to
be found. There was no tension there, no rub, no friction, no excitement." The misfortune of Eisenhower's presidency is that a man of such
immense popularity and good will did not accomplish more. All the
domestic problems which confronted the nation in the 1960s—the
unrest of the Negro, the decay of the cities, the mediocrity of the
schools, the permanence of poverty—were bubbling beneath the surface
in the 1950s, but the President never seemed quite sure that they existed
or, if they did, that they were problems with which he should concern
himself.

Richard E. Neustadt quotes an unnamed source (described as "one
official close to White House operations and decidedly in sympathy with
Eisenhower"):

"The process had been cumulative since the heart attack. Then there
were massive delegations which simply followed the existing lines to

Adams and on down. Those delegations were administered by men who told each other (and themselves), 'don't bother the boss,' 'can't do this to him now.' But the less he was bothered, the less he knew, and the less he knew, the less confidence he felt in his own judgment. He let himself grow stale. . . . That made the delegations irreversible. It made him cling the tighter to the judgments of the people already around him. The less he trusted himself, the more he *had* to trust them. And they thought the way to help him was to 'spare' him. A lot of this was very well intentioned."

Emmet Hughes tells of sensing in 1957 "a dispiritedness" among Eisenhower's staff, a "kindly but paralyzing consensus—to avoid 'upsetting the old man.'" Hughes, choosing his words carefully, writes of the staff's "solicitous, but destructive" concern for the President's physical welfare. He gives two examples.

Once in 1956 he entered Eisenhower's office on the morning after a presidential television appearance. He found the President happily reading a stack of telegrams. "Not a single bad one," Eisenhower exclaimed. This seemed unlikely to Hughes, and he found out later that the staff had filtered out all the unfavorable telegrams.

Late in 1958 Eisenhower told Hughes: "You know, I had an idea I thought was pretty good, but a bunch of the boys thought up too many objections to my going with it to the Hill. It was an offer to bring over here for one year, say, maybe ten thousand Russian students of college age who could handle some English—and let us put them through school here for a year. No reciprocity, no strings—just offer to do it."

Perhaps ten thousand was too many to start, perhaps reciprocity should have been involved—but it was a fine idea, far too good to be shot down by "the boys" without a hearing outside the airless offices of the West Wing. One wonders how many more of Eisenhower's worthy ideas may have been shot down by the boys over the years.

One of the major criticisms of Eisenhower's presidency has been that he delegated too much authority to his staff, and particularly to Sherman Adams. Eisenhower certainly never shared this view; to the contrary, his experience in the White House convinced him that the presidency had become too big a job for any one man to handle. He said candidly, "The President must have authority to delegate more work and responsibility to others."

Sherman Adams, after a talk with Eisenhower on this subject, wrote that: "Eisenhower believes that the stature and authority of the President's immediate assistants must be raised so they can free him of routine government management and give him time to concentrate on the bigger problems of world peace and disarmament, national security and domestic welfare."

Eisenhower, Adams recorded, believed the President should have a First Secretary in foreign affairs who would have responsibility for coordinating and directing the non-military overseas agencies, such as the foreign aid program and the U. S. Information Agency, and also the duty of representing the President at ceremonial functions with foreign heads of state.

Eisenhower never got such a First Secretary officially, but unofficially he had a First Secretary in domestic and political affairs. He was, of course, the dour, dedicated, ill-fated Sherman Adams.

2. The Incorruptible Man: Adams

Sherman Adams' story is a tragedy in the classic mold. The protagonist wins his way to honor and power, only to be struck down at the zenith of his career, not by his enemies, but by a flaw within his own character. Adams' tragic flaw was pride. He believed himself better than other men: stronger, wiser, more industrious, more honest. Such was his pride, and it led him to break the rules of moral probity he so sternly enforced against other men who served the Eisenhower Administration. For five years, as Eisenhower's deputy, he was obeyed and feared throughout the vast empire of government. Then, one day in 1958, his power began to crumble amid a shabby tale of vicuna coats, Oriental rugs, and pre-paid hotel bills. In the end, naked before his political enemies, deserted by the President he had served with such relentless dedication, Adams was forced to leave the White House after a humiliation so total, so abject that even his enemies pitied him.

He was born on July 8, 1899, in East Dover, New Hampshire. His father, a farmer and shopkeeper, was a descendant of the famous Adams family which gave the nation two Presidents. He became a campus leader at Dartmouth in the early 1920s, and was best known for his exploits as a hiker. When a hiking craze swept college campuses, Adams (who worked during summer vacations as a lumberjack) set an unequaled record by marching eighty-three miles in twenty-four hours. He refused to stop although wracked by painful stomach cramps for the last ten miles. It was an early example of the iron-willed, Spartan side of his nature.

After graduation he turned down conventional job offers to work instead as a scaler in a logging camp. Despite his small size—five feet seven and 140 pounds—his physical toughness and no-nonsense manner won the respect of the rough-and-tumble lumberjacks. He became timberlands manager for Parker-Young lumber company, with authority over dozens of lumber camps and hundreds of men.

Adams was a rising young executive with Parker-Young in 1938 when a hurricane uprooted thousands of trees in New Hampshire. He led a statewide campaign to salvage these trees and avoid forest fires. This effort involved numerous public speeches, and Adams acquitted himself extremely well. His superiors at Parker-Young were so impressed that they decided Adams should run for the state legislature, which he did in 1940. He thus entered politics at age forty-one not because of burning personal ambition, nor from any urge to serve the public interest, but for the good and simple reason that his bosses told him to.

He advanced in politics as rapidly as he had in the lumber business. He was re-elected to the state legislature in 1942 and became Speaker of the House. He was elected to Congress in 1944. In 1946 he challenged New Hampshire's incumbent Governor in the Republican primary and lost by only 157 votes. In 1948 he was elected Governor, and re-elected two years later.

Adams was a most uncommon Governor. On wintry mornings he would go ice-skating before breakfast on a frozen lake beside his home, gliding through graceful figure eights to the strains of Mozart recordings he had piped-out over a loudspeaker. Later, he would trudge to his office on snowshoes, carrying his lunch in a brown paper sack. He was known for economy and efficiency in government, and he did not mind making enemies to achieve those ends. Once when the leader of a political delegation told him, "We represent more than 30,000 votes for governor," Governor Adams snapped back, "Who the hell wants to be governor?"

In the summer of 1951, while in Gatlinburg, Tennessee, for the annual Governors' Conference, Adams attracted national attention by announcing that General Eisenhower's name would be entered in the New Hampshire presidential primary the following March. Adams' decision to cast his lot with Eisenhower rather than with Senator Robert A. Taft came after prolonged soul-searching. He did not know Eisenhower, who was still in Paris heading NATO, or what he stood for. But long talks with Senator Henry Cabot Lodge, the leader of the Eisenhower forces, persuaded Adams to swallow his doubts and back the General. One major factor in his decision, the pragmatic Adams later said, was simply that Eisenhower "looked like the fastest horse in the stable."

Adams' political management helped Eisenhower win a landslide victory over Taft in the crucial New Hampshire primary, and at the outset of the Republican National Convention in Chicago in July 1952 Eisenhower's backers chose Adams to be their floor leader for the convention fight. Adams barely knew Eisenhower, but his efficient, nononsense style of operation soon won the General's admiration. Eisenhower asked Adams to help in the campaign, and Adams took leave without pay from his duties as Governor of New Hampshire to do so.

Eisenhower's respect for Adams grew during the 40,000 hectic miles of plane and train campaign travel. Adams took charge of innumerable political and logistical details, and he would meet the big issues head-on as well. When the story of Nixon's "slush fund" broke and many Republican leaders were demanding Nixon's resignation, it was Adams' unruffled "wait and see" advice that carried the day. It was at Adams' advice that Eisenhower, although "smoldering with resentment" (Adams' phrase) at Senator McCarthy's abuse of General George C. Marshall, agreed to delete praise of Marshall from a campaign speech in Milwaukee. Liberal and moderate Republicans were shocked by this concession to McCarthyism ("Do I need to tell you that I am sick at heart?" the New York *Times* publisher, Arthur Sulzberger, telegramed to Adams) but Adams refused to view it as a moral issue. He dismissed the incident by saying that the Governor of Wisconsin had requested the deletion and "after all, he was the governor of a state where we were guests and some adjustments had to be made to party harmony."

On January 21, 1953, the day after Eisenhower's Inauguration, Adams was sworn in as The Assistant to the President, the office Truman had created for John Steelman, who never quite lived up to his imposing title. Adams was then fifty-four years old, white-haired, ramrod-straight, and as lean and hard as the young lumberjack he had been three decades earlier. The political world knew little of the taciturn Adams, but James Reston had already predicted that he would prove to be more influential in the new Administration than most Cabinet members. Adams was not long in proving him right.

Eisenhower had told Adams on the day after his election: "I could visualize you as a member of the Cabinet, but I need somebody to be my assistant in running my office. I'd like you to continue on at my right hand, just as you've been in the campaign. You would be associated with me more closely than anybody else in the government."

From the first, there seemed to be an instinctive understanding between Eisenhower and Adams as to their respective roles. Adams later recalled: "During the campaign, as later in the White House, Eisenhower never defined or outlined the precise duties and responsibilities that he wanted me to assume. Evidently I was supposed to know what I was supposed to do. Sometimes in taking a line of action on my own, I may have overstepped or fallen short of what Eisenhower had in mind, but I did not hesitate nor did I ever feel confused."

The essence of their relationship was simply that Adams did the work Eisenhower didn't want to do, mainly in politics and domestic affairs. Eisenhower was (and is) a supremely political animal, but one whose political advancement came outside the normal party framework. He found political patronage and most politicians distasteful, and since they needed him more than he needed them, he was able to use Adams to keep them at arm's length. He did not know much about domestic affairs, and his guiding principle was that less federal spending, coupled with increased local initiative, would solve most of the country's domestic ills. As candidate and as President, he did not propose any major new domestic initiatives (except for his highway construction program), and many historians believe that the most important accomplishment of his Administration in domestic affairs was a negative one: He resisted pressure from his party's right wing to dismantle the federal welfare-state programs.

Given Eisenhower's generally negative attitude toward domestic issues, it was not difficult for him to delegate to Adams the day-to-day housekeeping questions that arose. The Eisenhower-Adams arrangement was summed up by a remark Adams made to two feuding agency officials who had a personnel problem they wanted to take to the President for decision: "Either make up your minds or else tell me and I will do it. We must not bother the President with this. He is trying to keep the world from war."

Robert J. Donovan of the New York *Herald-Tribune* was in 1955 given access to Administration officials and files to write a semi-official account of Eisenhower's first term. In the resulting book (which did not entirely please the White House), he has this to say about Adams' role:

"With great exertion Adams has handled a considerable amount of the work that in past Administrations has been done by the President himself. . . . While it has not been an inflexible rule, it has been the general practice that almost everything of importance in the White House bearing on domestic and political policy clears through Adams.

He has been the pivot of political maneuver in the White House. He is the channel through which many of the most important projects in domestic affairs reach the President. What has been even more significant in fixing his influence is the fact that by the time many of these projects have reached the President they have already been shaped in part by Adams himself.

"Time and again when a caller or official springs an idea on Eisenhower, the President will tell him, 'Take it up with Sherman.' Almost invariably before Eisenhower signs his approval to a paper, he will glance over it for the familiar notation, 'OK, S.A.' If it is missing, the President will ask, 'Has Governor Adams approved this?'"

Eisenhower's supporters insist that the "OK, S.A." notation did not imply a substantive decision by Adams, as Donovan believed, only approval for the papers to go to the President.

It was often charged that Adams was overprotective of Eisenhower, that he shielded the President from problems he ought to know about, even to the extent of forbidding Cabinet members access to the President. Adams, asked about this in 1967, replied with his accustomed curtness: "What you say about shielding people from the President is essentially correct. Anybody who had legitimate business of sufficient importance to occupy the attention of the President got in; those that didn't didn't. I knew the difference."

Almost every President has had an assistant who did dirty work for him and took the resulting heat; this relationship was perfected by Eisenhower and Adams. There was little doubt that when Adams blocked access to Eisenhower, said "no" for him, fired officials who had erred, and otherwise did the dirty work, that he was doing what Eisenhower wanted done. Yet Eisenhower remained beloved, even by those who were fired or turned away; it was always Adams who was hated.

Eisenhower was the most beloved man of his time—not the wisest, not the most eloquent, but the most beloved. The people's affection for him was his strength, and he hoarded it like a miser. On the national scale he saw it as his mission to unite the nation, and on a personal scale it pained him, more than most men, to say "no" or otherwise give offense. All of this made Adams the perfect deputy for Eisenhower, for the two men were alike in one important quality and totally dissimilar in another. They were alike in their strict public morality, in their adherence to the traditional American virtues of hard work and thrift and self-sufficiency. Where they differed was in their attitudes toward their fellow men. Eisenhower wanted to be loved;

he was attuned like a seismograph to the reactions of those around him. Adams, by contrast, was an ultra-individualist; he didn't give a damn for the opinions of anyone outside his own family.

In his public life Adams seemed to glory in the ill will he created. It was a rare day when a "please" or a "thank you" or a "good morning" passed his lips. There was a grand egalitarianism about his rudeness; he bestowed it as casually upon secretaries and clerks as he did upon Senators and Cabinet members. Almost daily his gruff demands would have one of his secretaries in tears, and one day, according to *Time* magazine, he managed the impressive feat of having all five of them in tears at once. Only Adams' close friends were permitted to glimpse the caustic humor behind his icy exterior. Once he and Robert Cutler went to hear pianist Van Cliburn perform. As the concert ended, amid wild cheers, Cliburn and his conductor shook hands, embraced, and finally kissed one another. Adams, asked later what he'd thought of the young pianist, replied dryly: "He ought to do less kissin'."

But Adams' public arrogance made him the perfect foil for Eisenhower, and the government was so arranged that almost anytime it was necessary for Eisenhower to say "no" to someone, Adams could do it for him. The only exception was the Cabinet and NSC meetings, and even there, by encouraging debate on both sides of an issue, Eisenhower was spared the necessity of giving a direct "no"—he could simply say "yes" to the other side of the issue.

Adams viewed Eisenhower realistically but with great admiration. He was not a demonstrative man, yet sometimes at dinner parties with friends he would propose a toast: "To the President of the United States." His feelings were well summed up in a letter he wrote in 1967: "Remember that Eisenhower, a man of no political brilliance, exemplified the American character as no contemporary has approached, and as nearly attained the American ideal of what a President should be as any man since Lincoln."

Adams' second major area of responsibility was politics. Eisenhower hoped to remain above partisanship—there was a time when he had hoped to be the presidential nominee of *both* parties.

Eisenhower considered Adams a political expert, and he was happy to delegate many political decisions to him. Others in the Administration played a role in political planning, of course, including Vice President Nixon, Attorney General Brownell, and Republican Chairman Len Hall, but no one of them was as close to Eisenhower as Adams, and they generally took their lead from him.

Much of Adams' time was devoted to political patronage—the time-consuming business of matching deserving Republicans to the countless jobs and honorary appointments the President can award. Adams' former aide on patronage, Robert Keith Gray, wrote:

"On roughly seventy-five percent of the 15,378 civilian presidential appointments made in the six years Adams served the Eisenhower Administration, 'OK, S.A.' on the proposal memorandum constituted final approval for the preparation of papers. On names in this group, his 'No!' was as final."

Adams fired as well as hired. He fired a Secretary of the Air Force who was found to be accepting an outside salary. He fired Clarence Manion, former dean of the Notre Dame Law School, from a post as chairman of the President's Commission on Intergovernmental Relations, because Manion had made speeches in favor of the Bricker Amendment. Gray wrote of Adams' style of firing: "He had no patience with either sex's tears, he could match vernacular with a drunken sea captain, and he brooked no argument. He would say, 'It's settled,' when someone tried to continue a discussion of his case, and then without waiting for further comment would drop his telephone back on the hook."

Adams' own political views were a highly pragmatic, mildly progressive brand of Republicanism. The Republican Old Guard considered him a dangerous liberal, but Republican liberals were not so sure. He once summed up his political philosophy this way:

"Some people say that this is a renovated New Deal and that we haven't given them the change they voted for. We don't think this is so. What we have tried to do is to change the trend which was putting the government more and more in control of the individual and being a hard hand against the individual and his freedom of choice.

"You must have fifty-one percent of the voters behind you; otherwise, your adversaries will take over."

Two points must be made about Adams. First, there is an abundance of evidence to show he was an exceedingly influential man in the Eisenhower Administration, the recipient of a unique delegation of presidential authority. Second, it is still possible to overstate Adams' importance, and many observers have done so.

On one level, there was the grim joke of the 1950s:

First man: "Wouldn't it be terrible if Ike died and Nixon became President?"

Second man: "Yes, but what if Adams died and Ike became President?"

At a more serious level, there is the conclusion reached by Professor Louis Koenig:

"For the better part of President Eisenhower's two terms, Adams exercised more power than any other presidential assistant in modern times. He made decisions and performed acts which Presidents, since the establishment of the Republic, have been given to doing themselves. Indeed, it is demonstrable that his power and impact upon the national destiny have exceeded that of not a few Presidents of the United States."

There are several reasons why Adams' importance has often been exaggerated. First, despite his seclusion in the White House, his was a highly visible role. He dealt with Congressmen and job-seekers; he hired and fired; he said "no" for the President. These are tangible duties; they are easily understood. By contrast, the influence of someone like Secretary of the Treasury George Humphrey, Eisenhower's leading adviser on fiscal policy, is hard to pin down, for it was exercised in private, directly with the President. The biggest question facing the domestic departments of government in the Eisenhower Administration was not the day-to-day administrative matters that went to Adams for decision, but the basic issue of how much money they would receive, and on this the President turned to his conservative friend Humphrey for guidance, not to Adams.

Adams' role was overestimated, too, because as White House chief of staff he towered over the others on the staff and he tended to be blamed for negative decisions by the Appointments Secretary, the Press Secretary, the Legislative Assistant, the Special Counsel, and all the rest. Adams took the heat for everybody.

Finally, some critics have overestimated Adams' role for political reasons, as a means of indicting Eisenhower. This seems to be Professor Koenig's motive when he argues, in effect, that Adams was really running the government, not Eisenhower. Koenig declares: "It required the summoning of all of Adams' vast power to offset Eisenhower's intrinsic conservatism and its powerful insistent encouragement by influential businessmen around him." Actually, there is little evidence that Adams became significantly involved in liberal-conservative policy fights within the Administration, or that he ever ran counter to what he felt to be Eisenhower's wishes.

Similarly, when Koenig implies that Adams somehow was responsible for American failures in defense and outer-space programs, he goes beyond the facts—Adams had only minimal involvement in those areas.*

Adams was given considerable powers, but they were carefully circumscribed, and even within those limits he sought to do what Eisenhower wanted, not what he wanted. Implications that Eisenhower was putty in Adams' hands aren't supported by the evidence. Emmet Hughes, although often critical of Eisenhower's leadership, recalls that his strength of character was such that "he could shake even so strong a man as Sherman Adams—sharply asserting a will, an impatience, or a caprice that (as I witnessed more than once) would spin Adams completely around to reverse a decision already fixed in his own mind."

Hughes, a friend and admirer of Adams, stresses that the latter's duties were largely administrative and operational, and very little concerned with policy. Of the 1952 campaign: "Equally striking was the absence of Sherman Adams from all such strategy sessions. So burdened was Adams, as the candidate's personal campaign manager, with the mountainous labor of schedules and arrangements that he never attended a single discussion of the substance of what the candidate would endorse or decry. Like much else of these campaign weeks, this, too, foreshadowed the future—in this instance, the role, so largely administrative and operational, that Adams would fill in the Eisenhower Administration."

Adams reduced his role neatly when he described himself as "scrubbing the administrative and political back stairs" at the White House.

To define Adams' role is really to raise the question of how one defines "power" in a presidential assistant. There are two sorts of power available to a President and, by delegation, to his assistants: the passive and the active, the custodial and the creative. Such creativity as Eisenhower demonstrated during his presidency was largely in foreign affairs, an area in which Adams had little or no influence. In domestic affairs, Eisenhower delegated substantial authority to Adams, but it was custodial authority—a caretaker's power—for Eisenhower sought few innovations in domestic matters. To the contrary, he came to office pledged to slow the pace of federal involvement in social

---

* Adams says of Koenig's chapter on him: "He is manifestly so prejudiced that he has lost much of the effectiveness of his writing. Some of his conclusions are stupid, and so obviously the product of ignorance that they are worthless." Eisenhower similarly has strong words about "those damn professors" who write books about him without first talking to him.

welfare. Adams may have reigned supreme over the domestic agencies of government, but it was a barren empire that he ruled.

Adams' other area of importance was politics, and certainly, in the world of Republican political affairs, he was a powerful man in 1953–58. Yet it is not in the area of politics and patronage that a man can have (as Koenig put it) "impact upon the national destiny." In the long sweep of history, it little matters whether X or Y is appointed to be a postmaster or a federal judge. Indeed, there is a strong argument to be made that a modern President should not waste his time worrying about patronage and routine political affairs.

The kind of power that counts, in the long run, is the power to affect the course of the nation—how people live, how their children are educated, how their medical needs are met. Tugwell had this power in 1933–35, and Hopkins during the war years (although in a different way; he wasn't building a nation, he was helping save one by, almost literally, keeping Roosevelt alive), and Clifford to a lesser extent in 1946–49, and Moyers in 1964–66.

In these terms, Adams does not rank near the top of recent presidential assistants. In domestic affairs in 1953–58 Adams was a most influential caretaker, polishing the administrative and political back stairs, but his was not the sort of creative power that enables a man to leave monuments behind him.

Throughout his White House career, Adams operated in the utmost secrecy. He held no press conferences, he granted interviews rarely, he made few speeches, he declined requests to appear before congressional committees on the ground that his was a privileged relationship with the President. He felt, in short, no obligation to explain himself to the public in whose affairs he was so deeply involved.* Inevitably, this secrecy only fanned the flames of public and press interest, and in time Adams' "image" emerged—a public profile, part fact, part rumor, part press agentry. Adams was portrayed, more

* The first time I wrote Adams, he apparently got the idea I was connected with Jack Anderson, who is columnist Drew Pearson's associate. Adams therefore had his former secretary, a strong-willed lady who lives in Washington, investigate me. This lady called me one evening and announced: "We want to know who you are." She warned that unless "they" approved me, none of the Eisenhower people would talk with me. Since I had already had an interview with General Eisenhower, it seemed to me that I had sufficient clearance, and my conversations with the lady were unproductive. At one point, when I refused to take another of her calls, my wife spoke with her. "What right does your husband have to write about Governor Adams?" the lady demanded. This seemed to me to be a fair summary of Governor Adams' own attitude toward the press during his years in the White House.

or less correctly, as a flinty, hard-working, taciturn New Englander who sat at Eisenhower's right hand and exercised vast but undefined powers.

Most of all, Adams' image portrayed him as the Incorruptible Man. Not since the New Deal's Harold Ickes had so much been made of one government official's honesty. In part this legend sprang from Adams' idiosyncrasies: It was noted that he still wore the tuxedo he had bought in college, and that he drove his own car to work rather than be chauffeured by a White House limousine. Partly it was political: In 1952 Adams had been one of the most vehement critics of the Democratic "mess in Washington," and he became a natural symbol of the new "clean as a hound's tooth" regime. The dispatch with which he fired erring government officials was another oft-noted proof of his uncompromising ethical standards. And within the White House Adams' puritanical nature was well known. At the first meeting of the White House staff he had delivered a stern lecture warning them against "eccentric habits" in "deportment" such as gossiping by the secretaries, smoking in the corridors, or the men putting their feet on their desks. Once he had unsmilingly asked his well-dressed aide, Robert Keith Gray: "Where do you buy your suits? I hope you're working for them."

So grew the legend of the Incorruptible Man. A magazine writer called Adams ". . . a man with the dedication of a vestal virgin. . . ." Another quoted a presidential aide as saying: "I don't think he has ever made a decision here that he had allowed his personal desires to influence." Richard Rovere wrote: "No one who has ever seen Sherman Adams plain could possibly think of him as an influence-peddler. The idea is ludicrous; the imagination will not put up with it. It would be far easier to picture Dr. Norman Vincent Peale in a mood of black despair or Herbert Hoover angrily denouncing corporate wealth."

Then came the Goldfine affair.

In June, 1958, the House Subcommittee on Legislative Oversight, as a result of its investigation into federal regulatory agencies, let fire a double-barreled charge:

First, the subcommittee charged, Sherman Adams had allowed his friend, New England textile tycoon Bernard Goldfine, to pay hotel bills totaling some $3000 for him between November, 1955, and May, 1958. Moreover, Goldfine had given Adams a $2400 Oriental rug and a vicuna coat worth some $700.

Second, during the same period that Goldfine had been showering Adams with gifts, Adams had intervened on Goldfine's behalf with the Securities and Exchange Commission (SEC) and the Federal Trade Commission (FTC), when those two agencies were bringing charges against Goldfine for violation of federal regulations.

The shock that these charges caused in the political world was not caused simply by the allegation that Adams had brought pressure to bear on regulatory agencies. Indeed, two previous cases of Adams intervening with regulatory agencies had come to light.

In the first, House investigators revealed that in 1955 Adams had instructed the chairman of the Securities and Exchange Commission to postpone a scheduled hearing of the Administration's Dixon-Yates power project. The SEC hearing was set for the same day as House debate on a $6.5 million appropriation for Dixon-Yates, and a witness scheduled to testify before the SEC would have revealed information highly embarrassing to Dixon-Yates.

Also, early in 1958, House investigators made public two letters written by Adams in 1953 to Murray Chotiner, a lawyer who was Vice President Nixon's campaign manager in 1952. Chotiner was then representing North American Airlines, which had had its authority to operate as a non-scheduled airline revoked by the Civil Aeronautics Board (CAB) because of violations of CAB regulations. Adams told Chotiner, in a letter marked "personal and confidential," that he had spoken with the head of the CAB, who had advised him that "should North American consider the board's decision unfavorable, an appeal could be made to the U. S. Circuit Court, which might delay the operation of the order for as much as two years." In effect, courtesy of Adams, the CAB was advising an airline, which had violated its rules, on how it might escape enforcement of those rules.

However, neither the Dixon-Yates nor the Chotiner incident had much political propaganda value. Dixon-Yates was simply too complicated to become a mass issue, and although Adams had done Chotiner a favor, it was clearly a harmless favor, since the lawyer presumably already knew of his right to appeal the airline's case. Politically, the shocking fact about the disclosure of Adams' favors to Goldfine was that it was coupled with tangible evidence of personal gain—the hotel bills, the Oriental rug, the vicuna coat—that could be understood by every man, woman, and child in America.

Adams was in Maine on a fishing trip when the charges were disclosed. Many of his friends refused to believe they were true. Robert Gray said of the reaction within the White House: ". . . as the first rush of publicity subsided, Sherm's boys were too busy to do more than luxuriate in the delicious anticipation of the devastation the Governor would surely wreak on his antagonists when he issued a cutting and clearing denial. From the moment he gave, in lieu of the expected refutation, an explanation, his power was on the wane."

On June 12, Hagerty gave reporters a copy of Adams' letter to the House subcommittee in which he admitted accepting Goldfine's favors but denied exerting any improper influence on the textile tycoon's behalf. From that moment forward, for more than three months, there transpired a slow, relentless, semipublic stripping away of Adams' powers. It was an awful spectacle, like watching an incompetent matador butcher a bull who will not die. For Adams was a dead man politically. Everyone in Washington seemed to understand this except Adams and Eisenhower. And Adams, even in those moments when he contemplated resignation, faced a hard dilemma. To resign at once, and end the affair, would seem to be quitting under fire—an unthinkable alternative. Yet the longer he waited, the closer his resignation would come to the November elections, which of course were the real reason his fellow Republicans were clamoring for his head.

The White House had coupled Adams' admission that he accepted the favors with a statement of support from Eisenhower, but this failed to quell the widening storm of criticism. The Administration that had pledged to be clean as a hound's tooth had a scandal on its hands. *The New Republic* gave one reason for the furor: "Reporters had waited five years for this. There was a blood-lust beneath the professional suavity. The cleavage between what Washington correspondents think about the Administration and what back-home publishers allow to be published has widened. Now at last unction had stubbed its toe. It was not a lovely sight, perhaps, but the pack was pushing in for the kill."

Adams voluntarily testified before the House subcommittee on June 17. He admitted letting Goldfine pay his hotel bills. He said the Oriental rug in his home was a loan. He said the real value of the vicuna, coat was $69 rather than $700. He stressed his longtime friendship with Goldfine, and pointed out that he had sometimes given gifts to Goldfine. And he insisted that he had exerted no improper influence on Goldfine's behalf.

The facts about Adams' intervention with the FTC and SEC were largely undisputed. The FTC had issued a complaint against several of Goldfine's textile companies alleging false labeling. In 1954, Adams asked the FTC chairman to send him a memorandum explaining the charges against Goldfine. The chairman complied, and Adams passed the information along to Goldfine. In 1955, at Goldfine's request, Adams called the FTC and arranged a meeting between Goldfine and one of the FTC commissioners. (At the conclusion of this meeting, Goldfine picked up the phone and called Adams at the White House, but he later said, "This was not done in order to impress anybody at the meeting.") Although the FTC's legal staff had recommended a civil suit against Goldfine, their advice was ignored by higher-ups and instead in 1956 a milder settlement action was agreed to by the FTC and Goldfine's lawyers.

Goldfine's troubles with the SEC resulted from the failure of one of his companies, over a period of eight years, to file annual reports required by the SEC. In 1956, Goldfine complained to Adams about the treatment he was getting from the SEC. Adams asked Gerald Morgan, the Special Counsel to the President, to investigate. Morgan did and reported his findings to Adams. Although Adams later denied that he or Morgan exerted any improper influence, the proceedings against Goldfine's company ground to a halt. The SEC had previously obtained a civil-contempt conviction against Goldfine's company (and a $20,000 suspended fine) and had begun criminal-contempt proceedings, but suddenly on April 5, 1956, this action was called off.

Adams maintained during his congressional testimony that he had done nothing wrong. "I have no excuses to offer. I did not come here to make an apology. . . ." He did admit that if he had it to do over, "I would have acted a little more prudently."

On the day after Adams' congressional appearance, Eisenhower read to a news conference a self-written statement in support of his aide, one he hoped would close the issue. The statement's key sentences were: "I personally like Governor Adams. I admire his abilities. I respect him because of his personal and official integrity. I need him."

The words "I need him" were quickly seized upon by Eisenhower's critics as an admission of presidential weakness. Presidents are not supposed to need anyone. It was an honest and heartfelt remark—and it was politically unwise. A member of Eisenhower's staff told Emmet Hughes about the incident:

"Several of us had spent a night pondering what the President should say to help Adams in his press conference. And when we went in to the boss the next morning, he surprised us by reading what he himself had prepared. Not one of us caught the hollow ring of the words, 'I *need* him.' And we all just sat there—and said it sounded swell."

Hughes adds: "And so each passing month, it seemed, was deepening the disposition of the staff to dull its own faculties of criticism, to leave the President at peace in a world of gleaming and consoling assents."

The controversy raged into the summer. *Life* magazine called for Adams' resignation, but the New York *Herald-Tribune* backed him. Inevitably, Adams' influence was weakened by the controversy.

Robert Gray gives this portrait of Adams' declining power within the White House: "The Governor and his office had been the hub of White House activities. Now both were bypassed more each day as Presidential assistants, losing their awe of Adams-made-mortal, came to decisions without him and engaged in the plays for power which the superiority of Adams' position had quelled while he reigned. The President began to deal more exclusively on policy matters with members of the Cabinet and to use less frequently his phrase of five years, 'Check it with Sherm.'

"Adams reacted by drawing farther into his shell. In his last weeks at the White House he spent the hours discarding and sorting the avalanche of papers he had accumulated. In the preceding quarter of the year he had seemed to age a quarter of a century. Witnessing this accelerated physical aging made it easier to view without shock the striking changes in his personality. He was tired in spirit now as well as in body, his mood was mellow and his speech was slow. The old bark and bite were gone. The demanding commander issued few orders and those pathetically petty and awkwardly tempered with apology."

Adams fought back as best he could. He sent his Congressional Relations staff to Capitol Hill to ask Republican Senators to sign a statement supporting him. They found only four takers. The fact that the congressional elections were near made Adams' ouster inevitable. Every Republican in Congress feared that the Democrats would use Adams' coat and rug to cover them with corruption charges, just as they had used the Democrats' deepfreezes and mink coat six years before. (The Democrats kept quiet during this period; they were hoping Eisenhower would keep Adams.)

The clamor died down a bit in August, but it was revived in September when Senator Fred Payne of Maine, who had admitted accepting a $3500 interest-free loan from Goldfine, was defeated by a Democrat. After the primaries, Nixon reported to the President that unless Adams was removed, the Administration faced a full-scale revolt on Capitol Hill. Adams was not, as some of his friends suggest, simply a victim of the Republican right wing. The demands for his resignation came from all sides of the party. But it was true that the Old Guard strongly disliked Adams, and early in September Republican National

Committee Chairman Meade Alcorn anxiously reported to Eisenhower that major party contributors, most of them ultraconservative, were refusing to contribute to the campaign treasury until Adams was removed.

Finally Eisenhower, sick at heart, confused and repelled by the whole shabby affair, yielded to the political pressures. However, in his account of the episode in his memoirs, Eisenhower stresses his concern with Adams' judgment and minimizes the political aspect of his decision:

"In the meantime, in addition to the evidence in the press, I had been getting reports from individuals who knew of Mr. Goldfine and his business dealings in New England, that his reputation was not of the kind that should have encouraged Governor Adams to seek his friendship. (My own first impression had been—as I am certain Governor Adams' initial impression had been—that Mr. Goldfine was a high-minded and enterprising businessman. Now I was told that this first impression was far from accurate. This was serious because of the implication that the governor had been less than alert or wise in forming his friendships.)

"On September 4, I telephoned Meade Alcorn, Chairman of the Republican National Committee. His reports confirmed those I had been receiving: that the Goldfine case was a cause of 'hopelessness' in the Republican party all over the country.

"I had to conclude that, in spite of my deep conviction of Adams' honesty, his retention of his office would be a mistake both for him and the office.

"A few days later the results of the Maine elections became known. . . ."

Adams was vacationing in Maine when Alcorn reported to the President on the crisis the party faced. Next, as Adams later recounted the course of events: "Eisenhower asked Nixon and Alcorn to talk with me about it. But the President did not ask me to resign and neither did Alcorn or the Vice President. That decision was left to me."

The official Administration story is that no one ever "asked" Adams to resign, but one must have an extremely narrow definition of the word "ask" to accept this version. Another version, published in *Life* magazine and denied by the Administration, had the President assigning Alcorn the job of getting Adams' resignation, with the words: "You've got to handle it. It's your job." In other words, it was a political matter, to be delegated to a politician.

In either case, Alcorn got word to the backwoods of Maine. Adams returned to Washington immediately. Then Alcorn and Nixon relayed the President's concern over the situation to Adams. Eisenhower was in Newport. Adams decided to ask Gerald Morgan, the President's Special Counsel, to go to Newport and discuss the situation with Eisenhower, and to make his decision on the basis of Morgan's report. This was done. Adams writes: "Morgan came to me from Newport with a confirmation of what Alcorn had told me: The President was troubled by the feeling against me among the influential supporters of the Republican party but the decision on whether or not I ought to remain on the White House staff was still being left entirely up to me. It did not take me long to make the decision."

Adams resigned on September 22. He chose to announce his resignation in a televised statement in which he reasserted his innocence of any wrongdoing. Earlier in the day he had flown to Newport to clear the statement with Eisenhower. It was their first face-to-face meeting since the affair had come to a climax. Eisenhower told Adams he thought he had acted wisely, shook his hand, and wished him well.

The affair had cast perhaps more light on Eisenhower than on Adams. Eisenhower had mishandled the Adams case from start to finish, and in the process had revealed a woeful ethical and political confusion. If he had been serious about his Administration's oft-heralded purity, he should have fired Adams at the outset. Adams had fired many men for lesser offenses. Instead, by defending him, Eisenhower admitted to a double standard; Adams was above the law because the President needed him. Then, three months later, having refused to drop Adams for the right reason, he dropped him for the wrong reason—in the face of ugly, dollars-and-cents blackmail from the most reactionary elements of the Republican Party.

Adams made the ideal political scapegoat, both for the Republican Old Guard and for the Democrats, but he was not the only member of the Eisenhower Administration to demonstrate questionable judgment in accepting favors. The example started at the top. Eisenhower saw no harm in his accepting scores of expensive gifts for his Gettysburg farm from wealthy admirers.

It was a bit pathetic when the Goldfine investigation unearthed the fact that Goldfine's boundless largess had included $100 "Christmas checks" to Adams' secretary and to Appointments Secretary Thomas E. Stephens' secretary. But it was nothing short of incredible when, also in the wake of the Goldfine investigation, Press Secretary Hagerty confirmed a report that he had let the Ponte Vedra Inn in Florida pick up a $260.97 bill for a five-day visit by him and his wife. It almost defies belief that Hagerty, the shrewd political operative, the brilliant image-maker, would commit such a blunder, particularly only a few years after he had helped roast Truman's Donald Dawson for accepting free hospitality in a Florida hotel.

How had Sherman Adams, the Incorruptible Man, ever let himself get into such a mess? His friends and his enemies pondered that question, and they arrived at a multitude of answers. Richard Rovere suggested that Adams had never made the transition from the more flexible standards of state politics (all forty-eight state governors had gratefully accepted bolts of vicuna from Goldfine) to the more rigid, or at least more discreet, code in Washington.

Gray pointed out that Adams belonged to "that hard Yankee cult for which thrift is a religion" and suggested that he had viewed Goldfine's favors simply as "money saved." Koenig, in his sympathetic essay on Adams wrote that "the danger of hard work in a high and lonely station is that the toiling hero loses perspective, develops overweening self-righteousness and becomes uncritical of his acts."

All of the theories, in one way or another, lead back to a more basic answer: all-consuming pride, the pride of the youthful long-distance hiker, of the 140-pound lumberjack, of the Governor who trudged through the snow to his office carrying his lunch in a paper sack— pride that in time led Adams to believe he was not only above corruption, he was above even the appearance of corruption. Adams asked for no sympathy during his ordeal, yet he got much, for his was a universal weakness. He seemed to achieve in his disgrace a humanity that he had lacked during his years of arrogant power. Even his old critic, the columnist T.R.B. at *The New Republic,* wrote movingly of Adams' downfall: "The mood of the affair was sad, poignant, transcending politics, transcending Sherman Adams even. For who can see pride humbled without a tear or watch mistakes exposed without being himself in the dock?"

Adams stayed on in the White House for about a month after his resignation was announced. Then he returned to his Lincoln, New Hampshire, home for a life of strictly enforced privacy. Much of 1959 and 1960 were spent in writing *Firsthand Report,* which was published in 1961. In April, 1960, he attended a White House dinner for General de Gaulle. After that, as political power passed back to the Democrats, little was heard of Adams, only one- and two-paragraph notes in the New York *Times:* He had given his public papers to Dartmouth; he had had an operation; he would lecture at Dartmouth on the Eisenhower Administration; he was backing Nelson Rockefeller for the 1968 Republican nomination.

Perhaps the most suitable ending to the story of Sherman Adams is an incident that took place during his final days in the White House. He described it this way:

"Shortly after I resigned, the social secretary at the White House called to tell me that the President was arranging a dinner in my honor, with square dancing afterward in the East Room. I had no heart at that time for square dancing. I declined and the President understood how I felt. He had planned to present to me at the dinner a huge sterling-silver punch bowl. Instead he gave it to me privately one day in his office. On the bowl is inscribed:

To Sherman Adams
The Assistant to the President
1953–58
For Tireless Service to the Public
Brilliant Performance of Every Duty
and
Unsurpassed Dedication to his Country
From his devoted friend
Dwight D. Eisenhower

3. The National Security Council

Eisenhower's overriding concern was foreign affairs and it followed that his use of the National Security Council most completely reflected his theories of proper presidential organization. Moreover, his use of the NSC not only reflected his organizational theories, it also reflected his belief, based on first-hand observation, that both Presidents Roosevelt and Truman had failed to integrate political, diplomatic, and military decision-making, and that the national security had suffered thereby. To appreciate fully his use of the NSC, it is necessary to look back to its origins in the years preceding Eisenhower's presidency.

Every President since Franklin Roosevelt has faced problems in foreign affairs unimagined by Roosevelt's predecessors. Until the Second World War, ours was by tradition an isolationist nation. We came out of our shell once, to fight the War to End War, and then withdrew into Fortress America, proudly disdainful of the squabbling nations of Europe and the smoldering hotbeds of black, brown, and yellow men around the globe. The Second World War, followed by the threat of Russian expansion, ended our isolationist dream abruptly. Suddenly we were concerned with coups and revolutions and border disputes in scores of small and distant lands: Yemen, Lebanon, Laos, Korea, the Congo, the Dominican Republic, Cuba, Vietnam. In John Kennedy's phrase, "We find ourselves entangled with apparently unanswerable problems in unpronounceable places."

The first new problem facing Roosevelt's successors was simply one of quantity: The Presidents have had to have more information about more countries in order to make more decisions to be implemented by more foreign aid or, in some cases, more marines. President Kennedy's Secretary of Defense, Robert S. McNamara, underscored this fact when he noted that there had been 169 significant outbreaks of violence in the world between 1958 and 1966—each one of real or potential interest to U.S. policy-makers.

A second problem: time. Diplomacy once was a leisurely affair. Sixty years ago, when Theodore Roosevelt wanted to cut off Japanese criticism of U.S. segregationist policies, he could send the American fleet steaming toward Yokohama, confident that by the time it arrived, the Japanese government would have seen the light of reason (as it did), and confident that in any event the Japanese were powerless to retaliate. Today the world is different. Its leaders must live with the knowledge that a miscalculation in any far-off troublespot could lead to nuclear war within hours, even minutes. Today's President has little time for diplomatic courtesies or bureaucratic niceties; in a crisis he must have information with which to make immediate decisions.

A third fact facing postwar Presidents has been that the traditional institutions involved in foreign policy decision have often been unable to stay abreast of the fast-changing modern era. This failure has been most obvious at the Department of State, but the Pentagon has also had difficulty keeping pace with the rapid shift from "conventional" warfare to atomic warfare to guerrilla warfare.

Because of these problems, and more, each postwar President has had to improvise in a hectic, sometimes desperate, effort to ride the whirlwind of world events. The primary instrument the four postwar Presidents have used in this endeavor has been the National Security Council and its staff.

The NSC was created by the National Security Act of 1947, along with the Department of Defense. The original NSC had seven members: the President, the Secretary of State, the Secretary of Defense, the Secretary of the Army, the Secretary of the Navy, the Secretary of the Air Force, and the chairman of the National Security Resources Board.

Two years later, as part of legislation designed to strengthen the Secretary of Defense, the three service Secretaries were dropped from Council membership, and the President was given authority to appoint the Secretaries and Under Secretaries of other executive and military departments to NSC membership.*

In effect, the 1949 provision allowing Presidents to appoint other government officials to the NSC has made it an open-ended body, and Presidents have convened from three or four to thirty or forty officials as their National Security Council.

The NSC is clearly an advisory, not a policy-making body. Its stated purpose is "to advise the President with respect to the integration of domestic, foreign, and military policies relating to the national security so as to enable the military services and the other departments and agencies of the government to cooperate more effectively in matters involving the national security."

There is an obvious, built-in ambiguity about the NSC, in that it only formalizes pre-existing presidential powers—i.e., a President is presumably going to consult with his Secretaries of State and Defense, and other top officials, on national security, whether or not they are called the National Security Council. And if the President doesn't choose to consult with them, there is nothing in the National Security Act to force him to do so.

The explanations for this ambiguity, and for the creation of the NSC, are complex and often contradictory.

To a large extent the NSC was a reaction to the manner in which Roosevelt had directed the Second World War. Roosevelt, with his instinct for secrecy and personal leadership, had managed the war on a kind of *ad hoc* basis, coordinating the worldwide military-diplomatic campaign in part through the State-War-Navy Coordinating Committee and in part through such trusted advisers as Harry Hopkins, Sumner Welles, General George C. Marshall, and Admiral William D. Leahy. After the war, virtually every leading civilian and military official believed the machinery existing to create and coordinate national security policy was inadequate, and these officials were therefore eager to push for new machinery that might give them the President's ear.

The one individual in the Truman Administration who pushed hardest and most effectively for the NSC in 1946–47 was Secretary of the Navy James V. Forrestal, who, in addition to his concern for the national

---

* At the same time, the Senate added the Vice President to membership, a tribute to Alben Barkley, a former Senate leader. Later, the director of the Office of Emergency Planning replaced the director of the National Security Resources Board.

security, had a shrewd, selfish bureaucratic motive up his sleeve. The Administration was then also debating whether or not the armed services should be unified in a Department of Defense. The navy, accustomed to special status under Roosevelt, was fighting as hard as it could against unification, and Forrestal was its leading spokesman. One of his arguments against unification was that the creation of the NSC would provide top-level coordination of military affairs (since each service would presumably be represented on the NSC) and that additional coordination via a Department of Defense was therefore unnecessary. In Forrestal's strategy, support of the NSC was part of his resistance to a Department of Defense. Many powerful, pro-Navy members of Congress followed this line, thus adding to congressional support for the NSC. (The irony, as it turned out, was that after losing the fight against the Department of Defense, Forrestal became its first Secretary, and had to go back to Congress to seek legislation strengthening the Department so he could do his job.)

There have been suggestions that Truman was lukewarm to the idea of an NSC and that it was forced on him by Forrestal and a Republican Congress. There is much evidence to the contrary. Truman was an orderly President, one who like formal channels of communication and who didn't mind listening to advice. His Special Counsel, Clark Clifford, who drafted the National Security Act, says he saw no evidence that Truman did not want the NSC.

The fact remains that, until the Korean War began in 1950, Truman avoided NSC meetings as often as he could. Admiral Sidney W. Souers, Truman's first executive secretary of the NSC, says Truman avoided NSC meetings lest his presence impede free discussions. Clark Clifford says the reason Truman avoided NSC meetings was that he was briefed on national security developments early each morning and he therefore found NSC meetings repetitive and rather boring.

Beyond its obvious utility as a forum for debate and coordination, the NSC offers a President at least one major advantage and one major drawback. The drawback is that even if a President feels little need for a formal advisory forum (Kennedy and Johnson), he is not free to ignore or disband the NSC. That would give his critics a stout stick to beat him with: "The President is ignoring the National Security Council." Given widespread ignorance about the NSC, and given its imposing title, millions of voters would equate presidential indifference to it with high treason. So, Kennedy and Johnson called periodic NSC sessions, but more for window-dressing than for policy-making.

The NSC's major advantage to a President lies in the fact that it by law provides a permanent staff responsible to him. No President could fail to appreciate having a staff of foreign affairs experts to advance and protect his interests in the often hostile areas controlled by the military and diplomatic bureaucracies. The fact is that under Presidents Kennedy and Johnson (and some would say under President Eisenhower) the NSC staff has been more important than the NSC itself.

During Truman's Administration, the President and Admiral Souers, the NSC's executive secretary, tried to limit NSC meetings to nine or ten participants. Typically, if the Secretary of Defense wanted guidance on American policy in some situation, he would write Admiral Souers, who would send a copy to the Secretary of State and request him to submit a draft paper for consideration by the NSC staff. The paper would be prepared by State Department planners, in consultation with the NSC staff and officials from Defense and other concerned agencies. Finally, the resulting policy statement would be debated in an NSC meeting and passed upon by the President.

In other instances, policy papers would be initiated by the NSC staff itself. In either case, the policy papers tried to anticipate international crises and specify what U.S. policy would be. At the end of the Truman Administration, more than fifty national security policies had been fixed by the NSC, dealing with U.S. policy toward specific countries or toward policy toward larger geographic areas or various forms of aggression.

The decision to carry out the Berlin airlift was reached by Truman as a result of lengthy debate in an NSC meeting on July 22, 1948. In deciding to use an airlift rather than armed convoys to get supplies to Berlin, Truman overruled General Hoyt Vandenberg, the Air Force Chief of Staff, who argued that excessive use of planes in Berlin would leave the U.S. exposed elsewhere. Also that year, the NSC debated the terms of U.S. involvement in NATO, and Truman approved an NSC policy recommendation that the U.S. train and equip the South Korean army.

The outbreak of the Korean War in 1950 ended whatever indifference Truman may have felt toward the NSC. In the past, its policy debates had often bored him; now he and the Council had the urgent issue of war to focus on. Tightening up his decision-making process, Truman issued a memorandum ordering that all national security issues should be brought to him through the NSC mechanism. Throughout the war he met with the NSC as often as two or three times a week. In these sessions he wrestled with such difficult problems as the massive intervention of the Chinese army in Korea, General MacArthur's resistance to the Truman-NSC policy of a limited war, and the eventual firing of MacArthur.

Harry Truman had regarded the NSC with a Missourian's show-me skepticism; he used it when he thought he needed it and ignored it when he didn't. Dwight D. Eisenhower viewed it as the primary instrument by which he would be kept abreast of world affairs; Government officials would be informed of his thoughts on foreign affairs; departmental differences over national policy would be resolved; and policies would be defined and brought before the President for decision.

This is not to say that Eisenhower intended to surrender policy-making authority to the NSC, or that he expected it to guide his actions in fast-breaking international crises. He didn't. He saw it as an elaborate machine—a Rube Goldberg contraption, his critics said—that could sort out the countless worldwide issues and problems in foreign affairs and bring them before him for decision in an orderly, clearcut manner.

Reflecting on this point, he said to me during an informal conversation in June 1967:

"You walk into the presidency and you've got problems all over the world. You have to examine each one from every viewpoint—military, economic, political. How the hell can you do this for one hundred sovereign countries? We tried to use the NSC to keep our policies up to date. There is no single foreign policy—there are only basic national objectives—but there are individual policies to apply to each country. The NSC papers analyzed our position relative to each country. Regularly, you take the damn things out and you revise them.

"My successors either discarded or ignored the NSC and I think no greater mistake has been made. I suppose Kennedy thought one man could know all the answers, Heaven-sent, and not need the analysis the NSC could give him. He told me later, 'You don't understand the Presidency until you've been in it.' And he said to me, speaking of the Bay of Pigs invasion, 'I didn't have trustworthy information or I wouldn't have gone on with it.'"

Eisenhower's regard for the NSC was reflected in the quality of the men he chose to direct his operations, and in the fact that he created for them the new title of Special Assistant for National Security Affairs. The three men who filled this position were Robert Cutler, a Boston investment banker; Dillon Anderson, a Houston lawyer and writer; and Gordon Gray, who was Truman's Secretary of the Army and later president of the University of North Carolina. Cutler served from January, 1953, until April 1, 1955, when he was replaced by Anderson, who stayed until January 7, 1957. Cutler then returned for a second term that lasted until July 21, 1958, when he was replaced by Gray, who served out the remainder of Eisenhower's term.

Cutler, in particular, was an outstanding example of the quality of Republican businessman Eisenhower was able to attract to the government. Like McGeorge Bundy, his counterpart in the Kennedy Administration, Cutler was a prominent and proper Bostonian. Yet he defied the stereotype of the Boston banker. A Harvard graduate, he had started out to be a writer, and published two novels as a young man, turning to the law only after he had concluded that literature would not support him. (At a press conference in connection with his appointment in 1953, a reporter asked him what his novels had been about; Cutler replied: "Why, they were about love, of course. What else would a boy of twenty write about?")

His practice of law led Cutler, a lifelong bachelor, to become a Boston civic leader, patron of the arts, and popular after-dinner speaker. An active Republican, he was a prominent backer of Henry Cabot Lodge's political campaigns. Cutler had been a young army officer in Europe during the First World War, and during the Second he served in Washington on Secretary of War Henry Stimson's staff, rising to the rank of general. In 1946, he was elected president of Boston's Old Colony Trust Company, which he helped make the largest trust company in the U.S. outside of New York City.

Cutler had met Eisenhower a few times during the war and in the postwar years, and by 1950 he had decided Eisenhower was his candidate. He accompanied his friend Sinclair Weeks—Republican National Committeeman from Massachusetts, later Eisenhower's Secretary of Commerce—to the pre-convention sessions in Chicago at which Eisenhower's backers outmaneuvered Senator Robert A. Taft's men in disputes before the Convention's Credentials Committee.

It was, however, Cutler's personal charm rather than his political skills that most impressed Eisenhower at the Republican convention. Cutler was a witty, outgoing, rather flamboyant individual, and he struck Eisenhower as an ideal traveling companion. A few weeks after the convention, as Eisenhower was about to embark on his first national tour, Cutler got a call from his friend Henry Cabot Lodge.

"Bobby, the General has something he wants you to do."

"What's that?"

"After the Campaign Train leaves New York, it will be gone for over a month. A month packed with whistle-stops, major speeches, dealing with thousands of people, meeting more millions in rallies and in city streets and on farms. Something unique, unforgettable. Based on his experience of the first eight days of intensive campaigning, Ike telephoned me that everyone is so damn busy, there's no one who has time to talk to him. He wants you to go along on the Campaign Train's big swing and be there to talk with him."

Cutler protested that he had a trust company to run, but he succumbed a few days later when Eisenhower made the same plea: "Bobby, this is what I hope you can do for me. I need someone on the Train during the next month, whom I can turn to and talk with. Nobody had time to talk to the Candidate. And, by golly, the Candidate hasn't time to do anything except talk himself!"

As it turned out on the Campaign Train, Cutler's proximity to Eisenhower inevitably transformed him from a traveling companion into an Administrative Assistant, and in the end Eisenhower complained that not even Cutler would talk to him.

The experience impressed Eisenhower with Cutler's executive ability. Also, Cutler had worked with Eisenhower on campaign speeches that promised to turn the NSC operation from "shadow into substance," and this led Eisenhower to think of Cutler in connection with the NSC. As a result, in the early days of his presidency, he created for Cutler the new title of Special Assistant for National Security Affairs.

In his first weeks in the new job, Cutler prepared for Eisenhower a detailed recommendation on how the NSC should best operate. This report, which Eisenhower approved on March 22, included such rules on Council operation as: a forward agenda for presidential consideration; advance circulation to Council members of policy papers to be discussed; advance briefing on those papers for the President by the Special Assistant; regular weekly meetings of two or three hours; inclusion in each proposal of an estimate of its financial costs; opening each Council meeting with an intelligence briefing by the CIA director; following each meeting with a formal Report of Action prepared by the Special Assistant for the President.

Eisenhower also approved the upgrading of the NSC's "senior staff" (as it was called under Truman) into the Planning Board, and, later, the creation of the Operations Coordinating Board. These two groups had a "before and after" role in the NSC's operation; the Planning Board defined policy issues that would be placed before the NSC for debate, and the OCB's job was to see that presidential decisions were implemented by the departments.

Both were interagency, sub-Cabinet committees. Cutler presided over the Planning Board's deliberations, and the Under Secretary of State was chairman of the OCB, which also included the Deputy Secretary of Defense, the directors of the CIA and USIA, and the Special Assistant. The Planning Board met two or three times a week to try to thrash out interagency disputes over foreign policy; if they failed, the issues were set out for presidential consideration. The OCB usually met once a week.

Under Eisenhower, the NSC usually met once a week for about two hours. Issues to be discussed would be placed on the agenda several weeks or months in advance. The Planning Board would discuss the issues at a series of its meetings and prepare a "draft policy statement" to be circulated to the NSC members at least ten days before the meeting. This draft would also be sent to the Joint Chiefs of Staff for their "formal military views," which were also sent to the NSC members prior to their meetings.

The NSC meetings were semi-judicial in nature. As each item on the agenda was reached, Cutler would explain the reasons for examining it, summarize the highlights of the Planning Board's draft paper, and solicit the views of each NSC member. Sharp debate often followed. Eisenhower tried to remain silent lest his comments cut off the discussion, but sometimes he would be swept up in the debate. Often he would decide an issue on the spot; other times he would defer his decision for a few days. In either event, his decision became a formal document, circulated among the NSC members for comment, then signed by the President and forwarded to the OCB and the departments involved for implementation.

That was the way the NSC was supposed to work; it didn't always succeed. One enduring problem was that Eisenhower's high regard for the NSC made attendance at its meetings a prized status symbol in his Administration. He and Cutler fought a losing battle to keep down the size of the Council meetings. When Admiral Lewis Strauss, who rated a Council seat as chairman of the AEC, was nominated as Secretary of Commerce, he insisted that he should retain his Council membership. Eisenhower refused, noting dryly that pretty soon the Secretary of Agriculture would be wanting to attend. The problem was that oversized meetings cut down the free flow of discussion; Secretary Dulles, in particular, would refuse to talk openly if he felt too many outsiders were present. Sometimes as many as forty or fifty government officials would attend an NSC meeting, although these were usually meetings intended as briefing sessions rather than policy meetings. Cutler was sensitive on this point, and he would stress that twice as many people usually attended Cabinet meetings as NSC meetings.

The way Eisenhower used the NSC in a crisis can be seen by events on the morning he decided to send U. S. Marines into Lebanon to avert the possible collapse of its government. This crisis arose on a day in June, 1958, when an NSC meeting was already scheduled. (This, it happened, was to be the last NSC meeting Cutler would attend before his second retirement—his 179th NSC meeting, he noted.) The meeting was scheduled to have a much more prosaic focus—the presentation of civil defense studies. The meeting was to begin at 9:45 A.M. At 7 A.M. Cutler learned of the revolt in Iraq, and rushed to see Eisenhower, who was already in his office discussing the crisis by telephone with Secretary Dulles, CIA Director Dulles, General Nathan Twining, chairman of the Joint Chiefs of Staff, and Prime Minister Macmillan.

Eisenhower agreed that he should attend the regular NSC meeting, although Dulles had already said he could not arrive until 10:45 A.M. It was agreed that when Dulles arrived, Eisenhower would leave the NSC meeting and hold a smaller conference on the Mideast crisis in his office. In so doing, Eisenhower was able to have his cake and eat it, too: he maintained the elaborate, oversized NSC mechanism, but to deal with a pressing crisis, he ignored the multimembered NSC and dealt with a small group of officials of his own choosing. (Kennedy did much the same thing four years later when, during the Cuban missile crisis, he created the NSC's "Executive Committee.")

Those meeting in the President's office on the Lebanon crisis were Eisenhower, Nixon, the Dulles brothers, Treasury Secretary Robert Anderson, Deputy Secretary of Defense Donald Quarles, Generals Twining, Persons and Goodpaster of the White House staff, and Cutler and his successor, Gordon Gray.

Allen Dulles began the meeting with an intelligence briefing. Apparently, Eisenhower had already made up his mind, on the basis of the morning's phone conversations, about what he wanted to do. He turned quickly to General Twining, so quickly that Secretary Dulles had to ask: "Mr. President, would you wish to hear my political appreciation?" Eisenhower, a bit embarrassed to have ignored Dulles, asked him to proceed. The gist of his report was that Lebanon had asked for help from the U.S., and if she didn't get it, the government would probably

THE EISENHOWER STAFF   177

fall, and Jordan's, too. The U.S. had treaty obligations to aid Lebanon, and U.S. military action would probably not cause Russian intervention.

Eisenhower then proceeded, speaking in a calm and quiet voice, to question Twining on the military aspects of the situation. This was an area in which he felt entirely at home. At the end of his questioning, he asked Twining:

"How soon can you start, Nate?"

"Fifteen minutes after I get back to the Pentagon, sir."

"Sure?"

"Positive, sir."

"Well, what are we waiting for?"

The Marines landed in Lebanon the next day.

Criticisms of Eisenhower's management of foreign affairs did not focus on the times, such as the Lebanon crisis, when he acted quickly and decisively. To the contrary, his critics charged that he had become a prisoner of the elaborate NSC system, that it was a ridiculous "paper mill," and that—echoing Eisenhower's charge against Truman's NSC in 1952—it substituted shadow for substance in the formulation of foreign policy.

The primary source of criticism in 1959–60 was Senator Henry M. Jackson's Subcommittee on National Policy Machinery. With the 1960 campaign in the offing, and with Senator Jackson vying for the Democratic vice-presidential nomination, these hearings were not entirely innocent of political motive, yet they also reflected genuine doubt that Eisenhower's NSC got to the roots of thorny foreign-policy questions.

Nelson Rockefeller, who had assisted Eisenhower on international affairs, told the subcommittee: "I think the public does not recognize the degree to which the Planning Board really does ninety-five percent of the work. It is not very often that a paper is changed by the National Security Council." It was also charged that the Planning Board's policy papers were often compromises which only papered over disputes between agencies. The Jackson Subcommittee's report ridiculed Eisenhower's NSC as sitting atop Policy Hill with an army of papers marching up one side of the hill, receiving the NSC's rubber-stamp approval, and marching down the other side for implementation. Said the subcommittee: "The fact is that the departments and agencies often work actively and successfully to keep critical policy issues outside the NSC system. . . . They try to settle important questions in dispute through 'out of court' informal interagency negotiations when they are doubtful of the President's position. Or else they try 'end runs' to the President himself."

The subcommittee concluded that the Planning Board was nearly overshadowing the importance of the Council itself. It said of the Operations Coordinating Board: "Actually, the OCB has little impact on the real coordination of policy execution. Yet, at the same time, the existence of this elaborate machinery creates a false sense of security by inviting the conclusion that the problem of teamwork in the execution of policy is well in hand. . . . The case for abolishing the OCB is strong."

Above and beyond the purely political intent of the Jackson Subcommittee's report, it and the Eisenhower Administration seem not to have been talking about the same thing when they viewed the merits and demerits of the NSC. The Planning Board's job of grinding out policy papers, which the subcommittee ridiculed as a paper mill, was to Eisenhower (who was, after all, the President) a serious and useful function. Cutler put this well when he wrote: "Eisenhower's belief in continuous policy planning was based on his long experience with war planning. There is, of course, a difference between what you plan to do and what you actually do, because newly arising conditions may dictate what has to be done. . . . More important than *what* is planned is that the planners *become accustomed* to working and thinking together on hard problems; enabling them—when put to the ultimate test—to arrive more surely at a reasonable plan or policy."

In other words, as Eisenhower sometimes put it, the planning was more important than the plans.

The Kennedy Administration, it might be noted, swallowed whole the Jackson Subcommittee's criticisms and proceeded to abolish the Planning Board, the OCB, and, for all practical purposes, the NSC itself. Then, a few months later, after the Bay of Pigs disaster, the members of the Kennedy circle were saying that the tragedy had occurred because it came so early, because they had not "become accustomed to working and thinking together"—the very thing the much-despised Eisenhower system had been intended to provide.

During the 1960s, a number of students of foreign policy have expressed concern that the Kennedy and Johnson Administrations have had no ongoing, top-level mechanism to review foreign policy in depth and on a worldwide basis. Washington correspondents Charles Bartlett and Edward Weintal commented: "To the extent that the regular NSC meetings served to pull the government together, to insure that the President heard every side of an issue before he acted, and to examine danger spots before they erupted into crises, their omission is a risk in the operations of the Johnson Administration."

Another evaluation came from a former foreign-service officer, Smith Simpson. Simpson did not mind that the NSC system was complex and cumbersome; his experience had taught him that the government is complex and cumbersome and that fire may be needed to fight fire. He wrote:

"Being under a presidential agency—the Security Council—rather than under a department, the OCB was in a unique position to act as a clearinghouse and to mobilize resources. In many instances, its country committees did this admirably. Their systematic, country-by-country, subject-by-subject review of policy for the first time made available to those who were developing American foreign and diplomacy the vast resources of the Federal community. Ideas generated ideas, suggestions bred suggestions. No open and constructive mind participating in these committees could have failed to be stirred and enriched.

"For the first time in our history, the Federal Government came reasonably close to reconciling the needs for diversity and unity in the development of our foreign policy and diplomacy. For the first time, a nearly complete mobilization of Federal resources was brought to bear upon that policy and its execution. A way had been finally devised of assuring a careful enough study of every country of the world to uncover problems and needs before they became crises and to evolve basic, long-range policies. The Federal establishment began to look and plan ahead in unison."

Eisenhower, as he looks back over his eight years as President, is proudest of his record in foreign affairs. "The U.S. never lost a soldier or a foot of ground in my Administration," he declares. "We kept the peace. People ask how it happened—by God, it didn't just happen, I'll tell you that."

Eisenhower had his setbacks—the U-2 affair and the collapse of the summit conference, the widespread distrust of Dulles, the attacks on Nixon in South America, his own canceled trip to Japan—yet the fact remains that he embarked on no fiasco equal to Kennedy's Bay of Pigs and no tragedy of the magnitude of Johnson's land war in Asia. Historians will have to decide how much of Eisenhower's success was due to good luck, how much to his own judgment, and how much to the way he organized the presidential apparatus. In Eisenhower's own mind there is no doubt that his organization and use of the NSC contributed significantly to his ability to cope with the complexities of the Cold War, and his NSC operation must be viewed as a landmark in the history of presidential administration.

4. *The News Manager: Hagerty*

The coming of the Eisenhower Administration was like a dash of cold water in the collective face of the White House press corps. The reporters had for twenty years been spoiled by the informality and accessibility of Presidents Roosevelt and Truman. But Eisenhower had been spoiled, too, spoiled by an adoring press during the Second World War. In those days he and the press had been on the same team, but when the General began his 1952 political "crusade" he found that many of his old teammates had gone over to the enemy. A turning point came when the reporters on Eisenhower's campaign train foolishly let themselves be polled on their presidential preferences. They were overwhelmingly for the Democratic candidate, Adlai Stevenson, and Eisenhower never forgot it.

The press may have displeased the new President aesthetically as well as politically. A rumor spread soon after Eisenhower entered the White House that he was offended by the inelegant vista of several dozen reporters always lounging about the West Wing lobby, just a few yards from his own office, and that he wanted to move the press quarters out of the White House. The reporters were contemplating Gandhi-style sit-ins when Press Secretary Jim Hagerty came to their defense. But the episode was a straw in the wind, for the press soon had to accept several new realities in its relationship with the White House.

The first reality was that the new President not only didn't like the working press, he didn't need it. He had entered the White House with the support of eighty percent of the country's daily newspapers, and many Washington correspondents were most reluctant to send back critical dispatches that their publishers—and their readers—wouldn't like. One Washington columnist told *Time* magazine in October, 1953: "I don't think our readers are ready for critical reporting yet."

Eisenhower, in short, had little need to court the press, and he therefore withdrew from dealings with the press to a degree undreamed of by his two Democratic predecessors. Another campaign train episode had foreshadowed this withdrawal. Reporters had complained to Hagerty that they never got to see Eisenhower, so the Press Secretary urged the candidate to fraternize a bit. Eager to please, Eisenhower one day wandered back unannounced to the club car where the reporters were milling about, thinking he would smile, say hello, and shake a few hands. The moment he entered the car, reporters trapped him in a corner and began firing embarrassing questions about campaign finances at him. A stunned Eisenhower finally broke free and later told Hagerty: "I'll never do that again." He kept his word. During his eight years as President, Eisenhower almost never granted an interview to a member of the working press. His Cabinet tended to follow his example.

Another reality was television, which by 1953 was profoundly altering the balance of power between the President and the printed media. Television offered Eisenhower an alternative way to reach the people, one beautifully suited to his personal magnetism. Once Hagerty persuaded Eisenhower to open his press conferences to television, the bargaining power of newspapermen hit an all-time low. (Eisenhower's news conferences were filmed for later showing on television, with the White House retaining a theoretical veto power over the material; Kennedy was the first President to submit to live television coverage of his news conferences.)

A third new reality was Hagerty himself. His toughness, imagination, and zeal would soon make him the most effective—and, historically, the most important—of all the presidential Press Secretaries. Truman's Charlie Ross and Kennedy's Pierre Salinger were better liked, Roosevelt's Steve Early and Johnson's Bill Moyers had fuller understandings of public issues, but it was the tough-talking Irishman Jim Hagerty who would have the biggest impact on the delicate relationship between the President and the press.

He was the first presidential Press Secretary to be, both by instinct and experience, more of a professional public-relations man than a newspaperman. The homely, stocky, chain-smoking, hard-drinking Hagerty looked and talked like a character out of *The Front Page*, but his instincts toward news manipulation and techniques of mass psychology were as smooth and sophisticated as any Madison Avenue executive. He had spent eight years as a political reporter for the New York *Times*, where his father, James A. Hagerty, was a longtime political writer. But in 1943, the thirty-four-year-old Hagerty quit the *Times* to accept a better-paying job as Governor Tom Dewey's press secretary. He said the move was only temporary, but he had been with Dewey through nine years and two presidential campaigns when Dwight D. Eisenhower returned to the U.S. to run for President. Hagerty, having handled press relations for the Republican candidate of 1944 and 1948, was an obvious candidate to take over as Eisenhower's press chief.

It was Hagerty's achievement, during his eight years as Press Secretary, to manage the news to an unprecedented degree, and still maintain the confidence and good will of the regular White House correspondents. The primary reason he was able to do this was his unsurpassed mastery of detail.

Ninety percent of a Press Secretary's job is concerned not with policy but with endless routine: seeing that speeches and press releases are issued well in advance; arranging the press corps' travel plans on presidential trips; finding out what the President gave the First Lady for Christmas, and so forth. On such things Hagerty was unbeatable. A White House reporter compared him and Roosevelt's highly regarded Press Secretary, Steve Early, this way: "Early could give you a long think-piece on the Administration's attitude toward the gold standard. Hagerty knows just what makes a good still picture, the exact amount of lighting needed for television, and exactly when to break up a press conference in order to make deadlines for home editions on the East Coast."

On Eisenhower's frequent travels around the nation and the world, Hagerty saw to it that the White House press corps got red carpet treatment. He "advanced" the entire 22,000 miles and eleven nations of Eisenhower's December, 1959, trip to Europe and Asia, and on his return gave the departing reporters a thirty-seven-page, hour-by-hour itinerary. He would not only investigate such obvious matters as the availability of telephones and hotel accommodations, he would also find out where reporters could get their laundry done and whether the local voltage would power their electric razors. Hagerty sometimes filed stories for drunk reporters on campaign trains, and legend had it that he once stood on the railroad track in front of a campaign train to keep it from leaving the station until all the reporters were aboard. Newspapermen are not accustomed to such treatment, and in exchange for it they were willing to forgive Hagerty a great deal.

From where Hagerty sat, the key fact about Eisenhower as President was that—because of his illnesses, because of his vacations, because of his restricted concept of the presidency—he was not making much news. It became Hagerty's job to fill the void with manufactured news. He did this in several ways. He perfected a news-making device that came to be called "woodworking"—from Hagerty's good-humored line, "Boy, I sure had to dig into the woodwork for that one." Woodworking was the art of uncovering minor announcements—cost-of-living statistics, grants-in-aid, planned conferences, etc.—and having them made by the President, on slow days at the White House, instead of by the agencies involved. Over the years, the effect of Hagerty's woodworking was to give the casual newspaper reader an impression of ceaseless activity by the President; what Richard Rovere called "the spectacle, novel in the history of the presidency, of a man strenuously in motion yet doing essentially nothing."

Hagerty's supply of trivia was equaled, of course, only by the press's demand for it. During Eisenhower's 1959 visit to London, the Press Secretary informed 400 of the world's leading journalists:

"I have one bit of hard news. Mr. Berding [the State Department press officer] was asked this morning if the President was sleeping in a four-poster bed, and the answer is yes, and also if he had ever slept before in a four-poster bed, and the answer is also yes."

Hagerty's straight-faced renditions of such nonsense inspired a famous Art Buchwald column:

Q. "Jim, whose idea was it for the President to go to sleep?"
A. "It was the President's idea."
Q. "Did the President speak to anyone before retiring?"
A. "He spoke to the Secretary of State."
Q. "What did he say to the Secretary of State?"
A. "He said, 'Good night, Foster.'"
Q. "And what did the Secretary say to the President?"
A. "He said, 'Good night, Mr. President.'"

Hagerty, whose virtues did not include a sense of humor, was furious when he read this parody. He told a press conference it was "unadulterated rot" and in no way resembled anything he had ever said. He barred Buchwald from future press briefings and vowed to "get even with the *Tribune*," i.e., Buchwald's employer, the New York *Herald-Tribune*. Hagerty demanded equal space for a rebuttal, and the *Tribune* was delighted to give it to him. Arthur Krock commented that the Press Secretary seemed to be suffering from "caput magnus Potomacus," or "Potomac big head."

Another of Hagerty's techniques was called "blanketing"—manufacturing a favorable story to draw attention away from an unfavorable one. For example, in 1955, Sherman Adams ordered Secretary of the Air Force Harold Talbott to resign because of an apparent conflict of interest. With this unsavory affair about to hit the front pages, Hagerty

summoned five scientists to the White House to make a timely announcement of plans for America's first earth satellite. As a result,
although Talbott's resignation was carried under a one-column headline
on the New York *Times*' front page, it was "blanketed" by the satellite
story's five-column headline, half-page picture, and two related stories.

The reason Hagerty was able to dominate so completely the Administration's news output was that Eisenhower considered him—correctly—to be a genius in the art of public relations and therefore gave
him full trust and support. Hagerty attended Cabinet meetings and
spoke up vigorously on matters related to publicity, and the Cabinet
officials usually followed his advice. Hagerty had, by Eisenhower's
second term, his hand-picked men in charge of public relations at the
government's two biggest news sources, the Departments of State and
Defense. He was able to place himself, to an unprecedented degree,
in between reporters and governmental sources of information. For
reporters, the choice was often Hagerty—or nothing. His simplistic
version of controversial issues would be the only one available. One
newspaperman complained: "When the recession was on, I wanted to
talk to the group responsible for planning public works. I thought it
would be useful to know their outlook and the problems they faced.
They're in the White House so I went through Hagerty. For months
and months I tried to see someone. I never got past Hagerty."

Perhaps the central fact about the relationship between the White
House and the press is that no rules govern it. The President and his
aides do not have to cooperate with the press; the press does not have
to publicize the President. The relationship is based upon mutual
need, with hostility never far beneath the surface; it is a no man's
land of power and personality, bluff and bluster, experience and ex-
pedience. Hagerty understood this, and when he could not get his way
by other means, he was willing to pressure and intimidate the press.
His hot temper was real enough, but reporters thought he exaggerated
it to discourage unwanted questions. Once when a reporter wrote
that Eisenhower had exceeded the legal limit on a fishing excursion,
Hagerty roared at him: "From now on all you get is ——!" His power
to shut the doors to government news sources made it a meaningful
threat. His response to Buchwald's parody—barring the writer from
news briefings, calling Buchwald's editors to protest—was another instance of his pressure tactics. He ruled out most questions about Eisenhower's private life; when a reporter asked about the timing of the
polio shots for the President's family, Hagerty declared "That's out of
bounds and you know it." Because he was tough and because he held

most of the cards, Hagerty was able to enforce a very narrow, self-serving definition of what was and was not news about the President.

Hagerty's critics complained that the Press Secretary was unable to discuss national or international issues in any depth. They said Hagerty's genius did not extend beyond the realm of public relations; he was interested in affairs of state only insofar as they related to his job: to make Eisenhower look good. The end justified the means. He once told a reporter, laughingly, that if a certain story broke the wrong way: "We'll deny it—and then we'll deny the denial if we have to." He happened to have made a career of working for Republicans, but he tended to view domestic politics as a rather silly game: "They slap us, we slap them." As Eisenhower's spokesman, he once characterized a joint political statement by Harry S Truman and Adlai Stevenson as "a tale told by an idiot, full of sound and fury, signifying nothing"—and then attributed MacBeth's famous lines to *As You Like It*.

Hagerty's influence reached a peak in the weeks following Eisenhower's September, 1955, heart attack. Eisenhower had been vacationing in Colorado for six weeks when he was stricken at 2:45 A.M. on Saturday, September 24, as he slept in his mother-in-law's Denver home. Mrs. Eisenhower summoned the President's personal physician, Major General Howard Snyder, who immediately recognized symptoms of a heart attack. However, after treating the President, Dr. Snyder decided not to make known the nature of the illness immediately. News of the heart attack might upset Mrs. Eisenhower, he feared, or even cause excitement that would endanger the President. So that morning he told Acting Press Secretary Murray Snyder (Hagerty's assistant; no relation to Dr. Snyder) that the President had suffered a "digestive upset." Snyder passed this inaccurate information along to the press at 8 A.M.

By 2 P.M., the doctors had decided the President should be hospitalized, and at that time Dr. Snyder told the Acting Press Secretary the truth about the President's attack. Murray Snyder called his boss, Hagerty, at his home in Washington. Both men realized that the presidential circle stood in danger of severe press criticism for the twelve-hour delay in making known the heart attack. They agreed that a policy of maximum candor was imperative from that point forward. Snyder broke the news of the heart attack to the press at 3 P.M. as Hagerty was hurrying to catch a plane for Denver.

Eisenhower and Hagerty had several times talked about the possibility of Eisenhower's becoming seriously ill, and they had agreed that in such an emergency the government would have to follow a policy of complete disclosure. Hagerty recalled later: "When I arrived at Denver, I was armed ahead of time by the talks we'd had. We'd discussed what had happened to the country when [Woodrow] Wilson was sick, and the President had said, 'Jim, don't let that happen to me.'"

He arrived in Denver that night via Air Force Constellation and hastened to Fitzsimons General Hospital, where he was met with a scene of near chaos. Reporters were everywhere in corridors and waiting rooms. Rumor fed on rumor; tension on tension. The President was dead or dying. The President could not possibly run again. Nixon and Adams were struggling for control of the government. The national impact of the crisis was seen the next Monday when the stock market fell to its lowest point since the 1929 crash.

Dr. Snyder informed Hagerty that the President had told him: "Tell Jim to take over and make the decisions and handle the story." From the first, Hagerty was in complete command of the flow of news from Denver and to a large extent of the decisions that created the news. He was Eisenhower's only authorized spokesman and for nearly a week the only government official to see him. Hagerty's important achievement during those crucial weeks was to shrewdly and skillfully handle the news of Eisenhower's recovery on two distinct levels. The first level was personal, medical, and literal: the story of a sixty-five-year-old man recovering from a heart attack. The other level was public, political, and symbolic: the story of a national and international leader resuming the powers of command.

On the first level, Hagerty completely reversed his prior policy of reticence about the President's personal life. The press was deluged with details about every aspect of the President's waking and sleeping hours. The press was informed of Eisenhower's bowel movements (because, heart specialist Dr. Paul Dudley White told a press conference, "The country is so bowel-minded anyway.") and the exact number of hours he spent under his oxygen tent; in time, the press was told whether Eisenhower ate whole-wheat or white toast, the titles of the first records he heard ("Clair de Lune," "To a Wild Rose," "The Merry Widow," "Songs My Mother Taught Me," Beethoven's *Minuet No. 2 in G*) and the first book he read (Arthur Conan Doyle's *Sir Nigel*). Hagerty pored through medical books until he became a minor authority on heart disease. He missed his son's wedding rather than leave the President's side. He rewrote the doctors' three-a-day medical bulletins to achieve maximum clarity and, within the realm of honesty, maximum optimism.

Given the underlying fact of Eisenhower's amazing physical stamina, Hagerty was soon able to paint a favorable picture of a heart-attack victim moving toward recovery. But that was only part of Hagerty's job. At the same time, he and all other Eisenhower intimates were desperately seeking to convey the impression not only of a man regaining his health, which Eisenhower was, but of a President resuming the duties of office, which he was not in any meaningful sense. Such an impression was imperative if Eisenhower was to be renominated and re-elected the next year. At this point Hagerty encountered the confusing fact that presidential leadership is as much a matter of intangibles as of tangibles, as much shadow as substance. What a President does may matter much less than what the people think he is doing. For Hagerty to achieve his political ends, it was necessary for him to transform what were small steps in Eisenhower's physical recovery into significant steps toward his political recovery. A presidential letter had to be more than a letter, a bedside conference more than a talk. It was necessary, in short, for Hagerty to move beyond the literal level of his medical briefings into the more challenging realm of political symbolism.

This phase of the Denver drama began on September 29 when Hagerty announced that Eisenhower was about to perform his first official duty since the heart attack. He would write his initials—D.E. —on two lists of routine State Department appointments. The next day Hagerty dramatically announced that the President had signed *his full name*—Dwight D. Eisenhower—to the documents. Apparently the decision for the President to sign his full name, not just his initials, was Eisenhower's own, and in its small way it was a masterstroke—a little corny perhaps, but still spine-tingling when one imagines the old soldier, flat on his back, cut off from all other communication, grasping the pen and with that extra effort showing the world he was still in the fight.

In the next few days, Hagerty announced Eisenhower's signing of several more routine documents, but he and Adams agreed that the President's dispatching of letters and documents from his sickroom only underscored his state of disability. A better way to convey to the public an impression of a President resuming the burdens of office, they thought, was for leading Administration officials to visit Eisenhower for conferences on governmental affairs.

As soon as the doctors would consent to it, a procession of government officials to Fitzsimons Hospital began. There were several reasons for these pilgrimages, of course; they were good therapy for the patient, and good therapy for the anxious officials. Most importantly, they conveyed to the electorate an impression—a highly exaggerated impression—that the stricken President was once again directing the ship of state.

The first visitor was Vice President Nixon on October 8, and he was followed by Secretary Dulles and the rest of the Cabinet in the weeks ahead. Each visitor, upon emerging from the President's hospital room, would be led by Hagerty to a press conference. These press conferences, thoughtful observers soon realized, were both unprecedented and exquisitely staged productions. Unprecedented because in normal times no one imagined that reporters had a right to cross-examine Cabinet members about their private conversations with the President.

That the press conferences were carefully staged was clear. Attorney General Herbert Brownell, for instance, after a twenty-five minute visit with Eisenhower, announced presidential approval of a detailed seven-point program to improve the federal courts. Alert reporters noted that parts of the program had been announced weeks earlier; in any event it defied belief that the Attorney General would fly halfway across the country to the stricken President's bedside to talk about courthouse regulations. The problem was that the real significance of these visits—the expressions of confidence and loyalty between the President and Cabinet members, in what would have been a time of grave governmental crisis had that confidence not existed—was intangible. The public needed hard evidence that all was well, and such beautifully mundane matters as new courthouse rules sufficed nicely.

There was scattered criticism that Hagerty was using the press conferences to mislead the public. (Hagerty's case was not helped when he was seen giving one Cabinet member a prepared statement on the President's appearance before the man went in to see the President.) Hagerty had a ready reply to his critics: "Sure, those press conferences were unusual, but we put them on for a very simple reason. The President was getting better and we wanted to show he was taking up the reins. That was important not only for our country but for all the world."

Hagerty's tireless and forthright handling of the heart attack brought his standing with the press to an all-time high. Unfortunately, most of this good will was soon lost by his evasive policies on news of the

President's ileitis operation of June 9, 1956. Hagerty gave a reason for being less candid about the second illness: "A President's heart attack is the property of the people. But we did not consider the ileitis something that endangered the President's life."

One moves closer to the truth by noting, first, that the ileitis operation came with the 1956 Republican National Convention only two months away. Hagerty was under tremendous pressures to put the best possible face on the President's condition lest his renomination be lost. Moreover, while every American understood the severity of a heart attack, few had ever heard of ileitis or had any idea how serious it was. (It is an inflammation of the lower part of the small intestine, of unknown origin, and can be fatal unless relieved.) After Eisenhower's successful operation, a temptation existed for Hagerty to minimize the seriousness of the President's condition. Hagerty compared the President to a man who had suffered a bad cold and Secretary Dulles spoke of the President's "indisposition"—odd terms to use about a sixty-five-year-old man who has undergone major abdominal surgery.

Hagerty refused to make Eisenhower's doctors as accessible as they had been after the heart attack, yet he continued to flood the press with details. The President had taken his first steps . . . he had signed twenty-seven documents . . . he had eaten a soft-boiled egg and buttered toast. It was beginning to dawn on the press that a multitude of little facts could be used to obscure the absence of big facts. One reporter noted later: "In the ileitis case, when we wanted to find out about the possibility of recurrence, he refused to produce the doctors. Just because he was giving out so many other details, it was impossible to make a convincing case that we weren't getting important information."

Cabell Phillips wrote: "Hagerty attempted subtly and by implication . . . to minimize the seriousness of the President's attack and the possible effects of his illness on his future vigor and well-being. Within three days of the President's operation, he sought to impress on reporters that the President was resuming limited but important functions of his office. The reporters remained skeptical. . . ."

The New Republic's T.R.B. wrote angrily: "The ileitis-is-good-for-you pitch got a little too thick last week even for the White House hucksters. They finally toned it down to the extent of conceding that the President, even though back on the job at the White House, could not be said to have recovered fully from his operation. He was, as they put it, still convalescent. This is a spectacular reversal. Every day in every way, so Jim Hagerty said, the President had been getting better and better. He felt better now than he had after his heart attack, and everybody already knew how much better he felt after his heart attack than he ever had before it."

As in the heart attack recovery, every effort was made to dramatize the President's return to his official duties. Marquis Childs wrote: "It seemed that the patient had hardly come out from under the anesthetic when he was reported by Hagerty as conferring with Dulles and members of the White House staff." Hagerty was credited with persuading Eisenhower to make a non-essential trip to an OAS conference in Panama, only three weeks after he left the hospital, because the trip would dramatically demonstrate the President's physical fitness.

But if Hagerty came under fire for his handling of the ileitis operation, he had done his part in achieving the desired end: Despite two serious illnesses in less than a year, Eisenhower was renominated by acclamation and re-elected in a landslide.

During the second term, Hagerty's control over the press corps began to loosen a bit, and he and the Administration seemed to be easing up on their image-polishing efforts. Examples of this were seen during Eisenhower's two-week vacation at Secretary Humphrey's Georgia plantation in February, 1958. Throughout the fortnight, no pretense was made that Eisenhower was engaged in government affairs. There was no woodworking, no reports of telephone calls to Dulles. Hagerty simply had no news. Reporters saw the President only once, as he and Humphrey were starting out for a morning of quail shooting.

Toward the end of the vacation, the reporters were told that Eisenhower would fly back to Washington via Phoenix, Arizona, so he could drop Mrs. Eisenhower off at Elizabeth Arden's beauty resort. Hagerty, closely questioned by reporters about the propriety of such a government-financed detour, lost his temper. The trip was no business of the press, he declared; Eisenhower could fly where he pleased "because he's President of the United States." If Eisenhower knew of this criticism, he ignored it, for he flew to Phoenix, deposited his wife with Elizabeth Arden, and got in a round of golf before returning to Washington. During Eisenhower's first term, the White House reporters would probably not have had the courage to raise the issue of the Phoenix detour. But the mood of the press and the nation was changing a bit, and with the coming of the Adams-Goldfine case a few months later, a tempest of press criticism of the Administration would finally begin.

One of Hagerty's important contributions came in a memorandum he gave to the President in December, 1958, urging him to undertake worldwide travels during his last year in office.

The memo resulted from conversations between Hagerty and the President over a period of several months. Adams was gone, Dulles was dying (he died in May, 1959), and Hagerty's influence was proportionately greater. Hagerty perhaps viewed the proposed travels mainly in terms of "image"—he knew that Eisenhower possessed a vast reservoir of international good will, and he wanted to see it translated into acclaim for Eisenhower and into votes for the Republican candidate in 1960. Eisenhower's thoughts were no doubt on a higher plane, but he too believed he should do something to dramatize his own— and the world's—hopes for international peace. They discussed the matter many times, and finally Eisenhower asked Hagerty to write a summary of their discussions and his own recommendations.

The main thrust of Hagerty's memorandum was that Eisenhower should dramatize, in his final two years in office, his international standing as a "Man of Peace."

Specifically, he should move on three fronts. First, he should appear at the United Nations more often. Second, he should undertake worldwide travels, beginning with a trip to India. Third, he should welcome face-to-face meetings with Russian Premier Khrushchev.

Because Eisenhower was a lame-duck President, Hagerty continued, the nation and the world would recognize his actions as sincere and non-political. At the same time, his efforts on behalf of peace would inevitably assist the Republican candidate for President in 1960—indeed, they might make that election a ratification of the achievements of Eisenhower's two terms.

Hagerty pushed particularly hard on the trip to India. Eisenhower had a standing invitation to visit that country from Prime Minister Nehru. And if Eisenhower agreed to visit India, Hagerty knew, it would inevitably mean visits to many other friendly nations along the way. As it turned out, of course, Eisenhower's triumphant visit to India in December, 1959, was part of a 22,000 mile tour of eleven nations. This trip, and Eisenhower's other tours during his final years in office, and Premier Khrushchev's visit to this country in September, 1959, were all personal victories for Eisenhower (and to some extent, Hagerty) over a State Department that frowned on "personal diplomacy" and believed fiercely that diplomacy should be left to the diplomats. Dulles had vigorously opposed such political pageantry by the President.

Hagerty scored many successes as Press Secretary, yet there was one important area in which he—and Eisenhower—failed, and were hurt by their failure. Eisenhower in eight years had very few private conversations with reporters and columnists. The press had access to the President through his televised press conferences, and that was all. In time, the regular White House correspondents came to accept their lack of access to the President, and their occasional grumbles did not do the Administration much harm. But higher up in the journalistic hierarchy are men like Walter Lippmann, James Reston, Joseph Alsop, Marquis Childs, Drew Pearson, Richard Rovere, and Walter Krock, men who—if not accorded the deference they have come to expect from Presidents—can do a President much harm. Eisenhower ignored these men, and they, over the years, have done much to lower the nation's opinion of his presidency.

It may be that the columnists would not have thought or written any more favorably of Eisenhower if they had been given access to him. Yet everyone who has ever dealt with Eisenhower testifies to the immense personal impact of the man. It is possible to disagree with him, but it is impossible to doubt his honesty, his good will, his strength of character. Columnists are human, and they tend to think more highly of public leaders who seek their company and listen to their advice. A much less personable President than Eisenhower, Lyndon B. Johnson, has by virtue of favors and flattery managed to transform several syndicated columnists into semiofficial spokesmen for the White House Press Office. But—and it must have been immensely frustrating for Hagerty, the master of public relations—Eisenhower firmly refused to change his policy toward the working press.

Eisenhower relented just a little in his last year and agreed to hold several dinners for leading Washington correspondents. But it was too little, too late. The President and the press had been apart too long to come together gracefully; the dinners were stilted, and marked by the outcries of those who had not been invited.

Hagerty does not argue with this view, for he well understands the opinion-making power of the leading writers and columnists. He simply points out that he did all he could to bring the President and the press closer together, and notes that his greatest thrust was to make the fullest possible use of a new medium, television.

Washington correspondents generally agree that Hagerty was the most formidable, and most efficient, news manager of all the White House Press Secretaries. The point is certainly not that Hagerty was more venal than other Press Secretaries, only that he was more powerful. Roosevelt, Truman, Kennedy, and Johnson had all dealt with the press for decades before entering the White House, and all rightly felt that they could more skillfully persuade, inform, or deceive the press, as the case demanded, than their Press Secretaries.

Eisenhower was different. He disliked the cajolery, the deception, the self-promotion of press relations, and he was happy to delegate it all to Hagerty, as he delegated political affairs to Adams. Given Eisenhower's full trust, given Eisenhower's immense popularity, given his own technical skill and unsentimental outlook, Hagerty was able to become a news czar with unprecedented control over the public's "right to know."

Yet there was a certain rugged honesty about Hagerty's relations with the press. Hagerty would rarely prevaricate; he would simply tell reporters that certain matters were none of their damn business. Similarly, Eisenhower did not deceive reporters; he just wouldn't talk to them.

In the 1960s, some reporters, to their considerable surprise, found themselves looking back with a bit of nostalgia to the Eisenhower era, for they were confronted with one President who was fascinated by the endless subtleties of news manipulation, and another, less subtle President who viewed the press with open contempt. News management largely moved from the Press Secretary's Office across the hall to the President's office, and Hagerty's successors tended to be uninformed technicians or informed apologists (in Bill Moyers' case).

During the 1960s, after Hagerty had become a vice president of the American Broadcasting Company, there occurred throughout Washington a proliferation of government by handout, of public-relations techniques, of grandstanding and gimmickry, as must have shocked even Hagerty. Worst of all, while news management ran wild, no other Press Secretary ever came along who was fit to carry Jim Hagerty's coat when it came to getting a press release out on time.

V. THE KENNEDY STAFF

1. *The Band of Brothers*

John Kennedy's White House staff, despite the brevity of its time in office, was in some respects the most powerful, the most significant, and the most interesting of the five under consideration here. Powerful—because not since Roosevelt had there been a President so distrustful of the bureaucracy and so willing to let his personal aides prod, double-check, and bypass it. Significant—because in two major cases, McGeorge Bundy's National Security office and Larry O'Brien's Congressional Relations office, Kennedy reshaped and perfected presidential institutions of far-reaching importance. Interesting—because not since Roosevelt had a President attracted so many talented, ambitious, and strong-willed men, men whose dedication to their President was often equaled by their disaffection for one another.

The members of Kennedy's inner circle were, first and last, men of ability. As a group, they were not as glamorous as some writers have made them seem; as individuals they were often not terribly endearing; and several are of no particular interest either before or after their time in the White House. But during their thousand days of power, each was admirably cast for the role Kennedy gave him to play.

Unlike Truman and Johnson, who entered the presidency unexpectedly, and unlike Eisenhower, who returned from Europe to run for President, Kennedy had been carefully selecting his White House staff for years before he actually took office. As a result, there existed between him and his staff a rapport unique in White House history. His aides were not, like FDR's, constantly in the dark about his intentions. They were not, like Truman's, split into sharp liberal-conservative political cliques. They were not, like Eisenhower's dominated by a powerful chief of staff. Nor were they, like Johnson's men, often in fear of outbursts of presidential temper.

Nor was Kennedy's staff bothered by the generational gap that existed between other Presidents and most of their aides. Kennedy was young, and most of his men were his contemporaries, or not much younger. This resulted in an ease of communications between them, an informality, a common style. Yet there was never any doubt about who was boss. Kennedy had been a leader all his life, he had been in Congress for fourteen years, and he knew more about politics than his political advisers, more about foreign affairs than his national security chief, more about press relations than his Press Secretary. What he wanted, and got, were men who understood his style and his goals, and who could represent his interests in political and governmental affairs as he himself would have handled them if he had the time.

Kennedy was himself a generalist—an educated man, not a trained man—and his top aides were also generalists. Ted Sorensen was simply a young lawyer with Capitol Hill experience, but Kennedy valued his judgment and sought it on everything from farm policy to nuclear war. Similarly, McGeorge Bundy was made boss of the NSC staff—and considered for Secretary of State—with no more tangible qualifications than having been an excellent dean at Harvard. Kennedy had the generalist's suspicion of specialists and experts, especially the bureaucratic variety, and his worst fears were confirmed after experts helped lead him to disaster at the Bay of Pigs.

Kennedy's was a small staff, smaller by far than either Eisenhower's or Johnson's. Kennedy believed in holding all the strings of government in his own hands just as devoutly as Eisenhower believed in delegation of work—and of course neither man lived up to his belief entirely. Kennedy was at his best in crises, and the distinguishing mark of all the key crises was the presidential command post with Kennedy making the big decisions and many smaller ones as well.

"There aren't ten men in this country whose judgment I trust," a leading New Frontiersman once told me, and his was the prevailing view. Strangers were suspect; trust was hard-won. So Kennedy's remained a small staff, an overburdened elite, men whose ability had been tested. Knowing his men as he did, Kennedy could delegate authority to them with no fear that they would go against his interests or outshine him. He was a secure President; unlike Roosevelt and Johnson, he did not begrudge his men their press clippings. When the press made much of McGeorge Bundy's importance, Kennedy commented dryly, but not

THE KENNEDY STAFF   197

angrily: "I will continue to have some residual functions." The best statement of what Kennedy expected of his staff was made, not surprisingly, by the man who served him longest as a senior adviser, Theodore Sorensen:

"He knew that it was humanly impossible for him to know all that he would like to know, see everyone who deserved to be seen, read all that he ought to read, write every message that carried his name, and take part in all meetings affecting his plans. He also knew that in his Administration, Cabinet members could make recommendations on major matters, but only the President could make decisions; and that he could not afford to accept, without seeking an independent judgment, the products and proposals of departmental advisers whose responsibility did not require them to look, as he and his staff looked, at the government and its programs as a whole. He required a personal staff, therefore—one that represented *his* personal ways, means and purposes—to summarize and analyze those products and proposals for him, to refine the conflicting views of various agencies, to define the issues which he had to decide, to help place his personal imprint upon them, to make certain that practical political facts were never overlooked, and to enable him to make his decisions on the full range of *his* considerations and constituencies, which no Cabinet member shared."

Kennedy gave his men considerable trust and authority; in turn he received from them a high degree of personal loyalty. The fact that all his major aides were still with him when he was killed contrasts rather pointedly with the turnover on Lyndon Johnson's staff during its first few years. This was true, despite the fact that Johnson showers gifts, praise, and dinner invitations on his aides, and Kennedy did none of those things. One man who served both Presidents recalls: "I must have had dinner with Johnson a hundred times, and if you told me Sorensen never once had dinner with Kennedy, I'd believe it. Kennedy was more reserved, a strange man, he never asked you for anything, but he got absolute loyalty. It reminds me of what Freud said, that the great leader is often aloof from other men."

The loyalty ran both ways, and Kennedy's men knew they could count on his support in moments of stress.* He defended Bundy when he was

* There was another, almost feudal dimension to Kennedy's loyalty to his people. Those who served him faithfully were taken care of even if they had outlived their original usefulness. Ted Reardon, Kennedy's Administrative Assistant during his three terms in the House, stayed on through the White House years although his relative importance dwindled sharply. David Powers, who had volunteered to help Kennedy in his first political campaign, was on the payroll primarily because he amused the President. John (Muggsy) O'Leary, Kennedy's chauffeur and errand-runner in the Senate, was put on the Secret Service payroll, but his services re-

criticized for membership in a fashionable whites-only club in Washington; he defended Pierre Salinger when a Republican Congressman attacked him for dabbling in local politics; he defended Arthur Schlesinger when he was under fire for a fully clothed plunge into Robert Kennedy's swimming pool. "Congressmen are always advising Presidents to get rid of presidential advisers," he told a news conference in defending Salinger. "That is one of the most constant threads that runs through American history."

When Ted Sorensen apologized to him for stirring up trouble with a speech he made in his native Nebraska, Kennedy joked: "I don't mind. They can criticize *you* all they like." More seriously, he advised Sorensen when they entered the White House: "Every man that's ever held a job like yours—Sherman Adams, Harry Hopkins, House, all the rest —has ended up in the ————. Congress was down on them or the President was hurt by them or somebody was mad at them. The best way to stay out of trouble is to stay out of sight."

But it was not easy to stay out of sight, for Kennedy's was the most publicized White House staff in history. And, it should be said, much of what was written about them was awful nonsense. It was the good fortune of Kennedy's staff to become caught up in the glow that Kennedy and his wife brought to the White House—the New Frontier spirit and, later, the retrospective aura of Camelot. In fact, Kennedy's aides were efficient men, with nothing at all Camelotian about them. Permanent members of the White House staff found Kenneth O'Donnell's curt, abrasive manner indistinguishable from that of Sherman Adams. Bundy was a Beacon Hill Republican who might just as easily have been on Eisenhower's staff. Sorensen was a silent young man from Nebraska who seemed to dislike cocktail parties and most people. O'Brien was a shrewd, genial Irish politician who fit easily into the Johnson Administration when it took power. Evelyn Lincoln, Kennedy's secretary, was a plain, unsophisticated, kindhearted woman, indistinguishable in appearance from a thousand congressional secretaries. Yet somehow the whole was greater than its parts—and the reason was the Kennedy

mained personal to Kennedy. O'Leary's services included shagging golf balls for Kennedy on the White House lawn.

After Kennedy's death, Reardon entered private business in Washington, Powers was given a post with the Kennedy Library, and O'Leary remained in the service of Mrs. Kennedy. Probably the word "crony" was never used to describe Kennedy's entourage, but one can imagine the outcry if LBJ had employed a Powers or an O'Leary. As Harry Vaughan, a crony of yesteryear, puts it, one man's crony is another man's valued companion.

magic. David Powers, Kennedy's old Boston retainer, put it best: "He made everybody around him look ten feet tall. Now he's gone and they're shrinking."

Typical of the nonsense written about Kennedy's staff (by a man who writes very little nonsense) was columnist Joseph Kraft's declaration that its members "dazzled the nation by intellectual brilliance and social swank." Let us consider how some leading Kennedy aides in fact rate on the brilliance/swank scale:

Aide	Brilliance?	Swank?
Bundy	Yes	Perhaps
Goodwin	Yes	No*
O'Brien	No†	No
O'Donnell	No	No
Salinger	No	No
Schlesinger	Yes	No
Sorensen	Yes	No

Brilliance and swank are less useful words to describe this group than cold, practical, at times ruthless. Kennedy's rhetoric appealed to American idealism, but he did not surround himself with idealists or reformers. O'Donnell and O'Brien were political operatives—the Irish Mafia. Sorensen started life as a crusading liberal, but in Kennedy's employ he became one of the most cautious liberals who ever lived. Bundy was a brainy opportunist. Schlesinger, the most liberal of them, was the least influential. Goodwin, who tried some crusading at the State Department, was banished to the Peace Corps.

As friendly an observer as Richard Rovere has written of the Kennedy circle: "There was not a reformer among them, as far as anyone could tell. Pragmatism—often of the grubbiest kind—was rampant." When the Kennedy Administration encountered a real reformer, Senator Estes Kefauver, who wanted to stop the drug industry from selling dangerous drugs at outrageous prices, and the Administration deemed this goal contrary to its political interests, it stabbed Kefauver in the back.

The members of Kennedy's staff were sometimes credited with a fraternal spirit that distinguished them from, say, the Roosevelt and Truman staffs. Kennedy encouraged this fiction with such touches as his frequent quoting of Shakespeare's "band of brothers" passage from

---

* Goodwin was once rather accurately described as looking like an Italian journalist with a hangover.

† O'Brien is a political genius but that is not the same as intellectual brilliance.

King Henry IV. Actually, as Kennedy well knew, his staff hummed with an undercurrent of jealousy, rivalry, and friction. It was less a band of brothers than an unlikely assemblage of strong-willed individualists who were held in delicate balance by two factors.

The first was that they were disciplined men, able to submerge their animosities in the interests of getting the job done. They knew Kennedy had little patience with bickering. When now and then one of them would complain to him about another's actions, he would frown and say they would just have to work it out among themselves. After Kennedy was gone, it would have been hard to find a group of men less inclined toward brotherhood. Their memoirs and public utterances were discreet (the staff, Sorensen writes, was not "wholly free from competitive feelings or from scornful references to each other's political or intellectual backgrounds") but their private conversations were replete with acid comments about each other's faults, real or imagined.*

The second fact that kept this band together was John Kennedy's exceptional skill in handling men. His ability to cajole, to persuade, to soothe, to inspire, was effortless, virtually invisible. He was, in the best sense of the term, a master manipulator of men. Two main factors perhaps accounted for this talent, even before it was perfected by his years in politics.

The more obvious one was that he had grown up rich and, more than that, celebrity-rich, an Ambassador's son, a friend of the mighty. Throughout his youth he was sought after: Other boys (and girls) wanted to visit his home, to ride in his car, to meet his family, to be his friend. He learned early to measure what others wanted from him against what he wanted from them, and he learned that in these unspoken social negotiations, he held all the cards.

Had this been all, he might have grown into just another arrogant, spoiled young millionaire. But there was, I think, another important influence: the fact that in his formative pre-teen and teen-age years Kennedy was constantly bullied, beaten up, and generally made miserable by his aggressive, pugnacious older brother, Joe, Jr. This experience

---

* Examples: "Pierre came to us with holes in his shoes." "O'Donnell a great liberal? O'Donnell's not a great anything." "Powers was nothing but a court jester—and not a very funny one at that." "The trouble with Ted was that he thought the way to solve a problem was to write a speech about it."

The last illusions of brotherhood were cast away when several of John Kennedy's key aides joined Robert Kennedy's campaign staff in the spring of 1968. The early successes of Kennedy's campaign were achieved despite the fact that two of his top writers, Sorensen and Goodwin, and two of his top political advisers, O'Brien and O'Donnell, were not speaking to one another. Moreover, most of these older advisers were only barely speaking to the newer, younger men from Kennedy's Senate staff.

taught Kennedy something he might otherwise never have learned: what it is like to be on the short end of life's stick, to be the underdog, to be the victim of power's arrogance.* If his father's money had made him a manipulator, his brother's bullying added to his dealings a certain gentleness, a sensitivity to the feelings of others that some observers have thought lacking in other members of his family.

Kennedy's skill with people was often needed to calm the troubled waters of his inner circle. He knew, for example, that Sorensen was disturbed by stories that he had submerged his own personality in Kennedy's; once when one of Kennedy's friends jibed at Sorensen, "Say, you're getting more like Jack than Jack himself," the President pulled the man aside and said, "Don't. He gets that from all sides." Kennedy understood that various of his aides found it intolerable to have to ask the permission of his cold-eyed Appointments Secretary, Ken O'Donnell, each time they wanted to see him, so he sanctioned an informal arrangement whereby the aides bypassed O'Donnell and entered his office via Evelyn Lincoln's office. He knew that some of his aides viewed Arthur Schlesinger with ill-concealed disdain, and he often went out of his way to bolster Schlesinger's bruised feelings. He never called staff meetings, knowing they would only bring differences into the open; instead, he relied on one-to-one dealings with each aide.

By taking this trouble—and it was not much trouble for a man of Kennedy's sure instincts—he was able to keep peace. Often he added to staff conflicts by giving the aides overlapping assignments (and some of them, in turn, got in the habit of double-checking presidential assignments with their colleagues to save themselves extra work) but he had a reason for this annoying practice: "I can't afford to confine myself to one set of advisers. If I did that *I* would be on *their* leading strings." So he sought the often-conflicting views of staff members like Sorensen, Bundy, and O'Donnell, and then he balanced them off against those of Cabinet members, Congressmen, journalists, and old friends, and out of the whole elaborate process he took in the profusion of ideas and information from which, in his own way, he would make his own decision.

The main significance of Kennedy's staff lies not in its glamor, or lack of it, or in its members' lack of affection for one another, but in the way Kennedy used the staff to help him run the government. His aides were,

* Kennedy's first biographer, James MacGregor Burns, wrote: "Even today when asked whether anything really bothered him as a child, Kennedy can think only of his big brother: 'He had a pugnacious personality. Later on it smoothed out but it was a problem in my boyhood.'"

first of all, independent sources of information for him. Beyond this, they were valued advisers, particularly after the Bay of Pigs disaster had wiped out Kennedy's faith in the "expert" advice of the military, intelligence, and foreign-policy establishments.* Bundy and Sorensen soon came to have influence on Kennedy's policy decisions at least equal to that of most Cabinet members. Finally, Kennedy used his staff as an instrument to control the bureaucracy and to try to bend it to his will. One question Kennedy's presidency raised—and lacked the time to answer—is whether the Goliath of American government can be made to move fast enough to stay abreast of a nation and a world changing with unprecedented speed.

Kennedy took office pledged to "get this country moving again" and rightly or wrongly he viewed the bureaucracy—the "permanent government," as Schlesinger calls it—as a major obstacle in his path. Throughout his presidency he was engaged in two highly visible confrontations —with Communists abroad and with conservatives in Congress—and in a third, no less bitter confrontation with the Executive Branch bureaucrats. All his major White House aides were caught up in this unheralded struggle: Bundy by wielding unprecedented power over the departments and agencies involved in foreign policy; Sorensen and his staff by overseeing the domestic side of the government; O'Brien by making sure the Cabinet departments didn't put their own legislative interests ahead of the President's; Salinger by doing the same where publicity was concerned; O'Donnell, Schlesinger, and Goodwin by acting as presidential troubleshooters throughout the bureaucracy.

It is of course as mistaken to generalize about bureaucrats as about Negroes or writers or any group. Some are brilliant, some dull, some lazy, some zealous. But as Kennedy's men took over the government, fully believing that the same relentless energy that had won the election could now revive the nation, they instinctively viewed the men of the permanent government as their natural adversaries. It astounded the New Frontiersmen that the civil servants were disinclined to work until ten at night and all day Saturday, that they were somehow immune to the magic of the moment. The bureaucrats, many of whom had started in government as New Dealers in 1933, viewed their new masters with skepticism based on long experience. In time, of course, many alliances were formed between the two sides.

* Kennedy's associates stress that the Pentagon and CIA "experts" gave him bad advice on the Bay of Pigs invasion, as indeed they did. Kennedy's apologists less often mention that the real question was not military but moral—should the U.S. sponsor an invasion of a small Latin American nation whose government it dislikes? —and it was not the experts' fault that Kennedy gave the wrong answer on that one.

The Johnson Administration's attitude toward the bureaucracy has been more conciliatory. Johnson has increased the number of top appointments to career civil servants, and he has gone out of his way to meet with career officials and give them a feeling of participation in his Administration. Yet to a large extent Johnson could use the carrot in dealing with the permanent government because Kennedy had already used the stick. Kennedy's men, by fighting the hard fights in 1961, had to a considerable degree gotten the permanent government moving in the desired direction, if not at the desired speed.

This was particularly true of Robert McNamara's takeover at the Defense Department and McGeorge Bundy's attempts to revitalize State Department. Johnson carried this progress forward, as Kennedy surely would have if he had lived, by spreading McNamara's management concepts throughout the government and by moving toward a Bundy-style White House staff to coordinate the domestic side of government.

Kennedy's approach to the presidency, in theory at least, was one of total immersion in the affairs of state. In reality, he was much less interested and involved in domestic affairs than is commonly thought. But certainly in the foreign-policy field he wanted to soak up all the details, read all the cables, know all the policy-makers, and pass on all the issues. Insofar as this was impossible, he wanted his trusted aides to do these things for him. They were not to be simply middlemen; they were to seek out problems and propose solutions. If an aide told Kennedy of a problem, but offered no remedy, the President would snap impatiently: "Yes, but what can I do about it?"

Kennedy's restless curiosity was widely admired, yet not all students of the presidency agree that total immersion is the ideal style of operation. Eisenhower would say that Kennedy should have delegated more details to others. Surprisingly, two leading New Dealers, Tom Corcoran and Ben Cohen, once expressed this view in a talk with Arthur Schlesinger:

Cohen: "One of FDR's great strengths was a certain detachment from the details of his Administration. He did not try to run everything himself, but he gave his people their head. Sometimes he was criticized for letting them go off too much and squabble among themselves. But this was his way of trying people out."

Corcoran: "Also it reduced his responsibility for their mistakes. Since he wasn't directly involved, he could wash his hands of bad policies more easily."

Cohen: "Then, when it mattered, he was always ready to weigh in and settle things. We often wished at the time that he would get involved earlier; but in retrospect I think he was right. I am afraid that your man (Kennedy) in contrast tried to run too many things himself. He has too tight a grip on his Administration. He is too often involved in the process of shaping things which should be shaped by others before they are presented to a President. I doubt very much whether the Bay of Pigs decision would have been made if the President had not taken part in the preliminary discussions—if he had been confronted in an uncommitted way with the final recommendation. Kennedy is really a President on the model not of Roosevelt but of Wilson. Wilson also tried to run too much himself."

Schlesinger comments that Cohen had a point, although he thinks he "underestimated the extent to which the hardening of the permanent government since Roosevelt's day required presidential intervention at an earlier stage, as well as the extent to which the irreversibility of decisions in the nuclear age compelled a President to make sure that small actions at a low level would not lead ineluctably to catastrophic consequences."

But the debate, as Schlesinger notes, is an impossible one, for every President must govern in his own fashion. Kennedy, to help him get the country moving in the desired direction, assembled in his White House a team of aides who, however diverse they were in background, had in common ability, ambition, and commitment to Kennedy's cause. Not the least interesting of them was the least influential of them, his personal secretary, Mrs. Evelyn Lincoln.

2. *A Dancer in White: Mrs. Lincoln*

John Kennedy, after making an urgent call to his personal secretary, Mrs. Evelyn Lincoln, once told Ted Sorensen with mingled awe and amusement: "Whatever I do or say, Mrs. Lincoln will be sweet and unsurprised. If I had said just now, 'Mrs. Lincoln, I have cut off Jackie's head, would you please send over a box?' she still would have replied, 'That's wonderful, Mr. President, I'll send it right away. . . . Did you get your nap?'"

Evelyn Lincoln, sweet and unsurprised, was at Kennedy's side from his first day in the Senate until the day he died. She was a fixture outside his office, with candy for the President's children and cigars for his aides (cigars that had been given to Kennedy but weren't his brand). Ted Sorensen wrote that her "unfailing devotion and good nature more than compensated for a sometimes overly possessive attitude." Schlesinger praised her "welcoming patience and warmth," a compliment he might have regretted when he saw her devastating comments on him in her book. Ken O'Donnell sometimes grumbled that in her wide-eyed way she demanded too much of the President's good nature—first, at her request, Kennedy got her husband a job as a congressional liaison man with the Veterans' Administration, then she often urged Kennedy to attend VA ceremonies.

But for the most part, not much attention was paid to Mrs. Lincoln. Not until 1965, when she published her memoir, *My Twelve Years with John F. Kennedy*, did her old associates in the White House learn that Mrs. Lincoln, in her quiet way, was as ambitious and determined as any of them. And in 1968, when Mrs. Lincoln's second book appeared, with its sharply unflattering portrait of Kennedy's successor, even Lyndon Johnson learned that the mild-looking Evelyn Lincoln was not a woman one might misuse with impunity.

She was not the sort of woman one might have expected Kennedy to choose for his secretary, not beautiful or witty. Rather, she was a pleasant, birdlike, unsophisticated woman, a bit girlish, easily made happy or unhappy—Zazu Pitts might have played her in a film—but highly efficient and totally dedicated to Kennedy. She symbolized the clear-cut line Kennedy kept between his political and personal lives. Off-duty, he was second to no man in his appreciation of glamorous women, but during office hours he preferred efficiency to pulchritude.

Nor did Mrs. Lincoln have the slightest influence over Kennedy's decisions, in the way that Missy LeHand had with Roosevelt. Beyond the normal powers of a secretary—to admit visitors and relay messages —she neither had nor sought influence. Kennedy did not ask her advice on people or policies, and she would not have dreamed of volunteering any. In fact, she says that even on the minor, feminine matters about which he did sometimes consult her—what color some new drapes should be, for instance—it amused him to ignore her advice: "He would say, 'Which do you like, Mrs. Lincoln, the green or the blue?' I knew what was coming. If I said the green, he'd choose the blue. He'd do it every time. At first it hurt my feelings, but it was just his way. He was so independent-minded."

Mrs. Lincoln, like many others of her sex who have worked for the Kennedys, believes they have a prejudice against working women and refuse to give them important responsibilities. "The White House was a man's world," Mrs. Lincoln sighs, and offers a theory for the alleged attitude: "Franklin Roosevelt had a domineering mother, so he turned to women for advice. But Kennedy had a dominant father, so he turned to men."

Kennedy enjoyed teasing Mrs. Lincoln; her naïveté was a perfect foil for his dry sophistication. Her Methodism, as contrasted to his Catholicism, was a favorite topic for banter. Yet she remained, along with Dean Rusk, one of the few subordinates Kennedy did not call by his or her first name. It was always Mrs. (pronounced "Miz") Lincoln.

Her main importance in the White House, aside from the fact that she was almost the only person who could decipher Kennedy's handwriting, was that she guarded one of the two entrances to his office. Ken O'Donnell, the official Appointments Secretary, presided over the other entrance. A system soon evolved whereby persons refused an audience with the President by O'Donnell would appeal to Mrs. Lincoln, often successfully. Also, members of the White House staff preferred to slip into the President's office via the Mrs. Lincoln route rather than ask permission from O'Donnell.

Soon the legend was born of a hardhearted O'Donnell turning away presidential visitors, only to have a softhearted Mrs. Lincoln spirit them in for an audience. No one denies that O'Donnell's heart is several degrees harder than Mrs. Lincoln's, but she is quick to say that was not the reason for her open-door policy. "I only did it because he wanted me to do it," she says. "It was his way, not mine." In effect, Kennedy used Mrs. Lincoln as an escape valve from O'Donnell's stern protectiveness. O'Donnell was extremely useful to him in turning away unwanted visitors, but it would have been intolerable for such men as Sorensen, Bundy, and O'Brien to have to ask O'Donnell's permission each time they wanted to see the President.

(It should be noted, if only in parenthetical contrast to Mrs. Lincoln's gentle nature, that women in government, if there is malice in their hearts, can have a devastating impact on the fortunes of the men they serve. A classic instance was that of a well-known New Frontiersman. This young man had received a promotion from "Special Assistant to the Secretary" to "Assistant Secretary" in the department where he worked. Among other things, the promotion entitled him to have his own private bathroom. It developed that the only way to add a bathroom to his office was to move a wall so that one of the three toilets in an adjacent ladies' room was made part of his office, and the ladies were left with only two toilets. This was done, with the young Assistant Secretary blissfully unaware of the injury he had in-

flicted on the secretaries of his and nearby offices. Soon strange things
began happening. His phone calls were not returned. His memos were
lost on the way to the White House. Word began to spread that
he was inexplicably on the skids, and a promising career seemed face-
to-face with disaster. Then, in the manner of one of those "you-
have-bad-breath" television commercials, some kind soul told him what
was wrong. That same day, he had workmen move back the offending
wall, the ladies reclaimed their original equipment, and the New Frontiersman's star was once again in ascension.)

And so it went, with Mrs. Lincoln distributing candy, cigars, and
small favors, and not until Kennedy was dead and she had written a
book did anyone know what a remarkable woman she is.

My Twelve Years with John F. Kennedy can be read on several
levels. As political history, it is largely an exercise in trivia, i.e., she
tells us how Roger Blough looked as he went into Kennedy's office
to break the news of the steel price increase. As a source of Kennedy
anecdotes, the book is valuable, since she was in a position to observe
many incidents that others missed. For example, she tells of Kennedy,
waiting in anguish for news of his dying infant son, remembering to
send a note and a check to the family of a slain Boston policeman.

She displays an occasional knack for sharp descriptive writing, as
when she notes that O'Donnell's "heels never seemed to touch the
ground," whereas O'Brien "walked on his heels instead of his toes."
(Which brings to mind Merriman Smith's observation that Schlesinger
walked slowly and leaning forward, and Bundy walked rapidly and
leaning backward, so that when Bundy passed Schlesinger they formed
in profile a perfect X.)

Her book is distinguished, too, by the fact that unlike those written
by Sorensen, Schlesinger, Salinger, Paul Fay, and William Manchester,
it was not censored by the Kennedy family. By the time the Kennedys
asked to see her book, it was already set in type. Thus, although
her book is far from critical of Kennedy, it does capture touches of
humanity not always present in all the others. Her Kennedy is a demanding boss, one who pitted his employees against one another, one who
was easily irritated, one who sometimes lost his temper and bawled
out innocent bystanders. In a dramatic highlight of her book she tells
how Kennedy tried to fire her after she had undergone a serious
operation—and then lacked the guts to go through with it.

The real heart of the book, however, is not what she tells about
Kennedy, but what she tells about herself. Other former Kennedy

aides, in writing of how they were drawn to his side, tend to talk in terms of public service and political philosophy. Mrs. Lincoln is more candid. She sought out John Kennedy, she makes clear, because he could make her wildest dreams come true; her association with him rescued her from the humdrum life of a childless, middle-class, middle-aging woman and fulfilled her lifelong yearning to be someone important, someone the world took note of. If her prose is often that of *True Confessions,* her passions are sometimes those of *Madame Bovary.* We know, at the end of the book, all we need to know about Evelyn Lincoln, and it is a fascinating insight. American literature is awash with the soul-searchings of Jewish intellectuals, Southern alcoholics, and sexually tormented college professors, but where else, in fact or fiction, can one peer into the heart and soul of one of those thousands of anonymous women who sit behind typewriters outside the offices of the mighty?

She came from Nebraska, where her father, like Ted Sorensen's father, was a Progressive politician and follower of Senator George Norris. Her father, J. N. Norton, served in the state legislature, was elected to Congress for one term, and finally took a job in Washington with the Department of Agriculture.

Her father's political successes brought little joy to young Evelyn Norton. She lived on the family farm, attended a one-room country school, and dreamed of a bigger, brighter world. "I remembered the dream I had so often while going to school from our home on the farm," she writes. "It was of myself—Evelyn Norton—as a famous ballet dancer. When I was about ten years old, I saw a motion picture of a ballet, and from then on I dreamed that someday I would be dressed in white, dancing for the whole world." Then: "My dreams of becoming a ballet dancer began to fade for lack of encouragement, and I was far from happy in high school."

Her father's election to Congress took her to Washington, D.C., where she met the first of the two men who would dominate her life: Harold Lincoln, then a law student, also from Nebraska, a kindly man whose misfortune it is to be nicknamed Abe. They were married during the war, and returned to Washington in the early 1950s when Abe took a job with a congressional staff. Mrs. Lincoln decided to seek a job on Capitol Hill so she could be near her husband.

Although she was a college graduate and had attended law school, she found that congressional offices wanted women only for clerical jobs. The best job she could find was as the number-three girl in a Georgia Congressman's office, a status she rightly regarded as one step up from slavery. She was determined to do better, and one day in mid-1952 she told Abe: "I'm going to work for the next President of the United States."

"Eisenhower will be mighty pleased to have your support," Abe joked, but she meant the one after Eisenhower.

But who would he be? After pondering the complexities of Democratic politics for a few weeks, she told Abe: "I've decided that it is going to be young Franklin D. Roosevelt, Jr., or the Congressman from Massachusetts, John F. Kennedy." A few weeks later she announced to Abe: "The man I'm hoping to work for, and the next President, after the one elected this fall, is John F. Kennedy."

Obviously, her next step was to get a job with Kennedy. In this endeavor, she was aided by two circumstances. First, Kennedy was then beginning his campaign against Senator Henry Cabot Lodge, and he needed all the help he could get. Second, it has always been the Kennedy technique to make maximum use of volunteers during campaigns. Afterward, most are kissed off with a form letter of thanks (thousands of such letters, framed, hang on Massachusetts walls) and the few who make a strong impression can be singled out for later use.

Mrs. Lincoln volunteered her services to Ted Reardon, Kennedy's Administrative Assistant, and soon she was going to Kennedy's office every evening after her regular job and typing until midnight. She got no pay or promise of future reward for this, yet her service was not without its joys. One night, after she had been there a few weeks: "The Congressman was there. All kinds of thoughts rushed through my mind. Will he see me? What shall I say to him? My typewriter faced the door to his office; he couldn't help but see me when he came out. Then I heard footsteps coming across the room. I bent over my typewriter and kept working, hoping at the last minute he would not notice me. But I was so curious to see him, I looked up and there he was standing in front of my typewriter."

Kennedy, unaware of the consternation on the other side of the typewriter, favored her with small talk (beginning with "What's your name?" and ending with "Close the door when you leave") and departed, presumably to escort Jacqueline to Rive Gauche while Mrs. Lincoln burned the midnight oil.

Mrs. Lincoln was heartbroken when the Georgia Congressman required her to spend the fall in his home district, ending her volunteer work for Kennedy. Several times she called long-distance to his Boston campaign headquarters, desperately seeking news, and finally she sent Kennedy a telegram of congratulations—the day before the election.

With Kennedy safely in the Senate, Mrs. Lincoln writes: "One of my prayers was answered, but what about the other one? I still hoped to find some little niche in Kennedy's office, and I kept hounding Ted Reardon. But everyone there was taking it easy." Including the Senator-elect, who was relaxing in Europe and Palm Beach, his mind on matters other than the destiny of Evelyn Lincoln.

Unexpectedly, Kennedy's secretary, reflecting the strange customs of Capitol Hill, decided she would rather stay on the House side of the Hill than accompany him to the Senate. Evelyn Lincoln, giddy with disbelief, was suddenly recruited to be his personal secretary. There followed a period of adjustment, mostly on her part. "Once when things were somewhat more confused than usual," she says, "he looked at me and said, 'I don't believe you and I understand each other.' He saw how my face fell, and quickly added, 'See if you can't do a little better.'" She tried hard, and soon seemed securely enthroned outside his door.

But disaster struck. First, Kennedy underwent his near-fatal back operation. Next, in January, 1955, while Kennedy was recovering, Mrs. Lincoln was stricken. She collapsed at lunch one day, and an operation disclosed a duodenal ulcer. She fell into a fifty-day coma, unable to speak or move. A second operation revealed the cause of all the difficulty—a tumor on her spine.

There was doubt that she would walk again, and once back at her home she began a series of exercises to strengthen her back and legs. Kennedy had continued her salary during her long recovery, and her thoughts were often of him as she fought to recover her health: "During the time of his greatest pain, before he left a year earlier, I was very sympathetic about his health. But I couldn't know how much he was suffering until my own illness. I remembered how angry he made me by his irritation and I felt deeply ashamed of myself for having thought about quitting the job. 'I'll make it up to him as soon as I get back to work,' I told myself."

At that point her hopes were suddenly shattered. Kennedy, still on crutches himself, called her husband to his office to fire her:

"As he talked, Abe wondered what he was trying to get at. Then it came. 'In short, Mr. Lincoln, whoever is my personal secretary is going to have to be in excellent health to keep up with the job. We know what your wife has gone through.' Then he paused for almost a minute. 'She's got a lot of courage and she's the best secretary I ever had.' Another pause. 'But it just wouldn't be fair to her to have her come back. I don't think she could take it, and I think it would hurt her health to try. So, that's what I asked you to come in for. I want you to tell her what the situation is.'"

"You mean you want me to tell her that she's through?" Abe stammered.

"No, I didn't mean that. I'll always have a place for her in my office. But not as my personal secretary. That's what I want you to tell her."

There is a certain ambiguity in this passage. Did Kennedy intend simply to demote her, or did he set out to fire her but, faced with Abe's dismay, back down? Mrs. Lincoln believes the latter to be the case—Kennedy meant to fire her but couldn't go through with it. (Sorensen writes that Kennedy's biggest administrative weakness was that he couldn't fire anybody. Early in 1968 when the criticisms of President Johnson in Mrs. Lincoln's second book, *Kennedy and Johnson*, were an embarrassment to Robert Kennedy's political ambitions, the Kennedy people floated stories, anonymous but not necessarily untrue, in the women's pages of *The Washington Post* saying that for years Kennedy wanted to fire Mrs. Lincoln but because of his timidity or her tenacity, or both, he was never able to do it.)

In any event, to Mrs. Lincoln, demotion from his personal secretary to the typing pool seemed almost a worse humiliation than being fired outright. When Abe went home and told her of his talk with the Senator:

"I felt a kind of numbness stealing over me as he went on. It was like a tornado that once passed close by when I was a little girl in Nebraska. Unexpected, and destroying everything. I didn't say anything to Abe, just walked into my bedroom and started to cry. He said through the door, 'You didn't let me finish. He says he has another job open for you.'

"'Another job,' I thought. 'How can I go back there, just typing and filing? He's offered it out of pity. The way you find a job for the feeble-minded or a cripple.' I was too depressed and angry to cry. . . .

"Days later, still angry, I began to consider the future and what I would do. There was really no one else I wanted to work for, and even if there had been, jobs as personal secretary to a Congressman were hard to get. If I went to work somewhere else, I would be starting at the bottom of the ladder, and perhaps there would be no higher rungs on that ladder, or I might be working for a Congressman who had nothing to offer but routine and who had no great ambitions for his future. Pride, I decided, was the only thing keeping me away from the Senator's office, and I began to wonder, can I afford pride?

"I spent a week debating whether I would abandon that dream and go to work for someone else or return to my job in his office and be less than his personal secretary. I decided I would keep my dream and go back to work for him."

So she returned to Kennedy's office, and again fate befriended her. The girl who had replaced her as Kennedy's personal secretary displeased him, and one day: "Once again, I was his personal secretary." She was never in trouble again. A few years later, her 1952 political prophesy came true: "It seemed like a fairy tale. Here I was, a country girl from the plains of Nebraska, going to work for the President of the United States, as his personal secretary."

Soap opera? Perhaps. But it is the stuff of life to countless thousands of American women. I suspect that—granting that any book about Kennedy was a best-seller in 1965—the sales of Mrs. Lincoln's book were multiplied because so many women—housewives, secretaries, waitresses, salesladies—found in her a heroine who had shared their own shimmering dreams and ever-present frustrations.

Nor is the significance of Mrs. Lincoln's story limited to her and women like her. Her desperate instinct—to seek vicarious fulfillment, to make some great man the custodian of her dreams—was shared by other, more important members of the Kennedy entourage, and is shared by most of those who surround any President. They tend to be outsiders, geographically and spiritually, frustrated idealists, men and women from Nebraska and Iowa and Texas with little to lose and much to gain by playing a long-shot in the game of politics.

Ted Sorensen, another Nebraskan, a restless young government lawyer when instinct led him to Kennedy . . . Louie Howe, a youthful poet become a down-and-out journalist when he hitched his wagon to FDR's star in 1912 . . . Missy LeHand, a stenographer with a high school education who ended up advising a President . . . Harry Vaughan, back-slapper, tea salesman and National Guard warrior when Harry Truman yanked him from obscurity . . . Harry Hopkins, an Iowa social worker with half a stomach and ten men's hunger for power . . . Pierre Salinger, star reporter reduced to assistant news editor of *House and Home* magazine when the Kennedys' call came . . . Ken O'Donnell, a hero at war and football, a salesman for a paper company when Bobby Kennedy pulled him into the world of power . . . Jack Valenti, a Houston PR-man with a thirst for the big-time . . . Bill Moyers, preaching Baptist sermons in dusty Texas towns until Lyndon Johnson called him to Washington . . .

All are cut from the same cloth, all share Mrs. Lincoln's prairie dreams, her child's vision of a dancer in white, performing for all the world, whether or not they have the wit or the candor to admit it. It is one of the small drawbacks of being President, or even a would-be President, that you are expected to make dreams come true.

For Evelyn Lincoln, the dream ended, like so many others, in Dallas. She was riding a few cars behind Kennedy in the presidential motorcade. A few hours later, on Air Force One, Johnson kissed her on the cheek only moments after he took the presidential oath. But she would soon learn that although he needed Sorensen and Schlesinger and some of the others for political display, she was expendable. The next morning, a little before nine, he called her into the presidential office and, as she recalls it, said: "I need you more than you need me. But because of overseas"—presumably a reference to foreign opinion—"I need a transition. Can I have my girls in your office by 9:30?"

That was impossible but, efficient as always, she managed to get out by 11:00.

3. Gadflies: Schlesinger and Goodwin

From the outset there was an element of confusion as to the exact nature of Arthur M. Schlesinger, Jr.'s, duties in the White House. The press release of January 25 announcing the historian's appointment as a Special Assistant to the President stated only that he would perform "a variety of duties," including speechwriting. *The New Yorker*'s Richard Rovere rejoiced a few days later that Schlesinger would be "forcing the President to have some care for the morrow after the morrow, and for eternal, or at least enduring, verities. . . . It is an extraordinary assignment, and one that has no precedent in American history or, probably, in the history of any modern democracy. . . . The court philosopher went out of fashion with royal courts."

However, court publicist Pierre Salinger recalls Schlesinger in a less exalted role than that of court philosopher: "He was not a policy maker. His official role was that of White House liaison with United Nations Ambassador Adlai Stevenson."

Salinger also asserts that Kennedy and Schlesinger were "strong friends," but that is not the way Evelyn Lincoln saw it. Kennedy, she writes, "admired Schlesinger's brilliant mind, his enormous store of information, and his ability to turn a phrase . . . but Schlesinger was never more than an ally and assistant. . . . He knew that Schlesinger would have preferred to be working for 'President' Adlai Stevenson."

Ted Sorensen more generously recalls Schlesinger as Kennedy's "constant contact with liberals and intellectuals both in this country and abroad, as his adviser on Latin America, United Nations, and cultural affairs, as a source of innovation, ideas, and occasional speeches on all topics, and incidentally as a lightning rod to attract Republican attacks away from the rest of us."

At first, Schlesinger shared the general confusion about his duties. Kennedy told Schlesinger when he invited him to join his staff: "We won't say anything about this until Chester Bowles is confirmed. I don't want the Senate to think that I am bringing down the whole ADA." Bowles was quickly confirmed (as Under Secretary of State) and the anxious Schlesinger received a call from the White House press office telling him that his appointment was imminent and that he should contact Ralph Dungan, who was handling personnel matters, for details. Dungan responded to Schlesinger's query with "Your appointment as what?" But eventually he was appointed, announced, and assigned an office in the East Wing of the Executive Mansion, a location that ranks in White House prestige slightly ahead of an office in Baltimore.* Schlesinger recalls of those dizzy days: "The first days in the White House, as a Special Assistant without a special assignment, were uncertain and confusing."

Perhaps it should go without saying that the one man who never had the slightest uncertainty about Schlesinger's role in Kennedy's White House was Kennedy. He intended to be remembered as a great President, and he therefore thought it wise to have in attendance a great historian. Schlesinger, the Pulitzer Prize-winning historian of the Jackson and Roosevelt Administrations, and a strong Kennedy supporter in 1960, filled the bill. History, Kennedy remarked to Sorensen more than once, depends on who writes it. (How differently history might have been written if Schlesinger had been an admiring member of Eisenhower's staff and Emmet John Hughes had been a disillusioned speechwriter of Kennedy's.)

Schlesinger did not immediately grasp his place in the larger scheme

* Salinger says that when space became tight in the West Wing, O'Donnell moved Schlesinger to the East Wing ("whose calmer atmosphere he must have found more congenial to his cerebrations"); Schlesinger recalls that he was assigned an East Wing office at the outset.

of things, but Kennedy soon set him straight. In the aftermath of the Bay of Pigs, Kennedy said to him: "I hope you kept a full account of that." Schlesinger confessed he had not, and in fact he thought Kennedy did not want him or the other aides recording White House affairs. "No, go ahead," Kennedy commanded. "You can be damn sure that the CIA has its record and the Joint Chiefs theirs. We'd better make sure we have a record over here. So you go ahead."

Thus instructed, Schlesinger began keeping his historian's journal, and in time the result was *A Thousand Days*, his best-selling memoir of the Kennedy presidency. In writing this book, Schlesinger joined the small group of White House aides whose most important service to their President came not during but after his presidency. Two others were Robert Sherwood, whose *Roosevelt and Hopkins* is one of the major political biographies of modern times, and Emmet John Hughes, whose *The Ordeal of Power*, although often critical, does more than any other single book to show Eisenhower as a flesh-and-blood, believable human being.

To Kennedy, and even more so to his political heirs, Schlesinger the speechwriter-troubleshooter was expendable, but Schlesinger the historian was not. His *A Thousand Days* is one of those rare books with the power to create its own reality. Kennedy's undertakings were not all so successful as Schlesinger pictures them, nor his motives so noble, nor his appointees so able and idealistic, nor their wives so gay and lovely. Nor is there compelling evidence for Schlesinger's conclusion that Kennedy "transformed the American spirit." But because of Schlesinger's standing as a historian, and because of the skill and conviction with which he writes, countless thousands of readers will accept his judgments as the truth.

Certainly, it cannot be proved that Kennedy did *not* transform the American spirit, and if future generations choose to remember Kennedy's too-brief era as a golden interlude, a spiritual renaissance, a historic turning point in the American development, Schlesinger's writing will have done much to shape their judgment. No President could ask for more.

Besides his post-presidential writing, Schlesinger also performed valuable service for Kennedy during the pre-presidential period. As a founder of ADA, as a noted New Deal historian, as a liberal spokesman since the 1940s, as a member of Stevenson's campaign staff in 1952 and 1956, Schlesinger alone among the Kennedy entourage had a national following among liberals and intellectuals. His pen was well employed during the Kennedy campaign. Schlesinger authored an effective little campaign tract called "Kennedy or Nixon: Does It Make Any Difference?" (he said it did), and he "debated" conservative writer Russell Kirk on the same topic in the *New York Times Magazine* on the Sunday before the election.

To credit Schlesinger's pre-presidential and post-presidential contribution is not to detract from his actual service in the Kennedy White House. Essentially, Schlesinger had a dual role. First, he was an ambassador to the liberals. Second, inside the government, he was an intellectual gadfly, skitting here and there to seek out new ideas and to sting the slothful bureaucratic beast into action.

This was exactly the role Schlesinger wanted. There had been vague talk in the pre-Inaugural period of his becoming an Ambassador, or Assistant Secretary of State for Cultural Affairs, but he was interested in neither post. Schlesinger felt that the intellectual entering government must decide whether he wanted an administrative position (as Rexford Tugwell had chosen in 1933) or wanted to try the more hazardous but potentially more influential route of being a presidential troubleshooter without portfolio. He decided that he was by temperament and experience better suited to be a troubleshooter, or "floater" as he sometimes calls it.

A number of duties gravitated to Schlesinger because of his special interests. Kennedy asked him to keep an eye on Latin American affairs, along with Richard Goodwin, Ralph Dungan, and others, because of Schlesinger's longtime interest in Latin American politics. He was Kennedy's informal channel of communications to Adlai Stevenson because Kennedy found it hard to talk to Stevenson. Because he was one of the more cultured members of Kennedy's entourage, Schlesinger watched over cultural affairs.

Schlesinger gave Kennedy a good deal of political advice, generally unsolicited and rarely followed. In 1962, he argued that Kennedy should not risk his prestige by campaigning in the congressional elections, citing Roosevelt's 1934 precedent. He opposed Kennedy's appointment of John McCone, a conservative Republican, as CIA Director, but later admitted he'd been wrong about McCone. He unsuccessfully urged Kennedy to be more aggressive in his dealings with Congress, and he once intruded into a congressional matter with such a lack of finesse that O'Brien sent him a sharp note about it, with a carbon to the President, who was highly amused. Kennedy's political operatives had, and still have, a dim view of Schlesinger's political insights; one of them says, with eloquent disdain, "You have to understand that *Arthur* was over in the *East Wing*, drinking *tea* with *Jackie*."

If Schlesinger was never Kennedy's intimate, theirs was nonetheless a cordial relationship. Schlesinger understood that Kennedy to an extent discounted his advice because of the historian's well-known liberal bias, but he always felt that the President was willing to hear his ideas. Some evenings Kennedy would unwind by treating an entranced Schlesinger to long monologues on the problems and decisions of the day. And Schlesinger, more than any other member of the White House staff, was part of Kennedy's social life. He was friendly with Mrs. Kennedy and he was often the President or Mrs. Kennedy's guest for lunch or dinner. There are, after all, worse ways to spend one's time than drinking tea with Jackie in the East Wing.

Schlesinger had the distinction of being one of two men (Senator Fulbright was the other) who advised Kennedy against the Bay of Pigs invasion. In the bitter aftermath of that catastrophe, he saw his work cut out for him:

"The Bay of Pigs made us all more aggressive in defending the interests of the President and therefore in invading on his behalf what the foreign affairs bureaucracy too often regarded as its private domain. . . . We tried to become the President's eyes and ears through the whole area of national security, reporting to him the things he had to know—and this would sometimes include things which the department involved did not wish him to know until it had decided for itself what it wanted to do."

The Department of State became Schlesinger's special nemesis. He had little use for Dean Rusk, Kennedy's Secretary of State, and he soon developed an icy disdain for State's bureaucratic routines, its group decision-making, its possessive attitude toward foreign policy, its devotion to the past and fear of innovation. Nowhere, Schlesinger believes, is the conflict between the presidential government and the permanent government more sharply defined than in relations between the White House (if, like Kennedy's, it seeks innovation) and the State Department. Certainly no section of *A Thousand Days* is more memorable than his outraged analysis of the foreign-affairs bureaucracy.

He harassed the State Department on big issues and small, winning a few battles and losing others. He had some success, on a case-by-case basis, in forcing State to grant visas to foreign scholars and writers whose leftist politics the Department disapproved.

He writes of one fight he lost: "I spent three years in the White

House in a plaintive and unavailing effort to beg the State Department to stop using the phrase 'Sino-Soviet bloc.' This was a typical Foreign Service expression—barbarous in form (the parallelism would be 'Russo-Chinese' or, if absolutely necessary, 'Sino-Russian') and obsolescent in content." At one point in this dispute Schlesinger told the State Department that the term Sino-Soviet "suggests that those who use it don't know what is going on in the world. I assume this is not the case." It was in such intellectual self-indulgences that Schlesinger differed from really effective bureaucratic operators, such as Moyers or Bundy, who would know how to avoid petty disputes and horde their strength for important issues.

One important issue in which Schlesinger involved himself, and with some success, concerned Italian politics. He and others in the White House believed that the U.S. would be wise to encourage a political development known as *apertura a sinistra*—opening to the left—in Italian politics. This meant, essentially, that the ruling Christian Democratic Party should be encouraged to enter into a working alliance with the Nenni Socialists, led by Pietro Nenni, a formerly pro-Russian socialist who had begun to move away from the Communists after the Soviet intervention in Hungary. Schlesinger viewed Nenni in 1961 as a democratic socialist whose involvement in a center-left coalition government could speed political reform in Italy and provide a model for non-Communist coalition governments in other Western European nations.

Schlesinger, Robert Komer of the National Security staff, and others pressed this view on Kennedy, who in time accepted it and passed word to the State Department to act accordingly. But, says Schlesinger, nothing happened; it took two years to force State to do as the President wished it to do. Actually, no overt actions were required of State; all the White House wanted was for the Department and its embassy in Rome to quietly change their attitudes toward the Nenni Socialists and the *apertura*. The problem was, Schlesinger says, that State's experts on Italy still held fast to the Eisenhower-Dulles view that the Nenni Socialists were "not anti-Communist" and that their increased power would strengthen anti-NATO sentiment in Italy and otherwise weaken the Western alliance.

"Soon Komer and I enlisted Robert Kennedy, Arthur Goldberg, and Walter Reuther in the effort to cajole the Department into abandoning the legacy of the past," Schlesinger writes. "It was an odd situation. We had, of course, the presidential decision and the patient backing of McGeorge Bundy. . . . As for the Secretary of State, he did not have, so far as I could find out, any views on Italian policy. . . . But in a time when attention at the top was seized by major crises, policy toward Italy inescapably enjoyed low priority; and this gave the officers on the working level a chance to pursue their own preferences, which they did with assiduity.

"It was an endless struggle. Meetings would be called, decisions reached, cables sent; then the next meeting would begin with the same old arguments. One felt entrapped as in a Kafka novel."

Eventually, the State Department came around, but less because of the Schlesinger-Komer efforts than because of the skillful intervention of Averell Harriman, who became Under Secretary for Political Affairs in the spring of 1963. Yet Schlesinger's gadfly tactics had helped keep the issue alive, and had given assurance to Italian progressives that they had allies in the White House, if not in the State Department. When the Nenni Socialists entered the Italian government in December, 1963, it was with the State Department's approval.

Such experiences convinced Schlesinger that the textbooks err when they tell of three branches of government—executive, judicial, and legislative—for within the executive cosmos, the presidential apparatus and the permanent bureaucracy in fact constitute separate branches.

As a President confronts resistance within the fourth branch—the permanent bureaucracy—he must begin with the fact that the civil-service laws prevent him from removing all but a few of the bureaucratic officials who oppose him. There remain three main ways a President can try to control the permanent government. The first is the President's power to appoint his hand-picked men to the top policy-making jobs in each department: Secretary, Under Secretary, Assistant Secretaries, Special Assistants to the Secretary, and so on. The second is to use his personal staff to supervise, shame, and otherwise spur the bureaucracy along the desired path. The third is for the President and his staff to seek out allies in the permanent government. This is not as easy as might be imagined, for the career officer knows that he will still be at his desk when the new President and his followers are gone. The bureaucrat who gets too cozy with one Administration may find himself *persona non grata* with the next; State Department officials complain with cause that they were purged from the right during the Eisenhower-Dulles years and purged from the left during the Kennedy years.

Kennedy used all three of these techniques in attempting to control the permanent government. (A fourth technique is simply to bypass the bureaucracy by creating new agencies, as FDR did with his welfare programs, Kennedy with the Peace Corps and Johnson with his antipoverty program, but there are limits on a President's power to do this.) McGeorge Bundy's National Security staff was particularly active in seeking out careerists in State and Defense who wanted to play ball with the new Administration. The President's power of appointment was nowhere better used than in the Kennedy-McNamara takeover at the Defense Department. And Kennedy's use of staff troubleshooters was most prominently seen in the activities of Schlesinger and Richard Goodwin, and in a somewhat different way, Sorensen and and O'Donnell.

Predictably, the troubleshooters aroused strong resentment throughout the government and within the Cabinet. Schlesinger mentions Rusk's "bitter resentment over intolerable 'interference' by the White House staff." Another time Rusk complained that at Cabinet meetings "people like Sorensen and Kaysen (Bundy's deputy) with no responsibility were making academic comments." But Kennedy was willing to tolerate the friction in exchange for the independent judgment his troubleshooters were able to give him. And he knew that now and then his gadflies were able to prod the governmental beast an extra inch or two in the desired direction.

But for that extra inch or two, the gadfly had to be prepared to live a dangerous life. No member of Kennedy's staff illustrates this better than Richard N. Goodwin, its youngest, brashest, most ill-fated, yet perhaps most durable member.

Dick Goodwin, like Tom Corcoran three decades earlier, had the good fortune to combine a first-rate mind with an excellent education, a combination that carried him to the top layers of the political world at an early age. After leading his classes at Tufts and Harvard Law, Goodwin had become a clerk to Justice Frankfurter. From there he had joined the staff of a Senate subcommittee investigating the television quiz-show scandals. He was a native of Boston, and he had let Ted Sorensen know he was available to serve Senator Kennedy if he could ever be of use. The call came in 1959, and Goodwin, at age twenty-seven, joined Kennedy's staff as an apprentice speechwriter.

He proved to be a fine one, combining a sharp intellect with sound political instincts and a sure prose style. He was the only speechwriter Kennedy ever found who could rival Sorensen, a fact that did nothing to endear him to Sorensen. Even after Goodwin fell from Kennedy's favor in 1962, he continued as a valued writer for, successively, Sargent Shriver, Lyndon Johnson, Robert Kennedy, and Eugene McCarthy. Members of Senator Robert Kennedy's staff said that when Sorensen and Goodwin would both be called upon to submit speech drafts in the late 1960s, Goodwin's would almost always be more satisfactory. For whatever it is worth, Goodwin is probably the best speechwriter in America today.

But speechwriting was always just a base for the ambitious Goodwin. He never relished being Kennedy's number-two speechwriter, and from the first he was aiming for a substantive policy role. In this, he was remarkably successful, for late in 1961, at twenty-nine, he was named Deputy Assistant Secretary of State for Inter-American Affairs. He lasted in that post only about eight months, however, for Goodwin (again like Corcoran) combined considerable brashness with his considerable brightness. This combination was to lead him to a fate unique in White House history: at age twenty-nine he was a key Administration policy-maker; at thirty, as far as White House power was concerned, he was a has-been. (In 1964, he returned to White House prominence during the Johnson Administration.)

When Goodwin entered the White House in January, 1961, he was nominally a member of Sorensen's staff, but in fact his interests were wide-ranging. He worked some on civil rights, some on the foreign-aid program, but most of all he was caught up in Latin American affairs. He had no special knowledge of Latin America, but Castro's success in Cuba had made it a hot issue in 1960 and 1961, and Goodwin found himself often writing speeches on Latin America during the campaign. He had coined the term "Alliance for Progress" and during his first months in the White House he was increasingly the man Kennedy counted on to devise a program to fit the phrase. During the pre-Inaugural period he set up a high-level task force on Latin America, and in February he headed a White House review of hemispheric policy in preparation for a major presidential speech on the area. Much of the work for the Alliance had been done during the Eisenhower Administration. He sought ideas both from government officials and from foreign diplomats, and finally he secluded himself in his Georgetown home to write the presidential speech outlining Kennedy's Alliance for Progress. Kennedy went over Goodwin's draft carefully, but left it substantially intact when he delivered it to the Latin American diplomatic corps in the East Room on March 13.

The program he outlined to the diplomats stressed the need for self-help, for national planning, for regional markets, and for inter-American cooperation in education, technical training, and research. Kennedy promised that if the Latin American nations were ready to do their part, then the U.S. would "help provide resources of a scope and magnitude sufficient to make this bold development plan a success." These plans and promises were couched in dramatic terms. Kennedy spoke several key phrases in Spanish—once declaring ". . . progreso si, tiranía no!" and he concluded with the eloquent appeal:

"Let us once again transform the American continent into a vast crucible of revolutionary ideas and efforts—a tribute to the power of the creative energies of free men and women—an example to all the world that liberty and progress walk hand in hand."

Goodwin felt justifiable pride when he heard Kennedy speak those concluding words and watched the Latin American diplomats buzz with excitement. He had provided the unifying drive that had pulled together the Alliance for Progress, and he had fought hard to see that it was conceived as a true alliance, and as a political and social program as well as an economic program. His main opposition had come from pol- icy-makers at the State Department who had long-established ties to the right-wing governments of Latin America and shuddered to hear a President talk of "revolutionary ideas and efforts"—and apparently mean what he said.

Goodwin, at that point, was clearly Kennedy's man on Latin Amer- ica. His hand was strengthened by the fact that the Assistant Secretary of State for Inter-American Affairs resigned in March and was not re- placed for several months. During that period, Goodwin was fighting to turn the lofty sentiments of Kennedy's March 13 speech into reality. One fight he lost was to make the Alliance for Progress a separate agency, independent of the Agency for International Development (AID). One small victory he won was in setting up the Latin Ameri- can Policy Committee, which brought together in weekly meetings persons concerned with Latin America from State, AID, the Alliance for Progress, and other agencies.

Goodwin was becoming increasingly controversial within the govern- ment because of his advocacy of radical departures in Latin American policy, and it was inevitable that conservatives in Congress and the press—sometimes prompted by conservatives within the State Depart- ment—would make him a target of criticism. Goodwin gave them an opening when at the first Punta del Este conference in August 1961 he held a conversation with Cuba's Marxist theorist Ernesto "Ché" Guevara. There were widely divergent reports of this encounter. One of Goodwin's enemies, Delesseps Morrison, the U. S. Ambassador to the Organization of American States, later charged that Goodwin held a secret meeting with Guevara, in direct disobedience of the Secretary of State's instructions, and thereby caused irreparable harm to U.S. standing with anti-Castro governments in Latin America. Good- win's version, however, which *The Washington Post* accepted in an editorial defending him, was that he had simply encountered Guevara at a diplomatic cocktail party and listened while the Cuban talked. In either event, the damage was done: Goodwin would increasingly become a target of anti-Administration criticism.

The criticism did not prevent Kennedy, as a part of the Thanksgiving Day shake-up of the State Department in 1961, from appointing Goodwin as Deputy Assistant Secretary for Inter-American Affairs. The twenty-nine-year-old Goodwin (he turned thirty on December 7, 1961) was deputy to Robert Woodward, a competent, unaggressive career officer who had moved into the Assistant Secretaryship only a few months earlier. The next few months were Goodwin's heyday. In December, he accompanied Kennedy and Woodward on meetings with leaders in Puerto Rico and Venezuela. On February 18, he and Walt Rostow, chairman of the State Department's policy planning staff, flew to Paris to urge members of the North Atlantic Alliance to cut off trade with Cuba. Throughout the winter, the free-wheeling Goodwin made the most of his White House connections as he negotiated with foreign diplomats and government leaders, Cabinet members and agency heads, in furtherance of his Latin American aims. Woodward, the Assistant Secretary, soon had cause to wonder who was deputy to whom.

Goodwin had made the move to the State Department for several reasons. He wanted to get out from under Sorensen. He had felt he could do more to advance his views if he was actually in the State Department, involved in day-to-day decisions, rather than at the White House sending over policy guidelines that were often ignored. And, certainly, to become a Deputy Assistant Secretary of State at twenty-nine was quite an accomplishment for any young man.

Unfortunately, Goodwin lacked the tact that might have overcome his youth and his controversial views and made him effective at State. Persons who got in his way found him cold and arrogant. Goodwin, however, attributes his troubles at the State Department to idealistic fervor rather than rudeness, and pictures himself as a political innocent who was beset by right-wing wolves.

Goodwin went about his business at State with zest and conviction, but he was doomed to failure. In Schlesinger's phrase, Goodwin was "gradually weakened, cut off, surrounded, and shot down, as if by ambush, by the bureaucracy and its anti-New Frontier allies in Congress and the press." Goodwin at State was a gadfly enmeshed in miles and miles of flypaper. His radical strategies and aggressive tactics enraged the foreign policy establishment, and its members could find countless ways to ignore or dilute his instructions. Gradually the disturbance he was causing began to arouse concern at high levels of the State Department. Among those who disapproved of Goodwin's tactics was George Ball, who had been promoted to Under Secretary in the Thanksgiving Day shake-up; Secretary Rusk was also said to be annoyed at Goodwin's disturbing the bureaucratic peace. Eventually a decision was made to replace Woodward, who had tolerated Goodwin's wheeling-dealing, with a stronger figure, someone who (as a high official at State put it) "could clip Dick Goodwin's wings." Early in March, Woodward was made Ambassador to Spain, and replaced by Edwin M. Martin, the Assistant Secretary for Economic Affairs, an old friend of Under Secretary George Ball. Martin accepted the job only after receiving a firm commitment from Secretary Rusk that he—not Goodwin—would be the boss.

Martin insisted that Goodwin cease direct communications with the White House, that he not deal with Rusk, Ball, or other high officials without clearing with him first, that he report his activities to Martin in written memos and otherwise start working through regular channels. Goodwin says he decided to accept the new situation. He felt that he had had a free ride under the more tolerant Woodward, but now he had to face the fact that Martin was the boss, and the only way he could have fought back would have been to appeal to Kennedy on a "me-or-him" basis. This seemed unrealistic, so Goodwin tried to adjust to his reduced status, found his enjoyment of his job diminishing fast, and soon was looking about for new worlds to conquer. The New York *Times,* explaining the shifts at State in an April 29 article (based on background talks with top State officials), declared that "the Administration's procedures for planning policies toward Latin America are gradually being tightened after a long period of experimentation and what President Kennedy himself had called 'creative chaos.'"

It would seem that Kennedy, faced with increasing chaos in his much-heralded programs for Latin America, decided the time had come to put a strong administrator in charge of the effort. Martin was the best he could find, and to get Martin's talents as an administrator, he was willing to sacrifice Goodwin's talents. Goodwin does not agree with this interpretation. He says he never complained to Kennedy about his problems at State, and as far as he knows, Kennedy never knew about them. However, it defies belief that Kennedy, who prided himself on his intimate knowledge of foreign affairs, would remain ignorant of a major confrontation between his young protégé and his new Assistant Secretary of State.

It is instructive to compare two sharply differing views of Goodwin's decline, one by Schlesinger, observing the affair from the perspective of the White House, the other by a former foreign-service officer. Schlesinger wrote:

"The incident reminded one again of the limits of presidential power because, though Kennedy retained his fondness for Goodwin and often called on him for special jobs, he could not, without cost to other objectives, preserve Goodwin's usefulness in a department which did not want to use him. The government lost, however, the imagination, drive, and purpose Goodwin had given so abundantly to the Alliance."

Smith Simpson gives the Department's view:

"President Kennedy saw in the Alliance for Progress . . . one of the more promising advances in foreign affairs. Accordingly, he had his staff push on it. Unfortunately, the willingness of his staffers exceeded their experience and maturity. The harder they pushed, the greater the confusion they generated. Lines of responsibility became so fuzzed up that desk officers and office directors in State did not know which way to look for orders, to their own superiors or White House staffers.

"Unable to cope with the increasing anarchy, the Assistant Secretary in charge of Inter-American affairs, a career diplomatic officer [Woodward], was shored up by the assignment to his bureau of one of the White House assistants, who was to work as deputy. The deputy was ambitious, enjoyed the prestige of White House identification, and kept a communication line with the President's mansion. . . . The confusion increased. The unlucky Assistant Secretary was hoisted abroad as an Ambassador. . . .

"A competent, hard-nosed civil servant in the Department [Martin] was made Assistant Secretary, but he stipulated, as a condition of his acceptance of the post, that his deputy's White House line be transferred to him and all communications with Ambassadors go through his office. This restored order."

With order restored, Goodwin in July switched to a new job as a speechwriter and troubleshooter for Peace Corps Director Sargent Shriver. The opportunity so appealed to him that he never considered returning to the White House, he says, although he assumes he could have. Men who were at the White House at the time doubt that the assumption was correct. They say Kennedy still valued Goodwin's talents, but was annoyed at the controversy he had caused at State and felt he should be in a position where he would be less likely to embarrass the Administration. A second problem Goodwin faced was the ill-will of Ted Sorensen. After more than two years of cool relations, they had undergone a sharp break. Partly, Sorensen, speechwriter and idea-man, was reacting negatively to an equally accomplished and even younger speechwriter and idea-man; beyond that, there was simply an inevitable clash between two strong but very different personalities. It is safe to say that by July, 1962, Sorensen would not have gone out of his way to open up Goodwin's old job in the Special Counsel's office.*

Goodwin entered an enjoyable exile at the Peace Corps. After a year or so he got a chance to return to the White House in an entirely new role. Schlesinger had arranged for him to become Kennedy's Special Assistant on the Arts. The appointment was to be announced on the day the President was killed.

Goodwin's multiple talents were not unnoticed by the new President. As we will see in a later chapter, Goodwin returned to the White House as a speechwriter and as a leading architect of the Great Society's domestic programs, achieving more influence under Johnson than he had under Kennedy. The Goodwin who returned to the White House in 1964 was an older and wiser man than the Goodwin who had left it in 1961. Johnson, who admired his brains and versatility, once told him, "Dick, you're a bright fellow, but you're just a little bit anxious. I want you to do something for me. Every meeting you go to, you count to three before you say anything." Goodwin decided this was excellent advice, and he followed it.

But Goodwin left the White House in 1965 and not long afterward he openly broke with Johnson over the Vietnam issue. He remained close to Robert and Jacqueline Kennedy, and was one of their key operatives in the struggle with William Manchester over his book, *The Death of a President.* Early in 1968, Goodwin turned up in New Hampshire, writing speeches for peace candidate Senator Eugene McCarthy. He later returned to the Kennedy camp. His dynamic performance in New Hampshire moved one newsman to dub him—with reference to McCarthy's teen-age followers—"the Che Guevara of the teenie-boppers." In truth, the dark, silent, elusive Goodwin was building a legend as a political knight-errant, one that will be further enhanced if Goodwin returns to the White House under a third President.

* When Sorensen was assembling his staff in January, 1961, he felt it necessary to inform Kennedy that all three of his proposed aides—Mike Feldman, Lee White, and Goodwin—were Jewish. It is conceivable that this was an anti-Goodwin ploy, because if Kennedy had been concerned about this gathering in the Special Counsel's office, Goodwin would probably have been the one to be replaced by a Methodist. One of the trio later commented to me about this incident: "The irony is that Sorensen himself is half Jewish. His mother was a Russian Jew. So he should have told Kennedy he had three and a half Jews on his staff."

Schlesinger himself avoided the pitfalls that beset his young friend. At the outset, Schlesinger's instincts had warned him not to accept a post in one of the departments. He found life pleasant and secure in the East Wing. Yet even though he avoided the knives, he was fated, as Kennedy's most conspicuous liberal adviser, to be the target of considerable criticism from conservative spokesmen.

Schlesinger was a natural for this role, not only because of his politics and his haughty manner, but because physically—with his high forehead and oval face, his bow tie and pot belly, his horn-rimmed glasses and petulant, protruding lower lip—he seemed to some the very quintessence of an egghead.

The tone of the criticism was set during the 1960 campaign when Nixon, in a speech in the South, denounced the Democrats as "the party of Schlesinger, Galbraith, and Bowles," a trio whose infamy, one suspects, had not then penetrated deep into the mind of the South.

After he entered the White House, some critics questioned the propriety of Schlesinger's accepting money for magazine articles (their argument was that he was cashing in on his White House connection; actually, he had been writing for major magazines for a decade or more), but he blunted this attack by donating a few of his checks to charity. During this controversy a newspaper columnist named Henry J. Taylor (". . . well known for his belief in the existence of flying saucers," Schlesinger says) called and, as Schlesinger remembers it:

"When he made some particularly outrageous accusation, I said, 'If you believe that, you're an idiot.' Taylor soon wrote a column saying indignantly that my 'first words' when he called were 'You are an idiot.' Walter Winchell added his contribution: 'Schlesinger is haunted by intellectual snobbery, dominated by arrogance . . . as power-mad as he is venomous . . . a threat to fundamental American concepts.' A group of patriots in California founded the Organization to Remove Schlesinger from Public Life."

At about this time, at a dinner party at Robert Kennedy's home, both Schlesinger and his hostess slipped, jumped, or otherwise made their way fully clothed into the swimming pool. Their dip inspired a flurry of wildly imaginative stories picturing drunken degeneracy at the highest levels of government. As the hostile stories raged, with Schlesinger miscast as a sort of thinking man's Fatty Arbuckle, he one day received a call from Tommy Corcoran, who warned:

"I scent a manhunt. Whenever the market goes down, those fellows demand a human sacrifice, and they have nominated you. The play they gave the swimming pool story was the tip-off."

Schlesinger was already concerned to have brought bad publicity to the President, and Corcoran's tidings of doom did nothing to lighten his mind. In what he later remembered as "a lapse of humor," he glumly told Kennedy he was ready to leave the government. But Kennedy saw the matter for what it was and told his downcast historian: "All they are doing is shooting at me through you. Their whole line is to pin everything on the professors. . . . Don't worry about it. This is the sort of thing you have to expect."

Actually, Schlesinger was never an Administration whipping boy in anything like the sense that his fellow professor, Rexford Tugwell, had been during the New Deal. Schlesinger was not important enough, or radical enough, and in any event the Administration's critics had an infinitely more inviting target in the Attorney General, Robert Kennedy. Tugwell left the White House in near disgrace; Schlesinger emerged from it a celebrity.

Schlesinger's response to Kennedy's death was entirely that of a Kennedy loyalist. He was not concerned with continuity in government or with helping the new President assume command. Twenty-four hours after the assassination, Schlesinger called a luncheon meeting attended by Galbraith and other Kennedy loyalists at which he talked of the possibility of a 1964 ticket of Robert Kennedy and Hubert Humphrey. He had every desire to get out of the Johnson White House, yet on November 26, he was persuaded by Johnson to take back his letter of resignation and stay on. Johnson needed Schlesinger as a symbol of liberalism far more than Kennedy had. Typically, Johnson, after winning Schlesinger's promise to stay, ignored him. After four months in limbo, Schlesinger did resign.

He spent much of 1964–65 writing *A Thousand Days,* and after it was published in November, 1965, he returned to teaching, not at Harvard but at the City University of New York, as Albert Schweitzer Professor of the Humanities. By then Schlesinger was a bona fide celebrity. The serialization of his book in *Life* in the summer of 1965 caused a national controversy, particularly his assertion that Kennedy intended to oust Dean Rusk after the 1964 election, and the historian was soon under fire from President Johnson, Rusk, Vice President Humphrey, and other Administration spokesmen. Schlesinger responded via an appearance on "Meet the Press," and various newspaper and magazine interviews. He was on *Time*'s cover. As his book shot to the top of the best-seller lists, Schlesinger settled in to enjoy the good life in Manhattan. The chronicler was soon being chronicled as a companion of Mrs. John F. Kennedy, as a guest at Truman Capote's "party of the decade," as *Vogue* magazine's book reviewer—and there was talk that Schlesinger was on the road to becoming the Jet Set's intellectual. But between the dinner parties and television interviews and Broadway openings, Schlesinger was back at work on *The Age of Roosevelt,* and he hopes to publish its fourth volume in 1969. If it measures up to the first three volumes, and perhaps reflects new insights based on his own White House experience, the critics will be silenced.

If one had compiled, in the early days of Kennedy's presidency, a list of the men most likely to exert an important progressive influence on the new Administration, it would certainly have included Schlesinger and Goodwin.

Yet such a prediction would have been wrong. Tugwell altered Roosevelt's path, and Clifford altered Truman's, but neither Goodwin nor Schlesinger was destined to have any such degree of influence, for they served a President whose instincts were far more prudent than his two Democratic predecessors.

Goodwin started fast, with his skillful packaging of the Alliance for Progress plan, but after that his star fell just as fast. By mid-1962 he was far from the presidential orbit, a victim of his own tactlessness, of inexperience in high-level political warfare, and of presidential impatience and court politics. Ironically, it was in 1964–65, during Lyndon Johnson's presidency, that an older and wiser Goodwin (he by then was thirty-four) fulfilled his early promise and became a skilled and influential presidential adviser.

Perhaps Arthur Schlesinger would have fitted neatly into an Administration headed by Adlai Stevenson, but he was never at home in the Kennedy circle. Amid the prevailing pragmatism, the liberal Schlesinger marched to a different drummer and remained a sort of second-class citizen. Vainly he invoked the spirit of Franklin Roosevelt as he urged Kennedy to hew the liberal line, to meet congressional opposition head-on, to go to the people for support for legislation. But Kennedy's rule continued to be brave talk followed by cautious action, and Schlesinger remained on the periphery of events.

It must have been a frustrating time for Schlesinger, yet when it was over he allowed himself no rancor, neither at the Administration's many unfulfilled promises nor at his often less than gracious colleagues. To the contrary, it was as if he had determined with his writing to close the gap between what the New Frontier might have been and what it was.

A Thousand Days is a remarkable work, written in love and heartbreak, striking in style but misleading in substance, abandoning a historian's skepticism for a disciple's pure belief. For an inscription to the book, Schlesinger chose the famous passage from *A Farewell to Arms* that begins: "If people bring so much courage to this world the world has to kill them to break them, so of course it kills them."

Perhaps a more fitting inscription would have been the closing lines from Hemingway's earlier novel, *The Sun Also Rises*, the famous exchange in which Lady Brett says, "We could have had such a damned good time together," and Jake Barnes answers, "Yes, isn't it pretty to think so?"

4. *Falstaff and the Iceman: Salinger and O'Donnell*

Press Secretary Pierre Salinger and Appointments Secretary Ken O'Donnell, the two men who saw Kennedy most often each day, had come from far corners of the nation to be oddly paired on the New Frontier. Both were young veterans of the war, and politics-minded; both served an apprenticeship working for Robert Kennedy on the Senate Rackets Committee in the late 1950s. Yet beyond that point, it would have been hard to find two men less alike. O'Donnell, taut and silent; Salinger, plump and talkative. Pierre Emil George Salinger, a San Franciscan of French ancestry; Patrick Kenneth O'Donnell, Boston Irish. O'Donnell, the former Harvard football captain, lean and hard, Kennedy's bodyguard, sometimes carrying a gun; Salinger, a child prodigy as a pianist, the connoisseur of good food, wine, cigars, and women, who made a national joke out of his refusal to take a fifty-mile hike. Salinger, the jester, the political amateur, who became briefly a U. S. Senator soon after leaving the White House; O'Donnell, the political pro, who tried and failed to win his party's nomination for governor in Massachusetts. O'Donnell, the athlete, the Irish pol, the close-mouthed operative, the archetypal New Frontiersman; Salinger, plump, self-indulgent, and unathletic, the least likely of them.

To understand Salinger's unlikely presence in the Kennedy circle, one must first understand that, beneath the Camelot glitter, there was always a strong prep-school flavor about the New Frontier. The main promulgator of this atmosphere was Robert Kennedy (Milton Academy '43), who in his days as Attorney General liked to yank down his necktie, toss a football on the Mall, and hang out with athletes.*

At Harvard, one of the athletes Bobby Kennedy most liked to hang out with was the star quarterback, Ken O'Donnell. They palled around together, walked with a swagger and curled their lips at the Phi Beta Kappas. A decade later, with Kennedy as the thirtyish chief counsel for Senator McClellan's rackets committee, and O'Donnell as his Administrative Assistant, they continued to pull down their ties, walk with a swagger, and curl their lips as Kennedy applied his youthful piety and tough-guy manner to the complexities of labor-management relations.

As all students of prep-school literature will recall, tough guys must always have a foil, a comic character against which to measure their toughness. He is invariably called Tubby or Rollo; he has a round, open-mouthed face and a snub nose; he wears a beanie and short pants that reveal pink, stubby legs; and he is looked on by class leaders with mingled affection and disdain—affection for his eager loyalty, disdain for his inability to match their feats of physical prowess. From 1957 until 1963, Salinger played Rollo's role for the Kennedys and for O'Donnell. He was the fall guy, the butt of countless jokes. Since the Kennedys always liked a good laugh, and since Salinger was the only member of their senior staff with any noticeable talent for laughing at himself, he became an invaluable member of the entourage.

One of Kennedy's intimates recalls: "After the President had had a hard day, Pierre would wander into the office, and Kennedy would stick his cigar in his mouth and lower his voice and snarl at him, 'Dammit, Salinger, you've fouled us up again.' It didn't mean anything; it just helped him unwind." In one classic bit of Rollo-baiting, when Salinger turned up in Palm Beach wearing Bermuda shorts, Kennedy ordered him: "Get back into long pants; you haven't got the legs for shorts."

Salinger was a mediocre Press Secretary, but he could often brighten bad situations with a quip. Once O'Donnell passed on to him an unconfirmed report that the Dominican dictator Trujillo had been assassinated. Salinger foolishly blurted this report to the press, leaving the U.S. in an impossible position if Trujillo was still alive. Kennedy had never been more furious at Salinger.

"We now have later intelligence that Trujillo may not be dead," Kennedy raged.

"Mr. President," Salinger sighed, "if he's not, I am."

* This, at least, is the way he appeared to me when I had some dealings with him in 1962–63; apparently he changed considerably in his last years of life.

From the first, Salinger was acutely aware of his status as the new boy in class. In his book *With Kennedy*, he writes of the 1960 campaign: "I felt very much like an outsider during those first months." Later, however: "I began to feel more and more like a member of the team." Although he was often the butt of Ken O'Donnell's heavy-handed humor, Salinger always felt a special awe for O'Donnell's self-sufficiency and intimacy with the Kennedys.

"From my viewpoint, O'Donnell had the greatest responsibility, influence, and accessibility to the President. Ken is a slight man but tough and wiry with black hair and a disposition to match it. . . . He would never use five words if one would do, and that word was very often a flat 'no.' One could admire him immediately but it took a little longer to like him. . . . When the word came down from O'Donnell, that was it! . . . It was my impression that O'Donnell had the greatest influence in shaping the President's most important decisions. . . . Next to him I would rank Theodore C. Sorensen and McGeorge Bundy."

Salinger's declaration that O'Donnell had more influence than Sorensen and Bundy on Kennedy's major decisions is unfortunately not documented. Asked to give specific instances of O'Donnell's influence, Salinger said his statement was just a "general impression" based on the fact that Kennedy spent a lot of time with O'Donnell and had a high regard for his judgment.

Salinger's role as court jester largely concealed the fact that he was one of the most subtle, imaginative, and self-serving of Kennedy's men; in this he recalls Roosevelt's Pa Watson, who was often a clown but never a fool. "I may be plucky but I am not stupid," Salinger once said, and no one could disagree. Salinger was a down-and-out journalist when he joined the Kennedys, and in a half-dozen years he parlayed talent, shrewdness, energy, and good humor into, briefly, a Senate seat, and, more permanently, into the prospect of spending the rest of his life as a high-salaried business executive, best-selling author, and international celebrity.

As presidential Press Secretary, on a day-to-day basis, Salinger compared poorly with his predecessor, Jim Hagerty. Reporters had respected Hagerty professionally but not liked him personally; with Salinger the reverse was true. In sharp contrast to Hagerty's brisk efficiency, Salinger's briefings were often late, his press releases incomplete, his answers uninformed. Hagerty had known virtually everything that went on in Eisenhower's Administration; Kennedy, in such tense moments as the two Cuban crises, thought it wiser to keep Salinger in the dark.

Many better-known, better-qualified journalists than Salinger were available to serve as Kennedy's Press Secretary, but probably Kennedy got just what he wanted. If there was any aspect of politics at which Kennedy most excelled, it was his press relations. The last thing Kennedy needed was a powerful Press Secretary like Hagerty to stand between him and the press, or a knowledgeable one like Steve Early or Bill Moyers to explain his policies for him. Kennedy, aided by Sorensen, Bundy, and O'Brien, could charm and inform the press. What Kennedy needed, and got, in a Press Secretary was someone who was hard-working, loyal, and who could keep the press happy. This Salinger could do, for no matter how inefficient he sometimes was, reporters found it impossible to stay angry at Lucky Pierre for very long. Salinger's antics in the press office added the perfect touch to the White House image, serving to detract from the more serious business afoot elsewhere in the West Wing. He may have been Rollo behind the scenes, but up front he was Kennedy's Falstaff and he made the most of the role.

Moreover, despite his mediocrity on routine press matters, Salinger proved to be an inventive entrepreneur of media relations. Salinger had a knack for living by his wits. In the 1940s, he went from high school into the navy, then to the San Francisco *Chronicle* where, despite his lack of college training, he became a star reporter. In 1952 and 1956, he had served on Adlai Stevenson's campaign staffs. He had joined the staff of *Collier's* magazine and was writing a major piece on the Teamsters Union when *Collier's* folded in 1956. He had been reduced to a job as assistant news editor for *House and Home* magazine when early in 1957 Robert Kennedy, impressed by his investigations into the Teamsters, offered him a job as an investigator on the Senate Rackets Committee.

During Kennedy's pre-Inaugural period, Salinger persuaded him, over the objections of Sorensen, Bundy, and Dean Rusk, to open his press conferences to live television. Other advisers feared the repercussions of a presidential slip-of-the-tongue or indiscretion on live television, but Kennedy shared Salinger's belief that he could handle himself and that, in any event, if he made a slip the word would get out, TV or not.*

Newspapermen objected violently to the live TV, but Kennedy defended his decision on the ground that it provided "more direct

* Previous presidential slips had included Truman's scaring the wits out of European diplomats by saying that the U.S. might use nuclear weapons in Korea, and Ike's being quoted as saying about a Khrushchev remark, "I think he's crazy." A tape recording established that he had said "I think it's crazy."

communication" with the people. As one analyst pointed out, if Kennedy wanted "more direct communication," he should have ignored the reporters altogether and simply made speeches over television. The original idea and value of the presidential press conferences was that they provided *indirect* communication with the people—ideas could be explored, policies explained, advance information put forward without the problem of direct presidential attribution. But from Kennedy's viewpoint, the televised conferences proved to be a huge success, and Salinger's advocacy of them got him off to an auspicious start in the White House.

Encouraged, Salinger plunged ahead in his search for new ways to brighten Kennedy's image. Reflecting Kennedy's sensitivity to foreign opinion, he increased presidential access for foreign correspondents and hired an assistant to concentrate on them. He arranged Kennedy's superbly effective, hour-long chat with three correspondents on national, prime-time television. He eliminated Hagerty's rule that reporters must clear through the Press Secretary before seeing government officials—he couldn't have enforced it anyway. He increased the coordination of government information officers, and perfected Hagerty's policy of attributing agency news to the President.

Salinger's most surprising role, however, was as an impresario of Russian-American relations. He fell into this role more or less by accident during the Kennedy-Khrushchev meeting in Vienna in June 1961, and in rapid succession he debated two leading Russians on American television, became a drinking companion of Khrushchev's son-in-law and his press spokesman, served as a courier of secret messages between Kennedy and Khrushchev, arranged the first interview of an American President by a Russian journalist, and climaxed his adventures by spending fourteen hours with Khrushchev himself.

No previous Press Secretary, and no White House aide since Harry Hopkins, had been as directly involved in international diplomacy. The fact that Salinger was the emissary, rather than some more solemn figure such as Bundy, tended to detract from the fact that his exchanges with the Russians, and particularly with Khrushchev, were an invaluable source of information to Kennedy. Salinger was not the man Kennedy would have picked for the role, and he viewed his Press Secretary's adventures with misgivings, but the Russians liked Salinger and Kennedy would have been foolish not to make the most of this informal link with the Kremlin.

Salinger's exploits began in Vienna when Mrs. Lucy Jarvis, co-producer of NBC-TV's "The Nation's Future," asked if he would be willing to join a leading American journalist in debating two top Russians on the subject of a free press. Salinger was willing, but he doubted that the Russians she had in mind—Aleksey Adzhubei, editor of *Izvestia* and Khrushchev's son-in-law, and Mikhail Kharlamov, press spokesman for the Soviet Foreign Ministry—would agree. They did. Encouraged, Salinger asked Kharlamov about the possibility of a series of direct television exchanges between Kennedy and Khrushchev to be shown in both nations. He was also hoping to promote a deal whereby an American journalist would write on America for *Izvestia* and a Russian would write for a leading American paper.

The Vienna Conference ended on a chill note over the Berlin issue, but Salinger's plans bounced along undisturbed. A few weeks later Adzhubei and Kharlamov flew to New York to tape the debate—with Harrison Salisbury of the New York *Times* joining Salinger for the U.S. —and afterward the Russians flew to Washington for a party at Salinger's house in Falls Church, Virginia, where they drank vodka, ate barbecued chicken, swam in a nearby lake, and watched the debate on television.

The next day, Salinger took the Russians on a cruise up the Potomac, and the following day Adzhubei and Kharlamov spent an hour with Kennedy. The episode was a notable success except for one fact—the Russians broke their pledge to show the debate on Russian television.

Salinger's next exchange with the Russians came in September when he went with Kennedy to New York for the President's first speech to the UN. Kharlamov, back in this country, requested a meeting with Salinger to pass along an urgent message to Kennedy from Khrushchev: the Russian Premier was prepared to ease the Berlin crisis (presumably by backing away from his threat to recognize East Germany) but Kennedy must pave the way by avoiding belligerent statements in his UN address. Kennedy replied, via the Salinger-Kharlamov conduit, that a Berlin settlement would be more likely if Russia would honor its peace-keeping commitments in Laos.

While talking to Kharlamov, Salinger discovered that Adzhubei, Khrushchev's son-in-law, as a result of off-hand remarks during the weekend of the television debate, was expecting Salinger and his family to visit him in Russia the next summer. Salinger also prodded Kharlamov about letting a Russian journalist interview Kennedy for publication in the Russian press.

On September 29, six days after the New York exchange, Salinger got a call from Georgi Bolshakov, a Washington-based Russian editor and spy, urgently requesting an appointment. The next day, declaring, "Here. You may read this. Then it is for the eyes of the President only,"

Bolshakov handed Salinger a twenty-six-page personal letter from Khrushchev to Kennedy about the problems of Laos and Berlin. This was the beginning of an unprecedented secret correspondence between the two heads of state. Time after time Salinger would meet Bolshakov in bars or on dark streets to give or receive an envelope. On one rainswept streetcorner, as the melodramatic Bolshakov slipped an envelope into Salinger's pocket, he stage-whispered: "Every man has his Russian, and I'm yours."

Salinger says of the still-classified Kennedy-Khrushchev letters: "Khrushchev said, in effect, that you and I, Mr. President, are the leaders of two nations that are on a collision course. But because we are reasonable men, we agree that war between us is unthinkable. We have no choice but to put our heads together and find ways to live in peace."

During the first exchange of letters, Salinger learned that Khrushchev had agreed to let a Russian journalist interview Kennedy and had tapped his son-in-law, Adzhubei, for the assignment. The interview took place at Hyannis Port on November 25 and was printed in the Moscow edition of *Izvestia* three days later. Copies of the paper were circulated throughout Russia for months, and for the first time in the Cold War, the Russian people received a direct statement of the views of an American President on the issues of war and peace. Kennedy came across well as a man who knew the horrors of war and earnestly sought peace. World reaction was favorable; the *London Daily Mail* called the interview "the most remarkable event of its kind for many years." Even the State Department, which had grumbled at first that the interview should have been handled through diplomatic channels, admitted it had been a success.

While Adzhubei was in the U.S. to interview Kennedy, he told Salinger he had been unable to get approval for a plan to exchange sons for a summer. Salinger had been similarly discouraged by the Secret Service, which was not at all anxious to have to protect Khrushchev's grandchildren for several months.

There was good news on January 18, 1962, when Salinger had another urgent call from Bolshakov, the editor-spy: 1) Khrushchev had agreed to the series of televised exchanges between him and Kennedy, and 2) Adzhubei's invitation to Salinger and his family to visit him in Russia in April was official.

Salinger and USIA Director Ed Murrow met with Kharlamov in Paris on January 28 to negotiate details of the television exchanges, then Salinger hurried back to Washington for a luncheon Kennedy was giving for Adzhubei and his wife Rada. During the luncheon, Kennedy told the Adzhubeis that he would let Salinger accept their invitation to

Moscow, but without his family lest it be taken for a pleasure trip. Officially, Salinger would be conferring with Russian officials in search of increased communications between the two nations.

Salinger's diplomatic career received a cruel blow on April 5, when Khrushchev canceled the television exchange in retaliation for Kennedy's announcement that the U.S. intended to resume nuclear testing, as the Russians had done several months earlier. Kennedy was furious. His first reaction was to cancel Salinger's trip to Russia, but Charles Bohlen, the State Department's Russian expert, persuaded Kennedy to let the trip stand. Two months later, Salinger was in Moscow.

The announcement of the trip drew sharp criticism in Congress, the press, the White House, and the State Department. Asked about this criticism at a press conference, Kennedy defended Salinger: "I know there are always some people who feel that Americans are always young and inexperienced, and foreigners are always able and tough and great negotiators. But I don't think the United States would have acquired its present position of leadership in the free world if that view were correct."

O'Donnell, whose view of Salinger's political acumen was never high, grumbled that even if he did well in Moscow, "just the announcement that you're going has already been a political minus for the President."

When Salinger arrived at the Moscow airport on May 11, U. S. Ambassador Llewellyn Thompson met him with jolting news. Premier Khrushchev, who had not figured in Salinger's travel plans at all, had invited him to spend the next afternoon with him at the government *dacha* twenty-two miles outside Moscow. There was no question of turning down the invitation, so Thompson hurried Salinger to the embassy for a final briefing. Kennedy cabled instructions: Salinger was to discuss nothing substantive except communications; if Khrushchev wanted to talk about U.S. policies, Salinger was to listen but not venture opinions.

Actually, Khrushchev's intentions were mainly social. He wanted to show his gratitude for Kennedy's hospitality to his daughter. Their first marathon luncheon went so well that Salinger was invited back again the next day. In all, for fourteen hours they ate, drank, joked, talked, shot skeets, and walked in the Russian forests. They parted warmly after their second day together. "We have had good fun, yes?" the Russian leader said.

While Salinger was exchanging toasts with Khrushchev, much of the diplomatic world was up in arms. Salinger writes: "Ambassador Thompson had had a hectic day reassuring Bonn, Paris, and London that JFK's thirty-six-year-old Press Secretary had not spent the afternoon negotiating the future of Europe with Khrushchev." To Salinger's surprise, however, there was little domestic criticism when he returned to the U.S.

Salinger's exploits at home and abroad made him, to the man on the street, probably the best-known of Kennedy's aides, a fact that did not overjoy all his fellow staff members. O'Donnell in particular was annoyed when he and Salinger traveled together to advance Kennedy's trips and Salinger would get all the attention. This amused Kennedy, who jibed at O'Donnell: "How many times did Pierre get his picture in the paper this time?"

But inside the White House, O'Donnell remained the dominant figure, Salinger ever the eager outsider, still trying to prove himself. On March 17, 1964, when Salinger told O'Donnell he was thinking of entering the Democratic primary for the Senate in California, O'Donnell's reply was, "I don't think you've got the guts." Salinger proudly records that the next day, when he told O'Donnell he was definitely in the race: "He nearly fell out of his chair." Rollo—victorious!

Salinger beat his opponent in the primary, Alan Cranston, the state controller, by 174,000 votes. Soon thereafter, the ailing incumbent Senator, Clair Engle, died, and Governor Pat Brown appointed Salinger to replace him. He was sworn in on August 5. Unhappily for Salinger, who was only an amateur showman, his Republican opponent was professional song-and-dance man George Murphy, and Murphy proceeded to make him the youngest ex-Senator in American history.

As always, Salinger landed on his feet. Early in 1965 he took a job with the National General Corporation in Beverly Hills. Soon thereafter, having been divorced by his wife of eight years, he married an attractive young French journalist, Nicole Gillmann. His book *With Kennedy* became a best seller and he went to work on a novel. He is active in California politics and remains friendly with the Kennedys, although they blamed him for suggesting William Manchester as the author of the book on the assassination. He switched jobs to become Continental Airlines' vice president for international affairs, a position that allows him to continue as something of an international ambassador. In 1968, he joined Robert Kennedy's campaign staff, but journalists covering the campaign did not regard his role as a major one.

He has kept in the public eye by such high-level clowning as an appearance on the Batman television show as "Lucky Pierre," a comic lawyer, and an appearance on *Esquire* magazine's cover with Tony

Curtis, Kim Novak, and other celebrities who were supposedly protesting that they weren't invited to author Truman Capote's "party of the year." He even emerged as host of a television variety show.

Yet private life may never give Salinger the platform for international wheeling and dealing he enjoyed for his three years in the White House. In his way, he was one of the most imaginative of the New Frontiersmen. He had a fertile mind, limitless audacity, and a conviction that all things were, if not possible, at least worth a try. It can certainly be argued that in 1961–63 he personally did as much to improve U.S.-Russian relations as all the State Department's Russia desk men, policy planners, and diplomats. Getting Kennedy's views published in *Izvestia* was no small feat, his dealings with Khrushchev, Adzhubei, and Kharlamov were a step in the right direction, and, had the Kennedy-Khrushchev television exchange been carried through, it might have been a breakthrough of historic proportions. Salinger, with his bubbling optimism and his undercurrent of shrewdness, set a standard for future White House aides by demonstrating the excellent opportunity they have for doing good in the world if only they have the wit to try.

While Salinger was becoming the most public of Kennedy's men, O'Donnell remained the most private. His style was set in the 1960 campaign when he would laugh and turn away if reporters asked him what his job was. They saw him only, as Mary McGrory described it, as ". . . a dark-eyed man leaning over the railing, peering out into the crowd. Nobody knew whether he was counting the house or searching for bomb throwers. . . . If the man, whose name was Kenneth Philip O'Donnell [sic], did anything else in the campaign, most of the reporters traveling with him for hundreds of thousands of miles had no idea what it was."

It is a measure of O'Donnell's mystery that the astute Miss McGrory got his name wrong: It is Patrick Kenneth O'Donnell.*

O'Donnell looked the part of the presidential watchdog, with his skin stretched tight across his high cheekbones and his thin, small mouth. The eyes were small unsmiling slits in a flat, hard, defiant face—a taut, troubled, triangular face, not unlike that of the first Secretary of Defense, James Forrestal.

If O'Donnell was the most mysterious of Kennedy's men to the outer world, he was also the most controversial of them to the inner circle.

* At least it was then. When he ran for Governor of Massachusetts, O'Donnell had his name legally changed to Kenneth Patrick O'Donnell to ensure that the voters would recognize him.

Those who admire him—and the two ex-Stevensonians, Salinger and Schlesinger, express the most admiration for him—are lavish in their praise of his loyalty and liberalism; the larger number who feel no affection for O'Donnell are fierce in their denunciations.

At heart, the objections to O'Donnell rest simply on the fact that he was a rude, abrasive man to deal with, and that since he controlled access to the President (other than Mrs. Lincoln's bypass), use of limousines and helicopters, White House office space, and similar amenities, his unpleasantry was an inescapable fact of White House life. Certain other members of Kennedy's inner circle were not notably warmhearted, Bundy and Sorensen for example, but they at least found it expedient to maintain an external civility. O'Donnell rarely bothered. Like Sherman Adams, whom he resembled in many ways, he seemed to enjoy saying no. Like Adams, he bestowed his bluntness as casually on the mighty as on the humble. He was disliked by the clerks and administrators of the permanent White House staff, and at the other extreme he was disliked by the Vice President, Lyndon Johnson, and his staff. A typical O'Donnell affront to Johnson came in September, 1963, as the Vice President was preparing to leave for Scandinavia. Johnson, wanting the boost a send-off by the President would give his mission, asked O'Donnell if he might stop by Hyannis Port to meet with Kennedy before leaving. O'Donnell rejected Johnson's request without even consulting with Kennedy. However, Kennedy's military aide, Major General Chester Clifton, interceded on Johnson's behalf and arranged the meeting.

(How fleeting, power. I remember attending a party in 1962 at which both Johnson and O'Donnell were present; people were debating which was more important.)

Even within the Kennedy circle, O'Donnell's cold manner earned him the nickname of the Iceman. Once, a critical magazine article caused Kennedy to cut down the number of New Frontiersmen, and their wives and children, who could hitch rides to Hyannis Port each weekend on the presidential airplane. After the crackdown, all would-be passengers had to get advance approval from O'Donnell, and it was not lightly granted.

No matter how many enemies O'Donnell made, in the White House or outside it, it was his very singlemindedness, the peculiar fierceness of his loyalty, his proud indifference to the opinions of anyone except the Kennedys, that made him so immensely valuable to them. All Kennedy's top aides were ostensibly loyal to him, yet there were shades of difference. O'Brien's ultimate loyalty was to the Democratic Party; Schlesinger's to his liberal beliefs; Bundy's to a complex mixture of his own ambition and his concept of public service; even Sorensen might be suspected of having an ideological card up his sleeve now and then. But it was simply inconceivable that O'Donnell's advice to Kennedy would ever be based on any personal or political consideration except what he thought was best for Kennedy's interests. His commitment was total. If Kennedy had one day ordered his entire staff to leap from a fiftieth-floor window, O'Brien would have suggested they talk it over first, Bundy would have edged toward the door pleading a prior engagement, Schlesinger would have whipped out his notebook and begun scribbling, Sorensen would have started silently toward the window, Salinger would have cracked a feeble joke and looked to O'Donnell for guidance, but O'Donnell would already have raced to the window and crashed headlong through it, with only a brief, scornful glance back at those who hesitated.

O'Donnell had come to Harvard—where he met Bob Kennedy—from the wrong side of the tracks (his father, Cleo O'Donnell, was football coach at Holy Cross) but he made a name for himself as the football captain and star quarterback. O'Donnell's was a New Deal heritage, re-enforced by wartime service as an Air Force bombardier. His generation had not fought the war, he often said in his postwar years at Harvard, to keep America safe for the vested interests. Once when O'Donnell was visiting at Robert Kennedy's home, his fervent support of Franklin Roosevelt so angered Joseph P. Kennedy that the older man left the room.

After leaving Harvard, O'Donnell went to work for a Boston paper company, but he and Kennedy kept in touch; and in 1952, Kennedy recruited him to work in his brother's race for the Senate. O'Donnell, who was born on March 4, 1924, was then twenty-eight, and under Larry O'Brien's tutelage, he soon proved his aptitude for politics. By 1956, when Kennedy decided to fight it out with Congressman John McCormick for control of the Massachusetts delegation to the 1956 Democratic convention, O'Brien and O'Donnell were the two men he sent to do the job, and they did it. In 1957, Robert Kennedy brought O'Donnell to Washington as his Administrative Assistant on the Mc-Clellan Committee. The next year he was a key figure in Kennedy's re-election campaign, and in 1960 he emerged as the presidential candidate's schedule-planner, appointments-maker, and political confidant.

One journalist who knew O'Donnell during and after the campaign recalls: "I think Kenny wears better than any of the other Kennedy insiders. Beyond his loyalty, there was this fierce personal integrity that Kennedy respected. If Sorensen saw some corny campaign film that gushed about Kennedy, he'd say it was a work of art. If Kenny saw it and thought it was a lot of crap, he'd say so."

In the White House, O'Donnell decided who could and couldn't see Kennedy, and he took the heat from frustrated appointments-seekers. He had charge of physical matters in the White House—office space, limousines, staff hiring, and so forth. He was Kennedy's liaison with the FBI when security questions came up in government hiring, and he was active in dispensing patronage. He was Kennedy's top operative in national politics and kept in close touch with Democratic political leaders. Politicians who wanted Kennedy to campaign for them or do other favors had first to convince O'Donnell, who was not easily convinced. He had a long memory. "Don't try to con me," he would tell politicians. "I remember who you were for in 1960."

O'Donnell once told a reporter he wasn't entirely happy with his job—he would rather have an operational post someplace like the Defense Department—but as long as Kennedy wanted him in the White House, he would stay.

He stayed, because Kennedy liked to have him close by, liked to hear his judgments on people and policies, liked to bounce new ideas off the hard rock of his mind. Beyond these agreed-upon facts, just what specific influence O'Donnell had on Kennedy's decisions is a matter of dispute. Salinger, as has been mentioned, describes O'Donnell as Kennedy's most influential adviser but declines to document his assertion. Schlesinger, who also considers O'Donnell an important liberal influence on Kennedy, describes him as constantly urging the President, in so many words, "To hell with balancing the budget and keeping the conservatives happy—let's spend some money and help people." Schlesinger says that on domestic issues he generally found O'Donnell's views closer to his own than those of any other member of the White House staff.

Besides Salinger and Schlesinger, however, other Kennedy aides tend to minimize O'Donnell's influence on policy. One typical comment is: "Ken was oriented toward people, not issues."

O'Donnell had ample opportunity to express his views on people. As Appointments Secretary, he would often choose to sit in on meetings between Kennedy and political visitors, or come into the President's office at the end of a meeting if it needed breaking up. After the visitor left, Kennedy and O'Donnell would banter back and forth about him, analyzing his motives, joking about his hypocrisies. O'Donnell had no tolerance for phonies, least of all for big-shots who were phonies. Much of his advice to Kennedy seems to have been directed at warning him against possible injury from important people or institutions.

Like many liberals, he was vehemently opposed to Lyndon Johnson's nomination as Vice President in 1960. He was characteristically disdainful of the leading Establishment newspaper, the New York *Times*, and once told Salinger: "Nobody in Iowa or California reads the *Times* or even cares what it thinks editorially. You and the President exaggerate its importance." Another time he warned Kennedy in a confrontation with big business: "The worst thing we can do now is to put ourselves in a foot-kissing posture." Yet despite O'Donnell's liberal, New Dealish instincts, he always put Kennedy's political interests first, and he urged Kennedy to avoid civil rights legislation in 1961 and 1962, as he did.

The overlapping strands of O'Donnell's service to Kennedy, combining political advice, personal companionship, and logistical detail, were seen in his part in Kennedy's trip to Texas in November, 1963. At the outset O'Donnell, aided by O'Brien, handled the intricate negotiations required to paper over the bitter feud between Texas Governor John Connally and Senator Ralph Yarborough. Hour-by-hour details of the coming trip were plotted by on-the-scene advance men who reported to O'Donnell. When various persons urged Kennedy not to visit Dallas, because of its reputation for extremism, O'Donnell's advice was that the whole purpose of the trip—to build Democratic unity in Texas— would be defeated by skipping the state's second-largest city. Because the trip was political, both O'Donnell and O'Brien went along, and in Fort Worth on the morning of the 22nd, as the Yarborough-Connally feud flared anew, Kennedy angrily ordered O'Donnell to tell O'Brien to get Yarborough into a car in the presidential motorcade with Lyndon Johnson if he had to throw the Senator into the back seat.

O'Donnell surveyed the overcast Texas skies and instructed the Secret Service: "If the weather is clear and it's not raining, have that bubbletop off"—of the presidential limousine. Also that morning, he displayed one of his rare grins when Mrs. Kennedy told him and her husband that she would campaign actively in the coming year. O'Donnell did not know Mrs. Kennedy well—and, along with other Kennedy advisers, he considered her aristocratic appearance a political problem—but before that day ended, he would become a pillar of strength to aid her through the hours following her husband's murder. At Parkland Hospital, it was O'Donnell whom Press Aide Malcolm Kilduff came to for permission to release the news of Kennedy's death (O'Donnell told him to check with Johnson) and O'Donnell from whom Johnson sought permission to employ Air Force One for the return flight to Washington. It was

O'Donnell who assumed command of the Kennedy forces in the Kafka-like confrontation when Dallas officials refused to surrender the dead President's body. Finally, at midnight in a Washington funeral home, it was O'Donnell, O'Brien, and Powers who chose the coffin in which their leader would be buried.*

O'Donnell was not inclined toward reconciliation with Johnson during the latter's first hours as President. On Air Force One, he refused Johnson's invitations to come sit with him. When Major General Chester V. (Ted) Clifton, Kennedy's military aide, performed a chore for the new President—his Commander in Chief—O'Donnell snapped at him: "Why don't you get back and serve your new boss?"

Given this beginning, it was ironic that O'Donnell was to be among those who served the new President the longest. Sorensen, Schlesinger, and Salinger were gone within a few months, but O'Donnell stayed with Johnson through the 1964 political campaign and well into 1965. Theirs was an alliance of mutual need. Johnson needed O'Donnell as a link to the big-city Democratic leaders who were almost unknown to him. O'Donnell stayed on both out of party loyalty and because he hated to give up his role as a political power-broker in a national election year. He and Johnson treated one another with wary respect. It was no secret that O'Donnell's final loyalty was to Robert Kennedy; part of his usefulness to Johnson was in serving as a link, real and symbolic, to the Kennedys.

The Kennedy family's indebtedness to O'Donnell received a test in the fall of 1966 when he entered the Democratic primary for Governor of Massachusetts. His opponent was Edward McCormack, the Speaker's nephew, whom Ted Kennedy had trounced in a Senate race four years earlier. The Kennedys had no desire to alienate Speaker McCormack further, so they carried out a peculiar compromise in the O'Donnell-McCormack race. Senator Ted Kennedy of Massachusetts remained neutral, while Senator Robert Kennedy of New York endorsed O'Donnell.

O'Donnell lost, with 279,000 votes to McCormack's 342,000, but he had run a respectable race, and the fact that McCormack went on to lose to the Republican incumbent aroused speculation that O'Donnell might run again later.

He was prospering in Boston as a business consultant when Robert Kennedy announced for the presidency in March, 1968. O'Donnell im-

---

* It was a near-final moment of unity for this trio. Soon thereafter they agreed to jointly author a book on their experiences with Kennedy, but this venture fell through for a variety of political, financial, and personal reasons; so far, no one of them has yet published his Kennedy book.

mediately joined the campaign, and he will probably be active in Democratic politics for many years. Yet it may be that O'Donnell, like some other Kennedy men, lived his best years in 1961–63. Perhaps his finest hour came in Dallas when, blind with rage, he wrested John Kennedy's body from the grasp of the local officials. Or perhaps it came the next afternoon beside Kennedy's casket in the East Room. The assassination had struck O'Donnell like a lightning bolt—William Manchester pictures him as a "deaf mute" in Dallas—and it was not until the Saturday Mass that the tears came. Standing in the crepe-strewn East Room, he was overcome by the slow patter of the rain outdoors and the silent procession beside Kennedy's bier within. One of those who passed by the casket was Mary McGrory of the Washington *Star*. Two years earlier she had gotten O'Donnell's name wrong, but now she knew him better, and she had written in that day's *Star* that he "would have died" for Kennedy. O'Donnell embraced her and, weeping, thanked her for writing that. She said quietly, "Everybody knows that, Kenny."

5. The Bridge-Builder: O'Brien

Early in 1961, as Kennedy organized his Administration, he knew his two greatest challenges would lie in foreign affairs and in moving his domestic program through Congress. International affairs was his primary interest, and his determination to be his own Secretary of State left him with little time to be, as FDR had been, his own chief of congressional relations. Yet if Kennedy was to "get this country moving again," he had to move Congress first, and it was imperative that responsibility for directing his legislative program be entrusted to someone who combined political judgment, an ability to work effectively with members of Congress, and total dedication to Kennedy's goals.

Kennedy's inner circle was not bursting with qualified candidates for this job. Sorensen, Bundy, O'Donnell, and Robert Kennedy had many talents, but skill in charming elderly Southern legislators was not among them. Fortunately, Kennedy had one trusted lieutenant who was beautifully suited for the job: Lawrence Francis (Larry) O'Brien.

When Larry O'Brien was a small boy he often accompanied his father, an Irish immigrant turned hotel-keeper and Democratic organizer, on door-to-door canvassing through the poorer parts of Springfield, Massachusetts. Once, as they trudged along together, the elder O'Brien said something his son never forgot: "The votes are here, Larry, if we can only get them out."

O'Brien has been getting the votes out ever since. As director of organization for Kennedy's two Senate races and 1960 presidential campaign, and for Lyndon Johnson's 1964 campaign, O'Brien established himself as the foremost political strategist of the postwar era. As the Kennedy and Johnson Administrations' chief emissary to Congress, he became the architect of what was, despite some rocky intervals, an era of exceptional communication between the White House and Congress. Finally, by serving Kennedy's successor as faithfully as he had Kennedy, O'Brien became a symbol of loyalty and continuity within a Democratic Party shaken by dissent over the war in Vietnam.

He learned party loyalty early. "I got into politics because of my immigrant parentage," O'Brien says. "My father was typical of many immigrants. He saw opposition to his arrival. He saw the signs saying 'No Irish Need Apply.' The immigrants asked who was responsible for this, and they decided it was the party in power. Our state's politics was dominated by white, Anglo-Saxon Protestant Republicans, so our people became Democrats."

O'Brien's earliest memories are political: Boston Mayor James Michael Curley plotting strategy with his father in the O'Brien kitchen; his father coming home from the 1924 Democratic convention with campaign hats shaped like teapots; his father breaking with his closest friends to back Roosevelt over the Catholic Al Smith for the 1932 nomination.

Born in 1917, O'Brien served his political apprenticeship as a teenager during the '30s. As a result, he came to be a link between the past and present eras in American politics. In later years he would often be compared with Jim Farley, Roosevelt's political strategist and Postmaster General in 1933–40. Both O'Brien and Farley were immensely likable Irish politicians. Yet their similarities are less important than the one overriding difference between them: Farley was the last master practitioner of an old school of politics, and O'Brien became the first master of a new school. Farley's was the politics of exclusion; O'Brien's is the politics of inclusion. Arthur Schlesinger wrote: "The Roosevelt conception of the Democratic Party left professional politicians of the old school in a precarious and baffled position. They were used to dealing, not with coalitions, but with organizations; their lines of force moved from national committee to county courthouse, city hall, ward, and precinct, without regard to such odd groups as trade unions, nationality clubs, or women. . . . Some were flexible enough to make the adaptation.

Others were not; and among them was Farley, the last and one of the greatest of the classical school."

During the same Depression years when Farley was clinging to the old politics and consequently losing influence with Roosevelt, young Larry O'Brien was plodding the sidewalks of Springfield and pondering a new political strategy. Political bosses had always tried to keep the electorate small and manageable. O'Brien disagreed: "At an early stage in my career I saw two things that are accepted now but weren't then. First, that you should register everyone you could on the theory that registration will eventually help the Democrats. Second, that you need tight organization to register people and get out the vote. Doorbell ringing was relatively new then. I began to see what you could do if you combined an attractive candidate with an in-depth utilization of manpower."

After army duty during the war, O'Brien began to test his theories. He managed two congressional races for his friend Foster Furcolo. The first, in 1946, was a near-miss; two years later they won handily and O'Brien went to Washington as Furcolo's Administrative Assistant. In 1950, for reasons neither man has ever discussed, O'Brien broke with Furcolo and returned to Springfield, vowing that he was finished with politics. This retirement ended the next year when, in what seems in retrospect an inevitable union, Congressman John Kennedy asked him to organize his 1952 campaign against Senator Henry Cabot Lodge.

In Kennedy, O'Brien had a candidate who aroused enormous popular enthusiasm, and it was O'Brien's goal to harness every last ounce of that enthusiasm. Some politicians believe political campaigns should build gradually to a perfectly timed peak, but Kennedy and O'Brien shared a belief that there is no such thing as too much campaign activity, if it is properly directed.

Kennedy's problem in 1952 was that the state's Democratic leaders did not think he could beat Lodge and were concentrating on re-electing Governor Paul Dever. O'Brien's solution was to recruit in every community bright young men who would not seem to threaten the professional politicians and could therefore work both with them and around them. Some 340 of these "Kennedy secretaries" were appointed, and the fact that most were political amateurs inspired the now-famous O'Brien Manual, a sixty-eight-page political Bible that guided them from the first campaign tea to the last trip to the polls on election night.

O'Brien stressed the personal touch. When it came time to distribute a tabloid on Kennedy's war record, O'Brien decreed that rather than send it through the mail, volunteers should carry it door-to-door. "We wanted to get Jack Kennedy's name into conversation," O'Brien says. "Even if people only say, 'That S.O.B. Kennedy called me yesterday,' at least they're talking about you."

Farley had been contemptuous of women in politics, but O'Brien made "womanpower" basic to Kennedy's campaigns. The snob appeal of the candidate's mother and sisters was exploited to the hilt in the Kennedy teas and receptions. And every woman who came to a tea soon got a call asking her to perform volunteer work. Women who had to stay home with their children could nonetheless make campaign telephone calls or address and mail "Dear Friend" postcards—an O'Brien invention to ensure that there was some chore for every last volunteer.

A classic example of the O'Brien campaign technique came in 1952 when 1800 eager volunteers flocked to Kennedy headquarters and no one knew what to do with them. O'Brien remembered that 260,000 persons had previously signed Kennedy's nominating petition (only 2500 signatures were needed, but this was another way to give people a sense of participation). O'Brien's inspiration: to put the 1800 to work writing thank-you notes to the 260,000.

After Kennedy's victory over Lodge in 1952 he offered O'Brien a top job on his Senate staff, but O'Brien declined the offer, and throughout the 1950s he ran a public-relations firm in Springfield. Besides serving as director of organization for Kennedy's two Senate races, he was a key operative in Kennedy's 1956 takeover of the state's delegation to the Democratic National Convention. Then, in 1959, he joined the initial "Kennedy for President" team, and applied nationally the organizational techniques he had perfected in the two Senate races. The Kennedy teas might be retitled Kennedy weenie roasts in West Virginia but the principle remained the same. After the returns were in, the new President summed up his views on O'Brien: "The best election man in the business."

O'Brien says he never asked Kennedy for any appointment, but it is likely that he hoped to be repaid for his services by appointment as Postmaster General or as chairman of the Democratic National Committee. Instead, Kennedy chose to create for him the title of Special Assistant to the President for Congressional Relations, and to entrust him with mobilizing the full power, prestige, and persuasive ability of the executive branch on behalf of the New Frontier's legislative program. It was their goal, as O'Brien later put it, to build "an invisible bridge down Pennsylvania Avenue" from the White House to the Capitol.

O'Brien's bridge-building accelerated a trend that had been in progress since Woodrow Wilson's day. The nineteenth century had been a time of legislative supremacy, with the doctrine of separation of powers interpreted to mean that Presidents should keep their hands off congressional affairs. But the events of this century have helped break down the wall between the two branches of government. The growing complexity of American society has made Congress more and more dependent on presidential leadership in domestic affairs, and the press of world events has raised the President's stature as a leader in international affairs. Woodrow Wilson was the first President to be an active lobbyist, and he designated his Postmaster General, Albert Burleson, a former Congressman, to be his informal liaison with Congress.

Harding, Coolidge, and Hoover did nothing to further the evolution, but Franklin Roosevelt openly dispatched such aides as Tom Corcoran, Ben Cohen, and James Rowe to lobby for New Deal programs on Capitol Hill. Yet this remained an informal relationship; Corcoran, in his heyday as liaison with the Senate, was officially just a lawyer with the RFC. Harry Truman gave his Appointments Secretary, Matt Connelly, informal authority for congressional liaison.

Eisenhower was the first President to dispatch an official White House lobbyist to Capitol Hill. His choice for the assignment was his old friend and former military aide, General Wilton B. Persons. Persons, brother of a Democratic Governor of Alabama, was well experienced for the job; half his military career had been spent as a congressional liaison man for the Pentagon. Dapper and easy-going (his nickname was "Slick"), Persons was on a first-name basis with scores of Congressmen.

Persons had two main assistants. Bryce N. Harlow, formerly a staff member of the House Armed Services Committee, concentrated on the House, and I. Jack Martin, formerly Senator Taft's Administrative Assistant, was liaison to the Senate until his appointment to a judgeship in 1958.

Persons' office made an important beginning in molding the White House Office of Congressional Relations as an effective presidential instrument, but his operation was never as centralized, as systematic, as aggressive, or as strong as O'Brien's was. In effect, Eisenhower and Persons began the institutionalizing of the White House Congressional Relations Office and Kennedy and O'Brien perfected it.

One difference between the two operations was that Eisenhower's strong belief in the doctrine of separation of powers caused Persons and his assistants to stay away from the Capitol unless they had specific business there. Most often, they conferred with Congressmen by telephone. By contrast, O'Brien and his men spent up to half their time prowling the corridors of the Capitol.

Another difference was simply that the Eisenhower Administration had far less legislation to promote than those of Roosevelt or Truman, Kennedy or Johnson. Eisenhower came to office pledged to slow down the domestic social trends of the previous two decades, and his Congressional Relations staff was often more interested in blocking Democratic proposals than in promoting legislation of its own.

Finally, O'Brien was given a clear-cut authority that Persons lacked. Persons was outranked by Adams on the White House staff and often had to share his congressional-relations authority with Adams, Vice President Nixon, Postmaster General Arthur Summerfield, and Republican Chairman Len Hall. The title Kennedy gave O'Brien—Special Assistant for Congressional Relations—underscored the fact that O'Brien had no one between him and the President, and Kennedy backed this up with frequent expressions of confidence in O'Brien. In the early days of Kennedy's Administration, when even the most influential members of Congress made legislative proposals to him, his automatic reply was: "Have you discussed this with Larry O'Brien?"

At the same time that O'Brien's influence on Capitol Hill was being built up, that of another key Administration figure was being wiped out. Lyndon Johnson, in agreeing to trade his job as the Senate Majority Leader for the vice presidency, had deluded himself that he would continue as the new Administration's master manipulator on Capitol Hill. "Power is where power goes," he once boasted. In the pre-Inaugural period the Vice-President-elect hand-picked Mike Mansfield as his successor and arranged meetings between congressional leaders and Kennedy's Cabinet appointees. But Johnson went too far when he proposed that, as Vice President, he continue to preside over the Democratic caucus in the Senate. This proposal was voted on in caucus and actually received a majority, but the fact that seventeen Senators angrily voted against it was a moral defeat for Johnson. Stung by this rejection, and not wanting to risk another, Johnson thereafter rarely tried to wield power in congressional affairs during his vice presidency, unless called upon by O'Brien.

It is a measure of O'Brien's exceptional tact that he kept the thin-skinned Johnson's good will even as he took over the job the Texan coveted on Capitol Hill. In later years, he would be rewarded for his courtesy toward the brooding Vice President.

Kennedy and O'Brien made a nicely balanced team. At heart, both were unsentimental, disciplined, ultrapragmatic politicians, but in their styles of operation and their personal manners, they were as different as two Irish politicians could be. Kennedy, the Ambassador's son, was handsome, wry, sophisticated; O'Brien, the bartender's son, was homely, long-winded, folksy. Kennedy knew that O'Brien excelled in an area in which he himself was weak—in the ability to get along with the small-town, small-talking politicians who dominate Congress—and it is a measure of Kennedy's self-knowledge that he found an O'Brien for the job he lacked time, talent, or desire to perform.

Kennedy's appointment of O'Brien was not at all an obvious one. O'Brien was a regional political leader whose knowledge of Congress was limited to two years as the Administrative Assistant to a first-term Congressman a decade earlier. Kennedy could have entrusted congressional relations to many men with more contacts and experience on Capitol Hill. It did not necessarily follow that a shrewd campaign strategist could make the transition to being a solid salesman on the Hill.

But Kennedy knew his man; he knew it was O'Brien's skill to be not only a canny politician but to be a supremely Good Guy. Politics is a rough, often dirty business; in the showdowns, some people lose and some are hurt. O'Brien, more than any other politician since Farley, has the knack for putting a pleasant face on this business. The politicians he deals with, friend and foe, appreciate that talent, and they in effect become his constituency; he is a man they like to do business with. He set out from the first to establish personal contact with every member of Congress. In a series of get-acquainted cocktail parties, O'Brien proved himself to be a likable fellow, and a man of his word. His conversational style is a winning mixture of blarney, candor, and political insight. He listens as effectively as he talks. If there is malice in O'Brien's heart, he keeps it hidden from view. When he has to say No to a request, his anguish is so painfully obvious that the person making the request may end up apologizing. He plays the game of politics hard but clean, and as late as 1965 it was still possible for Tom Wicker to write that O'Brien's enemies could meet in a telephone booth.

Along with his popularity with members of Congress, O'Brien enjoyed press relations unexcelled among politicians. Reporters liked him, personally, in a way they never liked, say, Robert Kennedy or McGeorge Bundy or Richard Nixon. Moreover, O'Brien's encyclopedic knowledge of political affairs made him an invaluable source of information for key Washington reporters. After he became Postmaster General, his personal popularity with writers and editors undoubtedly did much to shield the Post Office from criticism for its increasingly snarled service in the late 1960s.

To aid his Congressional Relations program, O'Brien put together a small, talented staff. To oversee dealings with the Senate, he chose Mike Manatos of Wyoming, who had for many years been a Senate staff aide. To work with the House, he chose a young North Carolina lawyer and politician, Henry Hall Wilson, who had been a pro-Kennedy delegate to the 1960 Democratic National Convention. Wilson had no congressional background, but this was not necessarily a drawback, since it meant he had no vested interests in House affairs. The tall, hard-working Wilson did have a Southern accent, and that was important, for it was clear that the fate of Kennedy's program would rest with a few dozen Southern and border-state Representatives who fluctuated between modern conservatism and old style populism. On most issues, the House in 1961 had 180 members solidly for Kennedy, another 180 solidly against him, and about 70 others who held the balance of power.

O'Brien's immediate staff was only the core of his operation. Another important element consisted of forty congressional liaison officers from the federal departments and agencies. In the past, these agencies had often negotiated directly with their friends in Congress with little regard for the President's legislative priorities. O'Brien worked to weld their efforts into a single, O'Brien-directed operation that focused on the President's program, not the vested interests of the agencies. To this end he held weekly meetings with the forty or so liaison officers and required them to submit written reports to him on their dealings with Congress. Finally, in addition to overseeing his own staff and the agencies' staffs, O'Brien worked closely with private lobbies which were friendly to the President, particularly the AFL-CIO. Thus, on an important issue, O'Brien could bring to bear on a member of Congress the resources of the White House, of executive agencies, and of influential outside lobbyists.

Kennedy and O'Brien were in full agreement on the style of operation the latter should carry out in the furtherance of the President's program: patience was the byword, persuasion the goal. O'Brien would dangle or withhold patronage in specific instances, but the prevailing strategy was to try to win congressional support by persuasion and favors rather than by force or by Kennedy's bypassing Congress to appeal to public opinion, as Roosevelt and Truman had done.

Not everyone agreed with this strategy. One dissenter was Schlesinger: "At the time it seemed that Kennedy suffered from the illusion so common to new Presidents (even Roosevelt had it till 1935) that he, unlike any of his predecessors, could really be President of all the people and achieve his purposes without pain or trauma. Some of us, however, thought national argument the best way to break national apathy and communicate the reality of problems. We believed that the educational value of fights in drawing the line between the administration and its opponents would guarantee that, even if we did not have a law, we would have an issue. So we thought him mistaken in 1962 in making the entirely respectable, safe, and overrated trade expansion bill his top legislative priority instead of staging a knockdown-drag-out fight over federal aid to education or Medicare. To the President I would cite the Roosevelts, Wilson, Jackson, and so on in arguing the inevitability and superiority of the politics of combat to the politics of consensus. But, while he did not dispute the historical points, he plainly saw no reason for rushing prematurely into battle."*

Schlesinger was not alone in the view that Kennedy was overcautious. *The Washington Post*'s Carroll Kilpatrick commented: "It is in the use of public opinion to spur Congress that President Kennedy has most disappointed some of his supporters. . . . Unlike Wilson and the two Roosevelts, President Kennedy has refused to go over the heads of his former colleagues on Capitol Hill. . . . Instead, he has sought to win them over by the elements of compromise and adjustment he learned so well in the Senate."

The cautious Kennedy-O'Brien approach to Congress was all the more galling to liberals because of the brave rhetoric of Kennedy's campaign, which had contrasted his presumed fearlessness with Eisenhower's presumed timidity. ("In the decade that lies ahead, the challenging, revolutionary Sixties, the American presidency will demand more than ringing manifestos issued from the rear of the battle. . . .")

---

* Schlesinger's use of the word "prematurely" here is typical of the countless instances in *A Thousand Days* where he softens his criticisms of Kennedy. The question, in this context, was not whether Kennedy would rush prematurely into battle, but whether he would ever do battle at all.

Kennedy, it might be added, had a number of ingenious ways of rationalizing his reluctance to fight for his program on Capitol Hill. "Why fight if you are not sure to win?" he would ask. Or he would quote Thomas Jefferson's dictum that great victories can't be built on slim majorities. Or, resorting to Shakespeare, he would cite the exchange from *The Tempest* in which one character boasts that he can summon spirits, and another replies, Yes, but will they come when you summon them?

If one wishes to resort to aphorisms, literature and history contain many more exhorting courage than caution, from "Nothing ventured, nothing gained," to Harry Truman's comment that if you can't take the heat you shouldn't be in the kitchen.

Douglass Cater wrote of the contrast between the Kennedy Administration's "courageous expectations and cautious operations" and commented that "in a number of major battles Kennedy appeared to make a display more for the record than for anticipated results."

But Kennedy continued to agree with O'Brien that slow, day-in-day-out persuasion was the way to get legislation through Congress. O'Brien firmly believed that every member could be reached if you could only find the right key to his interests. O'Brien and his aides compiled an elaborate file on each Congressman's political background, prejudices, and pet projects. Every time a member asked a federal agency for a favor, or received one without asking, O'Brien was informed.

O'Brien's main tools as he sought to win over Senators and Congressmen were persuasion, patronage, and the President.

Persuasion—or education, as he sometimes calls it—is the means O'Brien most likes to discuss. He and his men did their homework (as the New Frontier jargon termed it) and were able to discuss how the Kennedy proposals would benefit individual members' states or districts. They would begin explaining important measures to the legislators months before the bills came to a vote.

In congressional showdowns, O'Brien had authority to negotiate substantive changes in Administration proposals in order to get them through Congress. He gives this account of the decisions he faced on the Administration's $1.25 minimum wage bill in the spring of 1961:

"The House Education and Labor Committee reported the Administration bill, but a canvass of Congress clearly showed that passage in its present form was doubtful. I can vividly recall a meeting in Speaker Rayburn's office, where Arthur Goldberg, then Secretary of Labor, the Democratic leadership and members of the Committee considered what we should do. Much to my discomfort, the final decision was left to me, because the tough decision was a political one. Should we compromise? And if so, where? Should we fight this issue out? And how should we best handle the bill on the floor of the House?

"I was the President's man in that meeting and while I could have picked up the phone and called him, I knew the choice was mine to make.

"So, I decided to hold to the $1.25 figure, but to agree to certain reductions in the number to be added to the minimum wage umbrella. Since we needed the votes of Southern Democrats to win this fight, I suggested that Carl Albert, the Democratic Whip from Oklahoma, be named as floor manager.

"When the bill came to a vote, however, we were defeated—186 to 185. I had to report this news to President Kennedy. I hated to go into that office and tell him that legislation he wanted so much for the workingman had been defeated by one vote. I can still see his reaction as I broke the news. 'One vote!' he said, and in frustration he plunged a letter opener into the top of his desk.

"There were two critical judgments to be made in the course of this legislation through the Congress. My first, that we should hold to $1.25 an hour, seemed to have been proven faulty.

"However, the Republican opposition, anxious to gain credit for some kind of minimum wage law, then introduced an amendment calling for $1.15 an hour, and a much scaled down extension to new groups. This passed the House and went on to the Senate. The Senate passed a bill calling for the Administration's proposal of $1.25 and extension to over four million new workers.

"The matter then reached a Senate-House Conference Committee. Again, I was asked to make a critical judgment. Should the Administration take a tough line, or modify its position? I knew that a tough stand was what the President wanted, but that we could agree to a two-step increase, first to $1.15 and then to $1.25. . . . The result was that the Conference Report was voted, 230 to 196, giving us substantially what we wanted, and involving no real compromise with the $1.25 minimum."

To get the support needed to pass the minimum wage bill, O'Brien had to agree to major concessions—140,000 laundry workers, 300,000 employees of auto dealerships, 15,000 cotton gin employees, and 17,000 local transit workers were dropped from the coverage of the bill. The Administration also had to agree to wait two years instead of one for the second-step increase from $1.15 to $1.25.

These were difficult and far-reaching decisions, yet in the heat of legislative battles O'Brien often had to make them and live with them. The experience sobered O'Brien. He freely admits that before 1961 he viewed politics as an exciting game—he was interested in winning elections, not what his candidates did after they were in office. Now, he says: "Working in the White House on legislation that affects millions of people has made a different guy out of me. Politics is no longer just a game, but a very serious business."

Yet despite his authority to make crucial decisions such as the ones on the minimum wage bill, O'Brien felt that his greatest importance was less in his influence on specific bills than in his providing continual, clear-cut lines of communication between the White House and

Congress: "For the first time, someone from the White House could sit in the Speaker's office with the congressional leadership and be recognized as a spokesman for the President. You weren't an errand boy or a head-counter, you had the authority to speak for the President."

Patronage is a weapon O'Brien likes less to talk about. Essentially there are two types of patronage available to the White House. The first is specific jobs: government appointments, postmasterships, judgeships, and so forth. The second is the infinity of government grants and contracts —the time-honored federal "pork barrel"—that has become increasingly important with the postwar proliferation of defense contracts and domestic welfare programs.

It was Kennedy's original intention to give O'Brien responsibility for both congressional relations and patronage. Two factors prevented this. First, O'Brien simply did not have time for both jobs. Second, O'Brien agreed with the adage that he who dispenses patronage usually winds up with "one ingrate and ten enemies." So an elaborate arrangement was reached whereby official responsibility for job patronage was given to John Bailey, chairman of the Democratic National Committee, but day-to-day supervision was assigned to Richard Donahue, who worked out of O'Brien's White House office. In effect, O'Brien managed it so he could take credit for the President for jobs given, while Bailey took the blame for jobs denied.

The second type of federal patronage, involving federal grants and contracts, is a more delicate matter, for two reasons. First, because such awards (unlike job patronage) are in theory made on a non-political basis; second, because they affect not just one job-seeking politician, but entire communities which may, in effect, be punished for their Congressman's political sins. Only a small minority of federal grants and contracts are awarded—or withheld—for political reasons, but the power existed for use in extreme cases.

O'Brien's office also expanded the practice of letting the party in power's Congressmen announce—and so take credit for—new federal grants and contracts in their districts.

On the other hand, when a federal agency was unable to approve some Congressman's pet project, O'Brien kept as far away as possible from the unpleasantry. "We let the agencies take the heat if we could," he once told me. "If not, my staff took it. If that didn't work, I took it. But in no case, if I could help it, did the President take the heat."

Finally, there was the power and the prestige of the presidency to apply to congressional persuasion. Both Kennedy and O'Brien agreed that this power should be hoarded, but at the proper moments there were favors to dangle: an invitation to a White House dinner, a seat in the presidential box at the baseball opener, morning coffee or an afternoon drink with the President. There were larger favors, such as the promise of presidential campaign help in exchange for support on a controversial vote. And for certain powerful members, such as Senators Russell of Georgia and Byrd of Virginia, and Congressmen Mills of Arkansas and Vinson of Georgia, there was careful, continual cultivation. Prompted by O'Brien, Kennedy would sometimes call these men, not to cajole, but just to chat with an eye to future needs. In one well-known instance, when Kennedy and Vinson were on a collision course over the controversial RS-70 airplane, Kennedy saved the day by taking the seventy-eight-year-old Congressman on the famous "walk in the Rose Garden" and persuading him to withdraw his demands.

O'Brien had an understanding with Kennedy that early in 1964 he would move from the White House to the Democratic National Committee to organize the 1964 re-election campaign. After that, O'Brien expected to return to private life. Kennedy's assassination suddenly changed these plans. Lyndon Johnson, on the flight back from Dallas, told O'Brien: "You have no constitutional obligation. You have signed no contract. You're an American citizen, free to do what you please. And I ask you to stand shoulder to shoulder with me. Your work in the White House should continue as is, and you have a blank check to carry it out."

At the time O'Brien was in a state of near-shock and had little interest in Johnson's rhetoric; he remembers thinking: Hell, let's talk about this later. But he soon found that Johnson meant what he said about a blank check. O'Brien's power and prestige increased under Johnson, who had never had working for him a politician of O'Brien's caliber. O'Brien was never exposed to the searing abuse Johnson sometimes pours on his employees. On the contrary, Johnson gave tangible recognition to O'Brien's senior status when he raised all the Special Assistants' salaries to $28,500 in 1965—except O'Brien's, which was raised to $30,000. Overburdened by the 1964 campaign, then by the 1965 escalation of the Vietnamese war, Johnson usually accepted O'Brien's recommendations on legislative decisions and priorities with only cursory reviews. In most cases, O'Brien's was the final word on what bills the Administration fought for or soft-pedaled.

After Johnson's election in 1964, O'Brien was ready to leave government, but at the President's urging he agreed to stay on through the 1965 legislative year. One main reason was that, with the new Democratic majorities created by Johnson's landslide victory of 1964, O'Brien saw an opportunity to help pass much of the Kennedy program that he had been fighting for since 1961. O'Brien's decision to stay in the Johnson Administration had caused him to take much abuse from some of his old associates. He had broken with Ken O'Donnell, and he knew that lesser Kennedy partisans were calling him "traitor" and "turncoat" behind his back. But as O'Brien saw it, he could make no finer gesture to the dead President's memory than to stay and do what he could to help pass Kennedy's legislative program. Moreover, above and beyond the legislative program, O'Brien saw his loyalty as being to the Democratic Party, whether its leader was named Kennedy, Johnson, Humphrey, or whatever.

His hopes for the 1965 legislative year were realized; he says with pride: "That year cannot be touched by any legislative year in history." But as it drew to a close, he was again ready to leave the White House. His prospects included several $100,000-a-year jobs, and the possibility of running for the Senate in Massachusetts. Then, in August, Johnson unexpectedly played the one card that could have kept O'Brien in the government: He offered him the post of Postmaster General, the job that since Andrew Jackson's day has traditionally gone to the top professional politician of the party in power.

As Postmaster General, O'Brien continued to direct the Administration's legislative program. In addition to the palatial Postmaster General's office, O'Brien kept an office on the second floor of the White House, and he was in it almost every day. Henry Hall Wilson, his chief assistant, took on increased duties. However, early in 1967, Wilson accepted a $100,000 position as president of the Chicago Board of Trade. He was replaced by H. Barefoot Sanders, Jr., a lawyer from Texas.

Soon after Johnson said he would not seek re-election, O'Brien left the Cabinet and joined RFK's campaign staff. After Kennedy's death, he joined Humphrey's campaign but will probably return to private life after the 1968 election. Thus, after his seven years' service in Washington, it is appropriate to ask what O'Brien's operation accomplished, and what its future prospects might be.

It is not at all easy to evaluate the legislative achievement of either the Kennedy Administration or the Johnson Administration at this early date. In Kennedy's case, the verdict largely depends upon whether one assumes his strategy of conciliation would have paid off with the passage of Medicare in 1964 and aid to education in 1965. O'Brien thinks it would have. Moreover, the experts are still disagreed on the importance of certain pieces of New Frontier legislation; one political scientist, for example, calls the Trade Expansion Act of 1962 Kennedy's outstanding legislative achievement, but Schlesinger calls it "overrated." It is necessary, too, for more time to pass before one can fairly evaluate the effectiveness of the major legislative accomplishments of either the Kennedy or the Johnson Administrations. After a few more years' experience, for example, both Kennedy's Alliance for Progress and Johnson's "war on poverty" may seem in retrospect to have been woefully misconceived.

Nonetheless, if one views the legislative record of 1961–67 as a single period—the O'Brien era, perhaps—it is clear that a great deal of legislation passed Congress, more than in any comparable period since 1933–37. Some of the major bills included the minimum wage increase, the trade expansion act, the civil rights bill, the Alliance for Progress, the nuclear test-ban treaty, Medicare, federal aid to education, the model cities program, the 1963 tax cut, and the creation of two new Cabinet-level executive departments. Whether or not this is all good legislation is debatable; if so, credit must go to the two Presidents and to men like Sorensen and Moyers who helped shape it. But regardless of the merits of the legislation, it is clear that O'Brien's quiet spadework did much to gain its passage. His job was not to write bills but to pass them, and in the service of both Kennedy and Johnson, he proved himself to be a political technician of unexcelled ability.

As he worked to pass legislation, O'Brien was shaping a new presidential institution and opening new possibilities of cooperation between the White House and Congress. Roaming the halls of Congress, huddling with congressional leaders on legislative strategy, O'Brien symbolized the virtual breakdown of the old concept of separation of powers; the modern President has become not only chief executive and commander in chief, but chief legislator.

Under Secretary of the Treasury Joseph Barr, a former Congressman and an informed (if not disinterested) observer of Washington in the 1960s, comments:

"This rather simple device of consciously building a bridge across the Constitutional Gulf has helped combine the advantages of a congressional and a parliamentary system . . . while maintaining the absolute independence of the individual Member of Congress, the O'Brien bridge has in effect opened a parliamentary dialogue in a congressional system. I mean by this that the politicians—the Members and the President—are now engaged in a direct dialogue as they would in a Parliament."

Whether or not the O'Brien bridge will survive O'Brien remains to be seen. It is unlikely that a future President or future Congress will want to return to the non-communication of the last century, or could do so even if the desire existed. But whether future White House liaison offices can have the influence of O'Brien's will depend on whether future Presidents have the good fortune to find someone equaling O'Brien's rare combination of talents. In his use of O'Brien—as in his use of McGeorge Bundy in national security affairs—Kennedy perfected a recent presidential institution, and did so by selecting a man so uniquely qualified for the task that his performance may never be equaled. Still, an important precedent had been set, and the way made clear for future presidential emissaries to march across O'Brien's bridge.

6. *Dean of the World: Bundy*

McGeorge Bundy, Kennedy's Special Assistant for National Security Affairs, brought to his job a sheer intellectual capacity such as had not been regularly employed in the White House since Tom Corcoran's heyday. Kennedy considered Bundy the second brightest man he knew (Kennedy's longtime friend, British Ambassador David Ormsby-Gore, ranked first) and he once said of Bundy's talents: "First, you can't beat brains, and with brains, judgment. Then, he gets the work done. He does a tremendous amount of work. And he doesn't fold or get rattled when they're sniping at him."

Beyond brilliance, Bundy was controversial—witty, acidulous, aristocratic, ambitious, overbearing, self-satisfied, self-serving. To those who had known him as Harvard's youthful Dean of Arts and Sciences (the university's number-two job) in the 1950s, and to those who were privileged to enter his sanctuary in the White House basement in 1961–65 for off-the-record insights into world affairs, Bundy was a multifaceted, always fascinating figure. Yet this very combination of personal fascination with the elusive, confidential nature of his responsibilities inevitably led journalists to write much more about Bundy himself—his wit, his brains, his background—than about the complex nature of his work. This was unfortunate because, as Bundy himself would say, the job was more important than the man.

Bundy's job was nothing less than to serve Kennedy as a kind of one-man National Security Council. In so doing he reflected Kennedy's administrative style as surely as Eisenhower's formal, systematic NSC process had reflected his administrative theories. Kennedy had agreed with the Jackson Subcommittee's criticisms of Eisenhower's NSC system. He was bored by the sort of large, roundtable discussions that Eisenhower so enjoyed. He wanted a faster, more flexible system. He wanted his personal representatives to prod and double-check the foreign affairs bureaucracy. Kennedy served notice that he had major changes in mind when he said, in announcing Bundy's appointment on January 1, 1961:

"I intend to consolidate under Mr. Bundy's direction the present National Security Council secretariat, the staff and functions of the Operations Control Board, and the continuing functions of a number of special projects staffs within the White House. . . . It is my hope to use the National Security Council and its machinery more flexibly than in the past."

At that point, Kennedy and Bundy were little more than acquaintances, and there was scant reason to think that Bundy would soon emerge as one of the most influential men in Kennedy's Administration. Yet once again Kennedy's instincts for men were sure; in Bundy's case, as in O'Brien's, the man and the mission were perfectly matched. Bundy, taking advantage of Dean Rusk's noncompetitive nature, would soon become Kennedy's principal adviser on foreign affairs, outshining the Secretary of State and the National Security Council. Many political observers were startled by Bundy's quick rise to power, but his old colleagues at Harvard were not. Bundy, one of them observed, had advanced as might be expected: from Dean of Harvard to Dean of the World.

It is probably McGeorge Bundy's destiny to become United States Secretary of State. He certainly thinks so, and so do many other, more objective observers. Any President, Republican or Democrat, who enters the White House after Johnson will have to give Bundy serious consideration for the post, for he has the brains, he has the experience, and like that other Establishmentarian of yesteryear, John Foster Dulles, he has been readying himself to be Secretary of State since the day he was born.

That day was March 30, 1919, and the place was Boston. His father was Harvey Hollister Bundy, a native of Grand Rapids, Michigan, who had become a prominent Bostonian by virtue of: 1) a distinguished law career and 2) a distinguished marriage—to Katherine Putnam, a niece of former Harvard president A. L. Lowell and of poetess Amy Lowell. Harvey H. Bundy three times left his law practice for public service: during the First World War as assistant counsel to the U. S. Food Administration, during the Hoover Administration as Assistant Secretary of State under his friend Henry Stimson, and during the Second World War as Special Assistant to Stimson when the latter served as Secretary of War.

McGeorge Bundy grew up, therefore, in a Beacon Street household where diplomatic and political affairs were staple, everyday conversation. He was a child of the Establishment, and his life was linked from the first with others who would in time assume prominent roles in national affairs. At age eight he entered the Dexter School, one class behind John F. Kennedy. His brother, William Bundy, married Dean Acheson's daughter. His sister married Hugh Auchincloss, a cousin of Jacqueline Kennedy's stepfather.

After prepping at Groton, Bundy enrolled at Yale, where he was the first freshman ever to receive three perfect scores on the college entrance exams. He majored in mathematics, wrote for the *Yale Daily News*, and was elected to Phi Beta Kappa and Skull and Bones. During the war he was an army officer who enjoyed what one writer called "a stylish service in the company of star-studded brass." Bundy's brother jokes that McGeorge, while stationed in London, "went to Harold Laski's soirees on Tuesday night and Lady Astor's on the weekend. It was a balanced ticket."

Just after the war Bundy helped his old family friend, Henry Stimson, write his memoirs, *On Active Service in Peace and War*. In April of 1948, he went to Washington to work on the Truman Administration's Marshall Plan. He was a Republican, however, and he left in the fall to join Governor Dewey's presidential campaign as a junior member of the foreign policy advisory team. Bundy later recalled: "We didn't demean ourselves writing speeches. We were too busy deciding on applications for ambassadorships."

After Dewey's bubble burst, Bundy prepared to return to Washington, but the Truman Administration decided it could do without one of Tom Dewey's unemployed speechwriters. He next took a job as a political analyst for the prestigious, non-governmental Council on Foreign Relations. Soon the tempo of his life increased. In the fall of 1949 he went to Harvard, where his "The U.S. in World Politics" soon became a favorite undergraduate course. In 1950, he married Mary

Buckminster Lothrop, then the assistant director of admissions at Radcliffe. In 1951–52, he edited Dean Acheson's papers, thereby making enemies in some Republican circles.

He had meanwhile advanced to a full professorship with astonishing speed, and in 1953 the thirty-four-year-old Bundy was considered for the Harvard presidency. But he was too young, and the prize went instead to Nathan Pusey, who quickly promoted Bundy to the university's number-two post, Dean of Arts and Sciences. He was a freewheeling manipulator of some thirty departments, forty faculty committees, and six hundred faculty members. His ability was everywhere respected, but his personality inspired conflicting views. One professor later recalled: "When Bundy was here, Harvard was like a glass of champagne and he knew every bubble by its first name." Another professor said: "I have great admiration for Mac Bundy. But I don't like him personally. He pays no attention to what the other fellow may think. He's as cold as ice and snippy about everything."

Although Bundy had supported Eisenhower in 1952 and 1956, the Eisenhower Administration never offered him a job of sufficient responsibility to lure him away from Harvard. When the Republicans nominated Richard Nixon in 1960, Bundy decided to support John Kennedy. He had known Kennedy casually at debutante parties in the pre-war years, and as a Harvard overseer in the 1950s. He did not play an active role in Kennedy's campaign, yet Kennedy instinctively wanted Bundy in an important post in his Administration.

He considered Bundy for Secretary of State, but there were too many strikes against him: his youth, his Republican affiliation, Adlai Stevenson's stated refusal to serve under him, his lack of national reputation, the likelihood that his crisp manner would rub Congress the wrong way.

Kennedy proposed to make Bundy the Deputy Under Secretary of State for Administration, Assistant Secretary of Defense for National Security Affairs, or head of the U.S. disarmament program, but none of these interested Bundy. Finally, almost by chance, they hit upon a mutually satisfactory job: Bundy would be Special Assistant for National Security Affairs.

From the first, Kennedy instructed Bundy to streamline the national security operation. Political scientist Richard Neustadt, one of Kennedy's liaisons with the outgoing Administration, delighted in introducing Bundy in the Eisenhower White House as the man who would personally replace five Eisenhower aides. Kennedy believed the Eisenhower system, with its policy papers by the Planning Board and coordination by the OCB, had sapped initiative from the State Department, so he abolished both boards. In abolishing the OCB—and some fifty interdepartmental committees that died with it—he stated: "We will center responsibility for much of the Board's work in the Secretary of State." (When the Secretary of State failed to accept these new responsibilities, much of the power flowed back to Bundy in the White House, but that came later.)

Bundy cut the size of the national security staff by about a third, from roughly seventy-five to fifty persons. Ten to fifteen of these were his professional staff—experts in such fields as European affairs, economics, intelligence—and the rest were communications and clerical personnel. There was no distinction, as there had been on the Eisenhower staff, between planners and implementers. Bundy's men were recruited from law firms, universities, and the government. They were young (average age around forty-three), well-paid, overworked, aggressive, and united in something close to fear of Bundy.

As Kennedy's disenchantment with the State Department grew, Arthur Schlesinger writes, he sometimes dreamed of starting a small, secret office to run foreign affairs "while maintaining the State Department as a façade in which people might contentedly carry papers from bureau to bureau." Bundy's office was the closest Kennedy came to realizing that dream. Its members were supposed to keep in touch with every aspect of foreign affairs: disarmament negotiations, NATO troop levels, the Common Market, Harold Wilson's political problems, the latest border dispute in Pakistan or Israel or Yemen, the intrigues of Buddhist leaders in Saigon, the state of the aid program in India, the probability of a coup in Greece. It was their job to know everything, because it is the President's job to know everything.

Obviously, Bundy's staff duplicated work done at the State Department. It was supposed to. Kennedy often had little faith in facts and opinions presented to him by career officials at State, men who were unknown to him personally and of uncertain loyalties, but he felt as confident as a President can feel that information coming to him from Bundy's office would be fully investigated and verified for him to act upon.

In the first months of the new Administration, Bundy was housed across the street from the White House in the Executive Office Building. But his importance soared in the aftermath of the Bay of Pigs disaster, and one of his first moves was to obtain offices in the West Wing basement. Soon Bundy scored again—in the establishment in the White House basement of a communications center (dubbed the Situation Room), with teletype machines receiving all important messages from military, diplomatic, and intelligence centers around the world simultaneously as they were received at State, Defense, and the CIA. In so doing, he did much to make Kennedy the master of his own house. At the same time, Bundy was strengthening his position, since he was now the President's primary source of official information. Immediate access to routine cables made it possible for Bundy and his staff to deal with the bureaucracy on an informed basis. One member of the national security operation recalls: "The communications center was a tremendous breakthrough, and they fought us like crazy on it. Over there, they think you should never let raw intelligence into the White House —those fools might push the button."

Although Kennedy's NSC maintained the same outward forms as Eisenhower's—the Council held meetings, the President had a Special Assistant who headed a staff of experts—the actual operation of the two systems differed as night from day. Eisenhower saw his first Special Assistant, Cutler, about four times a week; Kennedy was more likely to see Bundy four times a day. The production of policy papers, so vital to Eisenhower's system, was shifted to State's Policy Planning Council, and had little relevance to presidential decision-making.

The Council itself fell into disuse. Kennedy cut its meetings back to every three weeks or so, and tended to use them either as briefing sessions or to rubber-stamp previously agreed-on decisions. Yet during the Cuban missile crisis, Kennedy turned to the NSC to help him make the hardest decision of his life. Since two to three dozen officials had some claim to NSC membership, Kennedy had to make use of his NSC's flexibility: he called together the fifteen or so men whose advice he wanted and dubbed them the Executive Committee of the NSC.

Whereas Eisenhower had been content to let many foreign affairs problems ascend to him via the bureaucratic process and the NSC machinery, Kennedy dispatched Bundy and his staff to be spies in the hostile land of the permanent government, to zip in and out of it like PT-boats harassing an enemy armada.

Kennedy believed (like Roosevelt and Johnson, unlike Truman and Eisenhower) that a little high-level duplicity is needed now and then to lubricate the wheels of government. Roger Hilsman tells of the time early in 1963 when he was promoted from a lesser State Department post to Assistant Secretary for Far Eastern Affairs, and Sec-

retary Rusk told him that he had assured the Pentagon that Hilsman
would no longer intrude in military and strategic matters. The moment
Hilsman returned to his office, he received a call from the White
House; he does not identify his caller, but Bundy would seem a logical
guess. "By now you will have been told that you are to be the new
Assistant Secretary for Far Eastern Affairs," the caller said. "You will
also have been told to refrain from intruding into military and strategic
matters. Well, the President wants you to understand that it was
precisely because you have stood up to the Defense Department that
you were chosen, and that he expects you to continue."

An inevitable friction, a kind of love-hate relationship, existed between the Bundy operation and the State Department. At the highest
level, it was often said, probably correctly, that Bundy had more influence on Kennedy than Rusk did. This did nothing to endear Bundy
to Rusk, yet there is another side to the picture. Any modern Secretary
of State, overburdened with administrative, ceremonial, and congressional demands on his time, needs all the help he can get. The White
House staff can help the Secretary ride herd on his bureaucratic underlings, and it can relieve pressure on the State Department by attending to the President's immediate, personal needs for information,
for advice, for documents, sometimes just for someone to be mad at.
"The President," says one member of the Kennedy-Johnson NSC
operation, "is entitled to have a mattress—people he can kick the hell
out of and they won't do anything at all."

It was no secret that Bundy, like Kennedy, was more impressed by
McNamara's performance at Defense than by Rusk's at State, but Bundy
was too wise to be other than cordial and correct in his dealings with
the Secretary of State. Bundy and Rusk, like all Kennedy's people,
were disciplined men, able to conceal their inner feelings in the interests of getting the job done, and in many ways Bundy, Rusk, and
McNamara constituted a foreign affairs triumvirate of considerable skill
and strength. Nor should Rusk's talents be dismissed; he, after all, got
the job Bundy wanted in the beginning and still had it long after
Bundy had returned to private life.

Despite the fact that the National Security staff often lightens the
State Department's burdens, hostility is never far beneath the surface
in their relationship. The National Security staff members may pro-
claim—as Bundy's successor, Walt W. Rostow, often does—that they
are merely "messenger boys," but their personal talents plus their proximity to the President inevitably make them much more than that.
Presidents are likely to put more trust in someone they see every

day or two than to trust someone from State or Defense or Treasury whose face is only a blur to them. One member of Johnson's National Security staff put it this way:

"The point is that with his own staff the President is comfortable, at ease, he knows how far he can trust them and depend on them. All this is not true of an Assistant Secretary of State or Defense.

"Say you're writing a memo to the President. You don't know how much he knows, or how much he wants to know. You have to guess. There's something he needs to know, but you're afraid that, if you add those three extra paragraphs, you'll lose him. It's a gamble every time. But it's something an Assistant Secretary who sees him three times a year just can't do."

One reason Kennedy and Johnson increasingly depended on their National Security staffs was simply the time element. Kennedy once said, "Damn it, Bundy and I get more done in one day in the White House than they do in six months in the State Department." After Kennedy's 1961 meeting with Premier Khrushchev, the State Department took five weeks to produce an important *aide-mémoire* Kennedy wanted to send to the Russian leader.

Yet in the last analysis the National Security staff has to depend upon the State Department for most of the information with which it must make decisions and advise the President. To protect themselves, the National Security staff members will double-check with other agencies and will seek out members of the bureaucracy they think they can trust. One member of the Bundy staff told me: "The people at State have to decide. They can try to lick us, or they can join us. The good ones join us." Another says: "If you're any good, you have a spy system. You know whom you can trust in the bureaucracy. You have a system of rewards and punishments. If you tell someone, 'I misled the President today because you gave me bad information,' he shouldn't sleep very well that night."

Much of the National Security staff's work is concerned with helping the President decide between the conflicting advice given him by the various agencies of government. For although everyone agrees that State should take the lead in coordinating and arbitrating government-wide efforts in foreign affairs, State has not done so, and the initiative has often passed to the White House staff.

Late in 1966, for example, President Johnson faced a decision over the tactics he should follow in the "Kennedy round" tariff negotiations in Geneva. The Common Market countries had failed to meet a deadline for putting forth their proposals for agricultural tariffs. The U.S.

had to decide whether to go ahead and table its proposals, or to stall for more time. Dozens of political, agricultural, economic, and diplomatic elements were wrapped up in this decision, and Johnson received separate opinions from his special trade adviser William M. Roth and from the Secretaries of State, Agriculture, Commerce, and Treasury. Johnson in turn sought advice from Francis Bator, an economist from M.I.T. who was then Deputy Special Assistant on the National Security staff. Bator advised the President to go ahead with the U.S. agricultural proposals—thus siding with the Secretary of State and Special Adviser Roth, and opposing the Secretary of Agriculture. Johnson followed this advice.

Another time, Secretary of the Treasury Fowler handed President Johnson an extremely complicated, six-page memorandum seeking clarification of the U.S. position on increasing its contribution to the International Development Association, a World Bank subsidiary which (with forty percent U.S. funding) makes "soft" loans to underdeveloped nations. Again, Johnson passed the memorandum on to Bator for his recommendations. Bator told the President he could make a quick decision (as Fowler had requested) if he so desired, but he would urge that the President instruct him (Bator) to call an inter-agency meeting to discuss the matter. Johnson agreed, and Bator called together the Budget Director, the AID Administrator, and officials from State and Treasury. This meeting resolved differences and resulted in a joint memorandum from Fowler and Rusk agreeing on a U.S. policy toward the IDA. In essence, the agreement was that the U.S. increase its commitment to IDA from $250 million to $1 billion over a three-year period. The Rusk-Fowler memo recommended that this promise be communicated to officials of the World Bank.

Then Johnson surprised his advisers by refusing to follow their advice. Always sensitive to congressional feelings, Johnson told his advisers he would make no such commitment until they had discussed the issue with leading congressional leaders. Only after dozens of House and Senate leaders had been consulted, did the President give his approval to the Rusk-Fowler proposal.

In all such matters, the National Security staff members serve as "President protectors," making sure the President's interests take precedence. During the Kennedy and Johnson Administrations, virtually every memorandum to the President from the State Department reached him with a covering memorandum from the National Security staff. One of its officials explains: "We clarify issues, add facts, comment on political issues the State Department isn't sensitive to—in effect the

President gets a one- or two-page memo from this office, and the State Department memo becomes a back-up document. We honestly wish they'd do the job the first time, but they won't."

Doing it right the first time, in Johnsonian terms, means writing the document in the style which catches the President's eye. Typically, a State Department memorandum to the President will be six or eight pages long, with long paragraphs in a sort of essay style. The NSC staff's covering memo, by contrast, would be shorter, with short sentences and paragraphs, and with key words capitalized, underlined, or over-scored in transparent yellow with a felt-tipped pen for emphasis. The NSC staff memo, moreover, would be couched in plain political patois, with phrases like "If you want to make the Prime Minister happy . . ." or "We've got them where it hurts on this one. . . ."

The need for President-protecting was never more dramatically seen than in the midst of the Cuban missile crisis when Kennedy learned, to his total dismay, that America's obsolete Jupiter missiles were still in Turkey despite his specific instructions, months earlier, that they be removed. The missiles became an issue when Khrushchev demanded that they be withdrawn in exchange of his withdrawal of the missiles from Cuba. The State Department had dragged its feet in the matter because it feared the Turkish government would be angry at the prospect of losing the American dollars that accompanied the missile bases. Elie Abel writes in *The Missile Crisis* of the President's reaction when he learned his orders had been ignored: "Kennedy reflected sadly on the built-in futilities of big government, and, in the struggle to control his emotions, left the room."

For all these reasons, Kennedy deputized Bundy to help him stay atop fast-moving world events. Bundy decided what issues reached the President and what issues did not. Bundy was the bearer of news, good and bad; this fact was never more dramatically seen then when Bundy was informed one evening about the Russian missiles in Cuba, and calmly decided to let Kennedy get a good night's sleep before he broke the news to him.* Bundy became, in Joseph Kraft's phrase,

---

* Bundy's apparent audacity in keeping the news of the missile installations from Kennedy for some twelve hours has never ceased to astound some observers. Bundy first learned of the missiles from the CIA at 8:30 P.M. on Monday, October 15. He considered informing Kennedy immediately but decided against such action. Bundy later explained: "The President would have asked the inevitable question: 'Is the evidence hard enough to go on?' He would have asked us to double-check everything, to order more photographs. These in any case had already been ordered. I decided the bad news could wait until Tuesday morning." Bundy told Kennedy some months after the missile crisis: "I decided that a quiet evening and a night of

"an organizer of process." As Bundy once described his job, it was to "get to the bare bones of the problem as cleanly and clearly as you could and state the alternatives as sharply as possible."

He was a "traffic cop" on the path to the President, a trouble-shooter trying to keep the President's options open—yet he was also an adviser to the President as well. This basic duality in Bundy's role was underscored in the week-long debate during the missile crisis. His own position as an adviser shifted from an initial preference for a diplomatic response to support for an air strike against the missile sites. But more important than his own opinions, he felt, was his obligation to see that every view was examined: "I almost deliberately stayed in the minority. I felt very strongly that it was very important to keep the President's choices open. If we froze a minute before we had to, we might not be right."

A Defense Department official recalls that when asking Bundy to bring an issue to Kennedy's attention he was always careful not to offend Bundy by seeming to ask him to advocate one side or the other. By prizing his impartiality on routine matters, Bundy enhanced the value of his advice on important matters. Bundy's cards were always close to his vest; one of his colleagues says: "You don't know what he thinks. I don't know what he thinks. The President doesn't know what he thinks. And I sometimes wonder whether he knows what he thinks."

What Kennedy did know was that he had in Bundy a buffer between him and day-to-day military and diplomatic problems. Bundy was not afraid to make decisions on his own, and to stand by them when the heat was on. Nor was he afraid to bring the proper problems to Kennedy, and when he did, Kennedy could be sure the facts and alternatives would be set out for him with precision.

During Kennedy's presidency, Bundy's work was almost entirely behind-the-scenes. He would talk to important newspaper and magazine writers, but almost never for attribution.* Yet he was not lacking for friends in the press, and pieces by leading columnists, plus several newsmagazine cover stories, soon made it clear to the public that

---

sleep were the best preparation you could have in light of what you would face in the days ahead."

Bundy's critics have suggested that he should have let Kennedy himself decide whether he wanted to remain inactive for the first twelve hours of the crisis, but there is no evidence that Kennedy objected to Bundy's decision.

* Even today Bundy won't talk about his views on such matters as the 1961 Berlin crisis, presumably because he expects again someday to be negotiating with the Russians and he doesn't want them to know any more of his thinking than they already do.

Bundy was one of the powers in the Kennedy government. No journalist was more wholehearted in his praise of Bundy than Joseph Kraft, who termed him "perhaps the only candidate for the statesman's mantle to emerge in the generation that is coming to power." At the same time, reflecting both sides of the Bundy picture, Kraft added: "Few people who have been elected to office in Washington trust him very far."

For Bundy, after Kennedy's assassination, the crucial question became: How far did Johnson trust him? The answer was not simple. Johnson respected Bundy's abilities, and he desperately needed him during his first year in office, but he seems never to have much cared for him personally.

The new President must have appreciated Bundy's loyalty to him—or, more accurately, to the presidency—in the wake of Kennedy's death. Unlike Sorensen, or Schlesinger, or O'Donnell, Bundy was concerned with continuity in the government. When Johnson returned to Washington from Dallas, Bundy was waiting, ready for action. Bundy later wrote: "That night I followed the man, not the coffin. . . . The transition was easier for me. I hadn't given a year of my life campaigning for him."

Many observers say Bundy's power actually increased in 1964 as Johnson, preoccupied with the political campaign, left foreign affairs to Bundy, Rusk, and McNamara. Bartlett and Weintal relate two small but illuminating instances when Johnson backed Bundy in disputes with his State Department rival, Under Secretary George Ball:

"After Kennedy's assassination, a young foreign service officer named Lee T. Stull, who had previously served Vice President Johnson as a State Department briefing officer, was retained by Mr. Johnson on the White House staff. Ball saw a chance of bypassing Bundy and used Stull as a channel of communications with the new President. Simultaneously, one of Bundy's assistants noticed that the flow of State Department cables to Bundy's office had virtually ceased. An investigation disclosed that the stoppage had been ordered by Ball. Bundy called for a showdown and won his case with the President, whose final injunction was to be sure 'to find a good job for Lee.'"

A good job was found for the young man, in Pakistan, but shortly thereafter: "Ball challenged Bundy to prove that he spoke for the President when he opposed the famous MLF project in policy meetings. Bundy did."

The MLF (Multilateral Force) dispute is a good example of Bundy's role in holding open the door of decision for the President. The MLF was intended to quiet West Germany's yearning for its own nuclear capacity by giving its troops involvement in a sea-based NATO nuclear force. In reality, American fingers would be alone on the nuclear trigger, but it was hoped that the MLF's symbolistic value would appease the Germans. By the end of 1964, most officials in both the American and the West German governments thought that Johnson had made a firm commitment to MLF. Perhaps he had, but he was having second thoughts. Britain had a new Prime Minister, Harold Wilson, who opposed the scheme, as did France's de Gaulle. Moreover, leading members of Congress had misgivings about MLF, and Johnson sensed trouble there.

Bundy, for his part, felt that MLF was being pushed on Johnson, perhaps against his political interests, by leading Establishment figures and by pro-German forces in the State Department. Bundy began a holding action against the MLF, one which gave Johnson non-political reasons for mulling over his political doubts about the project. Bundy somewhere unearthed a note Kennedy had written on MLF, saying in effect: "If the Europeans don't want it, to hell with it." For weeks, Johnson showed this note to visitors as justification for his doubts about MLF. Bundy also dispatched a political scientist to Europe to consult with political leaders, giving Johnson another excuse to defer decision.

Eventually, Bundy got Johnson off the MLF hook by passing the buck to the British and the West Germans to resolve their differences over the scheme. They didn't, and MLF died, widely unmourned. Yet it might be alive today but for Bundy's determination that the President should not be forced into a premature or an unwise decision.

One of the things Johnson disliked about Bundy was that as an Establishment member he was something of an independent political force. Johnson likes his people to derive their power from him alone. Yet Bundy's prestige was also something Johnson could make use of, and he often called Bundy out of his basement sanctuary to be a public spokesman for the Administration. He dispatched Bundy to debate academic critics of his Vietnam policy, at Harvard and elsewhere. In May, 1964, he made Bundy the head of a top-level presidential mission to the Dominican Republic; in February 1965 he sent Bundy on a fact-finding mission to South Vietnam; he sent Bundy to Canada as part of his worldwide "peace offensive" in December 1965.

But, according to many reports, Johnson was abusing Bundy as well as using him. *Time* magazine reported that Bundy once stuck his head in Johnson's office while the President was talking to Henry Cabot Lodge, only to be met with a thundering: "Goddammit, Bundy, I've told you that when I want you I'll call you." Another time, Bundy and Moyers entered the President's office together to discuss a foreign policy matter, only to have Johnson declare angrily that he wouldn't have them ganging up on him.

An ability to absorb abuse has always been essential to success on Lyndon Johnson's staff, and Bundy didn't have it. Flexible politically, he was rigid personally. "The President consumes people emotionally," a Bundy associate recalls, "and Mac is not about to be consumed." One of the virtues of Bundy's successor, Walt Rostow, is a boundless optimism, an ability to roll with the Johnsonian punches.

There was another problem. Schlesinger and Sorensen have made it clear that if Kennedy had lived he would have named Bundy to replace Rusk as Secretary of State in his second term. But under Johnson, while Bundy's influence was gradually declining, Rusk's continued to soar as Johnson praised him as "the greatest Secretary of State in this century." When it became clear that Johnson had no intention of removing Rusk, Bundy decided to return to private life.

The job he entered in early 1966—the presidency of the Ford Foundation—could not have been better suited to Bundy's continuing needs as an aspiring Secretary of State. The Ford Foundation is a kind of government in exile, and its presidency gives Bundy involvement in nationwide and worldwide programs to improve education, urban life, cultural affairs, and almost every aspect of human relations. Moreover, personal association with Ford's multimillion-dollar largess should help brighten Bundy's rather austere image: Nobody hates Santa Claus.

It was Bundy's achievement to demonstrate, much as O'Brien did in congressional relations, just how valuable a White House aide can be if he has enough talent and enough presidential support.

Perhaps none of Bundy's successors will ever wield the same power he did during the Kennedy years, but it is unlikely that any future President will try to get along without a Bundy-style national security operation of some sort.

The insistent question in the post-Bundy era of national security affairs is whether we are evolving toward new institutions, whether much of the State Department may not be as outmoded in a nuclear age as the hoop skirt. Is ever-increasing power destined to shift to the White House? If so, won't its staff inevitably develop the same problems of bigness that now afflict the State Department?

Richard E. Neustadt addressed himself to these questions in testimony before the Jackson Subcommittee a few years ago and suggested there were three ways the present trends in national security matters might work themselves out.

One would be to continue to enlarge the staff of the Special Assistant for National Security Affairs. The trouble with this, Professor Neustadt said, is that the more the Special Assistant becomes an administrator of fifty, eighty, or a hundred subordinates, the less he can serve the President's needs for a personal assistant.

A second possibility would be to create an Office of National Security Affairs, staffed by career civil servants, separate from the Special Assistant's office, as a part of the Executive Office of the President. Such an office would be intended to coordinate and oversee national security matters, much as the White House National Security staff now does. The problem would be, if past experience is any guide, that the new office would soon develop its own interests to protect and be just another obstacle for the White House to have to deal with. Moreover, unless given an extremely strong director, a Bundy or a Moyers, someone with direct access to the President, such a non-White House office would lack the authority to enforce its mandate.

The third possibility is that the State Department might, over the years, be brought to abandon its parochial views and instead assume its rightful place as the first agency of government. In Professor Neustadt's words: "All one wants is that the staff in the Secretary's Office will, conscientiously and carefully, with a sense of serving the whole government, make sure that all the people with a right to know, a right to be involved and to express opinions, will get a crack at the right time and place. This is asking a lot, but this is all I am asking. The better the State Department is able to do this, the more confidence will develop in the Pentagon and Treasury."

If State would do these things, then the White House staff could be less and less involved in matters of intergovernmental coordination, and more in simply serving the President's personal needs. This is the course of action Professor Neustadt would like to see and, essentially, it is the one preferred by Bundy and his associates.

The basic concept of Kennedy's NSC system, however ably executed by Bundy, is open to serious questioning. Confronted with a State

Department he viewed as "a bowl of jelly," Kennedy chose the short-range expedient of bypassing it with Bundy's "little State Department" (Kennedy's phrase), rather than the more challenging, long-range alternative of building a strong, effective State Department. Kennedy knew that State desperately needed vigorous administration (of the sort he installed at the Departments of Defense and Justice) but he appointed a Secretary who was a mediocre administrator and an Under Secretary, Chester Bowles, who was no administrator at all. After ten months he replaced Bowles, but he never came to grips with the long-range problems at State, and in the end he left it weaker than he had found it.

There is a clear need today for a White House staff on foreign affairs to maintain effective lines of communication between the President and the bureaucracy, and to serve the President's immediate needs, but ideally it would not supplant the State Department and its Secretary to the extent that Bundy's operation did. Someday, some President is going to have to undertake the long, thankless job of reorganizing and rebuilding the Department of State. President Johnson has at least made a step in that direction by downgrading the post-Bundy NSC operation in the White House and moving in several ways to shore up Rusk and his department.

McGeorge Bundy would probably not argue with this analysis. Bundy, contemplating Rusk in 1961–65, was like an actor who, undercast as Laertes, steals the show from Hamlet. But Bundy, although he is an opportunist, is also a traditionalist, a man with a rigid sense of protocol, and probably, in principle at least, he didn't entirely approve of the extent to which he undermined the Secretary of State's prerogatives. Later, after he had left the White House, Bundy was asked if he thought the President's aides needed more status. "No," he said, "they need less." It was a characteristically shrewd remark.

One of Bundy's NSC associates, a man who in his mind's eye envisions the day when Bundy will be Secretary of State and he will be (at least) an Assistant Secretary, told me he believes that with proper staffing and assumption of responsibility by the State Department, a powerful, Bundy-style NSC staff in the White House would not be necessary. A small staff to serve the President's needs would suffice, he said. Well, I asked, how would he like it if he took command at State only to have the President install a Bundy in the White House basement? "Oh, no," he said, with something close to horror, "we wouldn't want that!"

7. The Alter Ego: Sorensen

A special sort of self-discipline, an extra degree of dedication is required to serve as a presidential aide very well for very long, for the job carries drawbacks along with its benefits. It is, first and last, a young man's game, with always an element of coat-holding in it. The aide must be willing to subject himself to another man's interests, to accept another man's decisions, to run another man's errands, to be permanently number-two, a second-banana, a satellite, an easy mark for the sort of criticisms men make of other men who do not quite stand on their own two feet. A gracious President may make the job more easy, a tactless one may make it more painful, but in either case the aide must, as Sir Francis Bacon warned Sir George Villiers, always remember his true condition.

Some men are simply not cut out for staff work, even at the White House level. The promise of power means less to them than the loss of their individuality, the freedom to speak their mind as they please. They say, with Cyrano de Bergerac:

> What would you have me do?
> Seek for the patronage of some great man
> And, like a creeping vine on a tall tree,
> Crawl upward where I cannot stand alone?
> No thank you!

Raymond Moley was one such man. He entered Roosevelt's Administration reluctantly and left it joyously—yet even Moley might have stayed on had not his conflict with Cordell Hull hastened his departure.

More often, talented young men enter the White House bursting with good intentions, but after a while it becomes a job like any other, the man begins to feel overworked and underappreciated, and he looks with interest upon the green pastures outside the White House gates. Clark Clifford and Tom Corcoran are only two prominent examples of men who, in the classic phrase, came to Washington to do good and stayed to do well.

Finally, among presidential aides, there are the true believers, the ones who have signed on for the duration. The reasons for their devotion will differ. Some are moved by personal affection for their

President; some hope to advance their political beliefs; others love the power that surrounds a President; still others stay because they know they'd be nobodies but for their presidential ties.

To the outsider, the total dedication of an assistant to his President— putting that bond ahead of family or friends or personal ambition— may seem unnatural. The aide may seem to be hiding from life's challenges in the vest pocket of his great patron. But few Presidents will question the motives of such men, for total dedication is rare in politics. Roosevelt received it from Howe, Hopkins, and several others; Truman could count on the loyalty of his friends; Eisenhower inspired devotion in many of his aides; Johnson, to the contrary, does not seem to inspire total commitment in those who work for him.

Kennedy had the gift; the men in his inner circle accepted his leadership and followed him unquestioningly. Of them all, the one who followed the longest and contributed the most was Ted Sorensen.

He was a loner from the first, part of a political family in the non-political community of Lincoln, Nebraska, a liberal crusader among middle-class Midwestern conservatives, a hero-worshiper who found few heroes fit to worship amid the dusty plains of Nebraska politics. It was his nature to cut against the grain. He grew up during the passions of the Second World War, yet in 1945 he registered with the draft as a noncombatant. He campaigned for Negro rights at a time and place where Negroes were seldom seen or worried about. Later, as a young Senate aide, he was a teetotaler in the country's hardest-drinking community, a curt, silent young man among the army of congressional back-slappers. One of the things he liked most about the White House was that he was no longer obliged to waste time with people he didn't want to see.

Yet however nonpolitical Sorensen's aloof, sometimes arrogant, behavior seemed, it masked deepset political concern. His boyhood friend, William Lee Miller, later a professor of divinity at Yale, has written, "The Sorensens came campaigning from the womb; there never was a more political family, nor one more explicit in its liberalism." His father, C. A. Sorensen, was a crusading lawyer and reformer—a pioneer for human rights and women's suffrage, the founder of Nebraska's all-public power system, an insurgent Republican Attorney General, an associate of the independent Senator George Norris (young Ted's boyhood hero, later one of the eight Senators included in Kennedy's *Profiles in Courage*) and a supporter of Franklin Roosevelt.

Ted, his older brother Tom, and a few friends were a lonely outpost of liberalism in Nebraska in the 1940s. They subscribed to *PM* and *The New Republic;* they belonged to ADA and started a Lincoln chapter of CORE. They brought about the integration of the municipal swimming pool and they protested discrimination against Negroes in the Big Six universities.

Sorensen received both his undergraduate and his law degrees from the University of Nebraska, the latter in 1951. At that point, because the legal horizons in Nebraska seemed narrow, he set out for Washington. He soon found a job as a lawyer for the Federal Security Agency, only to discover that being a government lawyer can be as confining as being a Nebraska lawyer. His next move was to Capitol Hill, where he worked for eight months on the staff of a temporary Senate committee studying the Railroad Retirement system. When the committee completed its work, he set out to find a job with a Democratic Senator. One of the first he talked to was the new Senator from Massachusetts, John Kennedy.

After two brief interviews, Kennedy hired Sorensen as his legislative assistant. Kennedy was impressed by Sorensen's academic record, and by the fact that he had published articles in *The New Republic* and the *Progressive.* Sorensen, for his part, questioned Kennedy about his stand on McCarthy and other issues. Their union thus began in January 1953 when Kennedy was thirty-five and Sorensen was twenty-four, and only eighteen months out of law school.

The ages were deceptive. Sorensen at twenty-four had been forming and practicing a political philosophy for a decade. Kennedy at thirty-five, although a Senator and a veteran of three terms in the House, had few political convictions and no political philosophy. He had, instead, wealth, restless ambition, curiosity, intellectual honesty, and—most important from Sorensen's point of view—an open mind. As Sorensen later put it in his book, *Kennedy:* "It seemed to me in 1953 that an inner struggle was being waged for the spirit of John Kennedy—a struggle between the political dilettante and the statesman, between the lure of luxury and lawmaking." Sorensen was not long in casting himself into the struggle.

The two men who did the most to shape Kennedy's political thinking were his father and Sorensen. Kennedy often enough credited—or blamed—his father for his early conservatism. "I'd just come out of my father's house at the time and these were the things I knew," he said of his House career. His votes as a Congressman were non-ideological.

He favored liberal federal spending in his own working-class district and limited spending elsewhere.

But beginning with his arrival in the Senate in 1953, and continuing until his death a decade later, Kennedy moved toward a political philosophy that, while founded on the hard rock of self-interest, was increasingly concerned with the problems of the poor, with racial discrimination, with civil liberties, with the search for international understanding, and other matters he had little noted in the House.

Certainly there were several reasons for Kennedy's evolution. As he said, he was emerging intellectually from his father's house. His mind was challenged and invigorated by the Senate. As his political ambitions took on a national dimension, it was imperative that he move leftward. Finally, there was Sorensen.

It is beyond question that Sorensen had an immense influence on Kennedy's thinking on such major issues as civil rights and international relations. There were, of course, matters on which Sorensen's views were virtually the opposite of those held by Kennedy's father. Still, Sorensen's impact on Kennedy cannot be measured precisely, for their intimacy was such that no one—not even Sorensen—was sure just where his thoughts left off and Kennedy's began.

There are some neat, clear-cut instances of Sorensen's influence. For example, when they met, Sorensen was a champion of the Rural Electrification Administration, whereas Kennedy had barely heard of REA, since it didn't operate in Massachusetts. Kennedy's subsequent support of REA, as Senator and President, clearly followed from Sorensen's proddings.

But their relationship was not often so sharply defined. Sorensen was not aggressive with his ideas, nor was Kennedy a man who could be easily pushed. Theirs was a gradual intellectual coming-together, with Kennedy moving toward the liberalism that was Sorensen's heritage, and Sorensen moving toward the realism that was Kennedy's heritage.

Not far beneath the surface, both men were pragmatists, practical politicians who did not necessarily think it better to be right than to be President. In some ways, Sorensen may have been more tough-minded than Kennedy, for the unusual circumstances of Kennedy's life enabled him to move from pragmatism in youth toward idealism in maturity, whereas Sorensen (like most of us) moved steadily from idealism toward pragmatism. It is fair on some issues to envision Sorensen leading Kennedy leftward, but one must more often imagine the two of them, arm in arm, picking a careful path along the middle of the political road.

Call it the politics of compromise, or call it the Golden Mean, the one unifying thread running throughout Kennedy's Senate career was an ability to stay squarely in the middle of the road, an instinct for seeking alliances on both sides of any issue. He did it on McCarthy in 1954, on civil rights in 1957, on the labor legislation he sponsored in 1959, and on a host of lesser issues. And more often than not, Kennedy's adroit fence-sitting was justified (or rationalized) by Sorensen's legal arguments.

Sorensen became an all-around adviser on national and international affairs, but at bottom, his influence with Kennedy always rested on his facility as a writer. Words are a politician's stock in trade, like bread to a baker or beer to a bartender, and those who try to minimize Sorensen's importance by saying he was "only a speechwriter" miss the point. In no way could Sorensen have had more influence on Kennedy than as his writer. Kennedy looked to Sorensen not just for pretty words but for ideas to advance his career. From Sorensen's viewpoint, the speechwriting process could be used to educate, persuade, and commit the Senator; he could put ideas before Kennedy and force him to accept or reject them; he could seize upon Kennedy's good intentions and translate them into specific policies.

Sorensen's influence is most clearly seen in the Senate years, for by the time Kennedy reached the White House he had necessarily acquired a circle of advisers and it was usually hard to tell which of them had influenced him on a particular issue. But in the Senate there was only Sorensen.

In 1954, the proposed St. Lawrence Seaway came before the Senate. For twenty years, on six previous votes, no Senator or Congressman from Massachusetts had ever supported the Seaway. New England shipping and commercial interests were convinced it would hurt them, as were dockworkers in Kennedy's old congressional district. He had opposed it during his 1952 campaign for the Senate.

Nonetheless, Kennedy asked Sorensen to make an objective study of the Seaway's merits. Sorensen reported back that it was without question in the national interest. After much soul-searching, Kennedy voted for the Seaway, declaring: "I am unable to accept such a narrow view of my function as a United States Senator." It was his first conspicuous profile in political courage.

The overriding issue of 1954, McCarthy and McCarthyism, was more difficult. Kennedy had ducked the issue in his 1952 campaign and walked a tightrope on it thereafter. McCarthy had a strong following in Massachusetts. Kennedy's father was friendly with McCarthy and his brother Robert had worked for him in 1953. Sorensen, of course, was deeply opposed to McCarthy, and did all that he could to win Kennedy to his viewpoint.

Kennedy followed a cautious line when issues involving McCarthy reached the Senate floor. Like most Senators, he voted to appropriate money for McCarthy's investigations. He voted with McCarthy on many issues involving the fine line between individual liberty and national security. However, he often voted against McCarthy on clear issues of civil liberties and on the appointment of McCarthy's friends to government office. These votes were not enough to satisfy many liberals, such as Eleanor Roosevelt, who criticized Kennedy for refusing to take a stand on McCarthyism.

On July 31, 1954, the Senate had scheduled a censure vote on McCarthy. Kennedy was ready with a Sorensen-written speech explaining his vote against McCarthy. But the vote was postponed and the speech never delivered. When the censure vote was finally taken in December, Kennedy was in Florida recovering from his near-fatal back operation. His condition was such that Sorensen, who was empowered to record his vote for him, could not discuss the issue with him. Sorensen was not willing to assume that Kennedy's intention to vote for censure four months earlier settled the matter, for the Senate had altered the charges against McCarthy.

Sorensen's explanation why he decided not to record Kennedy on the censure vote: "An absent juror, who had not been present for the trial or even heard the indictment . . . should not have his predetermined position recorded. . . . His failure to be recorded at the time of the vote, which was persistently raised against him in some quarters, was due to my adherence to basic principles of civil liberties and not to his indifference to them."

This is nice, persuasive lawyer talk, but it is as easy to imagine Sorensen having cast Kennedy's vote against McCarthy and then explained with equal piety: "I knew the Senator would have voted for censure had he been present, and I strongly felt he would have wanted his stand made entirely clear on this most vital issue."

It is not inconceivable that Sorensen, knowing how much Kennedy wanted to duck the McCarthy issue, decided it would be most prudent to use his illness as an excuse for doing so. Sorensen's decision was entirely consistent with Kennedy's habit of following the middle of the road: Kennedy could tell McCarthy's friends he had not voted against their man, and he could tell McCarthy's enemies he would have voted against him had his health permitted. It remains the supreme irony of

Sorensen's career that he, the devotee of civil liberties, made the decision on the McCarthy vote that did most to raise liberal doubts about Kennedy in the years ahead.

Kennedy and Sorensen both denied, many times, with much irritation, that Kennedy's book, *Profiles in Courage,* was written to atone for Kennedy's non-stand on McCarthy. But the fact remains that it was written between January and June of 1955, just after the McCarthy episode, during his convalescence from his operation. The book was published on January 1, 1956, and became a best seller, a Pulitzer Prize winner, and a milestone in Kennedy's emergence as a national figure.

There was much subsequent controversy as to whether Kennedy or Sorensen "wrote" the book. The simplest answer is that they both wrote it. Sorensen and others handled most of the research—which in a historical work is, of course, a major exertion—and rough drafting. Kennedy's main exertions came in translating draft material into polished prose.

Kennedy was a literate man and a student of history, and there is no reason to doubt that he inscribed on paper the last draft of *Profiles in Courage,* but to say he "wrote" the book is entirely a matter of definition. Had he and Sorensen been two professional writers, instead of Senator and aide, any publisher would have credited them as co-authors.

Sorensen expected no credit. Helping write the book was yet another way he could influence "the inner struggle for the spirit of John Kennedy" that had become his preoccupation in life. The writing of the book, like the writing of speeches, could be an educational process for the Senator. Sorensen hints at this when he says that Kennedy "developed, as he read and wrote, a far keener insight into his own political philosophy as well as the obligations of the office-holder in a democracy."

Profiles in Courage notwithstanding, when the political dynamite of the 1957 civil rights legislation reached the Senate, Kennedy exhibited his accustomed profile in prudence. At the outset, he voted with the Southerners in refusing to let Senate liberals invoke a procedural device whereby the civil rights bill might bypass the Judiciary Committee headed by Mississippi's Senator Eastland. This vote, Kennedy said, was based on Sorensen's warning that there was no precedent for the bypass maneuver.

Next, switching to the liberal camp, Kennedy supported a section of the bill authorizing the Attorney General to use injunctive power to enforce school desegregation.

The Senate showdown came over the O'Mahoney Amendment, a pro-

Southern provision for jury trials in criminal contempt cases involving voting rights. Over the furious protests of civil rights supporters in Massachusetts, Kennedy voted for the O'Mahoney Amendment. He gave two reasons: First, Sorensen and numerous legal scholars assured him it would not seriously weaken the bill; second, he didn't think the civil rights bill could pass without the amendment as a concession to the Southerners. In the end, following his usual pattern, Kennedy could tell Southerners he had backed them on two key votes, and he could tell liberals he had helped pass the strongest bill possible.

Just as many of Kennedy's followers were disillusioned by his willingness to compromise on the civil rights bill, many of Sorensen's old friends were disappointed by his intimate involvement in Kennedy's politics of pragmatism. Sorensen's friend William Lee Miller wrote: "The enthusiastic young advocate of racial justice in 1947 would become exclusively concerned with his boss's future in 1957, treating the Senate civil rights struggle strictly from a tactical angle of the double strike with the Southerners and Northerners that Kennedy forces hoped to make (and did) in 1960. They say, in general, that Sorensen's liberal beginnings were not very visible. Maybe not."

As Sorensen had steadily submerged his own interests in Kennedy's, he had begun a transformation from an eager, archetypical young liberal into a cool political pragmatist. His liberalism didn't die, but it was brought under strict discipline. Perhaps it pained Sorensen to see Kennedy equivocate on McCarthy and compromise on civil rights. If so, he kept his suffering to himself, for he was ever ready with the legal points and the soaring prose that would put the best face on Kennedy's acts of self-interest. It is easy enough to say that politics demands compromise, but Sorensen knew the exceptions to that rule—hadn't he and Kennedy written a book praising politicians who refused to compromise? Sorensen's childhood hero, Senator Norris, was one such man, and in the 1950s the tradition was carried on in the Senate by Kefauver of Tennessee and Douglas of Illinois.

But Norris was no longer Sorensen's model of political excellence. Norris had left the Senate in defeat, as Douglas would later; Kefauver had been denied his party's presidential nomination. Such were the fruits of crusading, and by 1956 Kennedy and Sorensen had their eyes on a goal that allowed for no set-backs—the presidency for Kennedy in 1960.

By the time Kennedy reached the White House in 1961 he was surrounded by political experts—O'Brien, O'Donnell, Bailey, Robert Kennedy—and Sorensen was most often thought of as an intellectual adviser and speechwriter. But Sorensen was also an astute political operator; in effect, he was the O'Brien/O'Donnell/Bailey of the crucial 1956–59 era when Kennedy laid the groundwork for 1960.

In 1956, Sorensen was in charge of Kennedy's unannounced bid for the vice-presidential nomination. Kennedy was not sure he wanted the nomination, but Sorensen was convinced that to become President he would first have to serve as Vice President to overcome the religious issue. Kennedy therefore approved Sorensen's trying to line up delegate support, but remained officially uncommitted and free to repudiate Sorensen's efforts if need be. This delicate arrangement was best expressed in this semi-joking exchange:

Kennedy: "You're responsible for the whole thing."

Sorensen: "No, I'm responsible only if you lose. If you win, you will be known as the greatest political strategist in convention history."

Despite Sorensen's best efforts, Kennedy lost the vice-presidential nomination to Estes Kefauver in a dramatic fight on the convention floor. Yet as it turned out, he won by losing, for his nip-and-tuck battle with Kefauver, followed by his graceful call for party unity, focused national attention on him and thereupon launched his drive for the 1960 presidential nomination.

Sorensen's Christmas gift to Kennedy in 1956 was a map of the U.S. indicating the sources of his support in the vice-presidential balloting. It was almost blank west of the Mississippi, so the small Western and Midwestern states became the focal point of an odyssey that included Kennedy's 150 speeches in 1957 and 200 the next year. Starting in 1956 Sorensen accompanied Kennedy on his travels. Partly he was a coat-holder—he saw to the baggage, hailed cabs, ordered breakfast—but increasing political responsibility fell to him as well. He would handle the advance arrangements, write Kennedy's speech, deal with the local press, brief his man on local politics, and afterward handle follow-up calls and thank-you notes. In time Sorensen built a card file on some 70,000 local contacts.

Sorensen, in those pre-presidential years, had become indispensable to Kennedy, as Louis Howe once had to Roosevelt. In the Senate years, when first-rate help was hard to find, Kennedy must have wondered at his good fortune in stumbling upon this young man who was intelligent, industrious, and totally dedicated. The lonely travels of 1956–59 had forged enduring bonds between them. Kennedy knew why he was pushing himself to exhaustion, deserting home and family, spending miserable nights in drafty airports—he wanted to be President—but he must have sometimes wondered that Sorensen would choose to share his quest. But Sorensen—still in his twenties, yet caught up in a political drama of a magnitude he could only dream of a few years earlier—had by then made Kennedy's ambitions his own.

The two men were, as Sorensen put it, "close in a peculiarly impersonal way." They knew each other's minds, and could communicate in gestures and clipped phrases. Sorensen had mastered Kennedy's prose preferences as no one else ever would. He had come to speak like Kennedy, to the extent that Kennedy sometimes had Sorensen take telephone calls for him. Sorensen imitated Kennedy's jabbing forefinger in conversation, and when seated, would drape one leg over the arm of his chair in the Kennedy fashion. When Sorensen took up social drinking, his favorite drinks were Kennedy's favorites: daiquiris and Heineken's beer.

He was often called Kennedy's alter ego—second self—and in many ways the term fit.* Kennedy could send Sorensen to represent him at a meeting confident that his reactions and decisions would be those he would have made himself. Sorensen took pride in this status. Asked if it never bothered him to be always in Kennedy's shadow, he says: "It never bothered me in the slightest." He was fond of Kennedy, he was advancing his political beliefs, and he was advancing his own career in the bargain.

Yet his relationship with Kennedy was always political, never social. Sorensen was not a part of Kennedy's social life and apparently never aspired to be. Once Sorensen was persuaded to attend a New Year's Eve party given by Kennedy's socially prominent friends the Charles Wrightsmans; he was bored and went home at 10:30. In later years, when Sorensen was asked if he ever sought out his old White House associates, he replied: "I really don't seek anyone out. I don't have very many intimate friends." He was completely dedicated to his work; if he had to stay at the office all night to finish a speech, he stayed without a second thought. The intensity of his dedication was indicated when he later told an interviewer: "I had given eleven years of my life to John Kennedy and for those eleven years he was the only human being who mattered to me." Presumably Sorensen's candidly declared preoccupation with

---

* Nonetheless, to call Sorensen Kennedy's alter ego is to overlook that Kennedy's real alter ego was his brother Robert. Had Robert Kennedy served on his brother's White House staff, rather than as his Attorney General, he would certainly have been the most influential staff assistant of all time. Even as Attorney General, he performed many troubleshooting assignments that had little to do with his duties at the Justice Department and much to do with his unsurpassed understanding of and loyalty to his older brother.

his work was a factor in his 1963 divorce from his wife, the former Camilla Palmer, a University of Nebraska professor's daughter whom he married in 1949. His second marriage also ended in divorce in 1967.

The Kennedy-Sorensen relationship was a marriage of sorts, a political marriage, a marriage of two kindred minds, and at bottom the union always rested on Sorensen's unequaled ability to produce the sort of speeches Kennedy wanted to deliver. Kennedy, as he pursued the presidency, was surely realistic enough to know he would have to sway the people with his words, for his deeds in political life hardly qualified him for the office. Between them, Kennedy and Sorensen succeeded in forging a style of public speaking that captured the national imagination as no politician's words had since Franklin Roosevelt's.

Throughout 1960, America began to move to the rhythm of the new political rhetoric sent forth by the dashing young Senator from Massachusetts. The contrast between Kennedy's speeches and Nixon's could not have been more striking: Nixon's was the familiar elocution of the Kiwanis Club; Kennedy's was an unfamiliar style, elevated, one in which his admirers found echoes of the classical Greek orators. It featured balanced, inverted, and alliterative sentences, often with internal rhymes and formal parallelisms. Over and over such sentences were featured as: "Mankind must put an end to war, or war will put an end to mankind" and "Let us never negotiate out of fear, but let us never fear to negotiate" and "While we do not intend to see the free world give up, we shall make every effort to prevent the world from being blown up."

There seem to be only a few of us who find this Kennedy-Sorensen style deplorable, and its popularity an example of the characteristic American weakness for phony eloquence. At best, sentences such as those quoted above—and there are hundreds, perhaps thousands, of them—are coarsely mechanical, and reveal an unfortunate willingness to let style take precedence over substance. At worst, Kennedy became a prisoner of Sorensen's mania for contrapuntal sentences, and was led by them into the most grotesque contortions, such as his declaration to the United Nations a few days after Dag Hammarskjöld's death: "His tragedy is deep in our hearts, but the task for which he died is at the top of our agenda."

Kennedy must accept the final blame for his style, but Sorensen was its architect. It is notable that he had declared, in delivering his high school valedictory address in 1945: "To prove ourselves we must improve the world." The line would have fit beautifully into Kennedy's Inaugural Address.

That Address, everywhere hailed as Kennedy's masterpiece, seems to me outstanding only for its hollow pomposity. The essential trouble with the speech is that Kennedy was striking a pose. He was not addressing the problems of the people who elected him; he was announcing himself as a statesman to foreign heads of state.* "Let's drop the domestic stuff altogether," he told Sorensen as they drafted the speech. "It's too long anyway." In other words, "Let's don't muck up my Big Moment with grubby details about jobs and schools and civil rights."

Sorensen tells us that the first line of the Inaugural went through three drafts, from "We celebrate today not a victory of party but the sacrament of democracy" to "We celebrate today not a victory of party but a convention of freedom" to "We observe today not a victory of party but a celebration of freedom."

It is difficult to see how the third version is any improvement over the first. There is an idea rattling around in that phrase—although a highly self-serving one—but it is so weighted down by elevated prose that it never quite emerges.

Thus begun, the Inaugural Address speeds along from pose to pose—"Let the word go forth from this time and place. . . . The torch has been passed to a new generation of Americans. . . . We shall pay any price, bear any burden, meet any hardship, support any friend. . . . Now the trumpet summons us again. . . . The glow from that fire can truly light the world"—to climax with the unforgettable banality of: "And so, my fellow Americans, ask not what your country can do for you; ask what you can do for your country."

The only man in recent presidential politics who could legitimately have admonished the nation to "ask not what your country can do for you" was Barry Goldwater, who really wanted individuals to do more and the government to do less. Kennedy was elected as a Democrat, solemnly pledged to expand and perfect the welfare state; in other words, to see that the country did more for its citizens, not vice versa. As it turned out, he never did make clear just what it was he wanted the citizen to do for the country.

The banality of Kennedy's formal style was underscored by his wit and spontaneity in press conferences and informal talks. Yet pomposity

* Some observers found the substance of the Inaugural Address as objectionable as the style. For example, William G. Carleton, a political scientist at the University of Florida, wrote in the *Antioch Review:* "His Inaugural Address was alarmist, already historically off key, more suited to the Stalinist era than to 1961."

remained the hallmark of his major utterances—who can imagine Lincoln or Wilson or Adlai Stevenson saying, "Now the trumpet summons us again . . ."? How much easier to imagine Kennedy wryly quipping "Now the strumpet summons us again," as he once commented that Hemingway's definition of courage—"grace under pressure"—reminded him of a girl he'd known.

Kennedy, with his excellent taste and his instinct for understatement, must have often been amused, if not pained, by the martial extravagances of his public prose. Indeed, at a Democratic fund-raising dinner soon after his Inauguration, he parodied his Inaugural Address—"And so, my fellow Democrats, ask not what your party can do for you, ask what you can do for your party"—and the parody was a far better piece of writing than the original.

But Kennedy and Sorensen were not writing to please literary purists. They were trying to capture the popular imagination. They were logical, precise men, but they knew that a nation is less often moved by logic and precision than by drama and overstatement. So they fashioned an oratory that not only won the election, it inspired a generation of Americans. Bad prose can bring good results, and Kennedy's exhortations did much to make public service respectable, even desirable, to the best people of his time. For this, he deserves full credit.

Nor were the Kennedy-Sorensen writings all bad. The last sentence of the Inaugural Address* was very good, and the American University speech of June, 1963, was magnificent. The latter speech, a plea for peace and international understanding, contains four brief sentences that are more eloquent than the entire Inaugural Address: "For, in the last analysis, our most common basic link is that we all inhabit this small planet. We all breathe the same air. We all cherish our children's future. And we are all mortal."

Sorensen, it should be added, agrees that the American University speech was Kennedy's finest, and with the forgivable pride of authorship he can recite its key passages from memory.

Throughout his years with Kennedy, Sorensen was known as a curt, aloof, often arrogant man. Only his closest associates caught glimpses of the relaxed, rather boyish side of his nature—as when he would amuse himself by writing political memos in very dry, very wry verse. For the most part, his preoccupation with Kennedy's interests left him little time

* "With a good conscience our only sure reward, with history the final judge of our deeds, let us go forth to lead the land we love, asking His blessing and His help, but knowing that here on earth God's work must truly be our own."

for the social niceties. He could exhibit considerable charm when it suited his or Kennedy's interests, but it did not seem to be his natural state. No doubt his behavior in large part reflected the inner uncertainties of a shy young Nebraskan who was suddenly thrust in close proximity to the top level of American society and politics. Some of Sorensen's associates felt that his apparent indifference to Kennedy's social life and society friends in fact sprang from an awe of them, and that by his all-work-and-no-play attitude he was trying to say to Kennedy: "I am a serious man doing important work for you, and these are frivolous people who will do you no good."

The campaign of 1960 was a painful time for Sorensen, for he had to face the new reality (as Louis Howe had in 1932) that he was no longer the candidate's only important adviser. Robert Kennedy had entered the picture full time, and O'Donnell, O'Brien, Salinger, and Goodwin. Bundy would appear a little later. Sorensen resented the newcomers and they resented him. In the months just before and after the election there was a multiplicity of feuds and in-fighting, with Sorensen and others from the old Senate staff resisting inroads by the various newcomers.

Yet Sorensen, however uncertain he may have felt at the time, had little to worry about. Kennedy wanted him to continue with his primary duties as speechwriter, policy adviser, and alter ego. Perhaps out of consideration for Sorensen's sensitivities, Kennedy gave him the title he most wanted—Special Counsel to the President—and the honor of being the first of the aides to be appointed.

During Sorensen's regime, the Special Counsel's office achieved more power than ever before or since. Sorensen and his two assistants were responsible for all presidential speeches and documents, and also, subject to the President's final approval, for shaping the Administration's legislative program. Sorensen prepared White House legislative recommendations, basing them on the suggestions of Cabinet officials and agency heads, but revising the suggestions in keeping with his understanding of Kennedy's wishes.

In addition to working with the Departments on legislation, Sorensen and his staff were the President's spokesmen on all but the most vital day-to-day issues. Kennedy had little time for or interest in domestic affairs—aside from civil rights, which was under the supervision of his brother, the Attorney General—and Cabinet members who brought their troubles to him were likely to be told: "Talk to Ted about it."

HEW Secretary Ribicoff was sometimes angered at having to deal with Sorensen when he felt he should see Kennedy. Secretary of Commerce Luther Hodges, similarly disgruntled, arranged to have put on the Cabinet agenda of June 15, 1961, an item: "A candid discussion with the President on relationships with the White House staff." Sorensen asked Kennedy if he should leave the meeting, but Kennedy ignored both his offer and Hodges' complaint.

It may be that Kennedy delegated to Sorensen nearly as much authority in domestic affairs as Eisenhower did to Adams. It will be difficult to judge this until more time has passed and Kennedy's former associates are willing to speak more candidly than they will today. Sorensen has written of the Kennedy staff: "We wielded no secret influence. We did not replace the role of Cabinet officers, compete with them for power or publicity, or block their access to the President." All the available evidence—including the necessity of Sorensen's making that statement—indicates it is close to being the opposite of the truth.

Sorensen's responsibilities as presidential speechwriter sometimes kept him incommunicado for hours or days at a time. Inevitably, much authority evolved to his two assistants, Myer Feldman, the Deputy Special Counsel, and Lee White, Assistant Special Counsel.

Both were men Sorensen had recruited to Kennedy's Senate staff in the 1950s and Kennedy had come to trust. White's duties in the White House included supervision of the Veteran's Administration, the Small Business Administration, civil rights, and maritime and natural resources. In 1966, President Johnson appointed White chairman of the Federal Power Commission.

Feldman and Sorensen had been friends since the latter arrived in Washington, and in the mid-50s Sorensen recruited Feldman to Kennedy's staff. In the White House, Feldman, a tall man with a hawklike visage, was liaison with the Post Office Department, and the Departments of Commerce, Agriculture, and (on most matters) Health, Education and Welfare. Sorensen would become involved only on the most vital issues —for example, the aid-to-education legislation.

In his capacity of overseeing HEW affairs, Feldman was the key White House operative in the Administration's 1962 clash with Senator Estes Kefauver, who was seeking legislation to increase federal control over drug prices and drug safety standards. President Kennedy, if one may judge by his deeds, not his words, wanted no part of a controversial fight with the powerful drug industry. The White House at first all but ignored Kefauver's efforts, then—after the widely publicized thalidomide tragedies made drug-control legislation a popular issue—supported a mild drug-reform bill and tried to steal credit for the issue from Kefauver.

Feldman was Kefauver's contact for dealings with the White House. On March 7, 1962, a month after Kefauver ended his two years of hearings on drug abuses, he met with Feldman in the White House do discuss Kennedy's forthcoming Consumer Message. Kefauver had hoped the President's message would endorse his drug-control bill; it did not. The message did support several of Kefauver's proposals, but gave the Senator no credit for them. And the message said nothing about Kefauver's main point—reducing drug prices. An angry Kefauver called Feldman and said he intended to make a statement criticizing the message for ignoring the issue of drug prices. Feldman assured him the Administration was behind his bill all the way. "I wish to hell you'd made that clear in the message," Kefauver said, and hung up.

A few weeks later, Kennedy, stung by a Drew Pearson column charging that the President was ignoring Kefauver on the advice of his White House staff, gave the Senator lukewarm support. But the White House still feared that Kefauver's bill was too strong, and in June, Feldman helped arrange a secret meeting at which representatives of Senators James Eastland and Everett Dirksen, of the Department of HEW, and of the drug industry, wrote a new drug bill that was acceptable to the industry. In violation of all political and congressional courtesy, Kefauver was not informed of this meeting until the new Eastland-Dirksen bill was sprung on him at a meeting of the Judiciary Committee. Kefauver immediately called Feldman and demanded to know what part he had played in the secret meeting. Feldman said he knew nothing about it.

Kefauver decided to protest this action in a Senate speech that very day. Feldman, learning of this, called the Senator and asked what he intended to say. Kefauver told him. Feldman protested that this would put him in an embarrassing position with the President. Kefauver replied, "I haven't been so shoddily treated in twenty-three years in Congress," hung up, and delivered his speech.

After the thalidomide tragedies, the Administration became more enthusiastic about drug control legislation and offered its own bill—Sorensen at this point became involved in the wording of the legislation—but again gave no credit to Kefauver. This shabby handling of one of the Democratic Party's most distinguished figures continued throughout the whole sorry affair.

As the drug fight reached a climax, Kefauver had to contend with another veteran of White House manuevering, Tom Corcoran, who was a top lawyer-lobbyist for the drug industry. Eventually, meaningful drug legislation was passed. The White House succeeded in taking most of the credit for it, but anyone with any knowledge of the affair knew the real victory was Kefauver's.*

Feldman, after serving briefly as Special Counsel to President Johnson, left the government in 1965 to begin a highly successful Washington law office. Another key member of Kennedy's White House staff whose role was similar to those of Feldman and White—although he was not a part of the Special Counsel's Office—was Ralph Dungan, who had also served on Kennedy's Senate staff. Dungan's duties included liaison with the foreign-aid program, recruitment of top-level government personnel, and liaison with organized labor and the Catholic church. In December, 1964, President Johnson made Dungan U. S. Ambassador to Chile, a post in which he was known for his outspoken support of political reform in Latin America. In June, 1967, Dungan resigned to become Chancellor of Higher Education for the State of New Jersey.

In his early months as President, Kennedy envisioned neat partitions between his various advisers' duties, and in this scheme he saw Sorensen as an adviser only on domestic affairs. As it turned out, much of Sorensen's time was spent in shaping the Administration's domestic program, and particularly in trying to put together an aid to education proposal that might win congressional approval. Sorensen's critics charge that as a political strategist he was overly cautious, and too often advised Kennedy to hold down domestic spending rather than offend conservatives in Congress.

Sorensen was often Kennedy's right hand in domestic crises. He coordinated the Administration's massive response to the steel industry's price increases in April, 1962. And during the debate over the Berlin crisis in 1961, Sorensen's was the deciding voice in a domestic matter of some importance. Kennedy had tentatively accepted his brother Robert's suggestion of a tax increase, one intended to distribute the

* This account is based upon Richard Harris' excellent book *The Real Voice*. Harris, a writer for *The New Yorker*, spent a year talking with scores of participants in the fight for drug control legislation, including Kefauver and Feldman. Sorensen, in his book, devotes two sentences to the matter: "By personally persuading Senator Eastland to report out a drug reform bill broader in its consumer protection provisions than the Kefauver drug bill, he gave both Kefauver and consumers a notable victory. Kefauver had been consulted all the way, but the Tennessean's aides denounced the Administration for not including their patent proposals, which would clearly have blocked the whole bill." Recent political writing contains no more ludicrous assertion than that Kennedy "gave" Kefauver a victory in the drug fight.

burden of the military build-up equally on all citizens. In a final meeting on the emergency plans, however, Sorensen declared: "I'm against the tax increase." He explained that he thought it was bad politics and bad economics. Kennedy's other advisers agreed, and the President dropped the tax increase.

Sorensen advanced from being an adviser on domestic affairs to being an all-around adviser in the aftermath of the Bay of Pigs. Kennedy had not consulted Sorensen (or Robert Kennedy) on that decision, and after the disaster he realized he wanted the advice of both on all matters, particularly foreign affairs.

Kennedy's first important post-Bay of Pigs decision concerned Laos, and he noted that the same advisers who had urged the invasion of Cuba were urging him to commit American troops to Laos. Kennedy instead agreed with Sorensen and others who urged a non-military solution in Laos.

Kennedy's decision in July, 1961, over the Berlin crisis was more difficult. At the Vienna Conference in June, Khrushchev had flatly stated that Russia was going to sign a peace treaty with East Germany and thereby end the American rights of access through East Germany to West Berlin. Kennedy asked former Secretary of State Dean Acheson for advice on the Berlin crisis, and he responded with two hard-line proposals that won strong support in the Departments of State and Defense: 1) the U.S. should declare a state of national emergency, call up one million reserves, and bring home American dependents in Europe; 2) no diplomatic initiatives should accompany the build-up lest Russia take them as a sign of weakness.

Sorensen and others on the White House staff were disturbed by these militant proposals. Sorensen wrote Kennedy a memo warning that a U.S. declaration of national emergency might "engage Khrushchev's prestige to a point where he felt he could not back down from a showdown." Moreover, he warned, a declaration of national emergency would "arouse those at home and abroad who are fearful of 'rash' and 'trigger-happy' actions by the U.S." Certainly this advice influenced Kennedy's rejection of both elements of the Acheson proposal—he did not declare a national emergency and he did stress diplomatic action as well as military might in meeting the Berlin crisis. Kennedy's July 25 address to the nation on the crisis, with its emphasis on peaceful solutions ("We will at all times be ready to talk, if talk will help.") was regarded by Sorensen and his associates as a victory for their view.

One basic fact underlies Sorensen's advice to Kennedy on Laos, on

Berlin, on the Cuban missile crisis and on the nuclear test ban, and that fact is simply that Sorensen is what is today called a dove. At eighteen he registered with the draft as a noncombatant; his first wife was a Quaker and he is certainly sympathetic to pacifism; he is deeply opposed to war and to the sort of mentality that extols war as a solution to international problems. As a realist, he appreciates the need for national strength to ensure national security. But in his advice to Kennedy, time after time, he urged him to avoid saber-rattling, to avoid bluff and bluster, to avoid a tough-guy mentality, to be always willing to walk the extra mile in search of peaceful solutions to world problems. Probably Sorensen's most important impact on Kennedy was on the issue of peace. He was a moving force behind the Administration's determined quest, in the face of countless Russian rebuffs and delays, for a nuclear test-ban treaty. Sorensen's influence was particularly strong on the American University speech, which did so much to gain Russian acceptance of the test-ban treaty—on the speech's tone, its substance, its timing, and on the fact that Kennedy delivered it at all realizing that he would be criticized (as he was) for sounding soft.

There is a good deal of evidence that Kennedy needed this sort of steady pressure toward moderation to counter his oversensitivity to charges that he was not as tough as he should be. Kennedy's friend Charles Bartlett had written that Kennedy increased the number of American advisers in Vietnam in 1962 to "prove his toughness" and improve his "image" after the Bay of Pigs fiasco. Other critics have suggested that he overreacted to Khrushchev's verbal threats over Berlin for the same reason, and that the U.S. response to the introduction of Russian missiles in Cuba was exaggerated, since the U.S. presumably could learn to live with hostile missiles in Cuba as easily as Russia had learned to live with U.S. missiles in Turkey. It is a matter of record that Kennedy's most rash, ill-considered international adventure— the Bay of Pigs invasion—was the one major decision about which he failed to consult Sorensen.

Throughout the winter of 1961–62 Kennedy wrestled with the decision of whether to resume U.S. nuclear testing. Russia had broken the moratorium in the fall of 1961. By the end of February Kennedy had decided he would have to resume testing, but the question of timing remained unresolved. The simplest answer would be to follow the announcement of the decision to resume testing almost immediately with the first tests, so there would be no time for world opinion to build up against the tests. The State Department favored this plan. Sorensen, still hoping new tests could be delayed or avoided entirely,

pressed on Kennedy the more complicated timetable the President decided to follow: Kennedy announced on March 2 that the U.S. would
resume testing in the latter part of April unless the Russians agreed
to a disarmament treaty at the Geneva meetings resuming on March
14. This plan made it possible for the Russians, by a show of good
will, to halt the new U.S. tests, but not for them to stall the tests
indefinitely. The Russians spurned the opportunity, however, and the
U.S. resumed testing on April 25.

Sorensen played a leading role in the deliberations during the Cuban
missile crisis in October, 1962. His biggest contributions were made on
Friday, October 19, and Saturday, October 27.

On Thursday the 18th, the NSC's "Executive Committee" had reached
an uneasy consensus in favor of recommending to the President that
the U.S. carry out a blockade of Cuba. A minority of the group
still favored an air strike against the missile bases and many uncertainties remained about the specifics of the blockade.

On Friday morning, with Kennedy away on a campaign trip, and
after the Executive Committee had conducted a rambling, inconclusive
debate of blockade vs. air strike, Sorensen—impatient, bothered by
his ulcer, afraid they were letting Kennedy down—said he would draft
speeches on both proposals as a means of focusing on specific issues.
He himself favored the blockade approach, but was uncertain how
it came to grips with the specific problem of the missiles. As he
later wrote:

"Back in my office, the original difficulties with the blockade route
stared me in the face: How should we relate it to the missiles? How
would it help get them out? What would we do if they became
operational? What should we say about our surveillance, about communicating with Khrushchev? I returned to the group late that afternoon with these questions instead of a speech; and as the concrete
answers were provided in our discussions, the final shape of the President's policy began to take form. It was in a sense an amalgam of
the blockade—air-strike routes; and a much stronger, more satisfied
consensus formed behind it."

The important result of Sorensen's drafted statement and the discussion of it was to make clear to the Executive Committee that the
proposed blockade was in reality more than a blockade—that if it
didn't force the removal of the missiles, an air strike would be the
next step. This was the heart of the plan Kennedy approved on Saturday and announced to the world the next Monday evening.

On the following Saturday, the 27th, Kennedy reached another crucial point. On the previous evening he had received a letter from Khrushchev containing the germ of a settlement: Russia would remove its missiles if the U.S. would agree not to invade Cuba. Kennedy's hopes were raised by this proposal, only to be dashed down the next morning, Saturday, by another Khrushchev letter stating the unacceptable demand that U.S. missiles in Turkey be removed as part of the deal.

How to reply to Khrushchev? The Executive Committee debated this dilemma angrily, aware that if the missiles weren't removed within a few days, Kennedy would be forced to escalate to the air strike. Finally Kennedy sent Sorensen and Robert Kennedy into another room to resolve the various proposed replies to Khrushchev. One or both of them (which one depends on whom you talk to) came up with the ingenious tactic of ignoring Khrushchev's second letter and proposing a solution based upon the satisfactory ideas in the first message. President Kennedy in effect accepted a proposal Khrushchev had never specifically made. But the ploy worked and the next day Khrushchev ratified the deal and the missile crisis was over.

At the height of the crisis, when its peaceful resolution was by no means a certainty, the President took Sorensen and Robert Kennedy aside. Both men—the brother and the alter ego—had been meeting with him privately every day since the crisis began, endlessly discussing and debating the hard alternatives. Kennedy told them then, and both would treasure his words in years ahead, that they two had done most to help him make the awesome decision he had had to make.

Sorensen's world fell to pieces in the latter half of 1963. In August his wife divorced him and took their three sons back to Nebraska. In November Kennedy was killed. President Johnson valued Sorensen's talents and wanted him to stay in the White House, but Sorensen knew that his services, unlike O'Brien's or Bundy's, were not transferable. He stayed only as long as courtesy demanded—and to give Johnson some much-needed help on his first speeches to Congress and the nation—then resigned in January.

Sorensen contributed nothing to the evolution of the presidential institution. Rather, his was an intensely personal role—and in this role, he was probably more essential to Kennedy than any of his other aides. Kennedy, over the course of a decade, was able to mold Sorensen into a slightly more reflective version of himself—and at the same time to learn from Sorensen many of the liberal lessons he had not learned at home or in school.

From Kennedy's point of view, theirs was an ideal relationship, and certainly it had many benefits for Sorensen as well. Yet there is something bothersome about Sorensen's attachment to Kennedy. Loyalty can be a vice as well as a virtue. What are we to think of a man who says publicly that his employer meant more to him than his own family? How much can we admire, much less rely upon, a man so devoted to someone else's interests—not necessarily the nation's—so emotionally immersed in his role as a politician's alter ego?

As a young man Sorensen showed signs of promise as a lawyer and writer—two pursuits that, more than most, hold out the possibility of individuality maintained—but at age twenty-four he began the process of submerging his personal ambitions in Kennedy's political ambitions. Kennedy once said that Sorensen had never been mad at him, and apparently it was true; the record of their decade together shows no signs of self-assertion on Sorensen's part. Ted Sorensen, the intense individualist from Nebraska, had in Washington become Ted-Sorensen-who-works-for-Jack-Kennedy, and as far as anyone could see he was willing to go on working for Kennedy forever.

Even after he left the White House Sorensen was able to defer personal decisions for a year by immersing himself in his book, *Kennedy*, which he said at the outset is "my substitute for the book he was going to write." This statement caused some other Kennedy intimates to ask "Who does he think he is?"—and to fear they knew the answer all too well. There is indeed a shadowy quality about Sorensen's book, for when he praises Kennedy's words and deeds, one senses a touch of self-congratulation, since many of the words and some of the deeds were Sorensen's own.

By mid-1965 the book was finished and Sorensen lectured and traveled, postponing decision on his own future. Friends said it was the first time they had seen him confused and indecisive. His brother said: "I think he really only wanted one job, and I kept telling him that the job of Special Counsel to John F. Kennedy was no longer available."

Sorensen did not lack for prospects. He might have been a university president, a foundation executive, a syndicated columnist, or a partner in almost any top law firm. He joined a leading New York law firm, Paul, Weiss, Rifkind, Wharton & Garrison. Sorensen was soon in demand as a lawyer, with many clients wanting him to represent them in Washington. For example, he represented a watch-making firm seeking federal approval to sell more watches in the U.S., a mortgage company seeking permission from the Department of Interior to build an apartment building overlooking the Potomac River in Washington, and a new magazine seeking Post Office approval to use second-class rates.

Sorensen's most celebrated case came in 1966 when he returned to Washington to sit beside James Roche, the General Motors president, when Roche testified before a Senate committee investigating charges that GM had hired detectives to harass auto critic Ralph Nader. Sorensen's appearance with Roche disappointed many of his friends, who felt that his prestige could be put to better use than aiding a giant corporation in its fight against a lone crusader for the public interest. Sorensen counters that he might be subject to criticism if he had defended GM's harassment of Nader, but that his advice to Roche was to do the decent thing—to apologize to Nader.

Sorensen soon became active in Democratic politics in New York. Although not close personally to Senator Robert Kennedy, he served him as an adviser and speechwriter, and represented Kennedy in seeking unity among state Democrats. Early in 1968, the ever-cautious Sorensen advised Robert Kennedy against challenging President Johnson for the Democratic nomination, while Schlesinger and Goodwin were urging Kennedy to enter the race.

Sorensen would like to return to public life, and his political celebrity is such that he must be considered a possible candidate for public office in New York in the years ahead. However, as Sorensen candidly weighs his prospects, he doubts that the voters would elect him to a major office, given his status as a newcomer to the state, his two divorces, and his lack of a military record.

There is also the fact that although Sorensen thinks like a politician, he has never learned to act like one. In his frequent appearances on public-affairs television programs, he has proved himself to be one of the least appealing performers in television history. He always seems to be performing by rote. His square, wintry, bespectacled face seems carved from ice, and his smile is as spontaneous as a bank vault swinging open.

All in all, Sorensen's political future would seem to lie in appointive office. Some future Democratic President may well decide he wants Sorensen in his Cabinet, as Robert Kennedy probably would have if he had become President. Such an appointment would have a double value. First, it would bring back to government a man of keen intelligence and rare experience. Second, it would give Sorensen, who for three years was a remarkable public servant as John Kennedy's shadow, a chance to show at last what he can do in his own right.

VI. THE JOHNSON STAFF

1. *Caligula's Court*

Lyndon Johnson is a hard-working President, and he is also the hardest President to work *for* since Franklin Roosevelt. These two facts help account for the most conspicuous fact about Johnson's staff: its ceaseless turnover.

When Johnson was thrust suddenly into the presidency he turned for help, as Truman had eighteen years earlier, to old and trusted associates. Walter Jenkins and George Reedy, who had served him since 1939 and 1951, respectively, were brought to the White House from his vice-presidential staff. Bill Moyers, a Johnson protégé since 1954, came over from his Peace Corps job. A new Johnson follower, the loyal and energetic Jack Valenti, arrived from Texas. These were the four men closest to Johnson during his first year in the presidency. Each was a friend as well as an aide. Yet one by one they slipped away: Jenkins in October 1964, Reedy in July 1965, Valenti in April 1966, Moyers in January 1967.

There were other losses. Horace Busby, a Johnson aide in the late 1940s and a friend thereafter, entered the White House staff in the spring of 1964, stayed eighteen months, and departed. Jake Jacobsen, a suave Texas lawyer and political figure, came in the spring of 1965, stayed twenty months, and returned to Texas. The departure of most of Kennedy's men was of course inevitable. But three of Kennedy's ablest men, O'Brien, Goodwin, and Bundy, tried to make the transition to Johnson's Administration. O'Brien endured as Postmaster General; Goodwin called it quits in September, 1965, Bundy early in 1966.

There is always a good reason given for each resignation. The departing aide had a financial problem. He was in ill health. He had received an opportunity too good to turn down. He had never intended to stay more than a year. Often the resignations were accompanied by an exchange of affectionate letters and declarations of mutual devotion. But when the soft music stopped and the last tear had been wiped away, the perplexing fact always remained: Another man had quit Johnson—or as was possible in several instances, been forced out by Johnson.

Johnson likes to compare himself to Franklin Roosevelt, but as regards his staff, he compares rather poorly. Roosevelt attracted men who were prepared, literally, to die for him. Several did. Johnson does not inspire that degree of dedication. Walter Jenkins' resignation was imperative after he was arrested on a morals charge in October 1964. But Reedy, Moyers, Valenti, Busby, and Jacobsen all left the White House because they had decided there were better things to do than work for Lyndon Johnson, even if he was President of the United States.

By 1968, new figures headed the White House staff: Special Assistant Joseph A. Califano, Jr., Special Counsel Harry C. McPherson, Jr., Special Assistant Douglass Cater, Appointments Secretary Marvin Watson, Press Secretary George Christian.

Despite the rapid turnover, some facts stand out about Johnson's staff. First, the best of his men—Moyers, Califano, Cater, McPherson—do not suffer by comparison with the outstanding aides of any recent Administration. Second, Johnson's is a strong staff, like Roosevelt's and Kennedy's, but strong in a somewhat different way. Johnson's men tend to be operatives rather than advisers. The one major exception was Bill Moyers, and after he left early in 1967 the staff contained no Sorensen, no Tugwell, or Clifford—no aide who was both a friend and an important influence on policy. Rather, the Johnson men's authority has been mainly operational—the not insignificant power to oversee, coordinate, and reorganize the federal agencies and departments.

Throughout his political career Johnson has surrounded himself with ambitious, aggressive young men who showed a talent for getting things done. Young men as superficially different as Bill Moyers and Bobby Baker, two of Johnson's protégés in the 1950s, could win his favor if they had the basic ability to move fast and produce results. But as Johnson has grown older, a generational gap has developed between him and his bright young men. When he wants advice, he tends to call on contemporaries, old friends like Clark Clifford and Abe Fortas. One of those senior advisers put it: "He looks to older men for advice and to younger men for action."

The contrast with Kennedy and his staff is apparent. Kennedy's aides were his contemporaries; he was the boss, but the fact remained that they knew as much about some matters as he did. Johnson, on the other hand, was a Congressman when most of his aides were still schoolboys. Time and again they run up against the fact that he knows infinitely more than they about the legislative process, the federal bureaucracy, and national politics. "We're always finding out that he's not as stupid as we thought," one admits. Probably aides to every President make that discovery.

Johnson's attitude toward the federal establishment is more complex —more devious, perhaps—than was Kennedy's. Kennedy and his men rarely bothered to hide their distrust of the bureaucracy. Johnson is more of a respecter of institutions, more given to formal chains of command. By his statements, his promotion policies and his use of non-abrasive liaison men like Cater and Moyers, Johnson has done much to win the good will of the bureaucracy. In one important instance, the State Department, he has propped up a faltering Secretary and cut back the influence exerted by the White House through the staff of the National Security Council.

Yet Johnson has employed the stick as well as the carrot. He has— quite rightly—given his aides virtually unlimited authority to carry out executive-branch reorganizations. He has used his White House staff extensively to watch over agency affairs. One of his assistants, Joe Califano, directs a five-man staff that is used as a "domestic Bundy operation," i.e., a White House staff authorized to oversee the domestic agencies. The prevailing attitude is summed up by one White House aide, who says: "The departments just aren't independent, however much they'd like to be. They have to act in the President's interests and the staff has to see that they do."

One of Johnson's former White House aides comments: "A President necessarily has an eye on his place in history, and that doesn't make him any easier to work for."

Johnson has never been easy to work for. Long before he became President, it was a Washington legend that Johnson ranked as an employer somewhere between Mr. Dithers and Caligula.

He raves, he rants, he ridicules. He brags, berates, bullies. He is impatient, imperious, impossibly vain. He seems determined to pass on to his underlings all the frustrations and uncertainties he himself has suffered in a lifetime of politics.

Johnson is the least predictable of masters. Louis XIV's most powerful minister, Jean-Baptiste Colbert, when on his way to visit the King at Versailles, would sometimes throw a piece of bread into a canal, on the theory that if it floated to the other side Louis would be in a good mood but if it sank Louis would surely be ill-humored. Eisenhower's aides believed that when the President wore a brown suit he was invariably in a black mood. But neither bread crusts nor brown suits have served to predict the Johnson temper; his men work in constant uncertainty. A man will be Johnson's fair-haired boy one day, then be haughtily ignored the next—the staff calls this game "the freeze-out." An aide, summoned to Johnson's presence, never knows if he will be lavishly praised or given a merciless, public dressing down.

Willie Morris, who knew the Johnson staff as editor of the *Texas Observer*, wrote of one of Johnson's able young lieutenants, Lloyd Hand: "The stories of how Johnson berated him before others for casual oversights became legend among us." After Johnson became President, Hand served briefly as U. S. Chief of Protocol, then departed to enter politics in California.

The story has often been told of the time Johnson, then Majority Leader, gave his long-suffering aide George Reedy a monumental chewing out. ("He was using language that I had never heard one human being use to another," said a witness.) A few minutes later, Johnson gave Reedy a Christmas present—a new station wagon—explaining: "You never want to give a man a present when he's feeling good. You want to do it when he's down."

Johnson's wrath can extend beyond verbal abuse. Douglass Cater noted in a 1953 magazine article that during the Second World War, Congressman Johnson discovered that a staff member of a House Committee had told a newspaperman about another Congressman's indiscretion. Johnson, knowing the offender to be a naval reservist, had him ordered to active duty in the Aleutian Islands.

Johnson is not the first President to have a hot temper. Consider this description:

"An unwelcome report of some baseless criticism or some unfinished labor or some blemished performance could ignite an explosion of temper almost fiercely physical. His voice would shout, his cheeks flame with rage, his arms wave threateningly. And I recall one of his oldest associates murmuring, after witnessing one such scene, 'My God, how could you compute the amount of adrenalin expended in those thirty seconds? I don't know why long since he hasn't had a killer of a heart attack.'"

Johnson in a rage? No—the "bland" Eisenhower as described by

Emmet Hughes. One might also cite Evelyn Lincoln's description of Kennedy dressing down an innocent naval officer after another officer gave him a faulty weather report. Or Paul Fay's story of Kennedy berating a navy cook who served him fried instead of broiled chicken.

But men who have observed Johnson over the years see more in his outbursts than just a fast temper. They see, rather, a petty, even a sadistic desire to elevate himself by degrading others.

A Washington correspondent says of one former Johnson aide: "He and I were friends when I was covering Capitol Hill. He was a good man and I liked him. But over the years Johnson systematically broke him down, destroyed him, left him a shell of what he had been. I avoid him now; it's too painful and embarrassing to talk to him."

There is, to be sure, another side to Johnson, a mellow, sentimental side. Sometimes he seems to regret his outbursts and to try to atone for them. Those who endure the trial by fire are rewarded by gifts and favors, by extravagant compliments, by personal intimacy. The aide and his family will be invited to the White House for Sunday dinner, or to the LBJ Ranch for a holiday. Again, the contrast with Kennedy is striking—Kennedy, a much more disciplined man, would not veer in either extreme, toward abuse or toward social intimacy with his staff.

Stories of Johnson's mellow side do not so often make their way into print, yet his aides tell many of them. Joe Califano recalls the time his father visited him at the White House and Johnson insisted on taking time to see him and have the three of them photographed together. Johnson inscribed one of the pictures for his aide: "To Joe, the pride of both of us." Later he reflected to Califano that, as a young man, Califano couldn't imagine what it meant to his father to see him succeed, and he spoke of his own pride at the way his son-in-law, Patrick Nugent, had handled himself during his much-publicized engagement to his daughter.

Some Johnson aides grow cynical, however, and they see his sentimental side as just the other half of his hot-tempered side. Either way, they say, Johnson has an instinctive desire to "devour" (sometimes they say "dominate" or "possess") the men who work for him. He wants to be the center of their universe, to put his brand on them as he puts it on his cattle or his monogrammed shirts, to have them on twenty-four-hour call, putting his wishes ahead of their own or their family or friends. His best aides fight a continuing battle to maintain social, intellectual, even spiritual independence. Some of his lesser aides, of course, are happy to be consumed by him.

The LBJ brand stays on some men long after they have left Johnson's employ. It is possible, in Washington and other cities, to find men whose entire lives are constructed upon their real or presumed intimacy with Lyndon Johnson. These men are usually found in large, comfortable offices with four or five autographed pictures of Johnson on the walls, and copies of his books in a prominent place near their desks. On the basis of their relationship with Johnson, these men command impressive salaries or fees. They are sought after socially and interviewed on television. Often they are intelligent, affable men who can speak with insight on many issues. There is just one topic on which they are absolutely no help, and that is their great friend Lyndon Johnson. To questions on that subject, they respond in the most solemn and intimate tones with the most absurd and pathetic nonsense. At such moments, the listener sees what the others have meant when they said that Johnson seeks to possess his men.

In one sense, Johnson's treatment of his men is irrelevant to the question of how he runs the government. If bawling out an aide is good for the President's mental health or his digestion, so be it. It's less time-consuming than golf, less harmful than whisky. If the aides can't take the heat, they can always get out of the kitchen. Still, *someone* has to serve the President, and how he treats his aides influences whom he gets, how long they stay, and how well they serve. Certainly the matter is, to the men involved, a serious one, one they have to come to grips with if they are to work for Johnson. For the most part, Johnson's men are realistic and candid about the difficulties involved in serving him, and they firmly defend Johnson's God-given right to be Johnson.

"If you looked out your window every day and saw a bunch of people singing 'Hey, hey, LBJ, how many kids did you kill today?'—you'd feel like giving somebody holy hell yourself," says one of Johnson's writers.

One assistant comments: "Johnson is a supercharged man. If you're a tender flower, you can get bruised. I find the relationship very invigorating. You don't goof off. He brings out the best in you. He works under enormous pressure; he has a right to be impatient. You and I think good and bad things every day—about our wives, for example—but we keep it all bottled up. Johnson thinks out loud—he says what's on his mind, good or bad, and then he forgets it. I find that people in government want to see more of him, not less."

Another says: "I've known him long enough that I know what it is when he loses his temper, and so does he. I get a tremendous amount of wind, but it doesn't hurt. It's not that I'm insensitive to pain; I'm not. But I know a lot of it is catharsis for him. When I came here, I made a conscious decision not to let myself, in my own mind, be made or unmade by him. And I like him, in an inexplicable way. I like the fact that he's human. He shows his warts. It's not like working for some bland, emotionless person. It's like a marriage; you have your scraps, but it's better than boredom."

Roosevelt, Truman, Eisenhower, Kennedy—each inspired love in the men who served him. Johnson does not. His men feel fascination, sympathy, respect, admiration—but not love.

However, although love may make the world go round, it doesn't make the government go round. Johnson, in his own way, has done an impressive job of that. He has done it because he works very hard, he demands to know every possible detail of governmental affairs, and he will not settle for vague or incomplete answers. The men who deal with him daily know what wrath they will encounter if they fail to meet his standards, and their determination to please him permeates outward through at least the upper levels of the bureaucracy. Few men who have dealt with him have failed to be impressed by the depth of his knowledge of governmental affairs—details of the budget, of domestic programs, of legislation, and of course of the war effort in Vietnam. Career officials with no special affection for Johnson say they have never seen a President who demanded to know so much.

As famous over the years as the Johnson temper has been the Johnson "treatment"—those occasions when LBJ focuses his entire verbal, political, and intellectual powers upon the conversion of one individual or group, usually with overwhelming effect.* Johnson has used fear to move the government but he has balanced it with his highly personal brand of persuasion. He often meets with second-level officials who

---

* I once had the pleasure of being the target of a brief version of one sort of Johnson treatment. In the spring of 1960, he was Senate Majority Leader and an undeclared candidate for his party's presidential nomination, and I was a reporter for the *Nashville Tennessean*, which backed him for President. One night Johnson's private plane was stopping briefly in Nashville on a flight from Texas to Washington and I was sent to interview him on the then-pending civil rights bill. As Johnson stepped out of his plane, I identified myself and my newspaper, and Johnson threw his arm around my shoulders and announced to Governor Buford Ellington and Senator Robert Kerr, who were also present, that I was one of the finest young men he'd ever encountered. The four of us started toward the terminal, Johnson still with his arm around me, and as we walked inside he whispered in my ear: "Boy, where's the men's room?" I led him to it, but stopped discreetly at the door. "Come on in, boy," he roared; inside, as he attended to other business, I completed my interview.

do not ordinarily enjoy presidential access, and these men rarely fail to come away impressed by his concern for efficiency and innovation in his government.

In his ceaseless effort to exert personal control over the vast reaches of the government, Johnson has had important help from his staff. His men, if less important than Kennedy's as policy advisers, have been more important as overlords of the federal empire. Bill Moyers, with his exceptional ability to deal with people smoothly and effectively, built a bureaucratic communications network such as Washington had not seen since Tom Corcoran's prime. Joe Califano, in a more systematic way, and aided by a sizable staff, has set out to institutionalize White House liaison with domestic agencies. McPherson and Cater have also been given responsibility for overseeing domestic agencies.

The extent to which some governmental departments have drifted out of the presidential orbit was dramatized in 1967 when the outgoing Secretary of Commerce, John T. Conner, stated publicly that he had lacked influence in what should have been the most important part of his job—formulation of basic governmental economic policies. This failure did not result from any lack of ability on Conner's part, but from the fact that in the past twenty years or so new presidential agencies have grown up to separate the Secretary of Commerce from the President.

Today, the three agencies that do most to help the President fix economic policy are the Council of Economic Advisers, which analyzes business trends; the Budget Bureau, which makes key decisions on government spending; and the Treasury Department, which has jurisdiction over tax policy. The Commerce Department, with its general duty to speak for business in government, but lacking the specific responsibilities of its three rivals, tends to be on the outside looking in when economic decisions are made.

More and more in recent years, as government has grown larger and the economy more complex, outstanding Budget Directors and CEA chairmen have functioned in effect as Special Assistants to the President on economic affairs. However, in the Johnson Administration, all the major economic advisers—the Budget Director, the CEA Chairman, the Secretaries of Commerce and Treasury—have routinely reported to Califano, who operates as a kind of Secretary of the Domestic Economy. Again, the need is for coordination, centralization, one key person to serve as a clearinghouse and a channel to the President on complex issues, and almost inevitably that role falls to one of the President's personal assistants.

One of the little-known facts about the Johnson staff is its size—it is easily the biggest in history. Hard figures are hard to come by: The White House is unwilling to publicize its growth, and exact head counts are difficult since many of the lower-level aides are paid by another agency, but permanently detailed to the White House (with office space, usually, next door in the Executive Office Building). It is a good guess, however, that Johnson's ten or so Special Assistants have a total of about thirty men helping them.

Often these younger, lesser-known aides are very able men. Ben Wattenberg, author of *This U.S.A.*, which combined painstaking analysis of the 1960 census figures with optimistic conclusions on the nation's future, one day received a call from Bill Moyers offering him a job as a presidential speechwriter. Joe Califano brought one of his law school classmates, John Robson, onto his staff, and Robson later became Under Secretary of the Department of Transportation. Clifford Alexander, Deputy Special Counsel while still in his early thirties, received a presidential appointment to be chairman of the Equal Employment Opportunities Commission, where he directs a staff of more than four hundred.

More often than not, these younger White House aides are recruited on the basis of ability rather than political connections. For example, Fred Bohen, a young political economist, was serving as assistant dean at Princeton's Institute of Policy Studies when he decided he'd like some Washington experience. He wrote letters to several friends in Washington asking for help. One of them passed his letter on to Califano, who called him sight unseen and offered him a job on his staff. Similarly, DeVier Pearson, a young Oklahoma City lawyer, was hired as Associate Special Counsel after he impressed Harry McPherson by the work he had done as counsel for a Senate subcommittee headed by Mike Monroney of Oklahoma. Tom Johnson, the young Associate Press Secretary, was a White House Fellow assigned to the press office, where he earned himself a permanent job.

These second-level aides have varying degrees of importance and access to the President. Some of the leading aides of aides, like Moyers' Hayes Redmon and Califano's Larry Levinson, wield considerable authority. Redmon, in particular, although virtually unknown outside the White House, was highly influential in coordinating Moyers' wide-ranging foreign affairs network. Other second-level aides necessarily have only limited access to the President, yet in a government so totally dominated by one man's wishes, even their access may seem impressive to officials who are even farther outside the presidential orbit. One young aide who is assigned to liaison with several agencies comments: "I may see the President only twice a month, but that's still more than the people I'm dealing with see him."

Johnson has made one or two mistakes in his hiring. In February, 1966, he hired Robert Fleming, director of the ABC-TV Washington bureau, and told reporters Fleming would be "my Press Secretary." Presumably he meant that Fleming would take over from Bill Moyers, the Press Secretary then, enabling him to perform other duties. But this arrangement didn't work out to Johnson's satisfaction, and when Moyers resigned ten months later he was replaced by a Texan, George Christian, with Fleming staying on to be Christian's assistant in charge of television relations.

Johnson's biggest fiasco came when he hired Eric Goldman, historian (*Crucial Decade*) and television performer ("The Open Mind") to be the White House intellectual-in-residence. Johnson brought Goldman aboard as a 95-dollar-a-day consultant early in 1964, and a White House spokesman proclaimed "a unique approach to channel the nation's best thinking into the White House." As it turned out, Johnson found Goldman impractical and pompous, and the resident intellectual drifted farther and farther into the limbo of the East Wing. Goldman's downfall apparently came when Johnson blamed him for the fiasco of the July, 1965, White House Festival on the Arts. The get-together for several hundred artists and writers was Goldman's project, intended to bring Johnson and the world of the arts closer together. As it turned out, the biggest news from the festival was 1) poet Robert Lowell refused to come, in protest against the war in Vietnam and 2) writer Dwight Macdonald came and spent most of the day circulating an antiwar petition. This duplicity inspired one of Johnson's most memorable remarks—"Some of them tried to insult me by staying away and some of them tried to insult me by coming"—and it also ended Goldman's influence, since Johnson blamed him for the whole absurd affair.

After that, Goldman couldn't get within a half block of the President. When he decided to resign, he sent a letter to Johnson, only to receive back a note from Mrs. Johnson saying how sorry she was that he was leaving. It dawned on Goldman that the President wasn't going to do him the courtesy of announcing his resignation. Goldman therefore announced it himself, at an off-the-record dinner with several reporters. He also spoke critically of Johnson and added that he intended to write a book about the Johnson Administration. The White House responded with Moyers' quietly scathing comment to reporters that

Goldman had spent most of his time working with Mrs. Johnson and her staff.

Undaunted, the President hired another intellectual-in-residence. This one, who has proved more effective than Goldman, is John Roche, a professor at Brandeis University who is a former president of ADA, sports a stylish mustache, supports the war in Vietnam, and devotes himself largely to presidential speechwriting. In his public appearances, Roche has struck some of us as having an unusual ability to appear intellectually arrogant without appearing intellectual.

Former ADA presidents aside, Johnson's staff, like Truman's and Kennedy's, has a strong home-state flavor. The Texans have included Jenkins, Moyers, Jacobsen, Christian, Valenti, Busby, Watson, McPherson, H. Barefoot Sanders, a young Dallas lawyer who works in congressional relations, Ernest Goldstein, a former University of Texas law professor who became a White House assistant in September, 1967, and Larry Temple, a young lawyer from Governor John Connally's staff.

The Texans are by no means a monolithic group. Some were liberal and Eastern-oriented, notably Moyers and McPherson. Others maintained strong ties to Texas' conservative political establishment—Watson was chairman of the Texas Democratic Executive Committee; Christian was press secretary to Governor Connally; Jacobsen was an aide to former Governor Price Daniel.

These political contrasts were reflected in sometimes bitter staff rivalry between the conservative Watson and various liberals, notably Moyers. Moyers was also involved in a quiet battle with Administration hawks on Vietnam war policy, whose ranks included White House national security aide, Walt W. Rostow. These and other White House feuds have been concealed by the consensus-conscious Johnson, but that they exist, often in highly intensity, cannot be doubted.

One Texan who never feuded, who only asked to serve, promote, and praise his President is Johnson's memorable friend, crony and sometime assistant, Jack Valenti.

2. The Hero-Worshiper: Valenti

All Presidents have their cronies, but they are not always called that. Indeed, although the dictionary defines "crony" simply as "an intimate companion," experience suggests that more precise definitions are in order. For example:

A "court jester" is a funny crony. (FDR's Pa Watson)

An "intimate adviser" is a powerful crony. (Harry Hopkins)

A "favorite presidential companion" is a rich crony. (JFK's Paul Fay; Ike's bridge partners)

A "longtime political retainer" is a crony reporters like. (JFK's David Powers)

A "political hanger-on" is a crony reporters don't like. (Truman's Harry Vaughan)

Cronies are almost part of the presidency. Since Presidents can't get out easily, their companions must come to them. When Harding was President and Herbert Hoover was his Secretary of Commerce, the strait-laced Hoover had to loosen his religious scruples and play bridge with Harding to gain his ear—but Hoover could never bring himself to stoop to poker. Silent Cal Coolidge had an old friend, Frank Stearns, whom he would summon to the White House during emergencies to sit beside his desk in unbroken silence.

One by-product of the modern staff system that began under Franklin Roosevelt is that Presidents, if they wish, can now have cronies at hand on a full-time basis. Some have chosen to do so. FDR's closest aides—Missy LeHand, Steve Early, Louis Howe, Tom Corcoran, Harry Hopkins—were also among the people with whom he most liked to spend his hours of relaxation. Similarly, Harry Truman numbered White House intimates like Vaughan, Matt Connelly, and Clark Clifford among those he most enjoyed as social companions.

On the other hand, both Eisenhower and Kennedy chose not to mix their staff assistants with their social friends. Eisenhower liked the company of wealthy businessmen, men who shared his political beliefs and his skill at the bridge table. Kennedy's off-hours companions included wealthy, longtime friends like Lemoyne Billings and Charles F. Spalding, plus newer Washington friends like journalists Charles Bartlett and Ben Bradlee.

Lyndon Johnson, so far as one can see, has no life, no thoughts, no interests that are not political. He does not read books, paint, enjoy movies or the theater, fish or collect stamps. He has been known to dance with women, ride in a speedboat, go deer-hunting and take an interest in the cattle on his ranch, but he is generally talking or (one suspects) thinking politics while he does these things. Johnson is not a man who savors either inaction or solitude. Throughout his career he has always had at least one aide who was a more-or-less constant companion, part sounding-board, part drinking buddy, part confidant, part errand-boy. This desire for round-the-clock companionship is one reason Johnson has had a long line of bright young men at his side—from Walter Jenkins, hired in the late 1930s, to Horce Busby, hired in the late 40s, to Bill Moyers hired in the late 50s. Young men, dazzled by the vistas of political power, are more likely to tolerate the foibles, the frictions, the frustrations that are part of intimacy with Johnson—or of any President.

Almost everyone in Lyndon Johnson's inner circle is a crony in one sense or another, but most of them have attained sufficient prominence —such as Moyers, Clifford, Fortas—to rate the more delicate designation of "intimate adviser" or some such. The one out-and-out crony who appeared at Johnson's side—and one of the most illustrious cronies in White House history—was an ambitious, energetic, irrepressible, emotional, shrewd Texas advertising man, Jack Valenti.

Valenti's White House career was brief but memorable. A Houston huckster who had married Johnson's favorite secretary and performed political chores for the then Vice President, Valenti happened to be at hand in Dallas when a stunned Johnson became President and reached out for familiar faces. Suddenly, like Dorothy swept up by the tornado and carried off to the Land of Oz, Valenti found himself aboard Air Force One headed for Washington. He arrived in the White House on the evening of November 22, 1963, and he stayed there as a Special Assistant until May of 1966, when he accepted a job as president of the Motion Picture Association of America, with a reported seven-year contract at $100,000 per year and another $50,000 for expenses. During his thirty months in the White House, Valenti became, excepting only Moyers, the most publicized of Johnson's aides. The publicity was not always to his liking.

During Johnson's first weeks in the presidency, when reporters were straining for clues as to the pecking order in the new Administration, Valenti was the man most often seen at the new President's side. There was an air of mystery about him—small and swarthy, moving crisply through the White House corridors, forever whispering in the President's ear, his dark eyes flashing. Tom Wicker called him "at once the most enigmatic and the most omnipresent of the Johnson men," and there were the inevitable comparisons with Louis Howe.

But the mists of mystery soon scattered, and Valenti, who had been a highly successful professional image-maker in Houston, proved to be a flop in molding his own image in Washington. By his second year in Washington, Valenti had succeeded in making himself an international laughingstock—with his famous "I-sleep-better-each-night" tribute to Johnson—and he was being cuttingly described in the nation's press as "a glorified valet" and "the President's favorite whipping boy." One of the President's Special Assistants told me he believes Johnson arranged for Valenti to get the movie post as "an act of compassion" because he was pained at seeing Valenti described as nothing more than a valet. (Then, reflecting on Valenti's new salary, he added: "I wish somebody would start calling me a valet.")

There was an essential paradox between Valenti's undoubted shrewdness and the apparent naïveté that caused his public-relations woes. The reason for this, I think, was the suddenness of his shift from Texas to Washington, and his inability to adjust to the different style of behavior expected in the White House. Texas is a land of overstatement, of tall tales, of unbridled enthusiasms, and Valenti—a natural booster and civic tub-thumper—fit in perfectly there. Washington is a different world. It is a place of whispered confidences, subtle suggestions, and ambiguous answers, of trial balloons and "official spokesmen" and "deep backgrounders." Valenti was a Texas bull in a Georgetown china shop—a hard-sell huckster in a soft-sell territory.

As he saw it, if he believed that Lyndon Johnson ranked with Abraham Lincoln and Winston Churchill among the great men of history—and he does believe that, most fervently—there was no reason for him to keep his opinion to himself. But in time, his unabashed, unalloyed devotion to Johnson made reporters unwilling to take anything he said seriously. As one put it, "If Johnson dropped the H-bomb, Valenti would call it an urban-renewal program."

I got a taste of Valenti's image-making early in 1966 while writing an article on him for the *New York Times Magazine*. Valenti had by that time been pretty roundly lampooned in various publications. Columnist Jack Anderson, for example, wrote: "A day seldom goes by without the President exercising his lungs berating Valenti. He has cussed out his handyman for everything from a malfunctioning doorknob to a slip-up of state . . ." And Valenti's praise of his boss, coupled with the hundreds of stories about Johnson's bursts of temper toward his aides, inspired a classic Herblock cartoon in *The Washington Post* titled "Happy Days on the Old Plantation," which pictured a blackfaced Valenti with lashmarks across his bare back bowing to a bullwhip-bearing LBJ.

Against this background of press abuse, perhaps Valenti saw me as his last chance of impressing the public with his importance in the presidential circle. When I asked him during our first interview to tell me about his duties, he began making statements that struck me as not only self-serving, but self-destructive. For example, in discussing the early morning sessions he, Marvin Watson, and Bill Moyers had with the President, he declared:

"The morning sessions are marvelous. . . . We are people who are intimately involved with the President, people he trusts who handle secret missions that few people know about, particularly in foreign policy. . . .

"I read every piece of paper the President reads. If he asks me to follow up a McNamara memo, I know what he means because I've already read it. I attend meetings of the NSC. I think the most significant things I do I really can't talk to you about—special projects involving Congress and national defense that are sensitive and often classified."

These seemed to me to be extremely foolish things for a White House aide to be saying. They might well be true, but you don't boast about such matters. I liked Valenti—it would be hard not to like him—so during our next interview I showed him my transcript of my notes and asked him if those remarks were what he had meant to say. Journalistic ambition should be made of sterner stuff, but I thought I would give him a chance to tone down his cloak-and-dagger comments.

With furrowed brow, Valenti studied the notes carefully.

"That's about right," he said finally. "Just one thing bothers me. Where I say the morning sessions are 'marvelous'—don't you think that word might sound a little effeminate?"

At that moment I decided I would not try to stand between Jack Valenti and his destiny. If he'd say it, I'd write it. After my article appeared, a perplexed Valenti told a friend: "That Anderson! I thought he was my pal—but he cut me up!"

Jack Valenti reached his destiny after a climb that was part Horatio Alger and part Sammy Glick. His father, the son of Italian immigrants, held a clerical job with the Houston city government. As a boy, Valenti sacked groceries, sold newspapers, and dreamed of attending Harvard. That fact in itself marked him as a young man of unusual ambition, for very few middle-class Texas boys in the 1930s had even heard of Harvard—and if they had, it was probably as a hotbed for Communists and degenerates. But Valenti had somewhere been told that Harvard was the nation's best school, and some spark in him aspired toward the best. Harvard was financially impossible, and he instead enrolled in 1936 in the University of Houston's night school. By day, he was an office boy for the Humble Oil Company. During the Second World War he flew fifty-one missions over Italy and was awarded the Distinguished Flying Cross. After the war, he returned to night school and was elected student body president. In the meantime, he had advanced from office boy to a promising job in Humble's advertising department.

He was doing well, but he still dreamed of Harvard, and the G. I. Bill made it possible. In 1946, he enrolled in the Harvard Business School. (Twenty years later, he still wore his HBS class ring.)

Upon graduation, he returned to Humble, but in 1952, he and a friend started what was soon a successful advertising agency. Valenti was anything but the prototypical Texan—he was not big or slow-talking or cowboyish, but small and glib and natty—but he was an engaging fellow, and industrious, and by 1956, he had been named Houston's Outstanding Young Man of the Year.

Throughout the 1950s, Valenti was active in the middle-of-the-road, Johnsonian faction of local Democratic politics. "I fell under the spell of Johnson before I ever knew him," Valenti recalls. In 1957, he met Johnson for the first time at a "get-acquainted" coffee for the Senator and leading young Houstonians. Valenti was then writing a weekly column for the Houston *Post* and he therein made public his first impressions of the Senator:

"There is a gentleness in his manner, but there is no disguising the taut, crackling energies that spill out of him even when he's standing still. And no mistaking either the feel of strength, unbending as a mountain crag, tough as a jungle fighter. . . .

"I left the gathering feeling good about our Senator. I liked him. He bears heavy problems, in times that shiver with chill tension. But he's a smart, tough, earnest man with both confidence and humility. He's going to need all this and more in the months and years ahead."

This analysis pleased the Senator, and Valenti found himself moving toward Johnson's inner circle of Houston allies. He would meet Johnson at the airport when he came to town, help with the luggage, handle details, and bask in reflected glory. Johnson liked Valenti, and appreciated his professional talents, for in 1960 when his political prestige depended on carrying Texas for the Kennedy-Johnson ticket, he chose Valenti's firm to handle the political advertising campaign in the state.

It is significant that Valenti was moving into the Johnsonian orbit when its central figure was in the temporary eclipse of the vice presidency and when some others (to their subsequent regret) were breaking away. Johnson as a powerless Vice President might hold less interest for Bobby Baker, his former Senate protégé, but in Jack Valenti's eyes he was still twenty feet tall. Johnson found out who his fair weather friends were, and Valenti was not among them.

An unforeseen factor entered the Johnson-Valenti friendship when Valenti began to court Johnson's attractive secretary of nine years' standing, Mary Margaret Wiley. They were married in Houston on June 1, 1962, with the Vice President (who briefly opposed the match because he didn't want to lose a good secretary) giving away the bride. "That was the beginning of my intimacy with Johnson," Valenti recalled later. "We often spent weekends at his ranch and he would sometimes visit us in Houston." The Valentis' first child, a daughter born October 30, 1963, was named Courtenay Lynda.

Then came what Valenti, in his characteristic hyperbole, calls "the act of inscrutable fate that changed my life." Valenti had handled the advance arrangements for the November 21 dinner in Houston attended by both President Kennedy and Vice President Johnson. When the dinner was over, Johnson urged Valenti to fly on to Fort Worth to keep him company. "My wife had just had a baby and she didn't want me to go," Valenti recalls. "But I said, 'Hell, it's just one night,' so I went on." The Vice President was in a good mood and once they arrived at Fort Worth's Hotel Texas he stayed up late entertaining Valenti and other followers with tales of his career in politics—a career that at the moment was at rock bottom.

In Dallas the next day, Valenti shared a car in the presidential motorcade with Evelyn Lincoln and several other women. After the shooting, when their car arrived at Parkland Hospital, Valenti was told that Johnson wanted him to return to Washington with him. It was not until he arrived at the hospital that he realized Kennedy was dead; the news was broken to him by Cliff Carter, another Johnson intimate, and Valenti virtually fell apart on hearing it, sobbing uncontrollably. Meanwhile, the new President had departed for Air Force One, and Valenti pulled himself together, raced to the airport, and burst into Johnson's presence with the declaration: "I got here as quick as I could, Mr. Vice President."

Valenti was Johnson's houseguest and constant companion during his first months in the presidency. "He gets up with me every morning, he stays up with me until I go to bed at night around midnight, and he is the only one who can really take it," Johnson declared.

Because Valenti knew a lot about Johnson, and nothing about the government, it was natural that his duties would be personal rather than governmental. (By contrast, Bill Moyers, who knew a great deal about the government, was busy building a bureaucratic empire during those early months.) Valenti arranged appointments, passed on messages, and was the President's companion for eating, drinking, swimming, traveling, and late-hour reminiscing.

In time, as Valenti learned his way around, his duties broadened. He was one of the President's top writers and editors. Valenti, a fan of Hemingway, had a knack for turning out the short, punchy sentences the President likes. Once, Johnson tossed Valenti a bone-dry farm message with the command, "Sex it up a little, Jack." One Johnson aide noted that, "The President might have a speech on Vietnam and say, 'Jack, put some more peace in it.'"

Valenti emerged as a wide-ranging presidential troubleshooter. Because he is a man of extreme tact and good nature, he was sometimes used in congressional relations and as a liaison with various members of the diplomatic corps. Ambassadors were more than glad to get Valenti's ear, for he was as likely as anyone to pass their views and problems along to the President.

This was the heart of Valenti's influence. He had little impact on national or world affairs, but he unquestionably was intimate with the President—he had access to the King's Ear—and in Washington this is a very formidable power.

Valenti was forty-two years old when he entered the White House, and the pressures there had soon put deep circles under his eyes and silver streaks in his wavy black hair. Yet the five-foot-seven, 145-pound Valenti maintained a jaunty attitude; he looked rather like an aging cheerleader. He was, as someone said, "a gutsy little guy," and he was generally liked by the press. One White House reporter recalled a colorful scene in Valenti's office:

"We were talking about the Dominican crisis and Jack said the trouble with the press is that it doesn't see the whole story. 'It's as if a band marched past my window,' Jack said. 'I'd see the drum major go by at the front, then the trumpets and trombones in the middle, then the drums at the end—but never the whole band at once.' Then, just in case I missed the point, Jack started marching around his office, imitating a band— the drums, the trumpets, the drum major, the whole thing. It was a magnificent, virtuoso performance. Of course, I didn't learn anything from him."

Valenti was even more popular with the other members of the President's staff. One reason for this was simply that he was no threat to their ambitions—as one of them put it, "Jack is simply not a Byzantine person." Because of his proximity to Johnson, he was often the victim of the Johnson temper—he took some horrid chewing-outs, say others on the staff, and they add that his taking the heat probably saved some of them from taking it. Moreover, when Johnson was angry at an aide or government official, Valenti would often warn the offender to lie low until the President's anger had passed.

It was Valenti's very intimacy with the President—an intimacy that might be envied by most Cabinet members—that in time created the image of him as a kind of valet. (In fact the President is served by two real valets.) It is the habit of the press to sum up political figures in one or two word capsules: Corcoran was a fighting Irishman; Hopkins a Svengali; Clifford a suave lawyer; Adams a tart New Englander; Sorensen an alter ego; Moyers a boy preacher; and Valenti was a valet. Once the tag was applied, it was as inescapable as quicksand; the more Valenti struggled, the deeper he sank. When the White House called in friendly propagandists like columnist William S. White to aid Valenti ("He is no drawing room card, maybe because he has too much work to do. He has the regrettable simplicity of the really competent man who needs no megaphone to establish his competence. He is only the 'little man' who is always there, always in there pitching for a President for whom he is glad to work"), it only stirred the flames of controversy.

An incident that Valenti believed typified his problem took place at the LBJ Ranch in the spring of 1964. The President, with Valenti at his side, was driving two reporters around the ranch. The President spotted a soft-drink bottle in his path on a desolate road and stopped the car, noting that the bottle could give someone a blowout. Valenti, who was wearing a golf cap and white buckskin shoes, hopped out and tossed the bottle off the road. While he was away, Johnson heaped praise on him: "Now there goes a valuable hunk of humanity. He can do anything for you and do it fast." When Valenti returned to the car, Johnson winked at the reporter and said, "I see you're still wearing those Harvard shoes." Valenti, the faithful second banana, smiled and replied: "Couldn't do without them, Mr. President."

This historic scene was duly reported by one of the reporters, and Valenti believed it left many readers with the impression that his main function was to pick up soft-drink bottles. "The reporters were our guests," he protests, "so what was I supposed to do—tell the President of the United States to go pick up the damn bottle?"

Valenti sealed his own doom when he delivered his remarkable speech before the Advertising Federation of America in Boston early in 1965, and there in Kennedyland described Johnson:

"He is a sensitive man, a cultivated man, a warmhearted and extraordinary man. . . . The full spirit of the man never seems to be captured. . . . [after the assassination] All around him everyone was in various states of shock, nearing collapse. But the new President sat there, like a large gray stone mountain, untouched by fear or frenzy, from whom everyone began to draw strength. . . .

"He began to give orders in clear, audible tones, yet the voice was soft, the words unhurried. And suddenly, as though the darkness of the cave confided its fears to the trail of light growing larger as it banished the night, the nation's breath, held tightly in its breast, began to ease and across the land the people began to move again."

Valenti said that Johnson "feels like a personal experience the giant agony of the world; there are not many in this aristocracy of humanity," and he continued:

"The President, thank the Good Lord, has extra glands, I am persuaded, that give him energy that ordinary men simply don't have. He goes to bed late, rises early, and the words I have never heard him say are, 'I'm tired.'

"I sleep each night a little better, a little more confidently, because Lyndon Johnson is my President. For I know he lives and thinks and works to make sure that for all America and, indeed, the growing body of the free world, the morning shall always come."

This speech was laughed at all over the world. Even Valenti's friends wondered how he could have made a statement so certain to be interpreted as the most extreme sycophancy. The answer, of course, is that Valenti had no idea it would be so interpreted. As he saw it, he had simply stated his honest opinion in his normal prose style. "What did they expect me to do?" he asked later, missing the point entirely. "Denounce the President?"*

To understand Valenti's confusion—and, in the last analysis, his woes in the White House—it is helpful to have read a little book called *Ten Heroes and Two Heroines*, a collection of Valenti's columns for the Houston *Post*. Cliché-ridden, melodramatic, these were the musings of a

---

* The fact that Valenti's speech was most famous for its "I-sleep-better-each-night" declaration was ironic in that Valenti certainly did not invent that tribute; it is a cliché of political rhetoric. For example, Robert Donovan, in *Eisenhower: The Inside Story*, quotes a White House official as saying: "The President has great faith in Adams and has told me many, many times that with Adams as his assistant he can sleep better at night."

man whose intellectual reach agonizingly exceeded his intellectual grasp. The most amazing thing is not that Valenti, as a Houston ad-man in his mid-30s would write the columns, or even that he would have them made into a book, but that ten years later, while serving in the White House, he would eagerly press a copy of his book on a visiting journalist. The vanity of writers knows no bounds.

As the book's title suggests, Valenti's weekly columns were usually about someone he admired—his heroes—from Alexander Hamilton, Beethoven, and Thoreau to Hemingway, Bing Crosby, and Joe Lewis. A few samples follow.

On Joe Lewis: "Time, that grim ravager, clutched him and slivers of skill began to shred off until one day Joe Lewis stumbled and fell."

On Bing Crosby: "How long, oh how long ago was it that this deceptively mild-appearing, jug-eared chortler with a flavorful groan two shades sweeter than the mew of a bull in a cave-in first burst on the entertainment scene?"

On the presidency: "I get a little groggy when the smart fellows talk about Oedipus complex or patria complex, but I vibrate tunefully when they talk about the President complex."

Valenti's deepest emotions, however, were reserved for history's statesmen, and most of all, for Winston Churchill, of whom he writes in the book's first essay:

"If the table of our memory could be swept clean, and if we could be born again in any age, to live in the same era as any man in history, there would be those who would choose to be fellow citizens of Napoleon, Alexander, or Pericles, or Caesar or Beethoven or Jefferson or Pitt, or perhaps in the perversion swimming in an idiot, Robespierre. But I am a Churchill worshiper, unabashedly so. To me one of the privileges of being alive in these lively and compulsive times is the nearness of the vibrant, electric figure of the noblest Englishman of them all."

Ten Heroes and Two Heroines confirms one fact about Valenti: He is a born hero-worshiper. Throughout his life he read history books and idolized the heroic men of past and present. Then, incredibly, he discovered a hero he could not only worship, but could *serve*, one he wholeheartedly believed would rank in the history books beside Caesar and Lincoln and Churchill.

Johnson and Valenti were made for each other; the one with a colossal vanity, the other with a limitless capacity for adulation. Others who had served Johnson had fought to maintain their individuality, but Valenti was content to let his hero engulf him. It became impossible to think of Valenti apart from Johnson. There is a Zen riddle that says:

"We know the sound of two hands clapping, but what is the sound of one hand clapping?" Jack Valenti without Lyndon Johnson is the sound of one hand clapping.

There was a special reason for Johnson to appreciate Valenti's dedication. Essentially, both men shared the same problem: their style of behavior was not one to which the Eastern-oriented (and Kennedy-oriented) press was accustomed, and their Texas manners were criticized and ridiculed. Johnson, as President, had resources to defend himself, but Valenti had none—once a presidential aide gets off on the wrong foot, his troubles tend to snowball. Valenti was one of the first victims of the merciless scrutiny the news media focus on today's White House. A more sophisticated man, a Bundy or a Moyers, can manipulate the media to serve his own ends, but a man like Valenti, unschooled in Byzantine maneuver, is likely to come to grief.

We need shed no tears for Jack Valenti, however. The film industry apparently decided it was worth many thousands of dollars a year to have as its spokesman a man who was well known as the President's friend and who, in moments of crisis, would have the President's ear. So Jack Valenti is doing quite well: globe-hopping to film festivals, making speeches to respectful audiences of filmdom's aristocracy, being photographed with various voluptuous movie queens. Whether LBJ actually sought the movie job for Valenti—as some in the White House say—or simply gave his approval when the offer came is really not relevant. In either case, Valenti has at last found his true milieu. In Hollywood, the land of make-believe, Valenti is valued as a profound thinker, a student of history, a master of prose, a subtle practitioner of the political art, and a cultured, if somewhat conservative, gentleman.

He has, meanwhile, maintained his close ties to President Johnson. Valenti and his wife and children—of whom the President is particularly fond—are the Johnsons' frequent guests at the White House and the LBJ Ranch. Valenti has, moreover, several times been called on to perform political chores for the President in California and New York, and to accompany him on trips abroad. Lyndon Johnson and Jack Valenti—hero and hero-worshiper—are deeply and genuinely fond of one another, and their affection is likely to continue as long as they are both alive. President Kennedy once said that the White House was not a good place to make new friends so he was going to stick with his old friends. President Johnson seems to have reached the same conclusion and to have decided that, although thousands at his bidding speed, he may never find a better friend than Jack Valenti.

3. The Preacher: Moyers

Bill D. Moyers was twenty-nine years old when he entered the White House with Lyndon Johnson on the night of Kennedy's assassination. He stayed there at Johnson's side until January, 1967, when he left to become the publisher of the Long Island newspaper *Newsday*. During those thirty-eight months his intimacy with Johnson, his influence throughout the government, and his impact on the course of national and international affairs were such that he became, in the opinion of some qualified observers, the most powerful White House assistant of modern times.

The New York *Times'* Tom Wicker, for example, calls Moyers "the most able and influential presidential assistant I have ever seen or read about." High Sidey, *Time-Life's* White House correspondent during the Kennedy and Johnson Administrations, shares this view. On the other hand, an older correspondent, the *Times'* Arthur Krock, casts his vote for Harry Hopkins. Comparisons lead nowhere, but it is clear that Moyers, if he was not *the* most influential White House aide of recent history, is one of the two or three top contenders for that title.

Moyers influenced almost every aspect of the Johnson Administration. He built a communications network that made him Johnson's chief emissary to the farflung federal bureaucracy. He was a central figure in the 1964 political campaign, and the architect of a merciless television attack on Republican candidate Barry Goldwater. Moyers organized and supervised the 1964 Task Force operation that produced much of Johnson's Great Society legislative program. He was named Press Secretary in mid-1965 when Johnson's press relations had reached a new low. Finally, he became deeply involved in foreign affairs, most dramatically in a little-known campaign against the escalation of the war in Vietnam.

Moyers tried to operate in total secrecy, and only since he has left the government has it been possible to uncover many of his activities, particularly in relation to foreign affairs and Vietnam. Yet while attempting to document *what* he did while in the White House, I think it is equally important to ask *why* he did those things, for Moyers seems to be a man who is motivated by something more than the expediency of the moment.

He came to Washington not, like Corcoran and Goodwin and Califano, from Harvard Law School, but straight from the campus of the Southwestern Baptist Theological Seminary, and many of his associates have felt that his basic motivation was more religious than political. Yet his idealistic impulses were blended with a sure instinct to survive and succeed in the dog-eat-dog world of politics. He once urged Peace Corps volunteers to pursue the ideals of Joan of Arc with the political prowess of Adam Clayton Powell, and the comment was something more than a joke. It was Moyers' rare mixture of realism and idealism, his capacity both to scheme and to dream, that made him so remarkably effective in Lyndon Johnson's White House. To find the source of that capacity we must look back beyond his Washington experience to the three major influences on Bill Moyers before he went to work for Johnson: his family, his hometown, and his religion.

He was born in Hugo, Oklahoma, on June 5, 1934, and grew up in Marshall, Texas, where his parents still live. His father, Henry Moyers, held a variety of unskilled jobs throughout his life; in recent years he has been a time clerk in a defense plant, and Mrs. Moyers has held a clerical position in a Marshall funeral home. His parents were hard-working, God-fearing people, whose fondest dream for their quiet, studious younger son, Billy Don, was that he might someday become a Baptist minister. Both Bill and his older brother, Jim, grew up feeling the intensity of their parents' hopes for them. James Moyers would later recall: "Our parents wanted so deeply for us to make some kind of mark. We felt that the worst thing in the world would be to disappoint them."

Although the Moyers family had little money, the Moyers boys never knew what, two decades later, would be called the culture of poverty. On the contrary, they grew up in a culture of opportunity. Marshall, located in East Texas near the Louisiana border, was in the postwar years a comfortable, relatively prosperous little town of 20,000. If it had all the limitations of smalltown America—smugness, narrowness—it also had the smalltown advantages. The community took note of its young people and if they did well—in school, in church, in sports—the community rewarded them with recognition and approval.

Bill Moyers discovered at an early age that his mind was a machine that worked better and faster than those of his contemporaries; grades came easy, so he was free to devote spare time to extracurricular activities and to work. At fourteen he worked part-time sacking groceries for the A&P store; he did so well that his supervisor urged him to enter the company's management training program. But the next year, at fifteen, Moyers got a job that opened broader vistas than the grocery business—he became a reporter for the Marshall *News-Messenger*, where his brother Jim, just out of college, was city editor.

Being a reporter sharpened Moyers' self-confidence; it gave him his first glimpse of the world of affairs; and it made him more aggressive in his school activities. His brother Jim later recalled: "I don't think Bill was a natural-born leader. I think it's something he set out to acquire."

In later years, Moyers would speak of his hometown's mobility and the opportunities it offered him, but there was another side to Marshall he also remembered. Not far beneath the community's surface was a hard core of materialism. Texas has never been noted for a social or intellectual aristocracy; rather, its aristocracy is one of money. In high school, Moyers began to realize that despite his top grades and extracurricular honors, a distinct social barrier existed between him and his classmates from the better-off families.

His soaring ambitions were destined to collide with the community's social realities in an incident, so trivial in retrospect, that seemed cosmic at the time:

"When I was a junior in high school I was outside the establishment of my school. It was made up of the affluent kids in the community. It dawned on me that to be on the inside I had to do so on some basis other than money. I couldn't get in unless I forced myself in. So I ran for class president—and lost. I remember writing my girl friend the next day, telling her that I'd lost that race, but I'd win the next one."

Years later, one of Moyers' friends suggested that he had always looked back on his hometown with a determination to "show those so-and-sos." Moyers vigorously denies any such sentiment. "There was an establishment," he says, "and I was determined to crack it, but not out of spite."

Whatever his motivation, Moyers' instinct was to work within the system, to make the system work for him. He was not a rebel, but a born bureaucrat.

In the fall of 1952, he enrolled at North Texas State College, a school of five thousand students located at Denton, a quiet college town thirty miles northwest of Dallas. North Texas was a good place for Moyers to pursue his political ambitions, for it was an inexpensive state school that attracted students much like himself, young people from small towns attending college on limited budgets. He ran for freshman class president and won. At the end of the year, he was named the Outstanding Student in his class. He repeated both honors in his sophomore year. He majored in journalism, made near-perfect grades, and held a part-time job in the school's publicity office.

In the spring of 1954, near the end of his sophomore year, Moyers wrote a long letter to his state's junior Senator. Moyers knew that Senator Johnson sometimes hired students as summer employees in his

Washington office and, after listing his many campus achievements, he asked for a job. Johnson, after checking with the publisher of the Marshall paper, hired him. It was a turning point in Moyers' life.

He spent the summer addressing envelopes in the Majority Leader's Washington office, and he often doubted that Johnson knew he existed. But Johnson was watching, and at the end of the summer he urged Moyers to transfer from North Texas to the more prestigious University of Texas, and he offered Moyers a $100-a-week job with KTBC, his television station in Austin, to help finance the move. Moyers accepted the offer. Among its other attractions, the job made it possible for him to marry Judith Davidson, the Dallas coed he had courted since their first week together at North Texas.

He worked a forty-eight-hour week as assistant news editor for the television station, and still managed to graduate as the University's senior journalism student with the highest four-year grade average. This won him the offer of a Rotary International fellowship to study abroad. He sought the advice of Senator Johnson, who urged him to accept the fellowship. He and his wife thus spent the 1956–57 academic year at the University of Edinburgh, where he studied religious history.

By the time they returned to Texas in the fall of 1957, Moyers had decided to make his career in religion rather than journalism. He turned down Johnson's offer of a permanent job with KTBC and enrolled in the Southwestern Baptist Theological Seminary at Fort Worth. He spent two pleasant years at the seminary. Bill was an outstanding student and a favorite of the school's younger, more liberal faculty members. He and his wife could live comfortably on his $6000 salary as the seminary's publicity director. Every other Sunday he drove sixty miles to preach at the small Baptist church in Brandon, Texas.

He believed, however, that his goal was to teach, not preach, and after receiving his Bachelor of Divinity degree from the seminary, he agreed to teach a course in Christian ethics at Baylor University, the large Baptist school at Waco. Then, in December, 1959, just as he was about to begin at Baylor, Senator Johnson called from Washington.

Johnson was gearing up for his push for the Democratic nomination for President the next year and he wanted Moyers around to help. For Moyers, it was a hard decision. He had spent two years preparing for a career in religion. But he had begun to feel restricted by the dogma of his church, and to fear that religion promised a life of "words, not action," and so he accepted the offer.

He left almost immediately to begin a hectic year of campaigning, first for Johnson's candidacy, then for the Kennedy-Johnson ticket. The

Sunday after Moyers left, his friend Olin Robison preached in his place at the Baptist church in Brandon. "So Mr. Moyers has gone to Washington?" reflected one of the parishioners, an elderly lady, with a shake of her head. "And he seemed like such a nice young man."

Moyers had moved into a world very different from that of the theological school, but he did not forget the lessons he had learned there. At that point he had had only minimal exposure to political theory, but his political beliefs flowed naturally from his theological studies. He once reflected when asked about this: "I had a gentle upbringing and gentle parents. I think I had basic humanitarian impulses, but I had no political philosophy. I think my political philosophy grew out of my religious training." Basic to his evolving philosophy was a belief that the duty of government is to do God's work on earth—and that God, in fixing His political priorities, is not overly concerned with the doctrine of States' Rights, the sanctity of private property, or other matters that might impede the state's concern for the care of human life and happiness.

Moyers' new job was in some respects not an especially desirable one. It was a young man's job—to be the Senator's personal aide, to hold his coat, arrange his schedule, run his errands—but it was a base from which to build. The older members of Johnson's staff were delighted to have Moyers "manage" the impulsive, often unmanageable Senator. They affectionately called the twenty-five-year-old Moyers "the preacher" and "the bishop." Soon the preacher was running the show. Within three months, Johnson increased Moyers' salary from $10,000 to $15,000. A little later, his title advanced from "Personal Assistant" to "Executive Assistant."

Tom Wicker, who covered the 1960 campaign, later wrote: ". . . As the campaign wore along I soon learned that young Bill Moyers was really running it, although amiable George Reedy was technically in charge. . . . A reporter had to latch onto Moyers to know what Johnson would be up to next. While Johnson would wander up and down the aisle of the Electra in vivid pajamas, or entertain the reporters with endless political lore and Stengelesque yarns, Moyers would be hard at work, helping with speech texts, radioing ahead to the next stop, passing out press releases, conferring with the staff. . . . Moyers could crack a joke, laugh at himself, kid Johnson a little when the latter was out of earshot, get his job done, and make things a little clearer for all."

One of Moyers' jobs during the campaign was to serve as Johnson's liaison with the Kennedy team, and despite his Texas accent, Moyers had no trouble communicating with men like O'Donnell and O'Brien. After the election, Moyers turned down a job with the new Vice President to join Kennedy's most exciting new agency, the Peace Corps.

He was a striking success there. At the outset, he won Peace Corps Director Sargent Shriver's favor by guiding him around Capitol Hill for a series of breakfast meetings with Congressmen who were dubious about the new program. Moyers soon became Shriver's Associate Director for Public Affairs, and in January, 1963, he was made Deputy Director, the agency's number-two executive.

The Peace Corps served Moyers well. It took him outside the world of Texas and showed him he could compete as an equal with the best-educated young men in America. It proved that his prior success had not been based (as some believed) on a mysterious Baptist spell he had cast over Lyndon Johnson, for the hard-driving Shriver admired Moyers purely for his ability to produce results. Finally, the Peace Corps enabled Moyers, for the first time in his life, to combine his ability to get things done with his idealism. In his previous work with Johnson, he had simply been a gifted operator, a young man with a knack for handling a dozen assignments at once. His personal philosophy, his instinctive liberalism, had been largely irrelevant. But at the Peace Corps his operational ability was harnessed to an idea in which he fervently believed. Second only to Shriver, Moyers molded the Peace Corps, and it taught him how political power can be channeled to do good on a worldwide basis. The Moyers who returned to Johnson late in 1963 was not the same man who had left him early in 1961; he was no longer content just to wheel and deal, but determined to have a hand in shaping the substance of things.

Early in November of 1963, Ken O'Donnell asked Moyers to go to Austin, Texas, and smooth over the political tensions that threatened to mar the President's dinner appearance there on the night of November 22. On the day of the dinner, Moyers was having lunch with Frank Erwin, chairman of the state Democratic executive committee, when the news came of the assassination.

Until that moment, Moyers had been uncertain and troubled about his future. Despite his success at the Peace Corps, he wondered where he was headed. He dreamed of being the Peace Corps' Director, should Shriver leave, but there seemed little chance that the Kennedys would bestow that prize on a young Johnson protégé. Restless, Moyers sometimes told friends he might accept an offer from an insurance company in Texas, or buy a small newspaper there.

In an instant, the assassination changed everything. Moyers raced to the Austin airport and chartered a plane to Dallas. His plane happened to land near Air Force One, but Moyers, unaware that Johnson was aboard, jumped into a state police car and ordered a startled state trooper to take him to Parkland Hospital. Halfway there, he heard on the police radio that Johnson was at the airport, so he ordered the trooper to turn around. He bounded aboard Air Force One unchallenged, but was stopped at the stateroom door by a security agent. He scribbled a note to Johnson—"I'm here if you need me"—and a moment later he was working for a President.

Moyers once said: "You aren't a man in your own right when you are working for a President. To be most effective you have to have an umbilical cord right to his character, nature, and personality."

An intimacy of this sort existed between Johnson and Moyers for most of their time together. Johnson was first attracted by Moyers' operational ability, and in time their relation took on what appeared to be father-son overtones. They became, despite the difference in their ages, close friends. They spent countless hours together—evenings in the President's office, midnight suppers, weekends at Camp David—mulling over ideas and problems, joking, planning, plotting, sharing their hopes and frustrations. Moyers understood the isolation that the presidency imposed on Johnson, and up to a point he was willing to serve as a safety valve, pincushion, and sounding board for his often lonely, often frustrated boss. In this sense, along with his political service to Johnson, Moyers played a psychological role, and at times he thought this was his most important one.

A central factor in their intimacy was Moyers' complete loyalty to Johnson, a degree of loyalty not shared by all Johnson's helpers. Bobby Baker, for example, was a skillful political operative, but Johnson realized that Baker was out for Baker. Moyers, by contrast, seemed interested only in advancing Johnson's cause. The only time their relationship faltered came near the end, when Johnson convinced himself that Moyers was putting his own interests first, and was cultivating Johnson's rivals, the Kennedys.

When problems arose between Johnson and Moyers, the friction usually came from without. Newspaper and magazine writers, in describing the two men, tended to polarize them, picturing an idealistic Moyers struggling for the soul of an iniquitous Johnson. There is an element of truth in this description, but it ignores the more subtle shadings, the fact that both Moyers and Johnson are complicated mixtures of the political and the idealistic. As story after story flattered Moyers at Johnson's expense, Moyers protested vainly to anyone who would listen that he and Johnson were very much alike.

Moyers and Johnson were alike in their enjoyment of power—the thrill of making decisions, taking risks, winning praise, controlling events, being at the center of things. They shared, too, an instinctive Populism that sprang from their early years as have-nots in small Texas towns. Where they differed was in the blending of pragmatism and idealism within their characters. Thirty years in the throat-slashing world of Texas and congressional politics have twisted and toughened Johnson; the impulse to do good is still within him, but it is buried beneath thick, protective layers of caution and cynicism.

When Moyers joined Johnson, the dew of theology-school optimism was still upon him and this, as well as Moyers' operational ability, appealed to the older man. Perhaps Moyers reminded Johnson of himself as a young man. Quickly, Johnson took Moyers under his wing.

Moyers soon developed a strong personal affection for Johnson, but I think that besides liking the older man, he feared him, feared that the driving force of Johnson's personality, his instinct to dominate, would break down Moyers' own individuality, as it had that of so many of Johnson's other protégés, and slowly remake him in his patron's image. I suspect that Moyers was fascinated by Johnson's power to create, yet fearful of his power to dominate, sometimes to corrupt.

For this is the most disturbing thing about Lyndon Johnson: it often seems that it is his tragic fate to corrupt almost everything he touches. He has corrupted men and women who have worked for him. He has corrupted American foreign policy. With his war in Vietnam he has corrupted even his own nobly conceived domestic program. There is much to dislike in Lyndon Johnson but—if one assumes he does these things not out of malice but out of ignorance and clumsiness and lack of foresight—there is also much to pity.

Moyers, when he hitched his youthful wagon to Johnson's soaring star, undertook a dangerous game: to share the power but avoid the corruption, to ride the tiger without ending up inside. For all his intimacy with Johnson, he fought to maintain his independence. More than any other member of Johnson's staff, Moyers would challenge The Man. "Bill would really go to the mat with him," one Special Assistant says, and another recalls: "I've seen them fighting like a couple of ten year olds."

Yet Moyers knew when to stop, too. He would offer up the small flatteries that helped balance his independence on large matters. Once a magazine writer agreed to let Moyers see in advance the direct quotations he planned to use from their interview. Moyers, scanning his quotations, had only one request. During the interview he had spoken of "Johnson," but he asked that this be changed for publication to the more respectful "the President."

Nonetheless, stories of Moyers' independence often appeared in print, and became a constant source of friction between him and Johnson. For example, one Saturday evening early in 1964, Johnson was unable to reach Moyers because he and his wife had gone out for a drive. A story spread, and later appeared in *Newsweek*, that Johnson gave Moyers a dressing down and ordered him to have a two-way radio installed in his family car. Johnson was doubly irritated by the *Newsweek* item: by the suggestion that he was a tyrant, and by the implication that Moyers himself had leaked the story. (Moyers later insisted that he himself had ordered the radio installed in his car. In any event, it was never installed, because his wife refused to have it.)*

Another instance occurred early in 1967 when Charles Bartlett and Edward Weintal's book, *Facing the Brink*, appeared, and included this anecdote:

"One day in his first year in office, Johnson lashed out bitterly at everyone around him. The victims of his spleen were startled to see Bill Moyers suddenly take the President of the United States by the arm and lead him out of the room with these words: 'We've had enough of this. You're wasting all of our time.' Later, when someone asked Moyers how he had the nerve to do this, he replied, 'It's easy—I'd rather be in the Peace Corps.'"

Moyers heatedly denies this story. Certainly it would have been more his style to speak to Johnson later, in private, and suggest a note or phone call to repair any damage done. But true or not, the anecdote appeared at the time Moyers was leaving the White House, his enemies made sure the President saw it, and it further damaged his relations with Johnson.

One part of the Bartlett-Weintal story was true—in his early months in the White House, Moyers made no secret of his wish to return to

* The car radio incident illustrates another peril that besets men around the President. Let us assume that, in the wake of the incident, Moyers' wife told one of her friends about it, the friend told her husband, and he passed the story on to one of his associates. Washington being the small, gossipy place it is, the story would soon reach some journalist's ear and find its way into print, perhaps embellished a bit in the process. There may be a way to stop this kind of leak, but no President has yet discovered it.

the Peace Corps, particularly if a chance came to replace Shriver as its director. This yearning amazed many people, and it points up one of the frustrations of work in the White House. By all Washington standards, Moyers' status would have dropped sharply if he had returned to the Peace Corps, but apparently he would have accepted that loss in exchange for the personal satisfaction it would have brought. At the White House he shaped and molded other men's programs; at the Peace Corps he would have had something to call his own.

Eventually, he put away that dream. He told me in 1966: "My hope of returning to the Peace Corps gave way to the realization that the real power to get things done was right here—in the White House."

Moyers began getting things done for Johnson during the tension-filled flight back from Dallas to Washington. He served then as the new President's emissary to the grief-stricken Kennedy circle (he was, in William Manchester's prose, "the gentle nexus") and he continued this role during the equally tense early weeks of the new Administration.

Moyers helped put the distinctive Johnson touch on the new President's first statements to the nation. Johnson was using Ted Sorensen as his primary speechwriter, but he called in Moyers to add the LBJ flavor. Johnson's speech to Congress on November 27 is a good example; it is fascinating to compare the familiar Kennedy-Sorensen cadences ("The greatest leader of our time has been struck down by the foulest deed of our time. . . . In this age where there can be no losers in peace and no victors in war . . .") with the new, plain-spoken Johnson-Moyers style ("I will insist that the Government get a dollar's value for a dollar spent. . . . The need is here. The need is now. I ask your help.")

Moyers, in those early days, was also helping Johnson address another unfamiliar group, the federal bureaucracy. Moyers had spent three years working within the bureaucracy, and he moved swiftly to build a communications network that became one of his main sources of power. Moyers understood that the government is not run by Cabinet officials, but by the Assistant Secretaries and top-level bureaucrats who make the day-to-day decisions, and he set out from the first to cultivate these men. "The bureaucracy has a life of its own," he reflected later. "It can be a President's worst enemy unless he can find means to stamp his own ideas and beliefs on it."

One reason he was effective was that it was his habit to deal with people in a manner that won them over to his side. A government official who has dealt with presidential assistants since the Eisenhower Administration says: "I never knew anyone else in the White House quite like Moyers. You find that most of the presidential expediters, men like Adams and O'Donnell, get in the habit of running over people. 'I'm the President's man,' they say. 'Do what I tell you.' Moyers was the very opposite of that. He was always receptive, he always made time to discuss an issue, and he wanted to involve himself in issues that other White House people weren't interested in."

Moyers' understanding of the bureaucratic process and his understanding of Johnson's wishes were the key elements enabling him, in 1964, to make one of his most important contributions to the Johnson Administration—his role in organizing and supervising the fourteen Task Forces that produced much of the historic Great Society legislation of 1965 and 1966.

In this undertaking, Moyers' closest associate was Richard Goodwin. After his downfall at the State Department in mid-1962, Goodwin had moved to the Peace Corps, where he had known Moyers. Soon after Johnson became President he began calling Goodwin in to help write speeches on Latin America, and in February, 1964, he joined the White House staff as a speechwriter and specialist on urban affairs.

The Task Force operation developed because Lyndon Johnson, as he settled into the White House in the early months of 1964, was a President without a program. There was no package of legislative proposals, no New Freedom or New Deal, that bore the LBJ brand. As it became apparent that Goldwater would be the Republican candidate that fall—and that a Democratic landslide was thus possible— it was imperative for Johnson to look ahead to a major legislative program for 1965.

One day in March, as Johnson splashed in the White House pool, he told Goodwin and Moyers of his desire for a dramatic new program to distinguish his Administration from Kennedy's. The President's mood was ambitious but vague. More than anyone else, it was Goodwin who conceived the specific idea of the 1964 Task Forces: to assemble the nation's leading thinkers, focus their attention on specific problems, and make their recommendations the basis of a presidential legislative program.

Johnson was excited by the Task Force concept, and on June 7 he sent Goodwin and Moyers to Cambridge, Massachusetts, to seek intellectual support. They met at John Kenneth Galbraith's home with about thirty professors from Harvard, MIT, and other institutions. Some of the academics feared that Johnson wanted to use them for intellectual window dressing, but Moyers and Goodwin did much to ease their fears. Some commented afterward that Moyers did not compare unfavorably with Sorensen, his counterpart in Kennedy's White House.

Goodwin had conceived the Task Force plan, but Johnson gave Moyers the responsibility of implementing it. Upon his return from Cambridge, Moyers wrote a memorandum setting forth guidelines for the operation. A key point was his requirement that government officials be mixed in, roughly half and half, with the outside experts. He did this because he believed the 1961 Kennedy Task Forces, consisting almost exclusively of non-governmental planners, had generated built-in resistance. Also, Moyers was able to appoint his own governmental allies to the Task Forces. Often, Moyers had made contact with progressive men within the bureaucracy whose proposals were regularly blocked by their cautious superiors. By putting his friends on the Task Forces, Moyers enabled them to side-step their bosses and deal directly with the White House.

By the end of June, the fourteen Task Forces, each with about twelve or fifteen members, were beginning to meet. They included several men who would later enter the Administration: John Gardner, as Secretary of Health, Education and Welfare; Robert Wood, as Under Secretary of Housing and Urban Development; and Harold Howe III, as Commissioner of Education.

Moyers, not wanting these men to operate in a vacuum, took steps to tie them in to the White House—and to him. Each Task Force had assigned to it a Bureau of the Budget man as its "executive secretary," and also one of the White House staff men as a liaison.

The panels deliberated in strict secrecy over the summer and fall, and made their reports on November 15—after the election was past, to forestall charges they were being used for campaign propaganda.

Moyers, preoccupied with the political campaign throughout the summer and fall, had had only occasional contact with the Task Force deliberations, but he again took charge when the reports came in on November 15.

First, he circulated the reports among Cabinet officers and other top officials for their comments. Next, he set up a second system of Task Forces, made up of Cabinet members, Assistant Secretaries, and Budget Bureau experts. These groups met for a series of sessions in Moyers' office to decide which ideas in the Task Force proposals had substantive merit, and, beyond that, were politically feasible. Larry O'Brien and his aides often attended to help weigh the latter point. These meetings inspired heated discussion, and Moyers did not hesitate to use his position with the President to get the results he thought desirable. When he said, "The President wants . . ." that would usually end the debate.

Given the decisions made and priorities set in these meetings, officials could begin to shape the final recommendations that would be presented to the President.

That led to the final step: presidential approval. In search of that approval, Moyers in mid-December began boiling down the scores of Task Force proposals into notebooks and charts that could present the new ideas to Johnson in clear, concise language. Moyers began his presentation during a flight to the LBJ Ranch and continued it through a Christmas visit there. Moyers had summarized the proposals into a fifty-page "Black Book," and he and the President pored over this notebook at length.

Johnson was enthusiastic about the proposals, and he dug deeply into them. Moyers recalls one scene when they talked outdoors, with Johnson relaxing in a hammock: "I thought I was being especially articulate, but when I looked over at the hammock, the President appeared to be asleep. So I stopped speaking, and for five minutes we sat in silence. Then bang, bang, bang, the President spoke—he had obviously heard everything—and he told us precisely why the recommendation would not work and how it should be repackaged. All the mulling in silence had paid off. The President had been able to chart the political terrain on education better than anyone else."

The Task Force operation was a success by any standard. In the field of education, it helped solve the church-state dilemma; it recommended the supplementary education centers; it focused Administration planning on the special problems of slum schools. The Urban Task Force recommended the rent-supplement program, the Model Cities program, and the creation of the Department of Housing and Urban Development. The Health panel provided impetus for more than twenty new health measures passed by Congress in 1965. Other Task Forces recommended legislation to combat air and water pollution, to improve the antipoverty program, and to clean up the cities and countryside.

Moyers' greatest contribution to this historic effort was not his impact on specific pieces of legislation, although that impact existed, but in creating the organizational framework within which the Task Forces operated with such notable success. His governmental genius was never more apparent. To overcome the skepticism of the Eastern intellectuals for their new, Texas-style President, to meld them with the best of the bureaucracy in an unprecedented process whereby their best ideas rose directly to the President's attention, to do all this in a campaign year with no leaks to the press, no backlash, no angry resignations, and in so doing to set a precedent for continuing communication between the academic community and government—this achievement may have been, as one of his friends insists, "Moyers' finest hour."

Underlying Moyers' organization of the Task Force system was a determination that the process should produce not just a jumble of unrelated proposals, but a coherent program flowing from a central philosophy. That philosophy, one he and Johnson had discussed for many hours, was a belief that Johnson's dreamed-of Great Society, besides perfecting the New Deal's programs for the poor, should go beyond it to deal with the quality of life enjoyed by all Americans. It was Moyers' hope, too, that the Great Society program, like the New Deal, would become an enduring part of American life, one that could not be repealed by conservatism at home or conflict abroad. Later, the war in Vietnam would seem to him and others to imperil this dream.

Throughout the summer and fall of 1964, as the Task Forces deliberated, Moyers concentrated on Johnson's campaign against Senator Goldwater.

He was, as Theodore White later wrote, Johnson's "chief idea channel of the campaign." Moyers directed all campaign speechwriting efforts, such as hiring writers and making assignments, and he helped shape the campaign issues. He was the White House contact for the numerous Democratic "advance men" in the field. And he was in charge of Johnson's multimillion-dollar media campaign.

At the Democratic Convention in Atlantic City in August, Moyers and Secretary of Labor Willard Wirtz wrote the party platform, which included the strongest civil rights plank in history. Moyers then was given the job of selling this platform to Southern political leaders. This led him into all-night bargaining sessions in smoke-filled rooms, and he was largely successful. (One Southern leader he couldn't sell was Texas Governor John Connally; bitterness between them grew in the months ahead, until Moyers decided he had no political future in Texas so long as Connally remained in power.)

Moyers' most interesting campaign job, however, was his direction of Johnson's television attack on Goldwater. Johnson could give Moyers virtually a free hand in shaping the television offensive because the two of them were in total agreement as to its goal: not simply to defeat Goldwater, but to destroy him and all he stood for. To this end, Moyers molded the most effective, most savage media campaign in political history. The ferocity of this onslaught may seem out of character for Moyers unless it is viewed as a corollary of his other preoccupation in 1964, the Great Society program. Goldwater was the dragon of reaction blocking the road to the Great Society, and if Moyers labored for the legislative program with the faith of a New Testament apostle, he set out to smite Goldwater with the wrath of an Old Testament avenger.

As his agent in the television offensive, Moyers installed at the Democratic National Committee an old friend from Texas, Lloyd Wright, whom Moyers had earlier brought to the Peace Corps. Moyers then chose Doyle Dane Bernbach, Inc., a New York advertising firm noted for its graphic handling of the Volkswagen account, to develop the television campaign. The agency would prepare specific presentations for Moyers to accept or reject. Moyers might or might not submit a proposed advertisement to the President for approval, as he saw fit.

The Democrats' $4 million TV offensive was divided into three phases.

First came the working-over of Goldwater. Moyers wanted, as he once put it, to hang the noose of nuclear irresponsibility around Goldwater's neck. His instructions to Doyle Dane were simple: Take the offensive, hit Goldwater where he's weakest, knock him off balance and keep him there.

Doyle Dane responded with a devastating political invention: the Daisy Girl. The Daisy Girl appeared on national television only once, for one minute on the evening of Monday, September 7, a little blond child, innocently plucking petals from a daisy. Suddenly her image melted into a shot of a nuclear testing site, and the entire scene was covered by a giant mushroom-shaped nuclear cloud.

Neither Goldwater nor the Republicans was mentioned, but no one doubted the intended victim of the advertisement. The next day, Goldwater and his campaign manager issued public protest. Moyers was overjoyed. He ordered that the Daisy Girl not be shown again—for as he saw it, newspaper and newsmagazine accounts of her fate had given the Democrats thousands of dollars in free publicity. (Moyers has later said that he never showed the Daisy Girl advertisement to the President before it was aired; had its savagery backfired on the Democrats, Johnson could have disclaimed it.)

Next in the television series came another little girl, licking an ice cream cone while a motherly voice discussed Strontium-90 and Goldwater's opposition to the nuclear test-ban treaty. Another TV spot pictured two hands tearing up a Social Security card—a silent reference to Goldwater's opposition to Social Security. Moyers also stressed regional TV spots. For example, one semihumorous one, shown in the South, pictured an auctioneer atop a dam—selling TVA, as Goldwater had once proposed. Another, also based on a Goldwater remark, showed someone sawing the northeastern states away from the rest of the country. (Moyers liked this one so much he authorized it to be shown once nationally.)

The TV campaign achieved its goal: Goldwater, shaken by the attacks on him, spent much of his campaign on the defensive, reassuring the voters that he *wouldn't* sell TVA, he *wouldn't* abolish Social Security. Then the television offensive could move to its less dramatic second and third phases: selling Johnson as President and hammering away at the peace-and-prosperity theme.

Moyers savored every minute of the campaign against Goldwater, but once it was over, he turned his attention back to the Task Force operation and the Great Society legislation. He recalls the first six months of 1965—"as bill after bill came down from Congress for the President's signature"—as the most satisfying period of his life. He once said: "The newspaper clippings in my wife's bureau drawer will fade, but no one can ever take from me that the Higher Education Act and the Elementary Education Act bore something of my mark, even if it was only a tiny toeprint."

Besides the legislative program, Moyers had many troubleshooting assignments. He kept a close eye on the "war on poverty." He was Johnson's "operating executive" in mobilizing the National Guard during the racial crisis in Selma, Alabama. During the crisis in the Dominican Republic, he and Bundy were credited with persuading Johnson to resist advice that he install a pro-U.S. military regime there.

When Johnson underwent his 1965 gall-bladder operation, it was reported that he had designated Moyers to decide, if an emergency arose, whether Vice President Humphrey should act as President. Moyers insists that he and Johnson never discussed the matter. However, he was the closest man to the situation, posted just outside the operating room, ready to give the good news to the press if the operation succeeded, or to take the bad news to the Cabinet if it did not.

It is interesting to speculate on what might have happened if Johnson had been temporarily disabled. Probably, as was the case during the Wilson and Eisenhower disabilities, the Vice President would not have taken command. Had Johnson been disabled, probably Robert Mc-Namara would have emerged as the strong man in foreign and military affairs, and Moyers in domestic affairs, with the First Lady also keeping in close touch with events.

Moyers' appointment as Press Secretary in July, 1965, came as a shock to him and almost everyone else in Washington.

The President's press relations were then in a state of rapid decline. With the initial, post-assassination honeymoon behind, with the Goldwater threat destroyed, with the escalation in Vietnam in progress, the press was beginning to take a new, hard look at Johnson. Johnson resented the outburst of criticism, and rather than blame himself, he blamed his Press Secretary, the long-suffering George Reedy. The unexpected resignation of Reedy, after fourteen years with Johnson, was blamed on a painful foot condition called "hammertoes," but most White House correspondents felt that, regardless of his health, Reedy was destined to be made a scapegoat for Johnson's declining popularity.

Moyers' first advice to Johnson as Press Secretary was to cut out two of the President's favorite practices: 1) long, mid-afternoon monologues with key correspondents; 2) walks around the White House lawn with thirty or forty reporters in tow. These exhibitions, Moyers knew, amused and annoyed more reporters than they impressed. Meanwhile, in his own dealings with the press, Moyers was trying to shift attention from Johnson's personality to Johnson's legislative program, which was then at its zenith.

Throughout his year and a half as Press Secretary, Moyers fought a losing battle to contain Johnson's exuberance, his secretive nature, and his rather obvious contempt for the press. During this period, there was much talk of Johnson's "credibility gap," but reporters tended to blame Johnson, rather than Moyers, for the Administration's inconsistencies on Vietnam policy and other issues. This was a source of growing friction between Johnson and Moyers.

Moyers, unlike Johnson, favored a soft-sell approach to the press. He thought that the one bright spot in the Democratic losses in the 1966 congressional elections was that the setback sobered and quieted the President. Moyers' parting advice to Johnson, early in 1967, was on the virtues of underexposure, understatement, and candor with the press.

Moyers soon grew restive in the Press Secretary's job. He was frustrated by its mechanical nature—the amount of time he had to spend chartering planes, arranging travel plans, and the like. He disliked having to tell half-truths for Johnson, and making himself look silly with obvious evasions—yet he realized this was part of the job.

He was continually embarrassed by the fact that the press often had kinder words for him than for the President. His background in the ministry proved irresistible to most writers, and an exaggerated, one-dimensional picture was drawn of him as "the boy preacher," "Johnson's Good Angel," "a political Boy Scout," "square," and "selfless."

Such descriptions overlooked other interesting aspects of Moyers' character. He had come a long way from the Baptist seminary: He smoked cigars, took a drink now and then, spiced his conversation with an occasional hell or damn, was once photographed dancing an energetic if inelegant Frug, and maintained outside his office one of Washington's most eye-catching secretaries. Nor can the man who gave American politics the Daisy Girl properly be called a political Boy Scout.

Moyers' most conspicuous quality in those days was his total self-confidence, a kind of moral and political certitude that annoyed some people but awed and persuaded many more. He was utterly unflappable. He explained the ways of Lyndon Johnson to the Washington press corps as confidently as, a half-dozen years earlier, he had explained the ways of God to Baptist churchgoers in Brandon, Texas.

Young men who achieve vast power sometimes succumb to pomposity, but Moyers' manner was the opposite of this.* If anything, he tended toward self-serving folksiness. He had a stock of self-deprecating anecdotes, apparently left over from his days in the pulpit; for example, his relationship with Johnson was compared with the mouse who crossed a bridge on the back of an elephant and declared: "We shook *that* bridge, didn't we?" He found it expedient to deal with writers at the lowest possible level of sophistication. To a reporter

* One aspect of Moyers' personality he brought to the White House from his undergraduate days was a love of practical jokes. There are many stories of his elaborate pranks; the most cosmic of them concerns his colleague of 1964–65, Dick Goodwin. One day Moyers had prepared a fake wire-service ticker story saying that Arthur Schlesinger, Jr., had quoted Goodwin as making numerous highly critical remarks about President Johnson. Moyers summoned Goodwin to his office, gravely showed him the news-ticker copy, noted that LBJ received the same wire-service copy in his own office, and suggested that Goodwin be ready with a good explanation. Goodwin, in panic, called Schlesinger—whom Moyers had recruited into the plot—and Schlesinger said, yes, he had made those remarks—and, after all, Goodwin *had* said those things about LBJ. Goodwin, all hope gone, had written out his resignation when Moyers finally told him it was all a joke.

who demanded no more, he would make as banal a declaration as, "I can't make the President do a gosh-darned thing he doesn't want to," but to the intellectual and introspective Murray Kempton he declared, speaking of his desire to return to the Peace Corps, "I sometimes feel the way Odysseus did when he said how he longed to see the smoke leaping from his own island."

The frequent folksiness of Moyers' public behavior contrasted sharply with the chilling candor he would sometimes display in off-the-record discussions of men and events. In such talks he would show himself to be—like Clark Clifford, when he wrote his 1947 political memorandum to Truman—a man who viewed the political process with piercing insight and entirely without sentiment or illusion.

All in all, Moyers was able to give reporters the impression that if he was not entirely candid with them, it was because he was working within a system that would not allow it, and that the situation caused him as much unhappiness as it caused them.

Moyers may have felt, deep in his heart of hearts, a bit like Prometheus Bound, as he struggled with the time-consuming trivia of the Press Secretary's job. He had, in the year or so before entering his new assignment, been instrumental in developing the most ambitious domestic legislative program since the New Deal. He was moving, even as he began the new job, into increased involvement in foreign policy, but his ambitions there were often frustrated by the mechanical demands of the press office.

Foreign policy had been his number-one interest for a long time, and it still is today. One day after the 1960 election, the twenty-six-year-old Moyers sat down with a manual listing all policy-level government jobs to see what positions, particularly in the State Department, he might shoot for. The one that caught his eye was Executive Secretary of the National Security Council, but upon investigation he saw that despite his excellent political contacts he had no credentials for such an important post. He therefore turned to the Peace Corps as a place to earn some credentials.

As soon as he entered the White House with Johnson, Moyers had a peripheral role in foreign policy, but in 1964 his preoccupation with the campaign and the legislative program kept it to a minimum. In February, 1965, after the start of the massive U.S. military build-up in South Vietnam, Johnson told Moyers he wanted him to become deeply involved in foreign affairs. Essentially, Johnson told him: "Listen, read, and tell me what you think. Don't worry if it's different from what a member of the Cabinet thinks." Johnson wanted ideas and information he might not have gotten through regular bureaucratic channels; it was to be a personal, informal arrangement, with Moyers expressing his views not in Cabinet or NSC meetings, but in private talks with the President.

It was probably inevitable that Johnson would call on Moyers to serve as an independent source of information, on Vietnam and on foreign affairs generally, just as the young assistant had already done so effectively in domestic affairs. Johnson had taken on in Southeast Asia the most dangerous venture of his life, and it was imperative that he have every viewpoint, every scrap of information upon which to base his decisions. Yet he surely knew that his government was so staffed as to favor hawk arguments over those of the doves. At the Pentagon, although the enigmatic McNamara had severe doubts about the war, the Joint Chiefs of Staff were united in pressing for expanded military action. Their hard-line views were shared by Secretary of State Rusk, National Security Adviser Rostow, and presidential intimate Clark Clifford.

Johnson thus had excellent lines to the hawks; what Johnson lacked was a pipeline to the younger, more flexible, second-level policymakers who had severe doubts about the war in Vietnam and about America's role as the anti-Communist policeman of the world.

Probably Johnson never expected Moyers to "serve up the options impartially," in the government jargon; he knew Moyers well enough to anticipate his reservations about the war in Vietnam, but he also knew he could not find a more fertile source of non-military ideas and arguments to balance against the hawks' urgings.

To carry out this assignment Moyers and his capable assistant, Hayes Redmon, built a network of trusted allies among the moderate, second-level officials throughout the foreign affairs bureaucracy. Their efforts focused on Vietnam, but Moyers was also deeply involved in such matters as seeking an East-West *détente*, the non-proliferation treaty, and African and Latin American affairs.

A dramatic instance of the way this system sometimes worked occurred one morning as Moyers prepared to go to the weekly Tuesday Lunch at which he (as Press Secretary), the President, Rusk, McNamara, Rostow, and military leaders discussed war policy. Through his foreign affairs network, Moyers was fully briefed on the matters on the agenda of each Tuesday Lunch, so much so that Rusk and military leaders sometimes bristled at the extent of his knowledge of what they viewed as their internal departmental affairs.

On the Tuesday morning in question, just before the luncheon began,

Redmon learned that a new item had been added to the agenda: whether or not the Air Force should resume bombing a certain type of target in North Vietnam. The ever-expanding bombing raids were a primary source of concern to Moyers and other moderates, and Redmon (who had been an Air Force officer stationed at the Pentagon before Moyers brought him to the White House) immediately began checking his sources for more information. He quickly learned of a new CIA report stating that previous bombings of this type of target had been ineffective. Redmon quickly got a copy of the report, scribbled down the key points, raced the hundred yards from the Executive Office Building to Moyers' office in the White House, and handed the paper to Moyers just as he was entering the elevator to go up to lunch. With this evidence in hand, Moyers was able to convince the President that he should strike the proposed target from the list submitted by the military for approval that day.

Such episodes caused Johnson to begin greeting Moyers' arrival at foreign policy meetings with "Well, here comes Mr. Stop-the-Bombing."

In a case like this one, Moyers was certainly doing what the President wanted him to do—seeking out information that could save Johnson from making grievous mistakes. But to many of the young moderates Moyers dealt with, who often felt that their hawkish bosses, Rusk or Rostow or the military chiefs, blocked their access to the President, working *sub rosa* with Moyers and Redmon was virtually an underground conspiracy against the war, and they speak of it in those terms. Moyers, as they saw it, was their only hope of getting their views to the President; they were thunderstruck when he left the government, and some of them resigned in frustration soon thereafter.

One close observer of Moyers' foreign affairs network describes it this way:

"Bill was able to recruit a network of guys throughout the government who thought the way he did on Vietnam. These were people at State and on the NSC staff and elsewhere who were sticking their necks out—risking their jobs—to deal directly with him. But by doing it, they were able to become an outside voice on Vietnam policy."

Another second-level official recalls:

"It was early in 1965 that I became aware of Moyers' role as an advocate of peace in Vietnam—a guy who saw this as a conflict that could not be resolved militarily, one that would eventually have to be negotiated. And this was at a time when negotiations were anathema to people like Rusk. Working with Moyers, you could conspire to outflank some of the more difficult customers at the top.

"In March, 1965, several of us who deplored the use of force in Vietnam wanted to suggest some more positive alternatives. We got our ideas to Moyers and a little later he wrote the six-point presidential statement that became the basis of the Johns Hopkins speech."

Actually, this man was not fully informed on what happened after he talked with Moyers. McGeorge Bundy, in collaboration with Moyers, was the main author of the six-point statement by the President, issued by the White House on March 25, 1965, which declared that "The United States still seeks no wider war" and "I am ready to go anywhere at any time and meet with anyone whenever there is promise of progress toward an honorable peace."

The Johns Hopkins speech, delivered by the President on April 7 and considered a major Administration peace overture, was written by Goodwin after discussions with Moyers and Bundy. It reiterated the pro-negotiations themes of the six-point statement, and suggested a billion-dollar American development program in Southeast Asia.

One undertaking that typified Moyers' style of operation concerned Johnson's July 12, 1966, speech on U.S. policy toward China. Johnson, prompted by Moyers and others, and encouraged by public-opinion polls that showed no great opposition to a more flexible U.S. policy toward China, had decided to advocate a liberalized policy but to couple it with a declaration of this country's permanent strategic interests in Asia. However, the State Department, asked to produce a first draft, proved either unable or unwilling to abandon the anti-Communist clichés which have distinguished its utterances on China for twenty years.

Johnson, dissatisfied with this first draft, one morning told Moyers to write him a better one. (When Goodwin had left in mid-1965, Moyers had replaced him as the President's number-one speechwriter; although already overburdened, he accepted this assignment gladly, knowing there was no way he could achieve more influence on foreign affairs.) Moyers quickly went to work on the China speech, eager to seize the opportunity presented by the President's mood. He was already in touch with State Department and NSC staff experts on China who opposed the government's long-standing policy against trade with mainland China or diplomatic recognition or UN membership for her. He immediately solicited speech drafts from these men. Their drafts came to him that evening, and he stayed at his office all night writing his own draft, which he took to the President's bedroom at 8 A.M. Johnson read the speech, liked it, and approved it.

Given that approval, Moyers was able to present his speech to the State Department as a *fait accompli*. Some of Moyers' close associates felt that he had scored a major policy-making coup not only over the State Department's hard-liners on China, but over Secretary Rusk personally. There is no question that Moyers (like Schlesinger, Bundy, Goodwin, and other White House aides) was in continuous conflict with the State Department bureaucracy—"the gnomes in the bowels of State" he sometimes called them. Moyers' relationship with Rusk is less clear. They differed on many issues, including Vietnam policy, but Moyers heatedly denies the assertion that he ever tried to outmaneuver the Secretary. Apparently, if they were antagonists, it was a muted conflict, for Rusk respected Moyers' intimacy with the President, and Moyers respected Rusk's official status, and also liked him personally.

There were two key passages in the President's China speech. First, Johnson declared that the U.S. seeks in Asia ". . . a peace that can only be sustained through the durable bonds of peace: through international trade; through the free flow of people and ideas; through *full participation by all nations in an international community under law*."

Second, Johnson said: "There is a fourth essential for peace in Asia which may seem the most difficult of all: *reconciliation between* nations that now call themselves enemies. . . . The greatest force for opening closed minds and closed societies is the *free flow of ideas and people and goods*."

The passages I have italicized struck the world's diplomats (not to mention the State Department) like a thunderbolt. The President seemed to be taking the first steps toward reconciliation with China, approval of her admission to the UN, and an end to the U.S. embargo on trade with China. Such steps were not likely with the war raging in Vietnam, but some diplomats predict that Johnson's speech will become the basis for future policy changes.

Moyers also played a central role in reviving the Nonproliferation Treaty with Russia in the summer of 1966. The President had long supported the principle of the treaty, by which the nuclear powers would agree not to give nuclear weapons to other nations. But a dilemma existed within the U.S. government: the concept of the Nonproliferation Treaty, to stop the spread of nuclear weapons, was incompatible with the Administration's long-discussed Multilateral Nuclear Force (MLF) by which the U.S. would, at least in theory, share nuclear control with its NATO allies. The MLF was then dying a slow death, but still had strong advocates (notably Walt Rostow) who were necessarily against the Nonproliferation Treaty.

Progress in the nonproliferation agreement with Russia had by the summer of 1966 slowed to a standstill. The State Department's pro-MLF theorists were throwing every possible roadblock in its path. At that time, the issue began coming to Moyers' attention from several directions. Spurgeon M. Keeny, Jr., a young disarmament specialist on the NSC staff, had a long talk with Redmon in which he argued that the decline of the MLF plan boosted the treaty's chances, but that clear-cut presidential action would be needed to overcome State Department resistance.

Meanwhile, Moyers had received a call from John McNaughton, the highly regarded Assistant Secretary of Defense for International Affairs (who died in a plane crash a year later), asking to see him about the Treaty. They met for two weeks in July, often in Moyers' office in the evenings over a glass of sherry, and McNaughton spoke urgently of the need to revive the treaty negotiations. He told Moyers: "Someone has got to show the President that this is not only the right thing to do but the best thing politically to do." Moyers tried to do this, advancing pro-treaty arguments to the President and suggesting that, at the level of national and international politics, the Nonproliferation Treaty would be seen in the same favorable light as John Kennedy's Nuclear Test Ban Treaty had been three years earlier.

At one point in exploring the issue Moyers consulted William Foster, the U.S. delegate to the Geneva disarmament conference, and was so impressed by Foster's pro-treaty declarations that he arranged for him to see the President—one of many examples of Moyers' trying to give access to the President to officials who might not otherwise have had it.

By August, the President had decided to revive the treaty, and he expressed his determination to Rusk (who, deferring to the strong pro-MLF, antitreaty forces within his Department, had remained neutral on the issue). Moyers, driving home the point, was inserting plugs for the treaty in the President's campaign speeches. For example, on August 26, at Idaho Falls, Johnson declared: "We are also seeking agreement on a treaty to prevent the spread of nuclear weapons. . . . I believe we can find acceptable compromise language on which reasonable men can agree." Such declarations were highly important, for they signaled to the State Department, and to the Russians, that the pro-treaty forces had carried the day. Rusk, given this clear signal of presidential intent, prodded his bureaucracy into action. Soon the treaty negotiations were brought back to life. A year later, on August 24, 1967, the U.S. and Soviet representatives at Geneva finally agreed to a draft treaty to ban the spread of nuclear weapons. There still remained the perhaps insurmountable problem of obtaining French and Red Chinese agreement, but the accord was a bright spot amid the prevailing tensions caused by the war in Vietnam.

This treaty case history is indicative of Moyers' role. Johnson favored the treaty, but more urgent business had crowded it from his agenda. Given Rusk's indifference and Rostow's hostility, it might have slipped from presidential view altogether had not Moyers served as an alternative channel by which pro-treaty advocates could get their ideas to the President.

Moyers' role was nowhere more intricate, more dangerous, or more important than in his efforts to move Johnson toward a negotiated settlement of the war in Vietnam. Much is still unknown about his role in the debate over Vietnam policy, but available evidence indicates that he, along with McNamara and perhaps one or two others, was among the most effective opponents of continued, mindless military escalation.

Moyers was not a party to the original decision to bomb North Vietnam, but he did participate in the decisions for the troop build-up in the spring and summer of 1965. He was convinced that the build-up was necessary to prevent the collapse of the U.S.-supported government in Saigon. But he soon came to have doubts that a military victory could ever be achieved in Vietnam, and to believe that a political solution was necessary—essentially, by supporting so liberal a government in South Vietnam that the Communist rebels would cease to attract the people.

In December, 1965, Moyers, along with Bundy, McNamara, Averell Harriman, and numerous others, helped persuade Johnson to call a Christmas pause in the bombing of the North and to use the pause as an opportunity to seek negotiations with Hanoi. Once Johnson agreed to the bombing pause—which he coupled with his celebrated "peace offensive," which sent various officials winging around the globe in search of peace "feelers"—the moderate forces' goal became to see that the pause was extended as long as possible. For example, on December 26, just after the pause was announced, one of Moyers' associates wrote a memorandum to the President which argued, on the basis of an analysis of public opinion polls, that there was widespread national support for dramatic peace overtures. Moyers, impressed by the memo, sent it to the President in Texas and followed it up with the message of his own restating his support of a long halt.

The President did continue the pause for thirty-seven days. But in the end, rebuffed by Hanoi, he decided it had been a mistake, he blamed Moyers and the other doves for misleading him, and he began to value more highly the views of Clark Clifford, Abe Fortas, and the military leaders who had opposed the halt in the bombing.

The way Moyers would boldly inject himself into matters of the highest import was seen in early 1966 when Senator Robert Kennedy proposed including the Viet Cong in a coalition government in South Vietnam. Kennedy's statement, delivered in a February 19 speech, caused a national furor. Vice President Humphrey proclaimed that Kennedy's proposed action would be like putting "a fox in a chicken coop." In television interviews on the twentieth, Under Secretary of State George Ball worried that a coalition government would soon become a Communist government, while McGeorge Bundy acidly cited President Kennedy's remark "I am not impressed by the opportunities open to popular fronts throughout the world" to refute Senator Kennedy.

Robert Kennedy had blundered politically. The "fox in the chicken coop" argument, however simple-minded it might be, had mass political appeal. The President was delighted to see Kennedy under fire, yet Moyers and others in the Administration were disturbed by the implications of the Humphrey-Bundy-Ball onslaught. Believing as they did that the creation of a truly representative government in Saigon was the only alternative to endless war, the moderates feared that the anticoalition declarations would have the effect of freezing the Administration in an untenable position.

On the Monday and Tuesday after his speech, Kennedy was scrambling to shake off the soft-on-Communism charges. He appeared on the "Today" television program, and called many newspaper columnists, trying to reinterpret his speech (which was ambiguous to start with) in a more favorable light.

Kennedy and Moyers both knew that the question of a coalition government was much more complicated than the public realized. Three separate issues were involved: Would the Viet Cong be admitted to peace talks? Could the Viet Cong take part in a post-negotiations, pre-elections coalition government? Could the Communists be admitted to the South Vietnamese government if chosen in free elections?

Kennedy and the Administration both answered "yes" to the third question; both gave a qualified yes on the second point; they differed on the first point. It was an ambiguous, hair-splitting situation, and Moyers set out at his Tuesday afternoon press briefing to blunt the Administration's criticism of Kennedy. He did this not as any favor to Kennedy, but because he believed it was in the President's best interest to keep his options open on a possible coalition government in South Vietnam. Among other things, Moyers told the reporters that he saw no disagreement between Kennedy and the Administration "if Senator Kennedy did not propose a coalition government with Communist participation before elections are held."

That left the next move up to Kennedy and he was quick to take it. Within minutes, the Senator telephoned Moyers for clarification of his comments to the press. Then Kennedy quickly called his own press conference, and told reporters: "In discussing with Mr. Moyers I find no disagreement between what Mr. Moyers said and what I have said." The result was the headline on the front page of the next day's New York *Times:*

> "Kennedy Agrees
> With White House
> On Vietnam Point."

Such headlines, bringing Kennedy back to political respectability, were invaluable to Kennedy; yet Moyers considered them valuable to the Administration, too; in effect, the White House had brought Kennedy around to its position. Moyers' goal was to protect the President's options on Vietnam. He had acted without any specific approval from Johnson, and because of Kennedy's involvement he was playing with political dynamite. If his remarks had backfired, the President might have repudiated him; moreover, he knew his enemies in the White House would say he was seeking favor with Kennedy. It was a dangerous game, but that was the way Moyers believed he should operate. When he decided that a course of action was right, and found that Johnson was uncertain or reluctant, he did not hesitate to try to persuade or prod his great patron to move in the desired direction.

Moyers wanted Bundy's job when the latter resigned early in 1966, but Johnson gave it to Walt W. Rostow.

When Under Secretary Ball announced his resignation in September, Moyers reportedly wanted that job, but it went to Attorney General Nicholas Katzenbach. Before Katzenbach was named, various figures prominent in foreign affairs, including Bundy, urged Johnson to give the job to Moyers. There was also newspaper speculation that Moyers would —and should—get the appointment. This pro-Moyers campaign, which Moyers said he did not encourage, was another source of tension between him and the President, who suspected that Moyers was trying to pressure him.

One morning, as he was shaving, Johnson settled the issue by calling to Moyers: "Bill, I don't want you over there; I want you here with me."

As it turned out, Moyers was not there with him much longer. In mid-December he shocked Washington by resigning to become publisher of *Newsday*.

Although only a few close presidential associates were aware of it, Moyers' influence with Johnson had been lessening during the summer and fall of 1966. Johnson had been treating Moyers with a touch of coolness—playing "freeze-out" with him, as he had with others in the past—and Moyers' absence was sometimes noted at meetings he would previously have attended. To some, it seemed that when Johnson and Moyers were together, there was a new note of restraint in the younger man's manner.

As best anyone could tell, Johnson was making Moyers the scapegoat for his again-declining popularity in the public opinion polls and with the press. The criticism of Johnson was made all the more galling by the many flattering articles about Moyers in leading newspapers and magazines. Moyers' shining "image" had become a Frankenstein monster that now threatened to destroy him. Even his friends on the White House staff were annoyed; one commented: "Moyers became the White Hat and Johnson was the Black Hat. If anything good happened in the government, it was Moyers. If anything bad happened, it was Johnson. If Johnson did something the press approved, they always assumed it was Moyers who had talked the old S.O.B. into giving Tiny Tim a Christmas present."

Johnson's coolness toward Moyers was intermingled with moments of their old intimacy, and Moyers continued to wield close to his accustomed power. But there were reports of Johnson's angrily dressing down Moyers for minor infractions. One writer who is close to the President later said he believes Johnson deliberately set out to force Moyers' resignation because of bitterness over his poor press relations. But Johnson, whatever his temper, respects talent, and it seems more likely that he simply meant to humble Moyers a bit, but pushed too far.

For Johnson was not the only one who was dissatisfied in the fall of 1966. Moyers was frustrated with the time-consuming limitations of the Press Secretary's job, and with his inability to play a larger role in foreign affairs. Also, he had personal and financial problems. His brother Jim, who worked as a White House Administrative Assistant, died unexpectedly on September 17. His death left Moyers contributing not only to his parents' support but to his sister-in-law and her children. It also was a painful reminder that since 1960 he had neglected his own wife and children to concentrate on his fast-moving career.

In August, seventy-six-year-old Harry F. Guggenheim, owner of

Newsday, asked Moyers if he'd like to direct his paper. Somewhat to Guggenheim's surprise, Moyers expressed interest. In December, Moyers accepted the offer.

When Moyers broke the news to Johnson, both men were emotionally moved by the sudden prospect of their parting. Moyers thought of retracting his resignation and staying, but realized it was too late. Johnson expressed pride that his protégé had received such a fine opportunity. There were tears in Moyers' eyes when he announced his resignation to the press.

But Johnson's mood soon soured, largely because so many newspaper and magazine accounts of Moyers' departure implied that Johnson wasn't quite capable of running the government without him. *The Washington Post*, for example, suggested that the loss of Moyers might cause Johnson not to run for re-election in 1968. (Johnson's eventual decision not to run was certainly not due to Moyers' absence, although it could be argued that had he followed the advice of Moyers and the other doves on Vietnam he would not have plunged on to his political destruction.)

The overpraising of Moyers was parodied by Art Buchwald in a piece that began: "Lyndon B. Johnson first came to Bill Moyers' attention about ten years ago when Bill discovered the tall, smiling Texan tucked away in a Senate office on Capitol Hill. Bill was immediately impressed by Johnson's spirit and willingness to do anything asked of him. 'Senator,' said Moyers, 'I think I can use you. . . .'"

All this did not amuse Johnson, and with the meanness of spirit that sometimes overcomes him, he began denouncing Moyers to reporters and to other aides: Moyers had always been more interested in promoting himself than in serving Johnson; presidential press relations had improved as soon as George Christian replaced Moyers; Moyers had always been trying to cultivate the Kennedys, and so on. These stories were eagerly spread by members of the Johnson entourage who had long resented Moyers' primacy with LBJ.

It was true that Moyers did not share the anti-Kennedy mania of the President, Marvin Watson, and others in the White House. Indeed, there were interesting parallels between Moyers and Robert Kennedy—both followed in the footsteps of a beloved older brother; both achieved power at an early age; both were ambitious and hard-driving and moralistic—but the analogy breaks down on their diverse backgrounds: the young Kennedy learned the uses of power and found they led to a measure of humility, while the young Moyers learned the uses of humility and found they led to a measure of power.

But politics is a great leveler and in the end they were much alike.

They shared political realism, and beyond that they shared a view of world affairs that set them apart from Johnson and his contemporaries on many issues. If Kennedy had become President, he might have wanted Moyers in his Cabinet, not as payment for past favors, but because Moyers is a man of demonstrated ability and the Kennedys respect ability.

The same might be said of Hubert Humphrey. Indeed, Moyers is probably closer personally to Humphrey than he was to Kennedy. When Johnson was thoughtless of his Vice President's feelings, it was often Moyers who would seek to make amends. Early in 1965, it was Moyers who argued vainly to Johnson that, if he could not go himself, he should send Humphrey to Winston Churchill's funeral. Johnson's failure to do so was one of his first acts to earn criticism during his post-election honeymoon with the press.

Whatever Moyers' standing with the next President (and within weeks of Robert Kennedy's death, Moyers seemed to be moving into the Humphrey camp), Moyers continues, as a newspaper publisher and well-known public figure, to have other political prospects. It is not unimaginable that New York's talent-starved Democratic Party may someday view him as a likely candidate for Senator or Governor.

Moyers was in a difficult position after he left the White House. He was hurt by the things Johnson was saying about him and he wanted to win back the President's good will, less for political reasons (in the circles he was starting to move in, Johnson's goodwill was a mixed blessing) than for personal ones. At the same time, he wanted to make it clear that he was his own man. He therefore set out, in his frequent writings and public appearances, to speak his mind objectively: to praise Johnson when he thought that was justified, but also to criticize him when that was called for. He soon discovered, as has many another journalist, that objectivity tends to alienate both sides of an issue: anti-Johnson observers viewed his praise of Johnson as an attempt to curry favor with the President, while super-Johnsonites in the White House cited his criticisms to the President as proof of his continued disloyalty.

Eighteen months after Moyers left the White House, there had been only minimal contact between him and Johnson. Moyers' friends in the Administration hoped Johnson might call him back to work on his re-election campaign, but Johnson's withdrawal ended that hope. There was a touch of the Stalinist era about the whole sad affair: the onetime favorite disgraced, denounced by court intriguers, accused of political heresy (consorting with the Kennedys), driven into exile (Long Island instead of Siberia), yet persisting in the hope that someday the Maximum Leader's face would again shine upon him.

Johnson's moods are mercurial; he may at any moment, in a burst of sentiment, return the lost sheep to the fold. But at this writing, in May of 1968, Moyers remains entirely out of favor with the man to whom he admittedly owes everything he has.

Even aside from his delicate relationship with Johnson, the transition from the White House to the newspaper business was a difficult one for Moyers, particularly when he found himself on the outside looking in at world events with which he had formerly been so involved. His emotional low point surely came during the June, 1967, weekend when Johnson and Soviet Premier Alexei Kosygin met at Glassboro, New Jersey. On the second afternoon of their meeting, as news announcers sent forth excited, minute-by-minute bulletins on every detail of the conference, a downcast Bill Moyers was only a few miles away, listening to the bulletins on his car radio, as he drove along the crowded New Jersey Turnpike, hauling furniture up to his new home in Long Island.

"I have no real interest in life except public service and I have no ambition but to return to it."

Moyers said that to me in July, 1967, and his declaration called to my mind George Orwell's opening remark in his essay on Gandhi, that saints should always be judged guilty until proved innocent.

I have tried to view Moyers with the skepticism that, as Orwell suggested, is deserved by those men who adopt a saintly mien while engaging in temporal affairs. When I first met Moyers, on a magazine assignment in 1966, I regarded him with suspicion, for I had been offended by the "boy preacher" and "good angel" publicity; in my experience, the political process in general and Lyndon Johnson in particular do not permit the degree of saintliness I had seen ascribed to Moyers. But in talks then, and more recently, I found Moyers not a boy preacher at all, but a young man possessed of an extremely quick and penetrating mind, a good deal of candor and detachment, an introspective nature, liberal ideals, and an ability to advance his beliefs both within the governmental structure and in society at large.

This opinion of Moyers is not unique; it is shared by other journalists who know him and by government officials who, now that he is gone, have nothing to gain by praising him.

Moyers is no paragon. He is tough, ambitious, and calculating. He can be glib and equivocal and, as Press Secretary, often was. Behind his smooth exterior there lurks, as Willie Morris said, "a certain necessary ruthlessness." Indeed, if Orwell's comment on Gandhi calls Moyers to mind, so does this description in Casanova's *Memoirs* of the intrigues in Rome two centuries ago:

"The man fit to make a fortune in this ancient capital of Italy must be a chameleon sensitive to all the colors which the light casts on his surroundings. He must be flexible, insinuating, a great dissimulator, impenetrable, obliging, often base, ostensibly sincere, always pretending to know less than he does, keeping to one tone of voice, patient, in complete control of his countenance, cold as ice when another in his place would be on fire . . . and, if he is an honest man, accept the painful necessity of admitting to himself that he is a hypocrite."

Yet, when all else is said, I think that at heart Moyers looks upon political power as a means toward the performance of good works, rather than, like so many ambitious young men, regarding the performance of good works as a means toward political power. This basic idealism, together with his operational talent, made him an exceptional White House figure for three years, and still makes him, as he looks ahead to his future, one of the most interesting and promising men of his generation.

4. *The President's Instrument: Califano*

On January 13, 1966, the day after he delivered his annual State of the Union Message to Congress, President Johnson convened one of his infrequent Cabinet meetings. In the message, he had announced his intention to ask Congress to create a new federal Department of Transportation. Now, in the Cabinet meeting, he made it perfectly clear that he intended to fight all the way for the new Department and that he expected every Cabinet member to support him, whatever his own bureaucratic interests might be. When he finished these remarks, the President turned and pointed to one of his Special Assistants, Joseph A. Califano, Jr., a stocky, round-faced young man who was sitting quietly in a chair against the wall. Califano, the President declared, was in charge of the fight for the Department of Transportation. And Johnson added emphatically: "When Joe speaks, that's my voice you hear!"

Later, when they were alone, the President laughed and asked Califano: "Do you think I've given you enough clout to do the job?" The thirty-four-year-old Califano, still a bit stunned by the President's endorsement, said Yes, more than enough. At that, Johnson laughed dryly and predicted: "Before you're through, you'll need it all."

Lyndon Johnson, Califano observed later, had never been more correct.

Califano had come to the White House—from his job as Secretary of Defense Robert S. McNamara's Special Assistant and troubleshooter—only six months earlier, in July, 1965, to take over coordination of the President's legislative program from Bill Moyers, who had become Press Secretary. The fight for the Department of Transportation (or DOT, as it became known) was only one of scores of projects he directed for the President, yet with its intense pressures—from the bureaucracy, from Congress, and from outside lobbies—it epitomizes the complexities and the dangers confronting a modern presidential assistant.

Not long after Califano arrived in the White House, President Johnson told him he wanted to have a major transportation program as part of his 1966 legislative package. The President gave no details and he made no final commitment, but he gave Califano the green light to explore the possibilities.

The President knew, as virtually every American knows, that the nation's transportation system is a mess. Streets are clogged; many highways are inadequate; railroads haven't improved in thirty years; subways are dirty and dangerous; airline facilities are already overburdened. Moreover, the President knew, as many citizens do not, that this chaos exists in large part because the federal government, while investing billions of dollars in transportation programs each year, had no central agency to fix transportation policy or to set priorities for the outlay of federal funds. Instead, thirty autonomous and semi-autonomous agencies were involved in subsidizing and regulating the transportation industries. These include the Interstate Commerce Commission, the Maritime Administration, the Civil Aeronautics Board, the Bureau of Public Roads, the Corps of Engineers, the Coast Guard, and the Federal Aviation Agency.

Obviously, logic called for a single, unified Department of Transportation to fix policy and priorities. Yet for many years, attempts toward unification in transportation had failed because of opposition from three groups. First, from the agencies themselves, whose officials preferred autonomy to being a part of the large, Cabinet-level department. Second, from many members of Congress, who for years had looked to these agencies for roads, dams, waterways projects, airport facilities—the historic federal "pork barrel"—and who feared that a Cabinet department might not be so generous or so malleable.

Finally, there was opposition from the powerful transportation industries themselves, who over the years have dominated the ICC, the CAB, the Maritime Administration, and other independent agencies that supposedly regulate them. The regulatory agencies are made independent to protect them from political pressure from the party in power, but the end result is to make them vulnerable to political pressure from private lobbies. These agencies find that, while few voices are raised for the public interest in transportation matters, the railroads and airlines and truckers can mobilize powerful congressional support for favorable decisions by the agencies on rates and routes and safety regulations.

These factors were working against President Johnson's desire for a Department of Transportation, but two others were working in his favor. One was the heavily Democratic majority he had carried into Congress in his 1964 landslide victory over Barry Goldwater. The second was simply that a prosperous nation was fed up with what *Newsweek* magazine aptly called "the agony of getting anywhere."

Such was the background when, in September, 1965, Califano called a meeting of top government officials to discuss what sort of legislation the Administration should propose—if any—in transportation. Those attending included Secretary of Commerce John T. Conner, whose department included an Office of Transportation; Alan S. Boyd, the Under Secretary of Commerce for Transportation; Charles Schultze, the Budget Director; and Gardner Ackley, chairman of the Council of Economic Advisers.

The group was in general agreement that the President should seek a Department of Transportation, but disagreed on details. One important disagreement was on whether the Administration should try to bring the two most important regulatory agencies, the ICC and the CAB, into the new Department. Ackley and Schultze argued that this was administratively desirable, while Conner believed it was politically impossible.

All agreed that a Department of Transportation lacked much political sex appeal, and this led to the idea of including an Auto Safety Bill in the transportation package. This idea was a good one. Aided by Ralph Nader's crusades, the Administration's auto safety bill proved to be potent politics.

After the initial meeting in mid-September, Califano sent a memorandum to the President summarizing the main points discussed. He suggested that regulatory agencies might be included in a new Department. He pointed out that the creation of the Department would be a major achievement both administratively and politically, and that the consolidation might save money for the government. Finally, he asked permission to go ahead with further discussions on the subject. The President wrote "Hooray!" across the bottom of the memorandum, and with that brief but enthusiastic endorsement, Califano moved ahead.

For the next thirteen months, until the Department of Transportation bill was signed into law by the President, Califano was intimately involved in its slow and perilous progress. He was far from being the only Administration official involved. Alan Boyd was the bill's chief public spokesman and Capitol Hill advocate (and the new Department's first Secretary); Charles S. Zwick, an Assistant Director of the Budget Bureau, was a principle draftsman of the legislation; Califano's assistant (and Harvard Law School classmate), Lawrence E. Levinson, represented him at many meetings; Larry O'Brien became prominently involved in selling it to Congress. But all of these men looked to Califano to decide the hard issues, or to go to the President for a decision if need be. He was, as Johnson had said at the outset, the President's voice in the matter.

Throughout the fall of 1965, before the President reached a final decision on whether or not to go for the legislation, Califano was working on two fronts. First, he and Lee White held a series of meetings with leaders of the transportation industries. Califano and White told these men the President had before him a recommendation for a Department of Transportation, and they tried to gauge the degree of their opposition to the proposal.

It soon became plain that any attempt to shift the regulatory powers of the ICC and CAB to the new Department—the power to fix rates and routes—would be met with total, last-ditch opposition from the transportation industries. This, then, became the first major decision facing Califano and his colleagues, and it was one Califano passed up to the President. Johnson, well aware of the political power of the transportation lobbies, took the position that if the Executive Branch would first get its own house in order, by creating a new Department, the rate-fixing authority could come later.

As something of a face-saving device, it was agreed that certain "executive functions" (as opposed to "regulatory functions") of the ICC and CAB would be transferred to DOT; primarily these involved safety enforcement.

Califano's second front was the bureaucracy itself; throughout the winter of 1965–66 he was calling in agency officials to gauge their resistance to the Department of Transportation. In brief, the bureaucratic problems he encountered were the following:

1. The Federal Aviation Agency (FAA) was created in 1958 as an independent agency to enforce air safety. It spends some $600 million a year for research and airport construction and equipment. Califano believed the FAA should be brought intact into DOT. This idea was at first vigorously resisted by its Administrator, former Air Force General William F. (Bozo) McKee, who feared that the move would put another layer of authority between him and the President. (There were already quite a few layers; during his negotiations with Califano, McKee was anxious to take his case directly to the President, but the President put off seeing him. This was typical; Johnson knew the re-organization would cause piteous cries and he didn't want to listen to them; that was Califano's job.)

It seemed to White House negotiators that two points particularly bothered McKee. First, that he might lose his Level Two (i.e., $30,000) salary rating; second, that he might lose authority for the development of the Supersonic Transport plane. Given Califano's assurances on both points, he came around to support of FAA's inclusion in DOT.

2. The Civil Aeronautics Board was more difficult. It was already agreed that CAB would not surrender its rate-fixing or route-granting authority, or its power to hand out to the airlines subsidies of some $70 million a year. Rather it was only to give DOT its safety authority —primarily, to investigate air accidents and to hear appeals from pilots who lose their licenses. But CAB Chairman Charles S. Murphy (the former Special Counsel to President Truman) was reluctant to surrender even those powers. Dozens of meetings were held with Murphy and his aides, and it was not until after January—when the President had positively committed himself to the new Department—that Murphy reluctantly gave it his support.

There was a very good reason why Califano expended such time and energy on winning the support of officials like Murphy and General McKee. Both men—Murphy because of his prominence in Democratic affairs; McKee because of his connections as an Air Force general—have many friends in Congress, and their opposition, expressed in closed hearings, could be fatal to the bill. Moreover, it seemed likely that their opposition, if it developed, would be phrased in terms of possible harm to air safety to be caused by tampering with their agencies.

3. The Interstate Commerce Commission (ICC) was to keep its regulatory powers over all forms of surface transport—trucks, buses, railroads—but surrender its safety functions. ICC Chairman John W. Bush met with Califano, agreed that the plan was good and persuaded a majority of the other ten commissioners to agree.

Also, the President originally declared in his Transportation Message that he would submit legislation to reorganize the ICC. The main problem is that the ICC Chairmanship rotates annually among its eleven members, preventing any chairman from ever becoming strong enough to stand up to industry pressures. The railroad and trucking industries recognized this proposed reorganization as a threat to their dominance of the ICC, and brought enough pressure to bear that the White House never sent the reorganization plan to Congress.

4. The Maritime Administration, a highly autonomous division of the Department of Commerce, at first seemed to present the least problem. Its Administrator, Nicholas Johnson, a Kennedy appointee still in his early thirties, fully agreed that the Maritime Administration belonged in DOT. His cooperation perhaps lulled Califano into a false sense of security, for on Capitol Hill, the unexpected loss of the Maritime Administration would be the President's most humiliating defeat.

5. The Coast Guard, in peacetime, operates as a part of the Treasury Department and concerns itself with water safety. Secretary of the Treasury Henry (Joe) Fowler was pained at the prospect of losing the Coast Guard to DOT. (One of his arguments was on historical grounds—the Coast Guard has, in peacetime, always been a part of the Treasury—but Califano's men rebutted this with their discovery that in fact it had once been switched to another department.) President Johnson was not interested in history, only in whether the move might in any way impair national security. When Califano obtained a memo from Secretary McNamara saying the move would probably enhance national security, the issue was closed as far as the President was concerned.

Secretary Fowler, like the FAA's General McKee, wanted to make a personal appeal to the President. His chance finally came during an end-of-year budget session with the President. When they came to the budget item on the Coast Guard, the President quipped: "Old Joe doesn't want to lose the Coast Guard and all those airplanes and ships with big flags he can ride in." Everyone present joined in the laughter, including Fowler, and he did not again bring up the subject of the Coast Guard.

6. Secretary of Commerce John Connor was at first reluctant to surrender his Office of Transportation—he suggested that the Commerce Department simply become the focal point for transportation, rather than a new Department—but he soon came around. His department was also required to yield its semiautonomous Bureau of Public Roads, which administers the $3 billion a year federal highway construction program.

7. Numerous smaller agencies, including the Interior Department's Alaska Railroad, the St. Lawrence Seaway Development Corporation, and the Great Lakes Pilotage Administration, came into the fold gladly, or at least without significant resistance.

8. Finally, one extremely important dispute was not resolved. The $130-million-dollar urban mass-transit program—grants for subways, expressways, and bus systems—had been previously entrusted to the new Department of Housing and Urban Development and HUD's Secretary, Robert Weaver, absolutely refused to surrender this program to DOT. Because of Weaver's intransigence, and because there were, in fact, difficult issues involved in whether HUD or DOT should administer the urban transit program, the President decided, as Califano once put it, "to finesse the issue." The President therefore appointed a high-level task force and gave it a year to come up with a solution to the HUD-DOT impasse. DOT finally won the battle.

The President listened carefully throughout the fall of 1965 as Califano reported to him on the bureaucratic problems and the industry opposition to the proposed Department. Finally, in December, during the preparation of his State of the Union Message, the President had to decide whether to go for the new Department or—as many suggested—to drop it as too big a political risk.

Califano had become committed to the proposal, but he nonetheless had to report to Johnson that it faced stiff resistance in Congress and from the transportation industries. Other advisers were less optimistic than Califano. Myer Feldman, the Kennedy aide who was then Johnson's Special Counsel, told Califano it would be "insane" to push for transportation reform that year. Bill Moyers had doubts about taking on such a hard fight so soon after the legislative battles of 1965.

Johnson made no commitment and gave few clues to his intentions. In mid-December he ordered Califano to seek the views of several key congressional leaders, and Califano took this as a sign that he was leaning in favor of the proposal. Throughout December, mention of the Department of Transportation was deleted from the drafts of the

State of the Union Message circulated among government officials, except the copies to Califano, Moyers, Secretary Connor, and a few others. (The President's secrecy was successful; news of the DOT proposal never leaked to the press, and that is rare for such a major proposal.) Not until Califano went to the LBJ Ranch on the day after Christmas for a last minute review of the entire legislative program did he learn that Johnson had decided to go for the new Department.

Once the President had made his decision—which was made public in his January 12 State of the Union Message—an interagency task force began drafting the Administration's bill.

This, along with a 3000-word presidential message on transportation, were sent to Congress on March 2. Johnson had postponed this step more than a week until his Congressional Relations staff contacted the forty or fifty members of Congress on the committees that would consider the bill and had reported to him on their views. Finally satisfied, Johnson permitted the message and the bill to go up to Congress, and the fight for a Department of Transportation entered its final phase, one that would soon make the earlier bureaucratic scuffles seem like child's play.

The President was himself intimately involved in the legislative struggle. He expected Califano to handle day-to-day developments, but to keep him fully informed on vital issues. Johnson brought the bill up often at his meetings with legislative leaders, and he was willing to meet privately with any important Congressman, journalist, or industry figure whose support might be won.

Lyndon Johnson is a master of the legislative process, and the thrust and counterthrust involved in so important a proposal as the Department of Transportation excited, delighted, and fascinated him. Like a football coach sending signals to his quarterback, he would shout warnings to Califano like (using the name of a prominent Senator): "Watch out for ——; he's going to get you!" Once, after Califano had been involved in weeks of fruitless negotiation with Senator John L. McClellan, chairman of the Committee on Government Operations, the President declared with keen amusement: "McClellan's taught Joe more about politics in four months than Tom Dewey learned in two campaigns for President."

Califano, unlike his colleagues Boyd and Secretary Connor, never testified before Congress on behalf of the bill, but he continued to direct the Administration's effort from behind the scenes. On March 1, the day before the message was sent to Congress, he briefed four important groups on its contents and implications: 1) the press, 2) congressional leaders, 3) leaders of the transportation industry, 4) thirty or forty officials from the agencies being transferred to DOT. (In effect, he told the latter group that everyone had been given a chance to express his views, and everyone was now expected to get behind the President's proposal. He also assured them that no one would lose his job or status in moving to the new department.) When congressional hearings on the bill began later in March, Califano's White House group cleared all prepared testimony by Administration witnesses and called several of the witnesses in to brief them on exactly what they should say.

California Democrat Chet Holifield, who skillfully managed the bill in the House, later commented, "In my twenty-four years in Congress I have never before encountered the atmosphere of pressure from lobbyists, such a barrage of distortion of the truth, as has occurred during the consideration of the Department of Transportation legislation."

As a result of these pressures, both from outside lobbies and from within the Congress, there were to be three changes of the utmost importance in the Administration's bill before it won congressional approval in October.

First was the loss in the House of the Maritime Administration. The proximate cause of this setback was two telegrams—one in August and another when the issue came up again in October—sent to each member of the House from AFL-CIO president George Meany declaring his opposition to the inclusion of the Maritime Administration in the Department of Transportation. This declaration, coming in an election year, with many Congressmen looking to organized labor for support, was more than enough to oust the Maritime Administration from DOT by a vote of 261 to 117.

Behind Meany's telegrams lay a complicated political and economic dispute, one which pitted the entire maritime industry—both labor and management—against the government. The federal government, through the Maritime Administration, has for years put out billions of dollars to subsidize an American industry that is incapable of competing in the world market; by one government estimate, federal funds provide $7200 of every $10,000 taken in by the maritime industry. Yet this generosity has not satisfied the industry, and its leaders set out to use opposition to the Maritime Administration's inclusion in DOT as a club with which to force a more generous program of federal subsidies. Long and elaborate negotiations took place in Califano's office and on Capitol Hill, but in the end the White House decided the industry wanted too much, so the negotiations broke off. The chief maritime negotiator, Paul Hall, president of the AFL-CIO's Seafarers Union, then made good on his threats by getting Meany to send the telegrams that blasted the Maritime Administration out of DOT.

The second issue on which the Administration was forced to give ground was the strength that should be vested in the Secretary of Transportation and, conversely, the degree of autonomy to be given to the various agencies that would make up DOT.

Califano naturally wanted DOT to have a strong Secretary, but DOT's opponents, once they accepted the inevitability of the new department, were out to gain maximum autonomy for its constituent agencies. The issue of autonomy became closely intertwined with the issue of transportation safety. In essence, many Congressman argued that the agencies responsible for enforcing transportation safety should be given maximum autonomy so there could be no possibility of a politically appointed Secretary overruling expert judgments on safety issues. Probably some Congressmen were quite sincere in this concern; probably others used the safety issue to shield their political motives for weakening DOT.

This issue came to focus on the FAA and one Senator, Mike Monroney of Oklahoma. Monroney had been called the "father of FAA"— he was instrumental in its creation in 1958—and he was disturbed at the prospect of his offspring's being swallowed up in DOT. His arguments centered on the safety issue, and in a series of meetings with Califano and O'Brien, he insisted that FAA should be dropped from the DOT package.

Califano responded that as long as agencies like the FAA are "independent" they will continue to be dominated by the transportation industries, and that if FAA were allowed to slip out of the DOT package, the whole thing might disintegrate. Califano's concern was genuine. The setbacks the Administration bill had already suffered were encouraging several agencies to hope that DOT might be defeated in Congress and that they thus might maintain their independence. FAA's loss might have triggered a full-scale revolt.

Alan Boyd, Charles Zwick, and Larry Levinson, representing the Administration, held long, unproductive sessions with Senator Monroney and his aides on the related issues of safety and agency autonomy. These sessions were stuck on dead center until at the end Califano became personally involved, for he brought with him the essential power the others lacked—power to make final commitments on the President's behalf.

The turning point came during a Saturday morning meeting at the White House during which Califano and his associates, along with Senate legislative aides, rewrote the bill in a manner that satisfied Senator Monroney and therefore guaranteed Senate passage. Essentially, the language Califano approved that morning was the language that became law. Two major concessions were made. First, Califano granted more autonomy than he wanted to grant to DOT's three major "modal administrations"—the Federal Highway Administration, the Federal Railroad Administration, and the Federal Aviation Agency. Second, all of DOT's safety enforcement authority was delegated to a five-man National Transportation Safety Board which, although technically "within" DOT, is virtually autonomous. (The law states: "In the exercise of its functions, powers, and duties, the Board shall be independent of the Secretary and the other offices and officers of the Department.")

Califano's view today on these concessions is: 1) that while he gave more autonomy to DOT's constituent agencies than he wanted to, the result is nonetheless workable, and 2) that while the Safety Board's autonomy weakens the Secretary's authority, there is much validity in the congressional aruguments about keeping safety outside the political domain.

Some critics disagree with Califano and have charged that the Secretary of Transportation is little more than a figurehead; *The Washington Post*'s Richard Harwood, for example, wrote that the new Secretary has "authority to assign office space and little else." The actual language of the bill is ambiguous on this issue; indeed, one Administration draftsman boasts that he and his colleagues "fuzzed up" the bill's language enough to enable a strong-minded Secretary to assert considerable authority. Probably it will take several years' experience to prove whether or not the Secretary can indeed exert effective control over his far-flung transportation empire.

The Administration's final setback centered about the bill's controversial Section 7, which proposed to give the Secretary of Transportation the authority to fix "standards and criteria" for spending federal funds on transportation. This issue was a simple one: should Congress or the Executive Branch have the last word on the expenditure of federal funds on transportation? The existing system of fragmentation had given that power by default to Congress, and neither Congress nor the transportation industries wanted to see that basic power given by law to the new Secretary of Transportation.

The reason for their resistance was simple. A Secretary empowered to set government-wide spending priorities in transportation spending would have endangered powerful vested interests. He might have decided for example, that some of the $3 billion highway trust fund should be used to build better railroads and subways. He might have decided that the government should stop pouring billions of dollars into a bankrupt maritime industry. He might have decided—and this possibility enraged Congress—to take a hard look at the costly inland-waterways projects that are carried out by the Corps of Engineers and that make up so much of the federal pork barrel.

The Administration never got over the first hurdle on this issue. The hurdle was Senator John McClellan of Arkansas, chairman of the Committee on Government Operations, which was in charge of the Transportation Bill. O'Brien and Califano met time and again with McClellan on this issue, until finally they realized he wasn't going to give an inch on Section 7. In the end, the Senate not only gutted Section 7 but added this blunt declaration to the bill:

"Nothing in this Act shall be construed to authorize, without appropriate action by Congress, the adoption, revision, or implementation of (A) any transportation policy, or (B) any investment standards or criteria" by the Secretary of Transportation.

Despite these setbacks, congressional passage of the Transportation Bill in October was considered a victory for President Johnson. He had succeeded in pulling most, if not all, of the government's transportation programs under one roof, and this would probably pave the way for the new department to take in the Maritime Administration and the regulatory powers of the ICC and CAB. Even at the outset the new department had 90,000 employees and an annual budget of about $6 billion; this made it the government's fourth-ranking department in personnel and fifth-ranking one in spending. Never before in this century had Congress approved a new Cabinet department within eight months of a President's request for it. The Department of Transportation had been weakened by Congress, but most political observers agreed it was a minor miracle to pass any bill, given the degree of resistance from Congress and the industries. Most authorities on transportation matters agreed with a New York *Times* editorial that "the gain far outweighs in importance the defects" of the new department.

Califano's part in the creation of the Department of Transportation typifies the role played in recent yers by such aides as Corcoran, Clifford, Sorensen, and Moyers. In this instance President Johnson set a goal and delegated to Califano the authority necessary to reach the goal. To do the job, Califano had to overcome bureaucratic resistance, arbitrate interagency disputes, negotiate with outside pressure groups, rally congressional support, and finally make a decision on how far the Administration could push a reluctant Congress without risking total defeat. Throughout this process he was continually incurring powerful enemies within the Administration, in Congress, and in the private groups he bargained with, and there was the constant danger that if he demanded too much—or achieved too little—he might lose the President's favor and with it his new-found prominence.

But Johnson had picked his man carefully, and in retrospect it seems that Califano won all that could be won in the fight for the new department. In the end, of course, the victory was the President's. It was he who had risked his political capital in a dangerous fight for the public interest against private powers, and it was Johnson to whom Califano looked for the half-dozen key decisions in the campaign. Yet Califano could not be blamed if privately he felt that the victory was in part his, too. If Johnson made the major decisions, Califano made a hundred lesser decisions that did much to shape the final result. When one considers the way the department turned out—with FAA and the Coast Guard in it, with the Maritime Administration out of it, and so forth—it is exceedingly hard to say just where Johnson's influence ends and Califano's begins. This is the way it must inevitably be for an active, ambitious President; in delegating the authority to get a job done, he must also delegate the power to do the job well or ill, and that is why the quality of the men around him is of such importance.

After the Department of Transportation was created, there was front-page newspaper speculation in New York and Washington that Califano was slated to be its first Secretary. This speculation, besides embarrassing Califano and annoying Alan Boyd, the front-runner for the post, underscored an awkward but undeniable fact: the Secretaryship was a step up in power and prestige for Boyd, but for Califano it would have been a step down in power, and probably in prestige as well. For Califano was by then second only to Bill Moyers on Johnson's staff, and after Moyers' resignation he emerged as the President's most influential White House assistant.

As such, Califano took his place among such past notables as Hopkins,

Clifford, Adams, Sorensen, and Moyers, yet he continued to seem out of place when considered alongside those predecessors. In part, this was because he enjoyed a warm social relationship with Johnson, but was in no sense an alter ego to the President in the sense that Hopkins or Sorensen or Moyers had been. Moreover, Califano had not attracted the degree of personal publicity that would make him a celebrity as well as a behind-the-scenes power. His round, forgettable face had graced no newsmagazine covers, as Moyers' had; his speeches, unlike Valenti's, set off no fireworks. In part, Califano's anonymity no doubt reflected a conscious effort on his part—he could hardly have ignored the President's response to the overpublicizing of Moyers.

Yet in larger part, Califano's lack of celebrity reflected his own personality. It would be unfair to call him colorless—most of us are colorless—but he does lack the exaggerated features that are so vital in the image-making process. He does not have Hopkins' sinister aura, or Clifford's glamor, or Adams' curtness, or Sorensen's status as alter ego, or Moyers' background as a Baptist preacher.

Rather, insofar as the term can be applied to a magna cum laude graduate of Harvard Law School, Califano is a rather ordinary young man. He is an inch or two under average, ten pounds or so over average. His looks are neither handsome nor unattractive, and his dark hair is cropped close in the Ivy League manner. He leans toward tasteful but conventional Eastern garb: dark suits, striped oxford-cloth shirts, ties with regimental stripes. His background is similarly unsurprising. He was born in Brooklyn on May 15, 1931; his father was of Italian descent and worked for IBM; his mother was Irish and taught school. He attended Catholic schools, Holy Cross, and Harvard Law. In 1955–58 he served as a legal officer for the navy, stationed at the Pentagon. (He once sued the navy for some back pay.) Then, completing the classic Flatbush-to-fortune pattern, he joined a prominent Wall Street law firm.

But in Califano's case, the conventional pattern had produced an unconventional young man, for beneath his unexceptional exterior lurked an exceptional talent for getting things done.

It was, moreover, a talent for getting things done with a maximum of discretion and a minimum of fanfare. One of Califano's Pentagon associates, asked for anecdotes about his performance there, replied: "There aren't any stories about Joe. He just performs."

A capacity for accomplishment is, of course, the one talent Lyndon Johnson most admires, and that he has encouraged in such diverse men as Bobby Baker, Moyers, and Califano.

Califano turned out to be one of those aides who, like Corcoran and Goodwin and Moyers, moved up the political ladder at a dizzying pace, pausing on each rung only long enough to note that the competition there wasn't so tough, then hurrying on up to test the next level. His restless ambition soon led him to become bored with the opportunities open to a young Wall Street lawyer, and led him, once he plunged into the Washington scene, to rise unswervingly to the top position open to a man of his age.

Califano credits his wife, Trudy, with causing his initial entry into the political arena, for in 1958–60 when he was busy handling tax cases and corporate law for Thomas E. Dewey's law firm—Dewey, Ballantine, Bushby, Palmer & Wood—she was becoming active in New York's Reform Democrat movement. As he describes it:

"I wasn't particularly interested in government or politics until Trudy became active in reform politics. I was just a busy New York lawyer. Then I happened to be home sick one day in February 1960 when she was having a meeting of the reform group. I got interested in what they were trying to do, and I worked a little for Kennedy that fall, but at the lowest level."

After Kennedy's victory, Califano became increasingly aware that: 1) "I was bored with splitting stocks for Tom Dewey's law firm," and 2) he was drawn to the excitement and promise of Kennedy's New Frontier. Therefore in January, 1961, he wrote Cyrus Vance, Kennedy's appointee as general counsel for the Department of Defense, outlined his experience and offered his services. Vance hired him as his Special Assistant, and in 1962 when Vance was promoted to Secretary of the Army, Califano rose with him, still with the title of Special Assistant. On July 1, 1963, Califano was promoted again, this time to be general counsel of the Department of the Army. At the time he was thirty-two years old.

Califano caught the eye of Secretary Robert S. McNamara, and in the spring of 1964 he became McNamara's Special Assistant and top troubleshooter, involved in everything from the development of the Supersonic Transport to the use of federal troops in Selma, Alabama.

Most important, Califano was the liaison between the Defense Department and the White House, and this job brought him into daily contact with Moyers, Bundy, and Valenti. On the day after the 1964 election, Moyers called Califano and asked if he'd be interested in coming to work at the White House. Califano said he'd have to talk to McNamara, and McNamara said the move was out of the question. Then, in July, 1965, when Moyers was unexpectedly made Press Secretary, he called

Califano and said the President wanted him to come take over his duties as legislative coordinator and top troubleshooter. At this point, all Califano could do was keep quiet while Johnson and McNamara decided his future. This time, McNamara reluctantly agreed to let him go, and Califano became a Special Assistant to the President.

In this new role, serving as the chief expediter for an impatient and demanding President, Califano has made many enemies. Cabinet members seeking to carry an issue to the President are often told to "talk to Joe" and this breeds resentment. Part of Califano's job is to knock heads together, and this wins him no friends among those whose heads are knocked. Some Cabinet members call him "Little Joe" behind his back, and they say it without smiling. Others who have crossed his path have called him a "hatchet man," and worse. Yet Califano is by nature a reasonable and agreeable man, and for the most part he is accepted as (to use a term he himself sometimes uses) "the President's instrument"—a man with a job to do, one he will do pleasantly if he can but effectively in any event.

It has been Califano's fate, as Moyers' successor, to be often compared with Moyers, and not always favorably. A typical pro-Moyers comment sounds like this: "Joe is a magnificent operator, a master of the governmental process, but he's not the philosopher Bill was. He's an excellent technician who sees it as his job to carry out the President's wishes, not to influence the President's course."

Califano's admirers disagree; one says: "When Bill left, a lot of people thought the Frank Lloyd Wright had departed and we were left with a contractor. I don't think that's fair. I've watched Sorensen and Moyers in the same job, and I don't think either of them has come up with better legislative proposals than Joe has. Of course, he's terribly frustrated now by the lack of money for the domestic programs."

Most people who know both Moyers and Califano would agree that Moyers is the more reflective, philosophical of the two, but the difference between their performances also reflects the changing times—during Moyers' 1964–65 heyday the Johnson Administration was in its creative phase; by 1967–68 the need was for implementation and Califano fills that need very well.

Califano, in his dealings with the President, is certainly not a yes-man, but it is generally felt that he is not inclined to challenge the President on major issues and that, more generally, his rise to power has been based not only on his intelligence, energy, and cool judgment, but on the prudence he exhibits in his dealings with the older, more powerful men he has served.

A significant example of Califano's caution concerns Vietnam. Coming to the White House, as he did, after four years in the Pentagon, Califano had the contacts and the knowledge to become one of the President's main sources of ideas and advice on the war. But Califano at the outset made a conscious decision to remain silent on Vietnam—unless asked a direct question by the President—lest he run any risk of conflict with Bundy, who was then the top staff adviser on national security.

Califano, of course, was not close to the President when he entered the White House and had reason to proceed with care. Moyers could risk violent disagreement with Johnson now and then, reasonably confident that their bond would survive. Califano had no such assurance. Califano once said he believes Johnson regards him "less as a son than as a McNamara," and the description seems apt. Paradoxically, Johnson has therefore treated Califano better than other aides he is closer to personally; Califano, "the President's instrument," is rarely subject to the abuse Johnson directs at others.

Not only Califano, of course, but every important presidential assistant must decide to what extent he will simply be an implementer of the President's wishes, and to what extent he will play the more dangerous game of attempting to influence the President's decisions. Moyers, who may have been the most effective combination of philosopher and activist of all the White House aides. Yet in large measure it was Moyers' desire to be more than an operative that caused his downfall with Johnson, a fact that has done nothing to encourage successors like Califano to interpret their jobs broadly.

Nonetheless, as Califano's confidence has grown, he has become, in the opinion of his associates, not only a gifted expediter but a creative force within the Administration. His former boss, Robert McNamara, has called him "the man who, next to the President, has contributed more than any other individual in our country to the conception, formulation and implementation of the program for the Great Society."

Califano's admirers suggest that the Administration's 1964–65 legislation was largely "a clearing-up of the old agenda"—i.e., long-awaited bills like aid to education and Medicare—whereas Califano proceeded in 1966 to develop a new and highly creative legislative program that included such new proposals as the Model Cities program, the Department of Transportation, the water pollution program, the reorientation of foreign aid toward health and education projects, consumer protection in pipelines, meat and other areas, and the civil rights bill that included open housing, jury reforms and protection of civil rights workers.

Califano continued to expand and perfect the task force system begun by Moyers and Goodwin; among other things, he found it useful to give the Task Forces bigger staffs and more specific assignments. Califano has met as often as possible with academic leaders, and he credits talks he had on college campuses with leading to his decision to include three year olds in the Head Start program and to propose the Child Health Act.

Califano and his staff exercise White House supervision over the Department of Labor, the welfare programs in Health, Education and Welfare, the poverty program, the AID program and all aspects of foreign trade, and the various agencies affecting the domestic economy, including the Departments of Commerce and the Treasury, and the Council of Economic Advisers. He is concerned with these agencies' legislative proposals and with their day-to-day activities, insofar as they need or warrant White House consideration.

Despite their differences in age and background, the President and Califano have one important quality in common: they are action-oriented men, men with a taste for the tangible, the immediate. This fact is seen time and again as Califano shapes the Administration's legislative program to Johnson's liking. When a proposed anticrime bill came to the White House from the Justice Department, it seemed to Califano to over-emphasize worthy but intangible goals, such as strengthening court procedures. He injected several immediate crime-fighting elements—money for police training and equipment—that suited the President's love of the visible.

Time and again, in developing and implementing the President's program, Califano must fight to impose Johnson's interests over the narrower interests of the departments of government. Late in 1965, Johnson told Califano he wanted a big, imaginative housing program, but the response from federal housing officials did not rise to meet the challenge. Califano then helped organize the Task Force which advocated the Model Cities program. He still had to push hard to overcome resistance from housing officials who insisted the Model Cities program was too big and controversial for them to undertake in the first year of the new Department of Housing and Urban Development.

For a time, Califano and the President were virtually the only two men in the Administration in favor of the $20-million-a-year rat-control legislation. White House sources say high officials of HUD were opposed, apparently because they found the subject of rats distasteful. This attitude infuriated the President. "Have you ever been scared of a wasp in your home?" he demanded of one official. "Scared he'd bite you? Well, how'd you like to have fifty rats in your home?"

In all this, Califano was following the traditional role set by Clifford and Sorensen of the White House aide who oversees and shapes the Administration's domestic programs. But in his two other areas of influence, Califano has been breaking new ground, for he has been trying to apply to the domestic side of government the two most important developments of the 1960s in the management of foreign and security operations: first, McNamara's reliance on a systems-analysis (or cost-effectiveness; Califano uses the terms interchangeably) approach to decision-making; second, Bundy's development of a small White House staff to oversee the foreign affairs bureaucracy.

One of Califano's goals is to have established, by the time he leaves the White House, a domestic equivalent to the Bundy NSC staff. Toward that end, he has assembled a little-known five-man group. He sees it as this group's job to help him: 1) spot crises before they erupt; 2) provide White House coordination of interagency programs; 3) provide well-informed information with which the White House can resolve disputes; 4) push for departmental follow-through on presidential decisions.

By 1968 Califano had assembled:

—Lawrence E. Levinson, thirty-six, Califano's classmate at Harvard Law School, holds the title Deputy Special Counsel, and is Califano's closest associate (he is sometimes called Califano's alter ego; today not only Presidents but their assistants have alter egos).

—Jim Gaither, thirty, who led his law class at Stanford and was a clerk to Chief Justice Earl Warren before joining Califano.

—Fred Bohen, thirty, a political scientist who came to the White House from a post at Princeton.

—Stan Ross, thirty-six, another Harvard Law graduate who taught at New York University before coming to Washington.

—Matthew Nimetz, twenty-eight, who led his class at Harvard Law School, studied at Oxford, and clerked for Justice John M. Harlan before joining the White House staff.

Califano's other major area of importance flows from his four years in Robert McNamara's Defense Department. McNamara in the early 1960s became the high priest of the facts-and-figures approach to military decision-making; Califano, one of McNamara's disciples in those years, has now become his evangelist in spreading the gospel throughout the government. Califano's shift from McNamara's office to the White House symbolizes Johnson's determination to apply McNamara's techniques, which have been credited with saving millions of dollars at the Pentagon, to the domestic side of government.

On August 25, 1965, Johnson initiated the controversial Planning-Programming-Budgeting System (PPBS) throughout his Administration. PPBS was first introduced by McNamara in 1961 at the Pentagon, and the fact that Califano had four years experience with it was certainly one reason the President brought him to the White House. Essentially, PPBS involved the utilization of computers and sophisticated statistical and mathematical techniques to provide objective evaluations of alternative courses of action. Critics of PPBS say that it may be possible to evaluate rifles or airplanes, but it won't work on, say, a Head Start pre-school program. Califano thinks it can work there, too. Other McNamara protégés have fanned out to the various government departments, where they keep in close touch with Califano's White House command post.

Califano considers both the Model Cities program and the Department of Transportation—two undertakings he was deeply involved in—to be prime examples of the new, "total approach" to problem-solving. He thinks they represent the "politics of innovation" and he thinks that is why both were resisted so vigorously in Congress.

As Califano looks to the future he has no doubt that the growing complexity of national life will force basic changes in the way the government makes decisions, implements programs, and evaluates their effectiveness. For example, it appalls him that the Labor Department, OEO, HUD, HEW, and other departments all have far-flung field offices with virtually no coordination among them. He thinks the Budget Bureau should be expanded to have men in the field to coordinate and evaluate federal undertakings at the grassroots level. He was involved in a reorganization of the Budget Bureau in 1967 that resulted in a new Division of Human Resources to oversee HEW, HUD, OEO, Labor, and Veterans Administration programs.

It is in matters such as this that Califano probably has had his most important influence on the Johnson Administration. Johnson spent two decades in Congress operating with a congressional view—asking what was good for Austin, or good for Texas, rather than what might be good for the nation as a whole. Now, as President, he must take a broader view, and he must reconcile his desires with his resources, and in doing this it has primarily been the McNamara-Califano approach that he has followed.

The accident of the war in Vietnam made Califano an immensely influential White House aide in domestic affairs. The point is not that Johnson isn't interested in domestic matters; he is, much more than either Eisenhower or Kennedy was. But his preoccupation with the widening war, and its political repercussions, cut very deeply into the amount of time he could devote to, say, the poverty program or the Department of Labor; he was forced to delegate, and Califano was there.

Califano's position was further strengthened by the fact that his job is more sharply defined than any of his predecessors. Unlike Sherman Adams, he does not have to deal with patronage or continuing political responsibilities. Unlike Sorensen, he is not called upon to write speeches. He has a larger staff than Moyers did. Most important, for a man who came to the White House a virtual stranger, he has had an excellent rapport with the President. Both men's liberalism is instinctive and pragmatic rather than intellectual and all-embracing. Califano, a driving and effective operator, has for the most part been content to let Johnson set the goals and to devote his energies to the not inconsiderable task of achieving those goals.

Probably Califano's preoccupation with organization, with systems, with decision-making will never make him appear a glamorous or heroic figure, as some of his predecessors have been. Yet it should be said in his favor that Presidents rarely lack for men with ideas about what the government should do, but that men with a real talent for getting those things done are always in short supply.

5. Quiet Men: McPherson, Watson, Rostow, Cater

It is best to begin this chapter on four current White House aides by saying that all speculation about the status and importance of incumbent White House aides is dangerous. This fact was nicely illustrated by the rash of magazine articles on Bill Moyers in 1965–66. Not one of these articles (and I wrote one of them) even hinted at what, we can now see, were the two most significant facts about Moyers' status then: his growing rift with Johnson, and his opposition to the war in Vietnam.

The presidential assistant is necessarily less concerned with the historian's curiosity than with his own survival, and he knows that secrecy is his surest self-defense. As long as no one is sure how far his mandate extends, he is free to extend it as far as he can. So long as he can avoid liberal-conservative, or hawk-dove labels, he can pose as everyone's ally and minimize partisan criticism. "The best way to stay out

el; W. Marvin Watson, Appointments Secretary; Douglass Cater,
pecial Assistant overseeing health and education programs; and
W. Rostow, the Special Assistant for National Security Affairs.

ry McPherson, who easily ranks as one of the most attractive,
ted, and well-intentioned men to grace the White House staff
ay years, made his way there in a roundabout, somewhat reluctant
r.

a in Tyler, Texas, in August, 1929, McPherson attended Southern
dist University for two years, then transferred to the University
South, a liberal arts school in Sewanee, Tennessee. He received
A. degree from Sewanee in 1949 and enrolled at Columbia Uni-
for graduate study in English literature. Midway through a
's thesis on the poetry of Dylan Thomas, he decided the academic
s not for him, and joined the Air Force. While serving as an
ence officer in Europe in the early 1950s, McPherson first became
y interested in public affairs. His concern was a negative one:
horrified at the spread of McCarthyism in the U.S. Often, unto believe newspaper accounts of the Senator's doings, Mc-
a would write to Washington for copies of McCarthy's speeches
nscripts of his hearings.

ly because of McCarthy, McPherson enrolled in law school at
iversity of Texas after his discharge from the Air Force in
seemed to McPherson that the Senator was going to lead
on into a reign of terror, one in which every liberal might
ed up before a political inquisition, and that the liberal's only
y in having the legal skill with which to defend himself. Given
nsity of McPherson's concern, he was dismayed to find that
school professors and classmates were more concerned with
d oil leases than with the threat of McCarthyism. When Mc-
got his law degree in 1956, McCarthyism was dying, but his
crest in politics had survived.

erson's cousin, Jack Hight, who was then working for Senator
B. Johnson, helped him get a job as assistant counsel for the
emocratic Policy Committee, then headed by LBJ. He became
mittee's general counsel in 1961. In August, 1963, he moved
entagon as Deputy Under Secretary of the Army for Inter-
Affairs.

months later Johnson became President. At that point Mc-
unlike many Johnson men scattered throughout the govern-
de no effort to climb aboard the White House bandwagon,

of trouble is to stay out of sight," Kennedy
the most capable White House aides have ur
stinctively. They will decline speaking invitati
public statements. If they must talk to repor
privacy of their offices, where they can exchang
tion for the reporter's promise not to attrib
them. They become "White House sources" c
President."

Yet it is almost impossible for a member
House staff to remain anonymous. Alert repor
the centers of power, will begin to pick up
aide's behind-the-scenes activities. An article wil
ton Post, or an item in one of the newsmaga
views will pile up. Realizing the inevitability o
will usually decide he had better make the best
reporters, his enemies will.

The human element enters the equation.
intellect urges secrecy, his ego may be cr
He may, being human, feel that he is doir
the credit is going elsewhere. He sees that
own horn, no one else will do it for him
anonymous," one influential but little-knowi
staff told me. "It's hell." A few months late

Johnson's staff has been less publicized
reason for this is not, as some Johnson mer
toil with a true passion for anonymity, wh
shameless prima donnas; the main reason is
a jealous master, one who believes there is
House who merits publicity. He often tells h
departure from the New Deal came soc
writing about "Corcoran's programs" and
son's aides get the message.

Moyers and Valenti were the two most
son's first term, and, in different ways, t
them—Moyers was made to seem more s
seem more foolish than he is. Califano,
top aide, has managed to stay largely be
maneuvers have attracted a scattering of
behind Califano in importance are four
siderable interest, who have operated ir
publicity as possible. They are Harry C

nor did Johnson send out a call for him. McPherson knew well all the drawbacks of working for Johnson—the long hours, the uncertain relationships, the flashes of abuse—and he was not eager to be exposed to them, even at the White House level.

In mid-1964, McPherson was offered a job that was most appealing to him, Assistant Secretary of State for Educational and Cultural Affairs. He called Jack Valenti and asked him to ask the President if he should take the State Department post. Valenti passed back word that the President said for him to take the job if he wanted it. He did.

Johnson's call came the next year, largely as a result of Moyers' efforts, and in August, 1965, McPherson assumed the temporary title of Counsel to the President. In February, 1966, he succeeded Lee White as Special Counsel.

In that position, McPherson was in some respects reminiscent of the younger Clark Clifford. Both were still in their thirties when they entered the White House; both were tall, handsome, charming, and politely evasive about their activities. McPherson, with his Southern courtliness, his love of music, art, and literature, and his relaxed, rather philosophical approach to the issues of the day, gives the impression of being out of his element in Johnson's inner circle. His chemistry must include a good dose of political pragmatism or he could not have maintained Johnson's favor for a decade, but McPherson lacks the driving instinct for power of a Corcoran or a Clifford or a Moyers.

As Special Counsel, McPherson, like Clifford twenty years earlier, served both as the President's lawyer and his speechwriter. However, McPherson did not, like Clifford and Sorensen, have primary responsibility for developing the President's legislative program. That power had passed to Califano, with McPherson taking a secondary role on legislation.

As the President's personal lawyer, McPherson negotiates and writes most presidential Executive Orders, and works with the Justice Department on presidential pardons, civil rights cases, and other legal matters. As a presidential liaison man with the agencies, McPherson's main responsibilities lie in urban problems, particularly education, employment, and antipoverty programs. These assignments overlap somewhat with Cater's and Califano's, but Johnson likes a degree of overlapping, and the three aides have managed to tolerate the situation.

It has been the trio of McPherson, Califano, and Cater that Johnson has dispatched to meet quietly with intellectuals at many college campuses in recent years. They were assigned to ask the intellectual community such questions as: Where does the Great Society go from here? What problems remain unsolved?

The campus visits have been a stimulating interlude for the White House trio, and they no doubt impressed the intellectuals with the quality of the men around Johnson. Just what concrete results, in terms of governmental action, have resulted from the trips remains a mystery. One member of the trio commented: "The trips proved that the intellectual community thinks the nation's number-one problem is that the President doesn't spend enough time listening to the intellectual community."

It is as speechwriter that McPherson has the potential for the largest impact on Johnson—if, like some earlier speechwriters, he can make the connection between what the President says and what he does.

McPherson's highly refined literary sensibility is often reflected in Johnson's speeches. When, for example, the President quotes Thomas Hardy, it is a good bet that the line came from McPherson, who has read Hardy, and not from Johnson, who may wonder why he is citing Hardy but not Laurel.

In the spring of 1967, McPherson sent President Johnson a memo which said in effect: "If I'm going to be writing about Vietnam, I think I should go there and get some feel for it." The President agreed, and on May 18, McPherson began a two-week visit to South Vietnam. He talked to political leaders and toured U.S. pacification projects. He returned to the U.S. via Israel, arriving there only hours before its war with the Arab nations began. He observed the war for four days before returning to Washington, where he worked with the Task Force headed by McGeorge Bundy that was trying to untangle the Mid-East crisis.

Asked later whether his visit to Vietnam altered his thinking on the war, McPherson commented: "Well, I came back with an increased existential awareness of the war."

It was a characteristic remark, evasive and intriguing; only McPherson among recent White House aides would speak of an "existential awareness" of the war in Vietnam. But whether, behind his charming, disarming façade, McPherson was having any substantial impact on the major issue of the day—Vietnam—remained unknown. Many moderates in the government, when Moyers left, looked to McPherson as the only man in the White House likely to replace him as an effective voice for moderation in Vietnam policy-making. But the indications are that McPherson, lacking Moyers' fierce, hungry aggressiveness, did not do so.

Lyndon Johnson has been kind enough, or shrewd enough, to provide political Washington with something it has needed and lacked for years —a conservative whipping boy in the White House.

He is W. Marvin Watson, a short, stocky, worried-looking Texas businessman who, since his arrival on the Washington scene in 1964, has been roundly and regularly denounced in the press and political circles for a multiplicity of real and imagined sins.

Joseph Kraft indignantly quoted an unnamed government official as saying Watson was the "crudest" man he'd ever seen in the White House. Joseph Alsop has blamed Watson's political ignorance for an alleged breakdown in communications between Johnson and the big-city Democratic organizations. Rowland Evans and Robert Novak declared, when Moyers left the White House: "At a time when Mr. Johnson desperately needs to broaden his political contacts, the new and stifling mood set by Watson is almost certain to narrow them even further." Various members of the Kennedy wing of the party describe Watson as a neo-McCarthyite out to purge all liberals from the government.

Watson endures the attacks with stoic resignation, bolstered by the support of the only man in Washington whose opinion interests him, Lyndon Johnson, who once declared:

"Marvin is as wise as my father and as gentle as my mother, and he is as loyal as another East Texan I know, Lady Bird."

Watson serves as the President's Appointments Secretary, performing the range of duties that have become traditional with that position. He handles the President's schedule, ushers visitors in and out of his office, juggles scores of phone calls each day, sees that papers and messages get to the President at the right time and that his replies go out promptly, oversees White House housekeeping details, has a hand in the hiring of top-level political and civil service employees, is the President's chief liaison with the Democratic National Committee and with Democratic leaders around the country, and serves as White House liaison with the FBI.

All this makes Watson the man who most often says "No" for the President and that makes him unpopular, as it did Sherman Adams and Kenneth O'Donnell before him. But Watson's unpopularity is intensified by his provincial nature and the extreme conservatism of his personal views. O'Donnell and Adams also did their Presidents' dirty work, but they were at least sophisticated men who spoke the language of national politics. Watson doesn't speak that language and apparently doesn't want to learn it. National Democratic leaders regard him as someone whose sensitivity to their problems was very slight.

When Johnson unaccountably designated Watson to be his representative at the funeral of former Pennsylvania Governor David Lawrence, the archetype of a Northern Democratic leader, columnists Evans and Novak declared: ". . . the President seems to delight in waving him (Watson) before the politicians like a red flag before a bull."

Watson, clearly, is out of step with such progressive, Eastern-oriented associates as Cater, Califano, and McPherson, and there have been frequent clashes between them. (Watson and Moyers, before he left, were particular adversaries.) Yet Watson's more liberal colleagues, when speaking of him, tend to stress that his actions spring not from any personal malevolence but from the extreme narrowness of his background. "Marvin has a good heart," one commented, "but you have to remember that he's just a boy from Daingerfield, Texas."

To some observers, Watson's background has not provided him with the ideal preparation for participation in national affairs. Born in Oakhurst, Texas, in 1924, Watson attended public schools in Huntsville, Texas, and, after serving in the Marines during the Second World War, he received Bachelor's and Master's degrees from Baylor University, the large Baptist school in Waco, Texas. In 1951, he became manager of the Chamber of Commerce in Daingerfield. In 1957, he accepted a position as executive assistant to the president of the Lone Star Steel Company, and it was from there that he came to Washington in 1964.

Lone Star Steel's president, it happened, was an ultraconservative figure in Texas politics—particularly noted for his opposition to organized labor—and he employed Watson as his chief emissary to Democratic Party gatherings. Texas liberals regarded Watson as one of their most dangerous adversaries in interparty power fights.

This training made Watson, in the words of another Johnson aide, "about as conservative as a man can be and still be an intelligent human being." Watson had received his political training in those ultraconservative Texas political circles whose members are deeply opposed to civil rights legislation, foreign aid, Medicare, federal aid to education, organized labor, welfare programs—in short, to everything the national Democratic Party stands for.

Yet Watson also had a reputation for party loyalty and dependability. He backed Adlai Stevenson in 1952 and 1956 because he was the Democratic nominee. He caught Johnson's eye in the 1950s and helped out on his 1960 campaign for Vice President. In 1964, Johnson recruited Watson to the White House staff, and once he arrived, Watson soon made a name for himself.

He first attracted attention in 1964 as the Johnson-appointed boss of the Democratic National Committee. At the party convention in Atlantic City in August, party officials were required to clear every detail with Watson. After the election, he began a purge of the committee's staff that soon made him one of the most hated and feared men in Washington. In doing this, Watson was only doing Johnson's bidding, for Johnson wanted to purge various Kennedy men and other unwanted individuals from the party payroll, but Watson wielded the ax with such efficiency that much of the ensuing backlash hit him, rather than Johnson. Similarly, Watson was widely credited with having engineered the removal of Abba Schwartz, a liberal Kennedy appointee, from his post as head of the State Department's immigration office.

Watson's first tactical error came when he enraged the Washington press corps early in 1966 in what might be called the Switchboard Affair. One day persons calling the White House found that its switchboard operators, instead of simply connecting them with the office they wanted, were asking each caller his name and number. Newspapermen, who value their freedom to call White House sources on a confidential basis, interpreted this as a crude attempt at news management. Watson, who had initiated the new procedure, insisted it was simply a study to determine whether some offices needed more or fewer telephones. He never made it quite clear why, to do this, he needed each caller's name and number. The press, largely undisturbed by Watson's firing of a few liberals, was outraged at this infringement on its presumed rights, and Watson was soon being called a "gumshoe," a "dictator," and worse. Eventually, Watson announced that he had completed his study, and he ended the procedure, except on calls to his own office.

Watson was also making enemies inside the White House by his zeal in enforcing the President's call for economy on his fellow staff members. As master of White House housekeeping, he restricted the use of limousines, the hiring of secretaries, and various lesser amenities. He turned a deaf ear to pleas that government economy should start somewhere else—like, say, the Labor Department. One former Special Assistant who has felt the hard hand of Watson summed up his complaint this way: "In government you don't have a union man's security or a professor's tenure. All you have is your status, and it's expressed in the size of the rug on your floor and your access to the limousines. When they take away your silver water jug, it's like cutting off your testicles."

Watson's role as presidential liaison with the FBI has brought him into frequent conflicts with others on the staff. All persons hired for top-level government jobs, or appointed to the various presidential committees and task forces, are routinely subjected to an FBI check, and the FBI reports are routinely submitted to the White House for inspection. Part of Watson's job is to study these reports and decide whether anything in them should disqualify the potential appointee.

The difficulty has been that using Watson as liaison with the FBI is rather like using General Curtis LeMay as liaison with the Air Force or Stokely Carmichael as liaison with the Black Power movement —he serves to magnify, rather than moderate, the problem he is dealing with.

To understand this, one must know a little about FBI reports. They are strange, surrealistic documents, conjuring up a world populated by Communists and fellow-travelers, pervaded by guilt by association and guilt by insinuation. I remember seeing the FBI report on one of America's most honored and distinguished journalists; he emerged from its pages as something close to a foreign agent, a man who "was known" to have spoken to this or that radical politician in 1935, who "admitted" contributing to some political journal in 1942, et cetera. More recently, and more amusingly, there was the case of the avant-garde artist, a noted abstractionist, who was nominated to an honorary committee. The FBI, in its field check, came across a traditionalist painter who told the FBI agent that the abstractionist was a Communist and that all modern art is part of a Russian-inspired plot to befuddle the American mind. This was solemnly recorded in the FBI report and sent to the White House for consideration.

Most White House aides know to take the FBI reports with a grain of salt, but this was not so easy for Watson, who came to the White House straight from a political ethos that is a shade or two to the right of J. Edgar Hoover. An example of the problems that have arisen was seen when Watson killed the appointment of a Columbia University professor to a presidential commission because the FBI had reported that the professor's brother was a Communist in the 1930s. Another Special Assistant, who knew the professor, and who didn't think his brother's politics thirty years ago were particularly relevant to the appointment, took it upon himself to check into the matter— and discovered that it wasn't the brother at all, but a man with a similar name, who had been a Communist. There have been numerous cases like this.

Some White House aides believe that Watson has deliberately used the FBI reports to block the hiring or appointing of liberals who are likely to advocate the sort of policies that he personally opposes. Others disagree, and think Watson is simply doing the best he can, given his inexperience in national politics. One White House aide says: "Marvin has learned a lot since he arrived here. The fact that somebody's brother was a Communist thirty years ago doesn't shake him up now the way it did at first."

Watson is not thought to have any direct influence on Administration policy. Nor is there any doubt that he tries to follow Johnson's orders faithfully, whether or not he agrees with them. He is said, for example, to have swallowed hard when Johnson told him to scare up some congressional votes to repeal the Taft-Hartley law's Section 14-b—the right-to-work provision—but he did as he was told.

Yet it is inevitable that a man with Watson's proximity to the President will have an effect. Many official memoranda reach the President via Watson, and if the President asks Watson for his opinion on them, he can hardly be expected to blot out all of his own political instincts. In his role as talent scout, Watson's prejudices are bound to affect his judgment. Similarly, it has become Watson's habit to invite persons appointed to top government jobs (GS 16 to 18, the so-called supergrades) to the White House for a little chat about "loyalty" to the President. Career civil servants have been known to go away unimpressed with Watson personally, fearful of his "Big Brother Is Watching" attitude, and indignant at the suggestion that their loyalty is in any way in doubt.

A man in Watson's position will inevitably, in gossip-ridden Washington, play a quasi-social, quasi-political role in determining who's in and who's out, who's up and who's down. This is particularly true in the Johnson Administration, because so many members of the President's Texas entourage have a rather paranoid view of Washington, the national press, and the world in general. Watson, who is nothing if not Texas-oriented, heads a Texas grapevine that reaches throughout Washington and follows a monolithic party line—at one time the grapevine trembled with righteous indignation at Mrs. John F. Kennedy's alleged slights to the Johnsons; later its members were busy denouncing the departed Moyers, whose manifold virtues they had all been praising to the skies a few months earlier. Several female members of the White House staff loom large in this network.

Most important, Watson's limited knowledge of national affairs and his conservative aura have worked in countless ways to widen the chasm between Johnson and the bureaucracy, the press, the liberals, and Northern political leaders. Often, labor leaders and Democratic politicians have tried to bypass Watson and deal with Johnson through Califano or O'Brien, which creates an unsatisfactory situation for everyone concerned.

In his role of the President's political troubleshooter, Watson is often blamed for outrageous acts performed by or on behalf of Johnson. One example was the smear campaign against Eugene McCarthy in the final days of the Democratic primary in New Hampshire in March, 1968. The attack featured radio commercials which implied that a vote for McCarthy was a vote for Ho Chi Minh—a direct and dirty attack on McCarthy's patriotism. Outsiders do not know to what degree this smear campaign originated with Watson, or with Johnson, or with the New Hampshire party leaders. But it was widely believed to be the sort of thing that Watson would approve, or at the very least, not disapprove. (And it was exactly the sort of presidential excess that the banished Moyers had always tried to prevent.)

Stewart Alsop has written that Watson's surly, suspicious behavior helped drive McGeorge Bundy out of the White House. It is undeniable that Watson has exercised virtually unlimited authority over many outstanding people in the government and throughout the Democratic Party, and he is regarded by many of them as a kind of small-bore Joe McCarthy working within the White House. Watson is no doubt in his personal life a fine fellow. But in his political life, he is out of his element, and he has shown himself to be a narrow, crude, and ignorant man. That such a man should exercise so much authority is one of the less happy chapters in the history of Johnson's Administration. The President's elevation of Watson to the Postmaster Generalship in April, 1968, can only be seen as his last, defiant pie-in-the-face to the liberals and Easterners whom he holds largely responsible for his political undoing.

Much as Watson has served Johnson as a shield to criticism on political affairs, Walt W. Rostow has become a whipping boy for critics of the war in Vietnam. For example, *The New Republic* of November 4, 1967, featured on its cover a drawing of Rostow looking like Fu Manchu and, inside, a piece by Alex Campbell which began: "Walt Whitman Rostow, the professor turned presidential assistant, is chiefly responsible for the bombing of North Vietnam."

At no point does Campbell offer evidence for this assertion, perhaps because there isn't any. It's true that Rostow advocated bombing North

Vietnam, and it's true that Johnson bombed it, but there's no known cause and effect relationship between the two facts. To the contrary, in 1964–65 when Johnson decided to bomb the North and otherwise escalate the war, Rostow was in exile in a relatively obscure policy-planning post at the State Department, grinding out policy papers that no one of any importance read.

The men whose advice to the President was influential would include Bundy, Moyers, Rusk, McNamara, the Joint Chiefs of Staff, a few senior Senators, Clark Clifford, and Abe Fortas, but not Walt Rostow. One member of Johnson's staff comments:

"I ask you, was Rostow in the White House when the bombing of the North began? No, he was in an obscure post at State; Bundy was in the White House. Was Rostow in the White House when the decisions were made for a massive build-up of troops in the summer of 1965? No, he was at State, not even a party to the discussions. Bundy was in the White House. Rostow arrived just in time to be blamed for foisting on the President policies upon which the President had already decided."

Nonetheless, ever since Rostow arrived in the White House in April, 1966, replacing Bundy as National Security Adviser, antiwar critics have made him a special target for abuse. Antiwar posters have listed his name alongside those of Rusk and McNamara, no doubt to the annoyance of the latter two gentlemen, who have little use for Rostow.

The anti-Rostow sentiment reflects the fact that certain of his qualities —an ingratiating manner, intellectual glibness, a passion for dubious causes—attract critics as a magnet attracts thumbtacks. Perhaps that was one reason Johnson wanted Rostow, rather than Moyers, as his National Security Adviser—he needed an effective lightning rod on Viet-nam. Rostow's critics, as Campbell says in his *New Republic* piece, have called him many unpleasant things over the years: "A compulsive fitter of discreet phenomena into a schema. A philosopher with a theory of history to which the facts fail to conform at their peril. A lightweight inventor of brand names and slogans (he is credited with the New Frontier, Pax Americana, and 'Let's get this country moving again')." Rostow's antiwar critics have resented the fact that, whether or not he really has had much to do with Johnson's decisions on Vietnam, he so zealously defends them. Rostow is a self-styled expert on guerrilla warfare, and as early as the spring of 1961 he was arguing that the only way the guerrillas in South Vietnam could be defeated was by bombing the infiltration routes from the north. After Rostow became an adviser to President Johnson, White House reporters viewed him as being more easily impressed than anyone else in the Administration by the questionable statistics sent from U.S. officials in Vietnam on the "kill-ratio," enemy weapons captured, enemy deserters, hamlets pacified, and so on. The general feeling was that, military advisers aside, Rostow was the man who most often assured Johnson that victory was just around the corner.

One notable example of Rostow's capacity for double-think was seen early in 1968, in the wake of the Viet Cong's devastating attacks on more than thirty South Vietnamese cities, when an untroubled Rostow assured the President and reporters that the enemy offensive had not only failed, but had left the South Vietnamese stronger than before.

Rostow was originally a Kennedy appointee. An economic historian and author, he was teaching at MIT's Center for International Studies when he became active in Kennedy's 1960 campaign. Kennedy planned to install Rostow in a job at the State Department, but Rusk didn't want him. He therefore became Bundy's deputy in the White House. In October, 1961, Kennedy sent Rostow and General Maxwell Taylor to Vietnam to review the situation there. Their advice, upon completing the mission, was that the U.S. send 10,000 men to aid the South Vietnamese army, and give serious thought to bombing infiltration routes. In November, 1961, reportedly because of friction with Bundy, Rostow was sent to the State Department to be head of its Policy Planning Council. There, in addition to advocating a hard line on Vietnam, Rostow worked on plans to strengthen West Berlin, advocated bridge-building to Eastern Europe, and was credited with forecasting Premier Khrushchev's fall from power in Russia several months in advance.

Soon after Johnson became President, Rostow joined General Curtis LeMay ("We are swatting flies when we should be going after the manure pile") and other hard-liners in urging him to bomb North Vietnam. Still, Rostow was then far from the center of decision, and Johnson's appointment of him to replace Bundy came as a surprise.

Perhaps Johnson saw in Rostow's appointment a means of rebutting the critics who said he had few men of ideas around him, for even Rostow's enemies concede that he has a fertile, imaginative mind. Perhaps Johnson saw Rostow, with his well-known pro-escalation views, as a lightning rod to criticism, and also as an adviser who would be expendable if the time came for a change of policy and personnel.

Probably the chief reason for Rostow's appointment, however, was Johnson's determination to bolster the prestige of his Secretary of State. One obvious way to support Rusk was to downgrade the status of his main governmental rival, the White House assistant for national security affairs. Johnson reportedly said, on the eve of Bundy's departure, that he didn't want "another Bundy" in the White House basement, and in Rostow he didn't get one. Rostow equaled neither Bundy's intellect nor his sheer force of personality. Bundy had dealt with Rusk and McNamara as an equal, but Rostow, after several years in sub-Cabinet posts, tended to defer to them. It was said that Rusk, before agreeing to Rostow's transfer from State back to the White House, had received a pledge from Rostow that he would forward to the President no paper involving the State Department's interests without Rusk's prior knowledge.

Still the physical fact of Rostow's move from the policy-planning post at State back to the White House inevitably increased his influence. His associates argue that, while he lacks Bundy's personal influence, their office as a whole has increased in importance because they are the President's agents and the President makes such exhaustive demands on the foreign affairs bureaucracy for facts, answers, and action.

And Rostow does have this undeniable significance: He has the President's ear, and he has spent two years reassuring the President that victory in Vietnam is just around the corner. David Halberstam, who won a Pulitzer Prize for his reporting in Vietnam, and whose record for predicting developments there is considerably better than that of the U.S. government, commented on Rostow's role in an article written in the spring of 1968. Halberstam noted the steady departure from government of the moderates on Vietnam—men like Moyers, McNamara, Goodwin, Roger Hilsman, Mike Forrestal. Then he noted:

"The slots that have been vacated can now be filled with men who have a stake in believing the war will be won, who have said publicly it will be won, and who look for evidence that they are right. Walt W. Rostow is the classic example; he has been predicting the imminent collapse of the Viet Cong since 1965, when he told a friend of mine that it would take only six weeks. He has made similar predictions ever since. The Viet Cong have not collapsed, but neither has Rostow. If a field official wants to report to Rostow, he must get the positive news in first, because Rostow will turn off once the darker side comes on. Thus does the team insulate itself from undermining doubts, from reality."

President Johnson had the good fortune to obtain in his Special Assistant for health and education programs, Douglass Cater, a unique combination of journalist, intellectual, academic, bureaucrat, political scientist, and presidential confidant. Cater and Johnson have known one another since the early 1950s, when the Alabama-born (in 1923), Harvard-educated Cater was a young writer for the *Reporter* magazine. In 1953 and 1955, Cater wrote sympathetic pieces on Senator Johnson, whom he viewed as a "politician's politician" and "a pragmatic 'centrist' for whom the mechanics of politics holds far more fascination than commitment to any particular brand of political philosophy."

Cater's writings reflected a sympathy, rare among journalists, for the problems facing those in government, and this led him in the 1950s to serve terms as a consultant to both the Secretary of the Army and the Secretary of State. He also received a Guggenheim Fellowship to study the interaction of the press and government, and an Eisenhower Fellowship for a year of world travel. His books have included *The Fourth Branch of Government*, a study of the press published in 1959, and *Power in Washington*, which he wrote in 1963 while a Fellow at the Wesleyan Center for Advanced Studies.

When the Kennedy Administration came to power in 1961, Secretary of State Rusk planned to hire Cater as Assistant Secretary for Public Affairs—the press-relations job—but Pierre Salinger maneuvered another man into the post. A year later, Cater had a second shot at the same job, but declined it. Not long after Johnson became President, he and Cater lunched together. A few weeks later, at a meeting with Johnson, both Rusk and McNamara commented that they hoped to hire Cater. "No, you're not," said Johnson, "because I'm going to hire him."

Cater was made a Special Assistant on May 8, 1964. His duties were not precisely defined. Johnson told him to "think ahead," and it was assumed he would be a campaign speechwriter and idea-man. He had a large hand in the production of Johnson's mini-book, *My Hope for America*. During the campaign, Cater's speechwriting came to focus on education. In time, the President came to think of Cater as his expert on education, with health added a little later. Cater, realizing that these were two areas that most interested the President, was quite content with his assignment. Part of his strength has been that he is not an empire-builder; he has been content to dig as deeply as possible into the two areas he has been given.

Cater was the White House liaison man with the 1964 Task Forces in health and education; in education, for example, he worked closely with Task Force chairman John Gardner and Commissioner of Education Francis Keppel to translate the Task Force recommendations into specific legislative proposals. He thus had an important role in shaping the some forty health and education bills that passed Congress in 1965 and 1966, including such landmark measures as Medicare, Elementary and Secondary Education, and the Heart, Cancer, and Stroke research bill.

It was Cater's intention from the first not to be an intellectual kibitzer but an insider who would work within the political and bureaucratic framework to help shape Administration policy. He tries to seek out ideas, both from the bureaucracy and from the academic community, and to present new ideas to the President in a form that he could use—not as vague suggestions, but as specific, well-researched proposals. In this role, he sees himself as a "packager" of ideas for the President.

In the winter of 1965–66, for example, Cater was the moving force in putting together the International Education and Health Acts, which Johnson sent to Congress on February 2, 1966. This legislation, which Cater hoped would project the President's concern with health and education on a worldwide scale, was essentially a grab bag of some forty actions, big and small, the government could take to foster international health and education, such as a Center for Educational Cooperation; a corps of Education officers in the U. S. Foreign Service; and grants to enrich the international studies curricula in U.S. schools.

The President's program, which was to cost $524 million in the first year, passed Congress amid much enthusiasm late in 1966 but, a year later, had been given no funds by Congress. It became one of the many victims of the budget cuts caused by the war in Vietnam. However, some of the President's proposals could be carried out administratively, without new appropriations, and Cater could thus transform at least a few of the ideas into governmental realities.

In addition to his day-to-day liaison with the Office of Education and the Public Health Service, Cater keeps an eye on health and education programs throughout the government. He requires the Agency for International Development to report to the President every six months on what it's doing in education. He keeps in touch with the Peace Corps' school-to-school program. He was a key figure in shaping the Administration's proposal for a public broadcasting corporation. When the news broke about the CIA support of the National Student Association, the President assigned Cater to head up the effort to unscramble the situation.

In all this, Cater has been an unusually effective presidential liaison man, not only because of his personal prestige, and his self-effacing manner of operation, but because he is, by White House standards, a specialist. Because his attention has been almost exclusively focused on health and education, he has become intimately familiar with the issues and personalities in the three or four agencies with which he most often deals.

Most White House liaison men have been spread impossibly thin. Sherman Adams often seemed like a man trying to hold back the governmental tide with a single bucket. Sorensen was often preoccupied with speechwriting, and his two aides, Feldman and White, more or less divided up the government between them. Similarly, Califano is overburdened and McPherson's duties as speechwriter cut into the time he has for liaison with the agencies asigned to him.

Cater's role suggests one pattern Presidents might follow in their efforts to exert control over the government: find men of ability, assign them to areas of specific responsibility, and back them up. Four or five such specialists, each with a small staff, coordinated by the President (or by a Califano if the President lacks time or interest), would probably be able to advance the White House interest in domestic affairs efficiently and effectively. Most recent Presidents have seemed to be moving in this direction, but they have found it difficult to recruit enough men with enough ability who would stay in the White House long enough to do the job. No recent President has exercised effective control over the bureaucracy, but Johnson, with his concern for domestic affairs and his hard-driving administrative style, might have given it a hard fight if he had ended the war in Vietnam and served a second term.

VII. TRENDS

The White House staff can be viewed in two lights, the personal and the governmental.

From a personal viewpoint, presidential assistants are generally more interesting and more likable than most men at the top level of politics. They tend to be young, highly intelligent, and unashamedly on the make. They take chances, they cut corners, and unlike most politicians they sometimes have a little spontaneity and irreverence left in them. This accounts for much of their charm and most of their problems.

Above all, to most of us who make up their audience, they are *familiar, understandable* men. Men who have made politics their profession learn to hide their true selves behind masks and mechanical responses, until the average man must despair of ever penetrating the mysteries of a Lyndon Johnson or a Robert Kennedy. But a President's assistants may have retained their individuality; anyone who has worked for a newspaper has known men like Hagerty and Salinger; any lawyer recognizes bright, hard-charging young men like Goodwin and Califano; any graduate of an Eastern college has known his campus versions of Tugwell and Bundy and Schlesinger.

We can see in such men, as we rarely can in Governors or Senators or Cabinet members, a bit of ourselves. In a government increasingly run by specialists, they are, like most of us, generalists, and we can tell ourselves, correctly or not, that they are doing about what we would be doing if we were in their shoes. The President, too, may find the reactions of a Louis Howe, a Charlie Ross, or a Pierre Salinger a better gauge to man-in-the-street sentiment than all the public-opinion polls.

At the personal level, the most striking trend of the White House staff has been its transformation from its original shadowy status to its place of prestige today. During the Roosevelt era, men like Tugwell and Hopkins were the victims of such unrelenting criticism that they were virtually unemployable when they left the government. Truman's men, with the exception of Clark Clifford (who left early, while his friends were still in power), did not walk into sudden prosperity when they departed in 1953. David Stowe, for example, lost $3000 in his first year as a labor consultant and had to sell his house to get by. The talented David Bell, similarly unencumbered by offers, returned quietly to Harvard.

As late as 1959, Professor Louis Koenig could write of presidential favorites: "Neither wealth nor high office will likely accrue from their travail." Yet in the 1960s we have seen a new situation develop. It is still easy for an unwary White House man to come to grief, as the Adams and Jenkins cases remind us, but if he plays his cards carefully he is on the high road to fame and fortune. Consider, for instance, the pre- and post-White House careers of several men who have served in the White House in the 1960s, when the staff positions had become an accepted, respected part of the presidential apparatus:

—Pierre Salinger—pre-White House, newspaper reporter, Senate investigator; post-White House, U. S. Senator, $50,000-a-year business executive, best-selling author, movie, and television performer.

—Ted Sorensen—before, a congressional aide; after, a $100,000-a-year lawyer, best-selling author.

—McGeorge Bundy—before, Harvard dean; after, $75,000 president of the Ford Foundation, aspiring Secretary of State.

—Henry Hall Wilson—before, lawyer in North Carolina; after, $100,-000 president of the Chicago Board of Trade.

—Jack Valenti—before, partner in a Houston advertising agency; after, $150,000-a-year president of the Motion Picture Association of America.

—Bill Moyers—before, theological student, deputy director of the Peace Corps; after, publisher of *Newsday,* at a salary reported to be near $100,000.

These are, in many ways, exciting precedents, yet to some of the more sensitive White House assistants, the pot of gold that awaits them at the rainbow's end is not an unmixed blessing. The aide may find, as he emerges from the White House, that he is not the same man he was a few years earlier and that, as Thomas Wolfe warned, he can't go home again. Clifford could not return to St. Louis, or Moyers to Texas, or Salinger to the city room of the San Francisco *Chronicle,* or Sorensen to those idealistic causes that had inspired his early manhood—if, in fact, any of those men ever wanted to return to those points.

The departing aide will have become acutely aware of status and image. He has spent several years dealing as an equal with the richest, most powerful men in America, and he may have come to savor the best clubs, the best cars, the best cigars, and other amenities of power. He has worked hard for a salary which, compared with his responsibility, is absurdly low. He may be in debt; he probably thinks he deserves some rewards after his years of sacrifice. His wife may have come to enjoy the pleasures of the most fashionable social circles.

In sum, as he leaves the White House, almost every pressure is pushing him toward the employer who can offer him the most money and respectability—the same private interests that, at least if he served a Democratic Administration, he has been opposing on behalf of the public interest while in the White House.

To take only the three most notable examples, we see Tom Corcoran, the flamboyant antibusiness crusader of the 1930s, leading the drug industry's fight against federal regulation in 1962; Clark Clifford, the onetime Fair Dealer, representing steel companies, airlines, gas producers, and other major industries resisting federal control; and finally, in one of the saddest sights of the 1960s, we see Sorensen accompanying his client, the president of General Motors, when the latter testified before Congress on GM's harassment of auto critic Ralph Nader—Sorensen, the young Midwestern idealist of the 1940s, advising Goliath on how to deal with David.

To be sure, the great corporations must have lawyers, and the former White House aides must be free to serve whom they please, yet it still seems sad that some of the brightest, most effective men of their time could find no other way to satisfy their social and financial cravings than by deserting the public interest for the service of the corporations.

From the corporations' point of view, the former White House aides are useful not only because they are well-known and have friends in power but because of their unique insight into the governmental mind and mood. Big business must make multimillion dollar gambles on such matters as the President's reaction to a price increase, or the Justice Department's probable view of a merger, and the likelihood that the former presidential adviser can predict, better than anyone else, what the government will do in a given situation more than justifies the five- and six-figure retainers that top Washington lawyers can command.

Whether the fabulous offers that now await departing White House assistants are good for the President or the country is another question. A young man who knows he can walk into a $100,000 job if he emerges from the White House with his reputation intact—if he does not make a name as a radical or a trouble maker—may become over-protective about his reputation. One of the virtues of many White House aides has been that they have had less to lose than most men around a President; they have been relatively idealistic, and willing to consider controversial ideas and espouse unpopular causes. There is too much caution built into the governmental system already, and any-thing that encourages increased caution among the President's staff is to be deplored.

Not all presidential assistants dash from the White House into the arms of business. Kennedy's Lee White has stayed in government as chairman of the Federal Power Commission. Larry O'Brien declined six-figure offers to become Postmaster General. Richard Goodwin, whose law degree and White House experience could no doubt have been parlayed into a blue-chip position, decided he would rather write than enrich himself (the two being generally incompatible) and has written on political affairs for *Life, The New Yorker, Commentary,* and other journals.

Even at best, the transition from the White House to private life is a painful one. The White House is the nerve center of the Western World and after its trials and triumphs a man is likely to find work in a Wall Street firm or a Long Island newspaper office to be weak wine indeed. The President, when he leaves office, has at least been President; the assistant, when he leaves, has been—what? A man who stood in the shadows of power, who played a mysterious role in a complicated process, a man who got little credit for his successes and ample blame for his mistakes, a man who will seem a braggart if he seeks credit, but whose good works will soon be forgotten if he does not. Like T. E. Lawrence or Charles Lindbergh or Jim Thorpe or Scott Fitz-gerald he may find that those first years of glory were the best and that those afterward become a long, slow decline. It is hard to think of a presidential adviser whose afteryears, insofar as one can judge from the outside, have equaled the satisfaction of his time in the White House. Clark Clifford, perhaps.

Finally, adding insult to injury, as the aide departs from the White House, bloody but not quite bowed, he must watch with envy as the new President's team marches in—crisp, confident, eager to clean up the mess in Washington, to get the country moving again, to build the

Great Society. The departing warrior's only consolation, in this dark hour, lies in the assurance that, as Emmet John Hughes put it, those who come to clean up the mess in Washington will soon *become* the mess in Washington.

A trend is emerging whereby young men make a name for themselves in government, either at the White House or one of the departments, then spend a decade or so in business attaining financial security, and finally, if the political winds blow favorably, return in their maturity to the top levels of government. Clark Clifford is one instance, and Charles Murphy and David Bell, who served on Truman's staff and returned to government during Kennedy's Administration, are two more examples of this process. Bill Moyers admits candidly that he hopes to follow this pattern, and Califano, Bundy, Sorensen, Goodwin, Cater, and McPherson all might attain high-level posts in some future Administration.

Such men, in selecting their post-White House jobs, must consider its political benefits along with its financial rewards. One might suspect that Bundy did not join the Ford Foundation entirely out of philanthropic impulses, for the job is sure to blunt the jagged edges of his image. Moyers, as a newspaper publisher, has an ideal forum for continued comment on, and involvement in, political affairs. Cater, if he secretly aspires to someday become Secretary of Health, Education and Welfare, would probably do better to become a university president or foundation executive than to return to his first love, writing. Lawyers like McPherson and Califano must decide whether to practice in Washington, and risk the lobbyist label, or in New York, or not to practice law at all.

Whether or not the young men of the Kennedy and Johnson Administrations later return to government, many of them will certainly remain prominent in Democratic politics for decades to come, just as Corcoran, Clifford, and James Rowe have done. No doubt some will seek elective office, as Salinger and O'Donnell did soon after leaving the White House. One can imagine the Democratic Party of New York turning to Moyers, or perhaps to Bundy or Sorensen, as a candidate for Governor or Senator. Similarly, either O'Brien or O'Donnell might make a successful race in Massachusetts, and Salinger might attempt a comeback in California.

If Clark Clifford had been elected to the Senate in the late 1940s, he would almost surely have emerged as a presidential prospect, and it is not inconceivable that someday in the future some former White House aide may return to 1600 Pennsylvania Avenue under his own steam.

There remains, after the personal aspects of the presidential assistants' roles have been considered, the larger equation in which those assistants are simply cogs in the increasingly complex machinery of government.

How do you run the American government? How do you make it work? The Founding Fathers pondered those questions at Philadelphia in 1787, and they are still pondered today by Presidents and the men around them.

A large, powerful White House staff has been one of the tools recent Presidents have built to try to control their ever-expanding bureaucratic empires. From where the President sits, the hard fact is that there isn't time for him to perform all the roles demanded of him—to be chief of state, chief executive, chief legislator, party chief, and commander in chief. He must fix priorities, decide where his time is best invested, and delegate duties accordingly. Inevitably, the men personally and physically closest to the Presidents, best known by them and most fully responsible to them, have been prime recipients of delegated authority.

The nature of the delegation varies with different Presidents, different aides, and different issues. There will be many matters the assistant will decide in the President's name, without consulting the President, but confident that he is acting within his mandate. This is possible because, on countless details brought to the White House for action, what is required is not *presidential* decision but just *decision*.

On other issues that come to the White House, the aide will conduct an investigation, arrive at a recommended course of action, and take it to the President for final approval. If the President skims a covering memorandum, or asks a question or two, before ratifying the aide's decision, it can be argued that the "decision" was his, although to say so is largely a matter of semantics.

Finally, there will be the larger issues, the ones that do demand careful presidential consideration, in which the aide's role will be to investigate and clarify the alternatives open to the President—not to make the President's decision but to make it easier for him. These are, of course, the hardest issues, the ones on which, as Harry Truman often said, the buck stops at the President's desk.

Most recent Presidents, Eisenhower excepted, have tried to maintain the pretense that they read every paper, examine every issue, and make every decision. In fact, at least the last three Presidents have, either by choice or necessity, concentrated their attention on foreign affairs and delegated substantial amounts of authority in domestic affairs to men like Adams, Sorensen, Moyers, and Califano. Moreover, Kennedy, disillusioned by the State Department, partially bypassed it by creating Bundy's "little State Department" in the White House basement.

The insistent question raised by the growth of the White House staff in the past thirty-five years, and particularly by the emergence in the 1960s of a powerful NSC staff and by Califano's staff of domestic specialists, is whether the White House staff has become a new, perhaps permanent instrument of presidential administration, one that is destined to supplant older instruments, notably the powers of Cabinet executives.

To an extent, it has. Since the New Deal, it has become normal practice for Presidents to have one or more staff assistants who are among the most influential members of their Administration. Moreover, in the 1960s, there has been a clear trend for the leading assistants not only to be powerful individuals, but to direct staffs that in effect institutionalize their authority. Bundy's and Califano's staffs represent a new layer of authority between the President and the agencies of government. Bundy's staff most often seemed to perform usefully in keeping open tangled lines of interdepartmental communication. It is too early to judge the effectiveness of Califano's operation. The unanswered question is whether a massive White House staff, as has grown up under Johnson, with a dozen Special Assistants and three or four dozen Assistants' assistants, is in fact an effective instrument of government. The danger of the fast-multiplying assistants to Assistants is that they really aren't the President's men, and they certainly aren't the departments' men, and they may fall into a kind of governmental limbo. There may be a point of diminishing returns, and Johnson's staff may be nearing it, at which an over-large White House staff creates more confusion than it eliminates.

The modern White House staff, although it may be big and powerful, has no guarantee of permanence. However efficient, it operates only a heartbeat from obsolescence. It is for this reason that detailed projections as to the future of the presidential staff in American government are unwise. Douglass Cater called the press the fourth branch of government, Arthur Schlesinger called the federal bureaucracy the fourth

Gardner. One major challenge facing the next President is to find a Secretary of State who can build a strong, viable Department of State.

President Eisenhower, when he left office, urged that the White House staff be endowed with more status. This could be done in various ways: by raising the staff's salaries, by defining their duties more clearly (perhaps by Executive Order), by submitting their appointments to the Senate for confirmation. Yet such moves would probably be unwise. The members of the White House staff should be exclusively the President's men, for him to use, abuse, or discard as he chooses. Insofar as they have independent status or permanent authority, their usefulness to him is lessened. They must remember their true condition: The President has been elected to lead the nation; they have been selected only to serve his convenience. If, in this era of the presidential mystique, there is any extra prestige available for the President to pass out, it would best go to those all but forgotten men, the Cabinet Secretaries and Assistant Secretaries, who now often wear the cloak of anonymity that the White House staff in recent years has cast off.

For the most part, the Presidents have brought men of outstanding ability onto their staffs. Sometimes, men of less obvious gifts have grown to meet the challenges of the job, just as Presidents have grown in office. It would be pointless to try outside regulation of the White House staff, as by Senate confirmation; the only way to get good men around a President is to elect good Presidents. And even then, even at best, the President's men will let him down from time to time. They will let old friends pay their hotel bills, or romance their secretaries, or enter into improper business deals, or make outrageous political statements.

Yet the same men will often perform admirably, even heroically, rendering genuine, little-known services to the country, with (in John Kennedy's phrase) a good conscience their only sure reward—and even that not always sure. These seekers of power are also men of paradox. Well-intentioned men generally, with a fair share of vanities and frailties, they operate within a political framework that offers many pitfalls and few protections, a system that does not always reward idealism and candor or punish deception and compromise. It is a system that allows for few whites, few blacks, and an infinity of grays. Small wonder that the best of the men described in this book fall well short of perfection, and the worst of them are not without their virtues.

While contemplating these interesting, paradoxical figures, I sometimes thought of the epitaph written by John Cleveland, the Renaissance poet, for the Earl of Strafford, whose politics caused him to be beheaded by Oliver Cromwell's government in 1641. The poem's last lines are:

> He spent his time here in a mist,
> A Papist, yet a Calvinist;
> His Prince's nearest joy, and grief,
> He had, yet wanted all relief;
> The prop and ruin of the state,
> The people's violent love and hate,
> One in extremes loved and abhorred.
> Riddles lie here, or in a word—
> Here lies blood; and let it lie
> Speechless still, and never cry.

Cleveland was once challenged to defend this poem's apparent ambiguity, and he replied, "It shows wherein the same man may both condemn and acquit the same man. Why is that such a riddle?"

SOURCES

The names of several persons interviewed who are still with the government have been left off this list for the obvious reason. A few of the interviews were conducted via long-distance telephone; one, with Sherman Adams, was an exchange of letters in which Governor Adams expressed himself with his accustomed bluntness and brevity.

No attempt has been made to list the hundreds of magazine and newspaper articles consulted.

I am particularly indebted to a number of outstanding Washington journalists who discussed various parts of this book with me; they include Tom Wicker and Arthur Krock of the New York *Times;* Marquis Childs and James Deakin of the St. Louis *Post-Dispatch;* Philip Geyelin of *The Washington Post;* Hugh Sidey and Neil McNeil of *Time-Life.* I am also grateful to my friend Dr. Otis L. Graham Jr., author of *An Encore for Reform,* for his advice on the New Deal.

The Roosevelt Staff

INTERVIEWS
Benjamin V. Cohen
Thomas G. Corcoran
Raymond Moley
Samuel I. Rosenman

BOOKS

Burns, James MacGregor. *Roosevelt: The Lion and the Fox.*
Daniels, Jonathan. *Frontier on the Potomac.*
                    The Time Between the Wars.
Farley, James. *Jim Farley's Story.*
Flynn, Edward J. *You're the Boss.*

Franklin, Jay. *The New Dealers.*
Freidel, Frank. *Franklin D. Roosevelt—The Triumph.*
Gunther, John. *Roosevelt in Retrospect.*
High, Stanley. *Roosevelt—and Then?*
Kennan, George F. *Memoirs 1925–50.*
Koenig, Louis. *The Invisible Presidency.*
Lilienthal, David E. *The Journals of David E. Lilienthal.*
Moley, Raymond. *After Seven Years.*
                    The First New Deal.
Richberg, Donald. *My Hero.*
Rollins, Alfred B., Jr. *Roosevelt and Howe.*
Rosenman, Samuel I. *Working With Roosevelt.*
Schlesinger, Arthur M., Jr. *The Age of Roosevelt.*
Sherwood, Robert. *Roosevelt and Hopkins.*
Sternsher, Bernard. *Rexford G. Tugwell and the New Deal.*
Tugwell, Rexford G. *The Democratic Roosevelt.*
Tully, Grace. *F.D.R., My Boss.*

The Truman Staff

INTERVIEWS

David Bell
Oscar Chapman
Clark Clifford
Donald Dawson
Charles S. Murphy
Richard E. Neustadt
John Steelman
David Stowe
Harry H. Vaughan

BOOKS

Allen, Robert S. and Shannon, William V. *The Truman Merry-Go-Round.*
Daniels, Jonathan. *The Man of Independence.*
Deakin, James. *The Lobbyists.*
Forrestal, James V. *The Forrestal Diaries.*
Kennan, George F. *Memoirs 1925–50.*
Lilienthal, David E. *The Journals of David E. Lilienthal.*
Neustadt, Richard E. *Presidential Power.*

Phillips, Cabell. *The Truman Presidency.*
Steinberg, Albert. *The Man From Missouri.*
Truman, Harry S. *Memoirs.*

The Eisenhower Staff

INTERVIEWS

Dwight D. Eisenhower
Sherman Adams
Robert Keith Gray
James C. Hagerty
Gerald Morgan
Arthur Minnick
Bradley Patterson

BOOKS

Adams, Sherman. *Firsthand Report.*
Childs, Marquis. *Eisenhower: Captive Hero.*
Cutler, Robert. *No Time for Rest.*
Donovan, Robert. *Eisenhower: The Inside Story.*
Eisenhower, Dwight D. *Mandate for Change.*
                        Waging Peace.
Gray, Robert Keith. *Eighteen Acres Under Glass.*
Hughes, Emmet John. *The Ordeal of Power.*
Koenig, Louis. *The Invisible Presidency.*
Morrow, E. Frederic. *Black Man in the White House.*
Neustadt, Richard E. *Presidential Power.*
Ross, Thomas and Wise, David. *The U-2 Affair.*
Rovere, Richard. *The Eisenhower Years.*
Simpson, Smith. *Anatomy of the State Department.*
Stone, I. F. *The Haunted Fifties.*

The Kennedy Staff

INTERVIEWS

McGeorge Bundy
Myer Feldman
Richard Goodwin
Evelyn Lincoln
Lawrence F. O'Brien

Pierre Salinger
Arthur M. Schlesinger, Jr.
Bromley Smith
Theodore C. Sorensen
Lee White
Henry Hall Wilson

BOOKS

Burns, James MacGregor. *John Kennedy: A Political Profile.*
Donald, Aida, editor. *John F. Kennedy and the New Frontier.*
Hilsman, Roger. *To Move a Nation.*
Kraft, Joseph. *Profiles in Power.*
Lincoln, Evelyn. *My Twelve Years with John F. Kennedy.*
Manchester, William. *The Death of a President.*
                    Portrait of a President.
McNeil, Neil. *Forge of Democracy.*
Salinger, Pierre. *With Kennedy.*
Schlesinger, Arthur M., Jr. *A Thousand Days.*
Simpson, Smith. *Anatomy of the State Department.*
Sorensen, Theodore C. *Kennedy.*
White, Theodore. *The Making of the President 1960.*

The Johnson Staff

INTERVIEWS

Horace Busby
Joseph A. Califano, Jr.
Douglass Cater
Lawrence Levinson
Harry C. McPherson, Jr.
Bill D. Moyers
James Moyers
Hayes Redmon
George Reedy
Jack Valenti

BOOKS

Bartlett, Charles and Weintal, Edward, *Facing the Brink.*
Evans, Rowland and Novak, Robert. *Lyndon B. Johnson: The Exercise of Power.*

Geyelin, Philip. *Lyndon B. Johnson and the World.*
Roberts, Charles. *LBJ's Inner Circle.*
Stone, I. F. *In a Time of Torment.*
White, Theodore. *The Making of the President 1964.*

Index

DATE DUE